The End of Value-Fre

"This book collects and expands on Putnam and Walsh's groundbreaking work exploring the philosophical background of economics and the nature of value judgments therein. Also, the contributions from their well-known peers in economics and philosophy, along with the authors' responses, provide a wonderful example of academic dialogue and exchange conducted with respect and dignity. This book will surely become an indispensable source of insight and inspiration for scholars working in the intersection of these two disciplines for years to come."

Mark D. White is *Professor in the Department of Political Science, Economics, and Philosophy at the College of Staten Island/CUNY*, USA, and author of *Kantian Ethics and Economics: Autonomy, Dignity, and Character*.

This book brings together key players in the current debate on positive and normative science and philosophy and value judgements in economics. Throughout their careers, both editors have engaged in the debate on the subject from its early foundations; both commencing in the early 1950s – Putnam as a doctorial student of Hans Reichenbach at UCLA and Walsh as a junior member of Lord Robbins's department at the London School of Economics,
    This book collects recent contributions from Martha Nussbaum, Amartya Sen and Partha Dasgupta, as well as a new chapter from the editors.

Hilary Putnam is Cogan University Professor Emeritus in the Department of Philosophy at Harvard University, USA.

Vivian Walsh is Distinguished Visiting Scholar in the Departments of Philosophy, Economics and The Wescoe School of Muhlenberg College, USA.

Routledge INEM Advances in Economic Methodology

Edited by Esther-Mirjam Sent
University of Nijmegen, the Netherlands

The field of economic methodology has expanded rapidly during the past few decades. This expansion has occurred partly because of changes within the discipline of economics, partly because of changes in the prevailing philosophical conception of scientific knowledge, and also because of various transformations within the wider society. Research in economic methodology now reflects not only developments in contemporary economic theory, the history of economic thought, and the philosophy of science; but it also reflects developments in science studies, historical epistemology, and social theorizing more generally. The field of economic methodology still includes the search for rules for the proper conduct of economic science, and it also covers a vast array of other subjects and accommodates a variety of different approaches to those subjects.

The objective of this series is to provide a forum for the publication of significant works in the growing field of economic methodology. Since the series defines methodology quite broadly, it will publish books on a wide range of different methodological subjects. The series is also open to a variety of different types of works: original research monographs and edited collections, as well as republication of significant earlier contributions to the methodological literature. The International Network for Economic Methodology (INEM) is proud to sponsor this important series of contributions to the methodological literature.

The End of Value-Free Economics

**Edited by Hilary Putnam
and Vivian Walsh**

With comments by
Harvey Gram,
Martha Nussbaum and Amartya Sen

Routledge
Taylor & Francis Group

LONDON AND NEW YORK

First published 2012
by Routledge
2 Park Square, Milton Park, Abingdon, Oxfordshire OX14 4RN

Simultaneously published in the USA and Canada
by Routledge
711 Third Avenue, New York, NY 10017

First issued in paperback 2014

Routledge is an imprint of the Taylor & Francis Group, an informa business

British Library Cataloguing in Publication Data
A catalogue record for this book is available from the British Library

Library of Congress Cataloging in Publication Data
A catalog record has been requested for this book

ISBN 978–0–415–66516–2 (hbk)
ISBN 978–1–138–79955–4 (pbk)
ISBN 978–0–203–15400–7 (ebk)

Typeset in Times New Roman
by RefineCatch Limited, Bungay, Suffolk

The authors lovingly dedicate this volume to Vivian Walsh's daughter Winifred Houldin; to his grandsons, Wiley and Warner Houldin; and to Hilary Putnam's children, Erika Chin, Samuel Putnam, Joshua Putnam, and Maxima Putnam; and to his grandchildren, Lauren Chin, Eva and Mara Putnam Steinitz; and Tani Elliott.

Contents

Acknowledgements

Taylor and Francis for permission to reproduce the following:

Vivian Walsh (2000) 'Smith after Sen', *Review of Political Economy* 12(1): 5–25.
Vivian Walsh (2003) 'Sen after Putnam', *Review of Political Economy* 15(3): 315–394.
Hilary Putnam (2003) 'For ethics and economics without the dichotomies', *Review of Political Economy* 15(3): 305–412.
Martha Nussbaum (2003) 'Tragedy and human capabilities: a response to Vivian Walsh', *Review of Political Economy* 15(3): 413–418.
Harvey Gram (2003) 'Openness versus closedness in classical and neoclassical economics', *Review of Political Economy* 15(3): 419–425.
Amartya Sen (2005) 'Walsh on Sen after Putnam', *Review of Political Economy* 17(1): 107–113.
Hilary Putnam and Vivian Walsh (2007) 'Facts, theories, values and destitution in the works of Sir Partha Dasgupta', *Review of Political Economy* 19(2): 181–202.
Vivian Walsh (2008) 'Freedom, values and Sen: towards a morally enriched classical economic theory', *Review of Political Economy* 20(2): 199–232.
Hilary Putnam and Vivian Walsh (2009) 'Entanglement throughout economic science: the end of a separate welfare economics', *Review of Political Economy* 21(2): 291–297.

1 Introduction

Hilary Putnam and Vivian Walsh

Few philosophical movements can have had anything like as great an influence on the mainstream economics profession as that of logical positivism from the 1930s until quite recently. It lasted long after the decline and fall of positivism among professional philosophers. Part of this longevity was probably due – ironically – to the fact that *most* mainstream economists never really mastered the logical and philosophical foundations of logical positivism,[1] as these were developed in the evolving works of the great positivist (aka 'logical empiricist') philosophers, such as Rudolph Carnap and Hans Reichenbach. Primarily, the economists seized onto one vital idea (as it seemed to them) and ran with it. Thus, they never experienced the long retreat of the great positivists, and never understood the significance of the bitter defeats that were suffered on that path. One of us (Hilary Putnam), on the other hand, having been a graduate student of Reichenbach's, and having come to know both Reichenbach and Carnap well, saw exactly what had to be given up. The other (Vivian Walsh), who was a junior member of Lord Robbins's department at the London School of Economics (and also of Sir Karl Popper's department of Logic and Scientific Method) from 1951 to 1955, saw something of the manner in which elements of a watered-down positivism were spreading among mainstream economics. Robbins's graduate and faculty seminar, in those days, was a stopping-off place for leading American economists passing through London – a notable example being Will Baumol, who later became a friend of both authors. In those days, Walsh was also attending Sir Alfred Ayer's seminar at University College, and they became friends – although Walsh never became a logical positivist.

The idea which the economists had taken away from their brief encounter with positivism was, of course, the claim that a science answered questions about what *is*, but was utterly silent as to what *ought* to be. This position, they gathered, was a fundamental result of logical positivism – and positivism was then the new and widely accepted philosophy of science. The influence of logical positivism on economics is usually attributed to Lord Robbins and his young 'Turks' at the London School of Economics. Based both on Robbins's written work, and on some years of frequent conversations with him, however, Walsh doubts that Robbins ever had more than a nodding acquaintance with logical positivism (see Walsh, 1996: 35, 179–183). Some of the young Turks in his department are a different matter, and those in Sir Karl Popper's department (of Logic and Scientific Method, as it was then called) would have read Freddy Ayer's (1952) book.

Robbins did, however, hold the view that interpersonal comparisons of welfare were value judgments. And value judgments were dismissed as meaningless by the logical positivists, so Robbins was objecting to interpersonal comparisons on grounds which the logical positivist young Turks would accept.

In a final, definitive statement of his position, Robbins chose to rest the exclusion of values from science on a much older tradition, that of David Hume (Robbins, 1971: 148). This enabled him, as it had Hume, to retain a role for values in *personal* life. Shorn of any scientific support, value judgments could express, and advocate, one's moral *sentiments*. So Robbins could insist that, although values had no place in science, 'this did not mean that economists should not have ideas of their own about ethics and policy' (Robbins, 1971: 148). Alas, Hume's gentleman's agreement that people brought up in the governing classes would share the same moral sentiments depended on eighteenth-century social relations *and* upon eighteenth-century metaphysics! Putnam, who also likes Hume, tries to put these ideas to rest (Putnam, 2002: 14–21).

In the Great Depression, the dogma of a fact/value dichotomy allowed economists who accepted it to wash their hands of any responsibility for the suffering of the poor and destitute. Robbins, however, was not one of these economists, sheltering from the storm under the massive wings of science. He was held back from this by his (Hume-endorsed) *personal* moral sentiments, and he stuck to his guns as he had done when he was a young British subaltern in the Royal Artillery near Armentières. His stance in the Depression, however, began with a serious mistake: publishing a work which *opposed* the Keynesian policies vital to recovery. But he quickly saw this mistake: 'I shall always regard this aspect of my dispute with Keynes as the greatest mistake of my professional career' (Robbins, 1971: 1954). He concludes: 'But it will always be a matter of deep regret to me that . . . I should have so opposed policies which *might have mitigated the economic distress* of those days' (Robbins, 1971: 155, emphasis added). Hume would have felt sympathy for his moral sentiments!

There were, of course, a few economists who never accepted the *logical positivist* ban on the making of interpersonal comparisons of welfare. At the London School of Economics, for example, were notably Lord Dalton and Sir Alan Peacock.

But neoclassical economists as a whole now had a doctrine which, having offered protection in the Depression, would also provide those who sought its aid a similar protection throughout the dangerous days of the Cold War. One of the present authors (Walsh) was once asked by a famous American economist: 'Do you know why we decided to refer to "social science" as "behavioral science"? It was to prevent backwoods congressmen from getting the idea that we were socialists!'

Thus the end of the Cold War offered an opportunity to neoclassical economists to explore the ethical implications of their policies. This did not depend on the fall of logical positivism among philosophers. The great battles which brought positivism down were fought on the terrain of exact science and there was no reason to expect economists to be keeping informed of these matters (philosophers who knew and philosophized about physics and mathematics, such as Quine and Putnam, played a leading part in those battles).

Instead, economists simply began to investigate the effects of changes in a broad spectrum of economic circumstances upon well-being, and to announce explicitly that they were introducing values into the assumptions of their models. Despite superficial appearances, however, this development by no means entailed that all logical positivist residues had been flushed out of neoclassical economic modelling. What had happened was that these economists had achieved a genuine ethical enrichment of *welfare* economics, which was now allowed to make interpersonal comparisons, not only of well-being but also of rights and capabilities. In the course of this, however, welfare economics had become a sort of 'red light district', to which mainstream economists could go in order to do things which were not allowed in pure 'predictive', 'analytical' or 'scientific' economics. The fundamental positivist notion which had survived in economics, that *sciences* were value-free was, if anything, *strengthened* by the setting up of a demimonde in which, by contrast, these naughty values were allowed.

This was possible because mainstream economists had not undertaken a systematic investigation of the logical nature of scientific claims in general, and specifically in economics. But, for at least two reasons, it would arguably have been unreasonable to expect such an investigation from the mainstream economics profession. For one thing, it would need to be led by a philosopher of science who had first-hand knowledge of how and why positivism had failed in the area where its great battles were fought – namely, in mathematics and physical science. And then it could hardly be expected that foundations, and other sources of funding for mainstream economics, would see such an essentially philosophical research project as constituting a high priority for financial support. So it should occasion no surprise that when such a project *did* begin, it began outside of mainstream economic theory. Even then, it required some unlikely events that in a work of fiction would be criticized as implausible!

It began when one of the present authors, a philosopher who had been involved in the battles which led to the fall of positivism, and had continued to contribute to the philosophy of mathematics and physical science – but with a growing interest in moral philosophy – was drawn to examine the specific situation in economics. In a book devoted to just these issues, Hilary Putnam explicitly sets out how he came to be so involved. He cites (Putnam, 2002: 30) a paper by Walsh which re-examines the original philosophical issues over which positivism fell, but which was written for a specifically economist readership (Walsh, 1987). The economists had sent up a signal, and Putnam was going to respond. He did so first in Putnam (1990: 163–165), then further aroused by Walsh (1996 and 2000: 5–25), he dedicated his book (Putnam, 2002) to this project. The aim of that book was, in Putnam's words, 'to present a philosophy of language very different from the logical positivist one that made [Sen's] enterprise seem so impossible' (2002: viii). He makes it clear that 'Walsh powerfully encouraged me in this' (ibid.).

Sen was quick to respond. Walsh had published 'Sen after Putnam' (2003: 315–394), to which Martha Nussbaum (2003) and Harvey Gram (2003) had responded, and Sen wrote that 'I regard myself as particularly fortunate that Vivian Walsh has given such careful and penetrating attention to my work in his new paper (Walsh, 2003) adding greatly to my personal debt to him, which is already large, because of his earlier critiques (Walsh, 1996, 2000), which had made me rethink and reassess my views' (Sen, 2005: 109). He added that 'I should also take this opportunity to record my enormous debt to Hilary Putnam' (2005: 109–110).

By 2007, Putnam and Walsh had published their first joint paper (Putnam and Walsh, 2007), and Sir Partha Dasgupta was the first to respond (Dasgupta, 2007: 365–372). Increasingly, the joint work of Putnam and Walsh is entering the on-going debate among economists who belong to the mainstream, but have an interest in values. Confusions still arise, however, because some of these writers still cling to the belief in a *separate* welfare economics distinct from purely 'predictive' or 'analytic' theory. Dasgupta, despite some splendid work (which belongs in the second wave of the classical revival), is a case in point of this.

These matters are further explored in Putnam and Walsh (2009) and in the final chapter of this book.

Note

1   There has always been a morally and philosophically serious minority among mainstream economists, examples being: K. Arrow, J. Coles, R. Frank, P. Hammond, I. M. D. Little, P. Samuelson and J. Stiglitz. Also, as the authors have stressed before, the *second* wave of the classical revival has returned to Smith's involvement with moral philosophy. Some examples are: P. Dasgupta, J. Eatwell, H. Gram, E. G. Nell, L. L. Pasinetti, B. Schefold, A. K. Sen and G. Steedman.

References

Ayer, A. J. (1952 [1936]) *Language, Truth and Logic* (New York: Dover Publications).

Dasgupta, P. (2007) 'Reply to Putnam and Walsh', *Economics and Philosophy*, 23: 365–372.

Gram, H. N. (2003) 'Openness versus closedness in classical and neoclassical economics', *Review of Political Economy*, 15: 419–425.

Nussbaum, M. (2003) 'Tragedy and human capabilities: A response to Vivian Walsh', *Review of Political Economy*, 15: 413–418.

Putnam, H. (1990) *Realism with a Human Face* (Cambridge, MA: Harvard University Press).

Putnam, H. (2002) *The Collapse of the Fact/Value, Dichotomy, and Other Essays, Including the Rosenthal Lectures* (Cambridge, MA: Harvard University Press).

Putnam, H. (2003) 'For ethics and economics without the dichotomies', *Review of Political Economy*, 15: 395–412.

Putnam, H. and Walsh, V. (2007) 'Facts, theories, values and destitution in the works of Sir Partha Dasgupta', *Review of Political Economy*, 19: 181–202.

Putnam, H. and Walsh, V. (2009) 'Entanglement throughout economic science: The end of a separate welfare economics', *Review of Political Economy*, 21: 291–297.

Robbins, L. C. (1971 [1954]) *Autobiography of an Economist* (Glasgow: Glasgow University Press).

Sen, A. K. (2005) 'Walsh on Sen after Putnam', *Review of Political Economy*, 17: 109–115.

Walsh, V. (1987) 'Philosophy and economics', in J. Eatwell, M. Milgate and P. Newman (eds) *The New Palgrave: A Dictionary of Economics* (1st edn), 3: 861–869 (London: Macmillan).

Walsh, V. (1996) *Rationality, Allocation and Reproduction* (Oxford: Clarendon Press).

Walsh, V. (2000) 'Smith after Sen', *Review of Political Economy*, 12(1): 5–25.

Walsh, V. (2003) 'Sen after Putnam', *Review of Political Economy*, 15(3): 315–394.

2   Smith after Sen*

Vivian Walsh

Introduction

> The support that believers in, and advocates of, self-interested behaviour have sought in Adam Smith is, in fact, hard to find on a wider and less biased reading of Smith. The professor of moral philosophy and the pioneer economist did not, in fact, lead a life of spectacular schizophrenia. Indeed, it is precisely the narrowing of the broad Smithian view of human beings, in modern economics, that can be seen as one of the major deficiencies of contemporary economic theory. This impoverishment is closely related to the distancing of economics from ethics.
>
> Amartya Sen (1987a, p. 28)

> These classical authors were deeply concerned with the recognition that we have reasons to value many things other than income and wealth, which relate to the real opportunities to lead the kind of life we would value living. In the writings of Smith, Mill, and other classical political economists, there is much interest in the foundational importance of our ability to do the things we value, so that they saw the freedom to lead valuable lives as intrinsically important—not merely instrumentally so.
>
> Drèze and Sen (1995, pp. 9–10)

I shall argue that the revival of classical economic theory in the twentieth century has successfully completed a first phase, in which the work of Ricardo was its main point of reference, and that it has, for some time now, been entering a second phase, in which the work of Adam Smith is gaining prominence. I shall then argue that a number of the works of Amartya Sen illuminate and develop certain of the ideas of Adam Smith. Sen's contribution to the development of Smithian ideas is, on this view, wholly to do with the second stage of the classical revival.

As I have noted elsewhere, 'David Ricardo never lost sight of the core of Smith's analytic contribution and its deepest moral implications . . . But Ricardo was not a trained moral philosopher, as Smith had been (and as Marx was to be). So Ricardo . . . confined his attention "to those passages in the writings of Adam

Smith from which he sees reason to differ" (Ricardo, *Works*, I, p. 6)' (Walsh, 1998a, p. 189). This had the (probably unintended) effect of concentrating 'a spotlight upon certain issues in the analytical core of Smith's economics, leaving a great part of his work in darkness' (Walsh, 1998a, p. 190).

This habit of concentration on a few key issues of classical theory was destined to reappear in those theorists who initiated the revival of classical theory around the beginning of the twentieth century, and their main preoccupation was naturally with Ricardo. (Although Rory O'Donnell has argued that a satisfactory account 'of the relation of Smith's work to the surplus theory of value and distribution was presented by Dmitriev as early as 1898' (O'Donnell, 1990, p. 222)). As the revival of classical theory gathered momentum, this Ricardian minimalism was a notable characteristic of Piero Sraffa (1960) as well as of John von Neumann and in some respects of Wassily Leontief (on their models, see Kurz and Salvadori, 1995). This is not intended as criticism: as I have remarked elsewhere, '[i]n fact such a minimalism reflected the most critical need for the successful revival of classical theory: the most precise possible mathematical development of the structure of the theory' (Walsh, 1998c, p. 4).

The reappraisal of Adam Smith, of course, is not the only context in which a second phase in the classical revival can be detected. But it can be argued that it is the case which highlights much of what is important *about* this newer phase. This is because Smith embedded a remarkable understanding of the core concepts of a classical theory of the reproduction of surplus, in the setting of a richly descriptive political economy whose implications for moral philosophy he understood and explored. The Smith texts as a whole offer a rich tapestry, interweaving threads of classical analysis, moral philosophy, jurisprudence, and history. It is when we are ready (as I believe we now are) to re-embed the bare bones of a present-day version of Smith's classical reproduction structure in a present-day version of its proper social and philosophical setting, that a number of concepts developed by Amartya Sen become both relevant and important.

Black with fact, white with convention, and red with values

A notable advantage with which Amartya Sen approached Adam Smith was virtual lifelong rejection of the neoclassical dogma of the sharp fact/value distinction and of the 'meaninglessness' of value claims: 'The peculiarly narrow view of "meaning" championed by logical positivists—enough to cause disorder in philosophy itself—caused total chaos in welfare economics when it was supplemented by some additional home-grown confusions liberally supplied by economists themselves' (Sen, 1987a, p. 31, cf. Walsh, 1987, pp. 861–869).

It should be noted that by the 1960s Sen had presented a sophisticated defense of his claim that reasoned arguments (for instance in economics) could contain an ethical component (Sen, 1967, pp. 46–62). He developed a complex taxonomy of different classes of the uses of ethical words in ordinary language, analyzing their respective openness to rational argument. He specifically used this to demolish Lord Robbins' well-known opposing position (Robbins, 1932, p. 132). It goes without saying that few indeed of the economists of the time could have followed Sen's early philosophical papers. I began publishing on philosophical topics in the mid-1950s (for references, see Walsh, 1996), but, alas, I did not come upon Sen's work until many years later. I have discussed the significance for economics of the collapse of the logical positivist/logical empiricist fact–value dichotomy on several occasions (Walsh, 1987, 1996, 1998a, 1998b, 1998c) and so will pass lightly over this here. What needs more detailed attention is that the character of the debate on facts and values has changed, and how this affects Sen's views concerning Smith.

In a volume edited by Martha Nussbaum and Amartya Sen (1993), Hilary Putnam has re-examined the issue of a fact–value dichotomy. Having quoted a passage from my (1987) argument against the old logical positivist fact–value dichotomy, he adds that 'as Walsh goes on to explain, by the end of the fifties "most of the theses necessary for this remarkable claim" [Walsh, 1987, p. 862] had been abandoned. The positivist theory of "cognitive significance" had fallen. The absolute analytic–synthetic distinction was seen to fail as an account of how scientific theories are actually put together ... Quine [1963] summed up its demise, writing, "the lore of our fathers is black with fact and white with convention, but there are no *completely* white threads and no quite black ones". Explaining the impact of all this, Walsh writes: "[...] To borrow and adapt Quine's vivid image, if a theory may be black with fact and white with convention, it might well (as far as logical empiricism could tell) be red with values."' (Putnam, 1993, pp. 143–144, emphasis in original).

Turning to recent developments, Putnam adds: 'The collapse of the grounds on which the dichotomy was defended during the period Walsh is describing has not, however, led to a demise of the dichotomy, even among professional philosophers. What it has led to is a change in the nature of the *arguments* offered for the dichotomy. Today it is defended more and more on metaphysical grounds. At the same time, even the defenders of the dichotomy concede that the old arguments for the dichotomy were bad arguments' (Putnam, 1993, p. 144, emphasis in original).

Sen's arguments against the fact–value dichotomy in neoclassical economic theory thus still stand, since the neoclassical position was based on versions of the old logical positivist/logical empiricist position. His support for 'a broad Smithian view' (Sen, 1987, p. 28) is, however, now in need of defense on a *different* flank. Before sketching such a defense, it is worth noting that those who have most wanted a purely positive economics are unlikely to be comfortable with the new 'support' for their position. This is for two reasons, which will be explained in what follows. First, the new 'dichotomy' does not in fact give one a *clear-cut* division in the way the old logical positivist argument appeared to do. Secondly, the new 'dichotomy' is only available if one adopts an *explicitly* metaphysical argument—something that was anathema to those who wanted a pure, 'value-free', 'scientific' economics.

As for the clear-cut division: the old hard insistence that ethical sentences were 'non-cognitive', i.e. that they were neither true nor false, is not maintained today.

'Today, philosophers like Williams [1985] do not deny that ethical sentences can be true or false; what they deny is that they can be true or false *non-perspectivally*. Thus, the position has been (appropriately) renamed . . . Relativism' (Putnam, 1993, p. 145, emphasis in original).

There are a number of reasons why the claim of non-cognitivism 'has given way to relativism' (Putnam, 1993, p. 145). But Putnam singles out a reason that will be deeply disturbing to economists who want something to take the place of the old dichotomy. This reason is 'an increased appreciation of what might be called the *entanglement* of fact and value' (Putnam, 1993, p. 145, emphasis in original). I had something of the sort in mind when I dropped some red threads into Quine's already entangled black threads of fact and white threads of (logical) convention.

Putnam notes the late Iris Murdoch's (1971) idea 'that languages have two very different sorts of ethical concepts: abstract ethical concepts . . . such as "good", and "right", and more descriptive, less abstract concepts' (Murdoch, 1971). It has been argued that there is no way of saying what the descriptive component of the meaning of a word like 'cruel' or 'inconsiderate' is without using a word of the same kind. What is more, as Putnam points out, 'Murdoch emphasized that when we are actually confronted with situations requiring ethical evaluation . . . the sorts of descriptions that we need—descriptions of the motives and character of human beings, above all—are descriptions in the language of a "sensitive novelist", not in scientific or bureaucratic jargon' (Putnam, 1993, pp. 145–146). This is strikingly close to Sen's concept of descriptive richness (see Sen, 1992, p. 118, note 4, referring to Dobb, 1937).

It is time to ask just what sort of dichotomy the new dichotomists *do* offer. It does not involve the old claim that ethical statements cannot be 'true'. For a person like Williams, 'Peter is cruel' can be true 'in the very same sense in which "snow is white" is true, while still being an ethical utterance' (Putnam, 1993, p. 147). The point, rather, is that for these philosophers *factual* statements in a natural language like 'snow is white', or 'grass is green', are not themselves treated as possessing the highest kind of 'truth'. According to Williams, Putnam argues, '[i]f I say that grass is green, for example, I certainly speak the truth; but I do not speak what he calls the *absolute* truth. I do not describe the world as it is "anyway", independently of any and every "perspective". The concept "green" (and possibly the concept "grass" as well) are not concepts that finished science would use to describe the properties that things have apart from any "local perspective"' (Putnam, 1993, p. 147).

So, according to the new dichotomists we are to wait around for finished science to tell us (presumably in a constructed language which it endorses) what things are absolutely true. Putnam does not mince words: 'This dichotomy between what the world is like independent of any local perspective and what is projected by us seems to me to be utterly indefensible' (Putnam, 1993, p. 148). He offers a brief and telling statement of his argument against such 'metaphysical realism', which interested readers should sample for themselves. It has been developed in a number of volumes, of which the most available for non-philosopher readers is, I believe, Putnam (1987).

The would-be 'positive' economist is unlikely to be cheered up by being offered a dichotomy that rests, not just on a metaphysical argument, but on a demonstrably bad metaphysical argument. But there is a more work-a-day objection that may be even more telling. Economists cannot afford to neglect the failure of an advertising campaign that tried to sell a shade of green which consumers rejected, or the devastating results of a record drought upon grasslands. The things consumers want, or buy, or have produced for them, are chosen or rejected in terms of features that arguably would not appear in 'completed science', if it should ever arrive. They live, move, and have their being, just like those who make moral statements, on the 'wrong' side of the dichotomy between 'finished science' and *everything else that anyone ever says*.

Putnam sums up: 'The failure of the latest attempt to find some deep truths in positivism is no accident. Although Williams tries to do justice to the entanglement of fact and value, he fails to do so, because positivism was fundamentally a denial of entanglement, an insistence on sharp dichotomies: science–ethics, science–metaphysics, analytic–synthetic. The science–ethics dichotomy that Williams wants to preserve presupposed the science–metaphysics and analytic–synthetic distinctions he rejects. This is why William's book-length attempt to spell out his position is either self-contradictory or hopelessly ambiguous at every crucial point' (Putnam, 1993, p. 155).

Entanglement, ethics, and rich description

We now have a sketch of some of the philosophical background needed for a present-day approach to Sen's understanding of the ethical implications of economics in general, and of Smith in particular. The early influence of Maurice Dobb is highly relevant here, and Sen explicitly draws attention to this in a number of places in his work (Sen, 1978, 1980, 1992, for example). Certain descriptions, Dobb had argued, have a vividness that makes it impossible to ignore some vital fact, and this rich and telling description elicits from us a moral judgement, sometimes against our wishes. In somewhat similar vein, Smith saw our recognition of moral obligations as dependent on our ability to enter imaginatively into another's plight or suffering. It is not, I believe, historically improper to use the present-day philosophical concept of the 'entanglement' of facts and values for this key property of classical political economy in its philosophically richest manifestation, namely in Adam Smith.

To apply this idea to the work of Sen himself, Sen's famous theory of famine, in terms of entitlement failure and the starvation set, *can* be—and is—presented as formal economic analysis (for the formal analysis, see Sen, 1981b, pp. 167–173). But the concept of entitlement deprivation focuses a spotlight upon exactly the falsity of an age-old popular evasion of responsibility: that people die in famine because there is not enough food in the region where they live. On the contrary, Sen demonstrates, there can be starvation in a region flowing with milk and honey. Entitlement failures can take place 'even when the ratio of food to population (on which Malthus concentrated) goes up rather than down' (Drèze and Sen, 1989,

p. 25). We shall return to famine and entitlements later, for now I close this section with an example of descriptive richness taken from Sen's work: 'in the Bengal famine of 1943 the people who died in front of well-stocked food shops protected by the state were denied food because of *lack* of legal entitlement, and not because their entitlements were violated' (Sen, 1981a, p. 49, emphasis in original).

Sen on Smith and self-interest

Amartya Sen's campaign against the dominant role of the concept of self-interest in neoclassical economics goes at least as far back as his Herbert Spencer lecture in Oxford in 1976, which was later published (Sen, [1977], 1982, pp. 84–106). He does not yet essay the rescue of Adam Smith from neoclassical interpretations, however. Smith appears only once, in a frequently cited passage from Kenneth Arrow and Frank Hahn, where it is claimed that there is a 'long and fairly imposing line of economists from Adam Smith to the present-day' (Arrow and Hahn, 1971, p. vi) who have supported the coherent results to be had in an economy motivated by self-interest. The focus of Sen's Herbert Spencer lecture, rather, is on questioning the adequacy of self-interest as an assumption which 'survives more or less intact in much of modern economic theory' (Sen, [1977], 1982, p. 87).

A crucially important distinction appears first in a footnote where he thanks the Oxford philosopher Derek Parfit for convincing him of the conceptual importance recognizing that 'there is no reason to presume that the future interests [of a person] *as assessed today* will coincide with those interests *as assessed in the future*' (Sen, [1977], 1982, p. 88, emphasis added). Later Sen quotes Henry Sidgwick, who had asked '[w]hy should I concern myself about my own future feelings any more than about the feelings of other persons?' (Sidgwick, [1874], 1907, pp. 418–419, cited in Sen, [1977], 1982, p. 105). This argument of Sidgwick's would be much developed by Parfit (1984, pp. 117–195) so as to demonstrate that one can split the set of presumed self-interested choices or actions into two disjoint sub-sets: truly self-interested actions, versus the pursuit of present aims. What is truly in our self-interest is to take account of all our foreseeable future needs.

But 'what people are often *actually following* when they *claim* to be pursuing self-interest are in fact simply their present-aims' (Walsh, 1994, p. 403, emphasis in original). Despite the unreality of neo-Walrasian models (now admitted even by their erstwhile strongest supporters) 'economists seem to enjoy wearing the garb of the "hard headed realist". It is just here that the proponent of the present-aims theory can steal their clothes' (Walsh, 1996, p. 129). Many of the most regrettable features of today's society are obviously, upon reflection, properly characterized as the unbridled pursuit of present aims—not the prudent following of lifelong self-interest.

What Smith meant by self-interest was by no means the pursuit of gross short-term self-indulgence. It was 'the pursuit of long-term enlightened self-interest properly restrained by prudence', a state of affairs 'moulded by just laws' (Walsh, 1998b, p. 274). Something which 'in no way licenses the vulgarizers of Smith, who try to interpret his system of natural liberty as a free-for-all of unbridled greed and swindling—a paradise for projectors, inside traders, takeover artists and barrow boys. Nor does it condone the squandering of the surplus—always the unforgivable sin for the classics' (Walsh, 1998b, p. 274).

Smith made very plain for all to see (if they take the trouble to read him) his utter contempt for gross self-indulgences; his deepest Stoic instincts rebel against the 'slothful and oppressive profusion of the great' (Smith, [1937], 1978, p. 566). He forthrightly condemns the monied man who 'indulges himself in every sort of ignoble and sordid sensuality, at the expense of the merchant and the trades man to whom he lends out his stock at interest' (Smith, [1937], 1978, p. 563). On the coherence of Smith's stoic hierarchy of virtues in the Smith texts as a whole, see Brown (1994).

The canonical Arrow–Debreu theory endowed each agent in one of its models with a ranking specified as having the nice properties of an ordering (most notably completeness and transitivity). The possibility that an agent might have to rank *several* orderings was not considered. By the time of his participation in the Bristol conference on practical reason, in 1972, however, Sen was working seriously on the need to analyze an agent's rankings of rankings (Sen, [1974], 1982, pp. 74–83). He observed that it is interesting to inquire 'whether morality can be expressed in the form of choice between preference patterns rather than between actions' (Sen, [1974], 1982, p. 78). In an earlier paper, I had considered the problems of an agent who is forced to choose between two incompatible rankings (Walsh, 1967). Using elementary lattice theory, I gave the agent comparability along one chain of a lattice, but incomparability between chains (cf. Walsh, 1996, pp. 104–107). But as Sen has noted, in expressing moral judgements 'a *dual* structure is deficient. Surely a preference ordering can be *more* ethical than another, but *less* so than a third' (Sen, [1977], 1982, p. 100, emphasis in original).

The idea of meta-rankings is, of course, an ancient one, familiar to philosophers at least since Socrates. But its formal embedability in mathematical choice theory is nonetheless far from trivial, since it tends to explode the narrow concept of rationality that has dominated such theories in economics, decision theory, game theory, political science and elsewhere since the imperial hegemony of the old canonical Arrow–Debreu models, and which is only now in decline. It offers the theorist an analytical apparatus wherein the self-interest theory, the present-aims theory, and sundry moral theories, are simply members of a set of putative rankings that a rational agent can rank. For present purposes, the significance of this development is that the apparatus it provides indicates ways in which Smith's concept of a hierarchy of virtues may be embedded in a present day model—made more or less formal as one's taste requires. (For references to some of the continually growing literature on meta-ranking, see Walsh, 1996, pp. 126–128). For Smith's explicit discussion of the ranking of various moral rankings, the leading source is, of course, the *Theory of Moral Sentiments* (Smith, [1790], 1976a). For a subtle and penetrating exploration of the significantly different voices that can be heard in the *Theory of Moral Sentiments*, noting that of the impartial spectator, the interested reader should consult Vivienne Brown (1994).

By 1987, Sen's critique of traditional views of the role of self-interest in Smith was in full flower. To begin with, self-interest (in Smith) is not to be confused with prudence (as it has been by some): 'Prudence is "the union of" the two qualities of "reason and understanding", on the one hand, and "self-command" on the other' (Smith, [1790], 1976a, p. 189). 'The notion of "self-command", which Smith took from the Stoics, is not in any sense identical with "self-interest" or what Smith called "self-love"' (Sen, 1987a, p. 22). Sen stresses the Stoic roots of Smith's position, citing Raphael and Macfie (1976, pp. 5–11). Using present-day concepts, we may say that Smith expected the ranking resulting from pure 'self-love' to be restrained by prudence. This would lower the grosser indulgences of self-love, on which we have seen Smith's opinion, and also, it may be hazarded, check improvident excesses which would otherwise divert to extravagant present-aims resources needed for the future. Thus, a ranking dictated by prudence dominates the ranking resulting from pure 'self-love'. But for a Stoic, prudence was a humble virtue. As Sen observes: 'Even though prudence goes well beyond self-interest maximization, Smith saw it in general only as being "of all virtues that which is more helpful to the individual", whereas "humanity, justice, generosity, and public spirit, are the qualities most useful to others" (Smith, [1790], 1976a, p. 189)' (Sen, 1987a, p. 23).

Thus, in Smith's implicit meta-ranking, the stoic higher virtues rank far above prudence. As Sen remarks, 'Smith chastened Epicurus for trying to see virtue entirely in terms of prudence' (Sen, 1987a, p. 24). Poor Epicurus had believed that a ranking of actions (by prudence) was enough—that there was no need for a meta-ranking of virtues.

Sen singles out a class of situations where it has been argued that the pursuit of the selfish interests of traders has led to desperate social hardship, unrelieved by policy makers persuaded by doctrines they believed were Smith's. He argues that '[o]ne specific field in which Smith's economic analysis has been widely misinterpreted with grave consequences is that of famine and starvation' (Sen, 1987a, p. 25). He shows that Smith did in fact discuss 'the possibility of famines arising from an economic process involving the market mechanism, without being caused by a "real scarcity" generated by a decline in food output as such' (Sen, 1987a, p. 26; see further Sen, 1986).

He quotes a lengthy passage from the *Wealth of Nations* in which Smith attributes starvation and famine to a situation 'where the funds destined for the maintenance of labour were sensibly decaying' (Smith, [1776], 1976b, pp. 90–91). He observes that, '[w]hile Smith was often cited by imperial administrators for justification of refusing to intervene in famines in such diverse places as Ireland, India and China, *there is nothing to indicate that Smith's ethical approach to public policy would have precluded intervention in support of the entitlements of the poor*' (Sen, 1987a, p. 27, emphasis added).

This claim is flatly opposed to the way Smith has been interpreted by intellectual historians during the neoclassical period. It is not made lightly, however, being in accord with the conclusions concerning theory and policy confirmed by Sen in his work, jointly with Jean Drèze, on the intricate dual role of markets and public policy in famine situations (Sen, 1976, 1977, 1981b, 1986; Drèze and Sen, 1989, 1990–1991).

Sen is quick to point out that Smith 'would have certainly been opposed to the suppression of trade, [nevertheless] his pointer to unemployment suggests a variety of public policy responses' (Sen, 1987a, p. 27). He adds that it is arguable 'that the real "Smithian" message regarding anti-famine policy is not non-action, but creation of entitlements of victim groups through supplementary income generation, leaving the market to respond to the demand resulting from the generated incomes of the would-be victims. This analysis has a good deal of bearing on policy debates that are taking place now' (Sen, 1987a, note 29).

Thus, Jean Drèze and Amartya Sen have argued recently that 'Smith's defense of private trade in food grains and criticism of prohibiting restrictions by the state have often been interpreted as a proposition that state interference can only make a famine worse. But Smith's defense of private trade took the form of disputing the belief that food trades produce serious errors of *commission*. That disputation does not deny in any way the need for state action, in tackling a threatening famine, to supplement the operations of the market by creating incomes (e.g. through work programs) because the market *omits* to do this. Smith's is a rejection of market excluding systems, but not of public intervention for market-complementary arrangements' (Drèze and Sen, 1995, pp. 23–24, emphasis in original).

They conclude that 'Smith's famine analysis is consistent with arguing for a discriminatingly activist government that would create incomes and purchasing power for the disentitled population, and then leave the supply of food to respond to the newly created demand through private trade . . . That combination was explicitly discussed by Smith's friend Condorcet, and Smith's own analysis is entirely consistent with taking that route' (Drèze and Sen, 1995).

I have concentrated here on famine-related issues, which, as has recently been observed by Siddiq Osmani, 'was of course the original terms of reference for the entitlement approach' (Osmani, 1995, p. 292). But it needs to be pointed out that, as Osmani observes, 'there is also a great potential for applying this framework in the study of long-term endemic hunger' (Osmani, 1995, p. 292) which, indeed, has been a major preoccupation of Drèze and Sen. (The interested reader will find in Osmani a helpful, brief, survey of the literature of the entitlement approach, a reply to some of those who have misunderstood it, and an indication of some of the areas where further theoretical development would be useful.)

Smith and the concept of capabilities

The capability approach to well-being has recently been described by James Foster and Amartya Sen as having 'clear linkages with Adam Smith's (1776) analysis of "necessities"' (Foster and Sen, 1997, p. 199, note 133). It was in his Tanner Lecture in 1979 (Sen, [1980], 1982) that Sen originally introduced what he has recently described as 'a particular approach to well-being and advantage in terms of a person's ability to do valuable acts or reach valuable states of being' (Sen, 1993, p. 30).

Even some of the more subtle implications of analysis in terms of capabilities can be found in Smith. As Foster and Sen observe, '*relative* deprivation in terms of *incomes* can yield *absolute* deprivation in terms of *capabilities*. Being relatively poor in a rich country can be a great capability handicap, even when one's absolute income is high in world standards. In a generally opulent country, more income is needed to buy enough commodities to achieve the *same social functioning*. For example, as Adam Smith (1776) had noted (pp. 351–2), "appearing in public without shame" may require more expensive clothing in a richer country than in a poorer one' (Foster and Sen, 1997, pp. 212–213, emphasis in original).

This result, owing to Smith, which we may express today by saying that relative deprivation in the space of incomes can map to absolute deprivation in the space of capabilities permeates much of Sen's analysis of the significance of the capability approach to poverty, inequality, well-being, and social justice, and reappears in a number of places in his writings on these issues over the years. Thus, Foster and Sen continue: 'If we wish to stick to the income space, these variations in the conversion of incomes into capabilities would require that the relevant concept of poverty be that of *inadequacy* (for generating minimally acceptable capabilities), rather than absolute lowness (independently of the circumstances that influence the conversion). The 'poverty-line' income can be, then, specific to a community, or a family, or even a person' (Foster and Sen, 1997, p. 213, emphasis in original).

Conversion from incomes into capabilities is particularly unreliable when we are dealing with people possessing 'handicaps that are not so easily compensated by higher personal income . . . conversion into income space can be less satisfactory, and the need to look directly at the capabilities achieved (or not achieved) may be inescapable' (Foster and Sen, 1997, p. 213).

If such situations render judgements based on income space unreliable, how might a space of utilities fare? As is well known, much of Sen's intellectual effort has been devoted to a sustained critique of the utilitarianism which has always been implicit in neoclassical economics (see, for example, Sen, 1970, 1973, 1982, 1984b, 1985b, 1987a, 1992, 1997b). A simple example vividly illustrates some of the differences between an argument based on the metric of utilities, and the capabilities approach. As Foster and Sen have observed, 'handicaps, such as age or disability or illness . . . make it harder to convert income into capability' (Foster and Sen, 1997, pp. 211–212). Now consider 'a case where one person A derives exactly twice as much utility as person B from any given level of income, say, because B has some handicap . . . In this case the [utilitarian] rule of maximizing the sum-total of utility of the two would require that person A be given a higher income than B' (Sen, 1973, pp. 16–17). Thus, instead of reducing the inequality that would have existed even with equal incomes, 'the utilitarian rule of distribution compounds it by giving more income to A, who is already better off' (Sen, 1973, p. 17). Thus, an analysis in terms of capabilities shines a bright light into some of the darker corners of utilitarianism (cf. Walsh, 1995–6, pp. 556–569; for a more formal analysis, see Sen, 1985a and Atkinson, 1995, 17–31).

Understandably, there has been some debate recently concerning the relationship between needs and capabilities. Present-day classical theory has tended to dichotomize commodities into basic and non-basic, following Sraffa. Sraffa himself, of course, made the decision not to retain the consumption basics (Sraffa, 1960, p. 10). Excluding subsistence requirements from the reproduction necessary for viability can be problematic, however, as indeed he recognized (compare Walsh and Gram, 1980, pp. 317–319). If one *includes* subsistence requirements, are these properly confined to what Smith would have regarded as necessaries? As Harvey Gram has observed, 'Smith distinguishes between necessities of the body and the necessities of a virtuous life. Only the former is implied by the usual meaning of "subsistence"' (Gram, 1998, p. 162). As Gram notes, there are a whole web of interdependent components needed for what we regard as a decent human life, and these 'conveniencies' should not be dismissed as sheer luxurious waste of the surplus. They are quite different from those vulgar extravagances that Smith frequently condemned.

This is clearly an area where the enrichment of present-day classical theory, which I have argued is a characteristic of its second phase, needs to proceed: 'Some concept of subsistence, and its relationship to such categories as "necessaries, conveniencies and luxuries", is central to the classical theory of value and distribution. Both the ancient concern with the reproduction of labour and the modern analysis of the reproduction of capital are intrinsic to maintaining an economy's physical, social and moral structure. No account of the general reproduction problem can proceed for long without taking into account the wide range of issues considered by Smith in TMS [Smith, A. ([1790], 1976a) *The Theory of Moral Sentiments*] . . . A theory of the social structure of demand, such as can be gleaned from TMS, is necessary to inform such investigations and thus to give firm foundations to a classical theory of demand' (Gram, 1998, pp. 165–166).

Clearly the functionings that have to be encompassed by such a theory go well beyond anything that could reasonably be described as the fulfillment of basic needs. One example of the current debate concerning needs and capabilities must suffice here. It comes from recent work of G. A. Cohen.

Cohen stresses that '[w]hen Sen first invoked capability it was in the context of a proposal that we attend to "*basic* capability equality". The relevant capability was of a fundamental sort, capability whose absence disables the person from satisfying his basic needs' (Cohen, 1993, p. 26, emphasis in original). Does the capability approach become problematic when we get above basic needs? In a slightly later publication, Cohen suggested that Sen's 'special interest in poverty is shown by [his] choice of capability as the premier space of advantage: capability provides a highly suitable measure of the deprivation that poverty imposes' (Cohen, 1994, p. 118).

Well, none will deny Sen's lifelong interest in poverty. But he is surely right to insist that, while the 'identification of minimally acceptable levels of certain basic capabilities' (Sen, 1993, p. 41) can provide an approach to poverty, nevertheless 'it is also important to recognize that the use of the capability approach is not confined to basic capabilities only' (Sen, 1993, p. 41). Recalling his earlier comments 'on the connection of the capability approach with some arguments used by Adam Smith and Karl Marx [Sen, 1984b, 1985b, 1987b]' (Sen, 1993, p. 46), he now turns to the powerful connections 'with the Aristotelian view of the human good' (Sen, 1993, p. 46).

Both Smith and Marx were Hellenists. They were hardly unaware of Aristotle's seminal discussion in the *Nichomachean Ethics*, which was the foundational treatment in the history of philosophy of the dependence of the good life on the availability of certain external means. Aristotle 'recognized that one may be prevented by the lack of various external necessities, or possessions, from leading what he regarded as the best kind of human life. In a later period of history, medieval philosophers were to recognize that much of what we call evil is more properly described as a privation of good. They were well aware that such deprivation could come from the lack of anything necessary to the flowering of our capabilities, whether or not what was needful was a physical object, or possession. Many years ago I began to explore this in a series of works [Walsh, 1958a, 1958b, 1961]. Kenneth Arrow later summed up what I was trying to explore, namely the "moral implications of the position that many attributes of the individual are similar in nature to external possessions" (Arrow, 1967, p. 21, note 10)' (Walsh, 1996, pp. 98–99),

From Aristotle through the medieval theorists of privation, to Kant's discussion of the loss due to the niggardliness of nature (see Walsh, 1954, pp. 627–637; 1961, pp. 67–101), to Smith and Marx, and down to present day discussion, the argument has never been confined to our bare capability for physical survival: 'To sustain such a claim, Cohen must meet, not Sen alone, but the whole tradition that runs from Aristotle, through Marx, to Sen' (Walsh, 1995–6, p. 561).

Certainly there is work still to be done: an enriched theory of conveniencies (in the sense of Smith) could be expected to body forth and strengthen the basis for capability analysis far beyond bare physical needs. Indeed, 'Smith's use of "conveniency" goes well beyond the desire to save time and trouble. It refers to "love of system", in the Stoical sense, well captured, according to Smith (TMS, VII. ii. 1. 52), by Seneca in the *Epistles*, where the Latin *convenientia* refers to proper, fit, decent and becoming actions' (Gram, 1998, p. 162). Thus are included, not just the necessities of the body, but the necessities of a virtuous life, of 'achieving self-respect, taking part in the life of the community, appearing in public without shame (the last a functioning that was illuminatingly discussed by Adam Smith)' (Sen, 1993, p. 367).

Needs, capabilities, and the dynamics of the wealth of nations

Bertram Schefold has remarked that '[t]here are certain hierarchies of needs, from basic needs up to higher needs such as the need for self-fulfillment' (Schefold, 1990, p. 187). This position, as we have seen, is perfectly consistent with Adam Smith, and it is quite natural that it should be on the minds of several people involved with what, I believe, are the early stages in the second phase of the revival of classical theory. Schefold points out that the presence of a hierarchy of needs implies a lexical ordering (Schefold, 1990, p. 185). Long dismissed as pathological by neoclassical theorists, lexical orderings have an important role in the enrichment of classical theory, as has been seen by Schefold. His work needs to be linked up with the rather extensive recent literature initiated by Sen and followed up by others (for sources and discussion, see Sen, 1977, 1981a, 1981b; Drèze and Sen, 1989; Coles and Hammond, 1995; Osmani, 1995; Walsh, 1996).

The concept of a hierarchy of needs, first for the most desperate necessity, then for less pressing necessities, and then for various levels of conveniencies, warrants the expectation that successive commodities will be added to a person's consumption and earlier inferior ones consumed less or given up completely, as income rises. Thus Schefold is right to expect 'shifts in the composition of output determined by Engel elasticities' (Schefold, 1990, p. 180). Here Schefold naturally turns to the work of Luigi Pasinetti (1981). Indeed this work, together with Pasinetti (1993) offers a striking example of a major effort to construct a rich, Smithian edifice upon classical (Sraffian) foundations (see Walsh, 1998c).

As Pasinetti has noted, technical progress gives individuals the possibility of acquiring 'entirely new goods and services altogether' (Pasinetti, 1993, p. 37). It thus becomes necessary to discuss the relation that exists between increases in real income, and expansion of demand for consumption goods. Neoclassical theory, however, 'on the dynamics of demand, is amazingly poor of information' (Pasinetti, 1993, p. 37). Thus, he argues that 'a dynamic analysis requires a decisive enrichment of the reference framework' (Pasinetti, 1993, p. 38). He expects various needs to be satisfied in 'a certain hierarchical order' (Pasinetti, 1993, p. 38); and that changes in consumption will also result independently of income, or price changes, as newly invented goods appear. Finally, he rightly expects that a saturation level will exist for any good or service. He does not explicitly discuss the role of lexical orderings in this context, although the possibility of their arising is clearly present.

Technical progress, in Pasinetti's system, brings a flow of new productive potential 'permitting us vast choices' (Pasinetti, 1993, p. 56). It imposes 'not just the possibility, but the *necessity* of making choices. There does not exist the alternative of not choosing!' (Pasinetti, 1993, p. 56, emphasis in original). He is depicting a vast field for the judgements of a classical theory of rational choice. Many of these new goods would be conveniences, quite possibly *not* previous luxuries but simply new goods. Responsibility for the non-damaging use of the surplus, in Pasinetti's society, would not be confined to a (relatively) tiny class as it was for Ricardo. Pasinetti observes that, in any community, there must be some channels 'through which the incomes, which flow only to some, provide the consumption that is needed by all' (Pasinetti, 1993, p. 109).

He discusses the social choice theory which 'we have inherited from current economic theory' (Pasinetti, 1993, p. 110). He finds that it has 'reached a rather unsatisfactory state. Arrow's remarkable "impossibility theorem" has put the whole field in a sort of state of frustration' (Pasinetti, 1993, p. 110). He adds, however, that 'a fruitful way out may come from an enlargement of the whole framework of reference' (Pasinetti, 1993, p. 110). He notes that '[t]he contributions of Amartya Sen, for example, are going in this direction' (Pasinetti, 1993, p. 110, note 7).

The literature on social choice theory, which has developed since Sen's critique of the neoclassical version of that theory, began to appear around 1970, and is, of course, immense. But a few points are worth making here. Kenneth Arrow's (1951) famous impossibility theorem on social orderings characterized rational choice by means of axioms that were similar to those underlying the formalization of choice in the canonical Arrow–Debreu models of general equilibrium. In both cases, the logical positivist precepts dictated what was allowed. Interpersonal comparisons of utility were disallowed as 'ethical'—all such judgements were regarded by logical positivist epistemology as 'meaningless'. So 'the surviving criterion was that of Pareto optimality' (Sen, 1987a, p. 31). Non-utility information about the agents was excluded, so that in fact 'the informational limitation of the Arrow format relates not merely to the poverty of the utility information but also to the eschewal of non-utility information. Most actual public judgements make extensive use of non-utility information, varying from relative incomes and ownership to the description of who is doing what to whom' (Sen, 1982, p. 18).

In the last 30 years or so, Sen has accordingly fathered a literature that defended interpersonal comparabilities (of varying degrees) and not just of utility; exposed the implicit utilitarian moral judgements hidden in even Pareto optimality; and led to the development of a wide variety of kinds of social choice results (see Sen 1997c, and other contributors to Arrow *et al.* 1996–1997). But all of this constructive development depended on a systematic rejection of the epistemology underlying the neoclassical theory of the canonical Arrow—Debreu models. Classical theorists, it will be seen, are well advised to shop carefully for any social choice concepts they need, and the tradition that has grown out of Sen's work is a good place to look.

Now Pasinetti's recent work embodies at its core an implicit rejection of logical positivist epistemology just as decisive as the explicit rejections evident in the remarks of Sen quoted above. Pasinetti tells us that '[t]he natural economic system represents so to speak the framework skeleton of the present theoretical construction. It is a set of relations that possess characteristics of analytical relevance and logical consistency, with *strong normative properties*' (Pasinetti, 1993, p. 117, emphasis added). He stresses that 'the natural system does not come into existence automatically' (Pasinetti, 1993, p. 117). It requires positive conscious policy: 'It becomes very important to single out those organizational devices that may continually search for, and lead to, the natural positions' (Pasinetti, 1993, p. 117). The debate of those engaged in such a search, turning on claims concerning the 'natural' system and what counted as 'natural' positions for it, clearly bodies forth Pasinetti's conception of an enriched classical model. Indeed, he explicitly compares his uses of the word 'natural' with the ways in which that word appears in the discourse of the original classics.

Compare some recent comments of Sen on how we should regard and evaluate the properties of a developing economy: 'The more conventional criteria of economic success . . . are to be valued only as means to deeper ends . . . The bettering of human life does not have to be justified by showing that a person with a better life is also a better producer' (Sen, 1997a, p. 6).

Concluding remarks

I have argued in this paper that the revival of classical theory in the twentieth century has essentially completed a first phase, which I have described as being one of minimalism. This must not be seen as criticism in any sense of the work of the great classics of the last century. I am completely convinced that what they did was right for their period, and for the specific tasks that they correctly saw as confronting them.

During the nineteenth century, after Ricardo's death, classical theory notoriously went into decline. The only truly great nineteenth century classic to succeed Ricardo, namely Karl Marx, was not published, or understood as regards his contributions to classical economics, until the end of the nineteenth century; but then his work was an important factor in stimulating the early beginnings of the classical revival. It is important to realize that the claim that twentieth century classics, by and large, tended to write minimalist models does *not* imply that they had narrow and confined theoretical or philosophical interests. The influence of Marx on the very earliest classical revival writers, just noted, illustrates the point at issue. Had the austerity which the early twentieth-century classical theorists insisted on in their formal models also limited their hearts and minds, they would hardly have been moved by Marx's great dark, richly tragic drama.

But the thinkers who revived classical theory were somehow aware of the emerging spirit of the new twentieth century: it would see the final triumph of modernist science, and the flowering and final fading of the pretensions of formalist mathematics. Classical ideas had now no chance of being taken seriously unless presented in the chaste garb of this intellectual puritanism. So they wrote within these conventions and, as we know, they did it superbly well, even if sometimes at the cost of an austerity and brevity that was a hardship for their readers.

The relationship between the work of Adam Smith and that of David Ricardo is very important for an understanding of the direction taken by the first wave of the classical revival, especially at Cambridge. Fortunately, Ricardo is on record as to how he regarded Smith, and it is worthwhile having the whole passage before us here:

> The writer, in combating received opinions, has found it necessary to advert more particularly to those passages in the writings of Adam Smith from which he sees reasons to differ; but he hopes it will not, on that account, be suspected that he does not, in common with all those who acknowledge the importance of the science of Political Economy, participate in the admiration which the profound work of this celebrated author so justly excites.
>
> (Ricardo, 1951–1973, 1, p. 6)

Smith had made some serious mistakes in the theory of distribution, which clearly affects the analytical skeleton of a classical model, and this had to be put right. On these, Ricardo concentrated his attention. Piero Sraffa took up Ricardo's lead, and followed the path leading to the certain key minimal properties of a classical reproduction system, leaving aside even the accumulation of capital. The view of Smith in Cambridge during those days can be seen very clearly in Maurice Dobb's well-known work (Dobb, [1937], 1953). Smith had made mistakes where it was vital not to, in the fundamental concepts of classical distribution theory. The great canvas of his political economy and its moral philosophy was not the pressing concern. Joan Robinson, when I came to know her well, used to say 'don't muddy the waters with a lot of stuff!' As she began to read and comment on our manuscript, Harvey Gram and I dropped a few chapters of a philosophical nature from the first draft (of Walsh and Gram, 1980). It was the right decision then.

But the time has come to focus our attention on the *praise* Ricardo had for Smith's whole political economy. And it is on this massive work, and not on Smith's now well recognized mistakes, that Amartya Sen's contributions concentrate. Smith is indeed the outstanding example of an eighteenth-century classical thinker whose texts offer a rich tapestry, interwoven with threads of analytic economics, rich description, and explicit moral philosophy. We owe to the recent studies of scholars like Vivienne Brown an illuminating analysis of the different voices to be heard at various points in the Smith texts, and of the consistency of the parts taken by different voices with the overall structure of Smith's moral philosophy.

I have stressed the importance—for his appraisal of Smith's total contribution—of Amartya Sen's remarkably early rejection of the fact–value dichotomy insisted on by logical positivism and similar movements that were prominent in the modernist scientific community of the last century. This made it possible for him to appreciate and develop ideas from Smith that were black with fact, white with convention, and red with values.

What is much less well-known is the significance for Sen (and also Pasinetti, Schefold, and others) working on second stage classical theory, of the rise and fall of what may be called the 'new dichotomy'. Two things need to be stressed right away: (1) the old fact–value dichotomy of logical positivists, logical empiricists, and such, is *not* defended today, *even* by proponents of the new dichotomy; and (2) the new dichotomy requires for its support arguments that would not have been accepted by the old positivists and their successors. Quite simply, the new dichotomy requires metaphysical arguments to support it, something that was anathema to the positivists and their allies.

Thus, even if the new dichotomy could be sustained (and Hilary Putnam has argued powerfully that it requires thoroughly *bad* metaphysics, and fails) it would not please the very economists who have clung so doggedly to the old fact–value dichotomy. What is more, the new dichotomy is not between facts and values. It is between everything that we ordinarily say about facts or values, and whatever 'finished science' will have to say, when (and if) it ever arrives. This prospect offers nothing to any kind of economist.

Also important is an idea that has risen to prominence among philosophers concerned with these issues: the increased appreciation of what Putnam calls the entanglement of fact and value. This has been especially recognized with regard to the more richly descriptive, less abstract ethical concepts. Which, of course, supports Sen's idea of rich description which in turn underlies many of his developments of Smithian ideas. Thus, concepts of entanglement and of descriptive richness facilitate and illuminate the re-exploration of a political economy *with an explicitly moral aspect.*

Consider for a moment, the concept of surplus—perhaps the most fundamental concept of all classical theory. Acute awareness of the role of surplus makes any classic alive to its misuse, or waste. Smith is savage where he sees the surplus being squandered by the profusion of the great. Closely related is the concept of exploitation, which pinpoints in one manner or another the extraction of the surplus from human labor, and its subsequent destination. Exploring this, of course, was one of the great contributions of the last great nineteenth-century classic, Marx. Exploitation, unfairness, and inequality, as well as the concept of the most vulnerable class, have of course been leading themes that sound throughout Amartya Sen's writings, but Sen's way of looking at exploited labor is highly characteristic. Just about every economic theorist I can think of who has cared about exploited labor, and also been a mathematical economist, has promptly reached for their mathematics. Sen, with the biggest guns one could wish for ready to hand, turns instead to certain features of natural languages.

Explicitly stressing his indebtedness to Maurice Dobb, Sen is unconcerned about the technical fact that reproduction prices in a classical model can be established without going through value magnitudes, since this 'does not affect this descriptive relevance of the labour theory of value in any way' (Sen, 1987c, 1, p. 911). The richness of the description of exploitation which one can give in terms of human labor, and its moral resonances, were what made the labor theory important to Dobb and Sen.

As far as the mathematics and analytic economics of reproduction models are concerned, any input can be said to be 'exploited'—that is to say, corn output is more than the corn input used in its production. But, '[i]n the case of human labour, unlike the case of a bag of corn or a machine, the use of the word "exploit" is a different member of its family of legitimate uses in English' (Walsh, 1998a, p. 191).

It is a property of natural languages that one can make many distinctions of this sort. The fact that the constructed language of commodity reproduction theory does not exhibit such distinctions should not be regarded as a defect of that theory: it does the jobs it was designed for, some of them so complex as to be beyond expression in a natural language. Artificial languages, including far more sophisticated ones, have been long known to be unable to replicate exactly many things which are easy to say in a natural language. One of the more hubristic enterprises of the last century, of course, was the attempt to construct an ideal language into which all that was truly the case could be translated. If you wanted to say something, and it would not translate into the 'ideal' language, so much the worse for the thing you had wanted to say. The logical positivists were at the forefront in the search for this Holy Grail, which 'underlay their belief in the desirability of translating things said in natural languages (seen as full of confusions and of primitive "metaphysical" notions) into the supposedly pellucid logical clarity of the constructed language whose chaste perfections were their goal' (Walsh, 1996, p. 92).

Recent philosophy has yielded several concepts that strengthen Sen's interpretation of Smith, notably one developed in a present-day guise by Derek Parfit. The vulgar (and interested) misunderstanding of what Smith meant by 'self-interest' is, of course, something that Sen has campaigned against for years. One of the many errors in the vulgar view is that it conflates self-interest and present-aims. A moment's reflection should be enough to show that many, if not most, of the obscene self-indulgences and wild financial gambles and swindles of recent years were in pursuit of immediate present aims at the *cost* of long-term, enlightened self-interest controlled by the humble virtue of prudence. Such actions are, it is evident, not even candidates for consideration as—what Smith made clear that he meant by—self-interest.

Another useful concept is that of meta-ranking, which formalized the ancient philosophical idea of a critical analysis and ranking of rival moral concepts. This shows how one might embed Smith's hierarchy of virtues in a present-day choice theoretical model, of the sort that Sen has made his own.

Interested misinterpretations of Smith, of course, are no monopoly of the last century. The ink was hardly dry on Smith's work before scribblers, politicians, and Colonial administrators were hard at work distorting his message. Sen makes excellent use of his well-known entitlement approach to famine in a spirited defense of Smith against his misuse by British Colonial administrators and others.

Ancient philosophy is, of course, the ultimate source for Sen's concepts of needs and capabilities. He turns to Aristotle for this, as we may well suppose Smith and Marx did in their turn, since they were both classical scholars. In working on the effect of various scarcities and deprivations in impeding our realization of otherwise possible moral attainment, I had also gone first to Aristotle, then to the medieval scholastic concept of privation, and finally to Kant's discussion of the loss due to the niggardliness of nature.

It is, I believe, very significant that a theorist who played one of the key roles in the *first* phase of the classical revival, and began to publish work some considerable time ago that had deeply 'second stage' characteristics—namely Luigi Pasinetti—has been exploring the concept of needs in a way that links up with Sen's writings. Bertram Schefold, long noted for his work in the first wave of the classical revival, has also been writing recently on hierarchies of needs and the significance of lexical orderings—the concept on which Sen has initiated a rather extensive recent literature.

Schefold naturally links his work on shifts in the composition of output to Pasinetti's studies of transformational growth. To me the most exciting thing about Pasinetti's work, especially on his natural system, is that it constitutes—as far as I know—the most sustained effort yet made to construct formal classical models which embed explicitly moral concepts in their structure. A number of questions have been raised about the natural system; whatever its present shortcomings may (or may not) be, however, it is certainly a vivid example of what a second wave classical construction may be expected to look like.

Note

* The first draft of this paper was presented to the *History of Economics Society* in June, 1999. I am grateful to my session Chairman, E. Roy Weintraub, and my discussant, Spencer Banzhaf for their encouragement and comments. Steven Pressman's advice played a key role in the writing of the present version, as did the advice and editorial assistance of Lisa Bendall-Walsh. The usual disclaimers apply.

References

Arrow, K. J. ([1951], 1963), *Social Choice and Individual Values*, 2nd (extended) edition (New York, Wiley).

Arrow, K. J. (1967) Public and Private Values, in S. Hook (Ed.) *Human Values and Economic Policy, A Symposium*, pp. 3–21, (New York, New York University Press).

Arrow, K. J. and Hahn, F. H. (1971) *General Competitive Analysis* (San Francisco, Holden-Day).

Arrow, K. J. Sen, A. K. and Suzumura, K. (Eds) (1996–1997) *Social Choice Re-examined*, Vols 1 and 2 (New York, St. Martin's Press).

Atkinson, A. B. (1995) Capabilities, exclusion, and the supply of goods, in: K. Basu, P. Pattanaik and K. Suzumura (Eds) *Choice, Welfare, and Development: a Festschrift in Honour of Amartya K. Sen*, pp. 17–31 (Oxford, Clarendon Press).

Brown, V. (1994) *Adam Smith's Discourse: canonicity, commerce and conscience* (London, Routledge).

Cohen, G. A. (1993) Equality or what? On welfare, goods, and capabilities, in: M. Nussbaum and A. K. Sen (Eds) (1993) *The Quality of Life*, pp. 9–29 (Oxford, Clarendon Press).

Cohen, G. A. (1994) Amartya Sen's unequal world, *New Left Review*, 203(1) (Spring) pp. 117–129.

Coles, J. L. and Hammond, P. J. (1995) Walrasian equilibrium without survival: existence, efficiency and remedial policy, in K. Basu, P. Pattanaik and K. Suzumura (Eds) *Choice, Welfare, and Development: a Festschrift in Honour of Amartya K. Sen*, pp. 32–64 (Oxford, Clarendon Press).

Dobb, M. H. ([1937], 1953) *Political Economy and Capitalism, Some Essays in Economic Tradition* (London, Routledge).

Drèze J. and Sen, A. K. (1989) *Hunger and Public Action* (Oxford, Clarendon Press).

Drèze J. and Sen, A. K. (Eds) (1990 and 1991) *The Political Economy of Hunger*, 3 vols (Oxford, Clarendon Press).

Drèze J. and Sen, A. K. (1995) *India: economic development and social opportunity*, (Oxford and Delhi, Oxford University Press).

Foster, J. and Sen, A. K. (1997) On economic inequality after a quarter century, in: A. K. Sen, *On Economic Inequality*, 2nd edn, pp. 107–219 (Oxford, Clarendon Press).

Gram, H. N. (1998) Necessaries, conveniencies and luxuries, in: H. D. Kurz and N. Salvadori (Eds) *The Elgar Companion to Classical Economics*, vol. 2, pp. 162–166 (Cheltenham, Edward Elgar).

Kurz, H. D. and Salvadori, N. (1995) *Theory of Production, A Long Period Analysis*, (Cambridge, Cambridge University Press).

Murdoch, I. (1971) *The Sovereignty of 'Good'* (London, Routledge).

Nussbaum, M. and Sen, A. K. (Eds) (1993) *The Quality of Life* (Oxford, Clarendon Press).

O'Donnell, R. (1990) *Adam Smith's Theory of Value and Distribution, A Reappraisal* (New York, St. Martin's Press).

Osmani, S. (1995) The entitlement approach to famine: an assessment, in: K. Basu, P. Pattanaik and K. Suzumura (Eds) *Choice, Welfare, and Development: a Festschrift in Honour of Amartya K. Sen*, pp. 253–294 (Oxford, Clarendon Press).

Parfit, D. (1984) *Reasons and Persons* (Oxford, Clarendon Press).

Pasinetti, L. L. (1981) *Structural Change and Economic Growth: a theoretical essay on the dynamics of the wealth of nations* (Cambridge, Cambridge University Press).

Pasinetti, L. L. (1993) *Structural Economic Dynamics: a theory of the economic consequences of human learning* (Cambridge, Cambridge University Press).

Putnam, H. (1987) *The Many Faces of Realism* (LaSalle, IL, Open Court).

Putnam, H. (1993) Objectivity and the science-ethics distinction, in: M. Nussbaum and A. K. Sen (Eds) *The Quality of Life*, pp. 143–57 (Oxford, Clarendon Press).

Quine, W. V. (1963) Carnap on logical truth, in: P. A. Schilpp (Ed) *The Philosophy of Rudolph Carnap* (LaSalle, IL, Open Court).

Raphael, D. D. and Macfie, A. L. (Eds) (1976) *Adam Smith, The Theory of Moral Sentiments* (Oxford: Clarendon Press).

Ricardo, D. (1951–73) *The Works and Correspondence of David Ricardo*, 11 vols, P. Sraffa and M. H. Dobb (Eds) (Cambridge, Cambridge University Press).

Robbins, L. (1932) *An Essay on The Nature and Significance of Economic Science* (London, Macmillan).

Schefold, B. (1990) On changes in the composition of output, in: K. Bharadwaj and B. Schefold (Eds) *Essays on Piero Sraffa: critical perspectives on the revival of classical theory* (London, Unwin Hyman).

Sen, A. K. (1967) The Nature and Classes of Prescriptive Judgements, *Philosophical Quarterly*, 17, pp. 46–62.

Sen, A. K. (1970) *Collective Choice and Social Welfare* (San Francisco, Holden-Day).

Sen, A. K. (1973) *On Economic Inequality*, 1st edn (Oxford, Clarendon Press).

Sen, A. K. (1976) Famines and failures of exchange entitlements, *Economic and Political Weekly*, Special Number, 11, pp. 1273–1280.

Sen, A. K. (1977) Starvation and exchange entitlements: a general approach and its application to the Great Bengal Famine, *Cambridge Journal of Economics*, 1, pp. 33–59

Sen, A. K. (1978) On the labour theory of value: some methodological issues, *Cambridge Journal of Economics*, 2, pp. 175–190.

Sen, A. K. (1981a) *Poverty and Famines: an essay on entitlements and deprivation* (Oxford, Clarendon Press).

Sen, A. K. (1981b) Ingredients of famine analysis: availability and entitlements, *Quarterly Journal of Economics*, 96, pp. 433–464

Sen, A. K. ([1974], 1982) Choice, orderings and morality, in: A. K. Sen, *Choice, Welfare and Measurement* (Cambridge, MA, MIT Press).

Sen, A. K. ([1977], 1982) Rational fools, in: A. K. Sen, *Choice, Welfare and Measurement*, pp. 84–106 (Cambridge, MA, MIT Press).

Sen, A. K. ([1980], 1982) Description as choice, in: A. K. Sen, *Choice, Welfare and Measurement*, pp. 432–449 (Cambridge, MA, MIT Press).

Sen, A. K. (1982) *Choice, Welfare and Measurement* (Cambridge, MA, MIT Press).

Sen, A. K. (1984a) The living standard, *Oxford Economic Papers*, 36, pp. 74–90.

Sen, A. K. (1984b) *Resources, Values and Development* (Cambridge, MA, Harvard University Press).

Sen, A. K. (1985a) *Commodities and Capabilities* (Amsterdam, North Holland).

Sen, A. K. (1985b) Well-being, agency and freedom: the Dewey Lectures 1984, *Journal of Philosophy*, 82, pp. 169–221.

Sen, A. K. (1986) Food, economics and entitlements, Elmhirst Lecture, 1985, *Lloyd's Bank Review*, 160, pp. 3–20.

Sen, A. K. (1987a) *On Ethics and Economics* (Oxford, Blackwell).

Sen, A. K. (1987b) *The Standard of Living*, Tanner Lectures with discussions, G. Hawthorne, (Ed) (Cambridge: Cambridge University Press).

Sen, A. K. (1987c) Dobb, Maurice Herbert, in: J. Eatwell, M. Milgate and P. Newman (Eds) *The New Palgrave: a dictionary of economics* 1, pp. 910–912 (London: Macmillan).

Sen, A. K. (1992) *Inequality Reexamined* (Cambridge, MA, Harvard University Press).

Sen, A. K. (1993) Capability and well-being, in: M. Nussbaum and A. K. Sen (Eds) *The Quality of Life*, pp. 30–53 (Oxford, Clarendon Press).

Sen, A. K. (1997a) Radical needs and moderate reforms, in: J. Drèze and A. K. Sen (Eds) *Indian Development: selected regional perspectives*, pp. 1–32 (Oxford and Delhi, Oxford University Press).

Sen, A. K. (1997b) *On Economic Inequality*, 2nd edn (Oxford, Clarendon Press).

Sen, A. K. (1997c) Individual preference as the basis of social choice, in: K. J. Arrow, A. K. Sen and K. Suzumura (Eds) *Social Choice Re-examined*, Vol 1, pp 15–37 (New York, St. Martin's Press).

Sidgwick, H. ([1874], 7th edn 1907, pp 418–419) (London: Macmillan).

Smith, A. ([1937], 1978), An early draft of part of the *Wealth of Nations*, in: W. R. Scott (1937) *Adam Smith as Student and Professor* (Glasgow, Glasgow University Publications). Cited from Smith (1978) pp. 562–586

Smith, A. ([1790], 1976a) *The Theory of Moral Sentiments*, vol. 1 of *The Glasgow Edition of the Works and Correspondence of Adam Smith*, A. L. Macfie and D. D. Raphael (Eds) (Oxford: Clarendon Press) referred to in the text as TMS.

Smith, A. ([1776], 1976b) *An Inquiry into the Nature and Causes of the Wealth of Nations*, vol. II of the Glasgow Edition, R. H. Campbell, A. S. Skinner and W. B. Todd (Eds) (Oxford: Clarendon Press).

Sraffa, P. (1960) *Production of Commodities by Means of Commodities: prelude to a critique of economic theory* (Cambridge, Cambridge University Press).

Walsh, V. C. (1954) The theory of the good will, *Cambridge Journal*, 7, pp. 627–637.

Walsh, V. C. (1958a) Scarcity and the concepts of ethics, *Philosophy of Science*, 25, 249–257.

Walsh, V. C. (1958b) Ascriptions and appraisals, *Journal of Philosophy*, 55, pp. 1062–1072.

Walsh, V. C. (1961) *Scarcity and Evil* (Englewood Cliffs, NJ, Prentice Hall).

Walsh, V. C. (1967) On the significance of choice sets with incompatibilities, *Philosophy of Science*, 34, pp. 243–250.

Walsh, V. C. (1987) Philosophy and economics, in: J. Eatwell, M. Milgate. and P. Newman (Eds) *The New Palgrave: a dictionary of economics* 3, pp. 861–869 (London: Macmillan).

Walsh, V. C. (1994) Rationality as self-interest versus rationality as present aims, *American Economic Review*, 84, pp. 401–405.

Walsh, V. C. (1995–6) Amartya Sen on inequality, capabilities and needs, *Science and Society*, 59(4), pp. 556–569.

Walsh, V. C. (1996) *Rationality, Allocation and Reproduction* (Oxford, Clarendon Press).

Walsh, V. C. (1998a) Normative and positive classical economics, in: H. D. Kurz and N. Salvadori (Eds) *The Elgar Companion to Classical Economics*, vol. 2, pp. 188–194 (Cheltenham, Edward Elgar).

Walsh, V. C. (1998b) Recent interpretations of Adam Smith, in: H. D. Kurz and N. Salvadori (Eds) *The Elgar Companion to Classical Economics*, vol. 2, pp. 270–275 (Cheltenham, Edward Elgar).

Walsh, V. C. (1998c) Rationality in reproduction models. Conference on Sraffa and Modern Economics, *Centro Studie Documentazione 'Piero Sraffa'*, Rome, Italy.

Walsh, V. C. and Gram, H. N. (1980) *Classical and Neoclassical Theories of General Equilibrium: historical origins and mathematical structure* (New York: Oxford University Press).

Williams, B. (1985) *Ethics and the Limits of Philosophy* (Cambridge, MA, Harvard University Press).

3 Sen after Putnam[*]

Vivian Walsh

I shall examine the work of a great economist-philosopher, Amartya Sen, with the aim of seeing how the very nature of 'classical theory' in economics becomes transformed in his work and how that transformation is a direct function of the collapse of the fact-value dichotomy.

Hilary Putnam (2002, p. 9)

[W]e have to grapple with the sad fact that contemporary economics has not yet put itself onto the map of conceptually respectable theories of human action. (Indeed, it has repudiated the rich foundations that the philosophical anthropology of Adam Smith offered it).

Martha C. Nussbaum (2000a, p. 122)

Sen and 'second phase' present day classical economic theory

In his recent book, Hilary Putnam (Putnam, 2002) collects together his *Rosenthal Lectures* (Putnam, 2000) and other relevant writings, some of which have not previously been published. In this work he provides, directly and indirectly, an explicitly philosophical analysis of ideas that are crucial for understanding the work of Amartya Sen. He defends the important role of moral concepts and arguments in Sen against a posture of denial among economists whose sole logical foundation he shows to be dependent on unsustainable ideas borrowed by economists from philosophy. This illuminates and supports Sen's analysis of human well being and of development in terms of the achievement of capabilities to function.

In this enterprise, Putnam makes use of the argument to be found in the article 'Smith after Sen', published in this *Review* two years ago (Walsh, 2000, pp. 5–25). In doing so he explains that: 'Vivian Walsh . . . has recently traced the development of what he calls "the revival of classical [economic] theory during the twentieth century" with special attention to Amartya Sen's place in what Walsh sees as the emerging "second phase" of that theory' (Putnam, 2002, p. 47).

I had argued in that article that the reappraisal of Adam Smith (in which Sen had been a major force) highlights much of what is important about the second phase of the classical revival because 'Smith embedded a remarkable understanding of the core concepts of a classical theory of the reproduction of surplus, in the setting of a richly descriptive political economy whose implications for moral philosophy he understood and explored' (Walsh, 2000, p. 6).

Putnam comments that 'if we are to understand Sen's place in history, the reintroduction of ethical concerns and concepts into economic discourse must not be thought of as an *abandonment* of "classical economics"; rather it is a *reintroduction* of something that was everywhere present in the writings of Adam Smith, and that went hand-in-hand with Smith's technical analyses. This is something that Sen himself stresses' (Putnam, 2002, p. 48).

This reintroduction of ethical concerns and concepts is a key distinguishing characteristic of what I have been referring to as the 'enrichment' of present day classical theory. Agreeing with this, Putnam concludes that Walsh's term 'second phase classical theory' is thus the right term for the Senian program. That program involves introducing ethical concerns and concepts without sacrificing the rigorous tools contributed by 'first phase' theory (Putnam, 2002, p. 49). Actually, I began arguing for the need for an 'enrichment' of present day classical theory some years ago, pointing out that

> there *are* technical distinctions between a present-day classical model (in the tradition of Sraffa) and a standard neo-Walrasian model . . ., such as the different treatment of inputs, and the rather prominent role of surplus and economic class in the classical models and their absence (to say the least) in the neo-Walrasian models. But if one presents the differences purely in technical terms, one offers Hamlet without the Prince of Denmark. Just as neo-Walrasian models are an incredibly subtle set of variations upon the deep (and morally non-trivial) ideal of methodological individualism, believed in but not adhered to by neo-Walrasian theory, so in their turn classical models are a set of variations upon the ancient theme of the ultimate significance of economic class, economic power, and the moral implications of the control and disposition of the surplus.
>
> (Walsh, 1996, pp. 259–260)

I first devoted my whole attention to the enrichment of present-day classical theory in a paper for the Sraffa Conference in Rome (in 1998). I had been persuaded by many conversations with Lisa Bendall-Walsh that I had devoted enough time to the criticism of the standard formulations of rationality in neoclassical (or neo-Walrasian) economic theory. In contrast to the neoclassics: 'Rationality claims, in the original classics, primarily concerned what they regarded as the reasonable, responsible use of the surplus in the accumulation of capital' (Walsh, 1998a, p. 1). It was time to explore how the claims to rationality and moral responsibility implied in *present-day classical theory* could be developed and enriched, and to consider what Alan Hamlin called 'the more constructive discussion of the appropriate reform of the idea of rationality within economics' (Hamlin, 1997, p. 1593), to begin to address the need 'for the reintegration of a richer and more philosophically attractive notion of rationality into economic theory' (Hamlin, 1997, p. 1592).

A review by Nicholas Baigent also drew my attention to the importance of asking, when considering any account of rationality, what are the *purposes* for which it was constructed. As he put it, 'many neoclassical economists will argue that, for their purposes their narrow characterization is appropriate while they may well agree . . . that for other purposes, their characterizations are too narrow' (Baigent, 1997, p. 550).

Well, my purposes would not be the 'narrow' concerns of neoclassical concepts of rationality, but rather the enrichment of present day classical theory, and the drawing out of its implicit moral position, and thus of the claims to rationality of that position. I began this task in the next year (Walsh, 1998b, pp. 188–193; 1998c, pp. 270–275). In 'Smith after Sen' (Walsh, 2000) I first presented explicitly the concept of a developing second wave in the articulation of present day classical theory, using the work of Amartya Sen as my chief exemplar of this.

How a minimalist classical theory arose

Why should it be necessary to 'enrich' a classical theory that descends to us from the morally deep and explicit political economy and moral philosophy of Adam Smith? A few historical facts are necessary to make this clear. We need to begin by comparing Adam Smith with the work of the great early nineteenth-century classic David Ricardo. Thus, Putnam observes that: 'As Walsh has noted elsewhere [Walsh, 1998b, p. 189], Ricardo himself never lost sight of the deep moral implications of Smith's analytic contribution. But Ricardo knew that he was not a trained moral philosopher, and so (as he himself tells us [Ricardo, 1951, p. 6]) he "confined his attention to those passages in the writings of Adam Smith from which he sees reason to differ"' (Putnam, 2002, p. 47).

After Ricardo's death in 1823, his mantle 'fell upon lesser men, and the light was gradually extinguished. Rather as the British army after the death of the Duke of Wellington retained in atrophied form only the great duke's defects, and not his brilliant leadership, so the classical school after Ricardo preserved . . . only his weaknesses' (Walsh and Gram, 1980, p. 121). Manchester school vulgarizers, especially, had no interest in reviving those parts of the works of Smith which Ricardo's modesty had led him to leave aside. Later, at the beginning of the twentieth century, when classical theory began to be revived, it *might* have been done through a philosophically enlightened reexamination of the neglected parts of the Smith canon. But such an enterprise would not have been in tune with the spirit of the age. Thus, when classical theory began to revive around the beginning of the twentieth century, it was at the hands of theorists who wanted to free Ricardo from charges of inconsistency, and to establish exactly what was sound in his system. The stress was on mathematical proof, and minimal explanation. (The little known history of the early twentieth-century beginnings of the revival of classical economics is explored in detail, and related to the mathematical exposition of present day classicism, in Kurz and Salvadori, 1995, pp. 379–423.)

Discussing this, Putnam correctly observes that

> this 'Ricardian minimalism' was a notable characteristic of the work of Piero
> Sraffa, von Neumann, and others, but this is not a criticism of Sraffa or von
> Neumann or their contemporaries. As Walsh says, 'In fact such a minimalism
> reflected the most critical need for the revival of classical theory: the most
> precise possible mathematical development of the structure of the theory
> [Walsh, 1998a, p. 4]'. A similar point is made by Sen himself (note that Sen's
> term for what Walsh calls minimalism' is 'the engineering approach'!):
> 'There are many issues on which economics has been able to provide better
> understanding and illumination precisely because of the extensive use of the
> engineering approach [Sen, 1987a, p. 8]'.
>
> (Putnam, 2002, p. 47)[1]

Despite what could be achieved by a strictly minimalist analysis, however,
Putnam concludes that '[i]f it was important in the twentieth century to perfect the
mathematical tools of the "minimalist" approach, Sen insists that something additional is needed now' (Putnam, 2002, p. 48).

Sen, it should be noted, was not a major participant in the discussions of the
minimalist phase of the classical revival. Again, a few historical remarks may be
helpful. As Kurz and Salvadori show in detail, the revival of classical theory can
be seen in the work of Vladimir Karpovich Dmitriev just before the beginning of
the twentieth century, and was developed in the early twentieth century in the
work of Ladislaus von Bortkiewicz, Georg von Charasoff, Wassily Leontiev,
Robert Remak and John von Neumann, to name only a few of the most important
contributors (Kurz and Salvadori, 1995, especially pp. 176–178, 379–426). Most
of this work was written in German (Dmitriev wrote in Russian), and took place
in Germany and Austria. It became impossible to continue this in the mid-1930s.
Neumann and Leontiev were among those who came to America. Piero Sraffa,
however, was in England, at Cambridge, from the 1920s, and in the 1950s he was
at the center of a group of people vigorously reviving classical theory under his
inspiration and that of Joan Robinson. Since a number of them were Italian—such
as Pierangelo Garegnani and Luigi Pasinetti—the Cambridge school of modern
classicism came to be known also as the Anglo-Italian school.

Sen was a graduate student in Cambridge and Robinson was supervising his PhD
dissertation (Sen, 1960), together with Amiga Dasgupta, and he was studying
economics with Piero Sraffa and Maurice Dobb, just as the Cambridge contributions
to the classical revival were in full flood. It was thus *this part* of the twentieth-century
classical revival that lay in the youthful Sen's immediate intellectual environment.

The Cambridge controversies (between Cambridge, UK and Cambridge, MA)
on the nature of capital, as they came to be called, became a bitter cold war battle-
field of ideas. The fact that Sraffa's classical model (Sraffa, 1960) was a valid
piece of economic theory, and should simply be treated as such, though obvious
now, was rendered obscure by overheated emotions. Among the less intelligent
neoclassic economists, the views of Sraffa and Robinson and the Anglo-Italians

came to be treated as the Victorians treated sex: something not to be mentioned in polite society, and especially not in front of the young. (An up-to-date account of the controversies can be found in Kurz and Salvadori, 1995. On classical theory, see also Kurz and Salvadori, 1998b; Walsh 2002a, pp. 327–342.)

Sen's position on these matters, however, cannot, I believe, be made clear simply by looking at the ideological battle being waged around him. As for the questions of economic theory, he has throughout his life consistently recognized the analytical rigor of the arguments of Sraffa and Robinson (see for example Sen, 1960, 1974, 1975, 1989). But he devoted himself to intense work on theoretical issues which (to Robinson especially) seemed a waste of time.

The situation has some ironic elements. Two profoundly *Cambridge* influences were tending to move him away from participating deeply in the minimalist phase of the classical revival. The first of these has been commented on by Steven Pressman and Gale Summerfield; citing A. Klamer (1980, p. 139), they note that Robinson had 'attempted to move his research away from "ethical rubbish" and toward abstract theory' (Pressman and Summerfield, 2000, p. 91). Dasgupta, it appears, was more supportive of Sen's interest in ethics and the philosophical foundations of economic theory. That Robinson would take a sharply negative, logical positivist position towards any entanglement of economic theory and ethics, however unfortunate, was certainly to be expected. As I have noted else-where, she was quite definitely influenced by the logical positivism which infected debate on economic theory in the 1930s (Walsh, 1996, pp. 258–259, 2002b, pp. 186–187). No economist, of course, ever *needed* to insist on the entanglement of fact, value, and theory more than Robinson did, and no economist ever cared more passionately for social justice. So I agree with Daniel M. Hausman that her positivism seriously impaired the consistency of her position. But he is surely also right in saying that is would be unfair to 'take Robinson to task for espousing the philosophical orthodoxy of her day' (Hausman, 1980, p. 822).

A salient characteristic of Robinson was her single-mindedness. During the last decade of her life, when with great kindness (but critical judgment!) she read and discussed successive versions of the work Harvey Gram and I were writing, until satisfied with it, (Robinson, 1980, pp. xii–xvi), he and I had numerous opportuni-ties to see her pursuit of the essential theoretical argument and her refusal to get sidetracked by what she regarded as unnecessary digressions. We learned to avoid philosophical debates—which indeed suited a study of the minimalist phase of the classical revival. Our classical model, stripped down to its bare essentials, was a blend of Neumann and Sraffa (Walsh and Gram, 1980). This blend, much embel-lished, is incidentally the one used later by Kurz and Salvadori, who remark that '[t]he most important proximate sources of inspiration for the present inquiry are the contributions to economic analysis by Piero Sraffa (1898–1983) and John von Neumann (1903–1957)' (Kurz and Salvadori, 1995, p. 34).

While seeking the essentials of minimalist revived classicism, Gram and I could not have had a better guide than Robinson. But she would not have done at all for the young Sen. Her ferocious logical gardening would have rooted out as weeds what were some of his finest flowers. For it is a great feature of Sen's work that one finds it hard to think of any of it which is *not* directly or indirectly shot through with moral issues—however abstract the mathematics! *Minimalism* was not for Sen.

But now there was another Cambridge force—this time a positive one—also strongly drawing Sen away from the capital theory debates. This was a man whose influence surfaces here and there throughout Sen's work: Maurice Herbert Dobb. It is important to see that Dobb had first-rate *Sraffian* credentials—he was firmly on the Anglo-Italian side of the debate! Writing of Dobb's last book (Dobb, 1973), Sen remarks that in this Dobb had responded 'to the new developments in Cambridge political economy, including the influential "Prelude to a Critique of Economic Theory" by Piero Sraffa (1960). Maurice Dobb's association with Piero Sraffa extended over a long period, both as a colleague at Trinity College, and also as a collaborator in editing *Works and Correspondence of David Ricardo*, published in eleven volumes between 1951 and 1973' (Sen, 1987b, 1, p. 910).

So certainly the young Sen was not coming under the influence of a neoclassical opponent of Sraffa and Robinson! But what Sen calls Dobb's 'deep involvement in descriptive richness' (Sen, 1987b, 1, p. 912) would help to sustain Sen's confidence in the legitimacy (and necessity) of what we would now call the entanglement of fact, value and theory. In fact, Dobb's influence took a more specific and decisive role: as Pressman and Summerfield point out 'It was Dobb, and Dobb alone, who encouraged Sen to pursue his interest in the work of Arrow, and Dobb who spent time with Sen talking about the implications of Arrow's theorem' (Pressman and Summerfield, 2000, p. 91). Dobb saw clearly that Arrow's theorem would be seen as a great barrier to the claim that a rational social policy could be found. He also saw that Sen had just the talents needed to take the theorem apart at the seams, as of course Sen later did. Cambridge had done the necessary work on *minimalist* classical theory (if the neoclassics would just listen). Sen, he may have felt, was not needed for this. Sen *was* needed to rescue the possibility of social choice. Arrow's dramatic negative result on the possibility of social choice had depended on certain axioms. After Sen had gone to work on these, things were never the same. As Putnam remarks, '[t]he truly vast literature that has grown out of Sen's critique of the various axioms involved in social choice theory is indicated by the references to be found in his work' (Putnam, 2002, p. 165, note 3). Instead of the supposed impossibility of any rational social choices, the prospect had opened up to reveal a widespread proliferation of different social choice models, whose different axioms had been designed to suit different classes of social problems. One after another the fortifications built by neoclassical theory to prevent itself from having to deal with any non-trivial issues concerning human well-being were falling, and Sen was making possible the development of an enriched economic theory that would be able to undertake a re-examination of long neglected aspects of Adam Smith. Maurice Dobb had set him on a path leading far away from Ricardian minimalism!

For the second phase in the revival of classical theory to flower freely, however, certain old philosophical dichotomies with roots going back all the way to David Hume needed to be demystified and rendered ineffective. This Putnam sets out to do in the Rosenthal Lectures.

Metaphysical dichotomies versus ordinary common sense distinctions

Putnam remarks, of giving the Rosenthal Lectures, that 'it seemed to me – and Walsh powerfully encouraged me in this! – that this was a perfect opportunity to present a detailed rebuttal of the view that "fact is fact and value is value and never the twain shall meet", a view that implied that the Senian enterprise of bringing economics closer to ethics is logically impossible, and, more particularly, to present a very different philosophy of language from the logical positivist one which made it seem so impossible' (Putnam, 2002, p. viii).

He adds a point of great importance concerning *rationality*—namely, that in effect, having a fact/value dichotomy, impoverishes and trivializes one's view of rationality, since it is then assumed that 'rationality' has to do only with judgments concerning *facts*. Whereas, '[o]f course it is clear that developing a less scientistic account of rationality, an account that enables us to see how reasoning, far from being impossible in normative areas, is in fact indispensable to them, and conversely, understanding how normative judgments are presupposed in all reasoning, is important not only in economics, but—as Aristotle already saw—in all of life' (Putnam, 2002, p. viii).

Several aspects of what Putnam is about to do need to be stressed. First, the philosophical trouble is caused by *more than one* dichotomy. The claim that there is a dichotomy between facts and values is *intimately* connected with the claim that there is also a dichotomy between facts and tautologies. Secondly, the problem over metaphysical dichotomies will be traced back to Hume—it is an ancient philosophical disease. The logical positivists were simply the leading early twentieth-century examples of the dichotomy disease, and the cause of economists becoming infected. And now a dichotomy disease of virulent metaphysical characteristics has quite recently broken out, with which economists do not seem to be widely infected yet.

Some philosophically trained economists, of whom I am happy to say there are increasingly many, may be initially surprised that their field should *still* be accused of logical positivism. But the claim is not that *philosophers* of economics are positivists—they would not have been caught dead with it for years (apart from one or two diehards).[2] Nor is the claim even that working economists still accept *all* of the positivist theses. The claim is that a fact/value dichotomy (of which logical positivism was the early 20th century version) still underlies the beliefs and intended practice of economists today. They probably do not see this as positivism, but rather as a matter of scientifically informed common sense, and would perhaps be surprised to discover some of its more ancient philosophical roots. As Putnam remarks, '[t]he idea that "value judgments are subjective" is a piece of philosophy that has gradually come to be accepted by many people as if it were common sense' (Putnam, 2002, p. 1).

As for common sense, the economist who hankers after some of this after recent invasions of the field by exotic philosophical imports will find that, in fact, Putnam is a true friend of common sense, offering a position that respects the major results of mathematics and science, and contains no support for the *nihilistic* side of post-modernism. Indeed, he has argued for years, and still does, that 'what is wrong with relativist views (apart from their horrifying irresponsibility) is that they do not at all correspond to how we think and to how we shall continue to think' (Putnam, 1987, p. 70).

Now, ordinary common sense distinctions are not at all Putnam's target. The distinctions which we make in a natural language have some limited range of application, there are areas where they do not apply, others where their relevance is hazy. We expect no more of them, and use them while aware of their limitations. Philosophers, however, elevate some distinctions into absolute 'dichotomies' or 'dualisms'. Such metaphysical 'dichotomies' are Putnam's targets.

Finally, Putnam is concerned with *all* sorts of values, not only with those normally regarded as 'ethical' or 'moral'. He argues, following Charles Sanders Peirce and the other classical American pragmatists, 'that science itself presupposes values—that *epistemic* values (coherence, simplicity, and the like) are values too, and in the same boat as ethical values with respect to objectivity. Chapter 8, my concluding chapter, fleshes out this argument by looking at twentieth century philosophy of science and its sorry history of trying to evade this issue' (Putnam, 2002, p. 3). I might note here that for a number of years Hilary and Ruth Anna Putnam have been working on a reappraisal of the classical American Pragmatists (see, for example Putnam, [1992], 1995). Philosophical readers will be able to pick up pragmatist influences here and there throughout the book we are discussing.

The analytic/synthetic dichotomy

Before launching his main attack on the dichotomy that will most concern us (that supposedly existing between facts and values) Putnam suggests that it will be useful to examine another distinction 'that has also been inflated into a dichotomy and wielded as if it comprised an exhaustive classification of all possible judgments, namely the distinction between analytic and synthetic' (Putnam, 2002, p. 7).

The terms 'analytic' and 'synthetic', borrowed from Kant, came to be used in early analytic philosophy for tautologies and for empirical statements, respectively. Famous examples were 'all bachelors are unmarried' and 'the cat is on the mat'—the former true simply in virtue of its meaning, while the latter is open to immediate empirical testing. The logical positivists, it should be noted, in borrowing these terms analytic and synthetic adopted a 'vocabulary that had passed through and, on the way, been transformed by Frege' (Putnam, 2002, p. 8). Famously, Kant had believed that the truths of mathematics were synthetic a priori—*both* synthetic and necessary. The positivists, on the other hand, 'following Wittgenstein in the *Tractatus*, tried to combine Frege's claim (as against Kant) that mathematical truths are analytic, while agreeing with Kant (against Frege) that all analytic judgments are merely explicative and not ampliative' (Putnam, 2002, p. 148, note 1).

In a significant way, the logical positivists were thus more extreme than Frege. In describing all mathematical truths as analytic, Frege meant simply that they could be derived from the basic laws of logic—he believed that such mathematical truths *did* extend our knowledge (they were *ampliative*). This the positivists denied. It was thus in this *narrow* sense of analytic (explicative but *not* ampliative) that they proceeded to attempt 'to expand the notion of the "analytic" to embrace all of mathematics (which they claimed to be, in effect, a matter of our linguistic *conventions* as opposed to *facts*)' (Putnam, 2002, p. 8, emphasis in original).

So the logical positivists confront us with a pair of dichotomies, each sharply contrasting *facts* with something opposed: in one case facts are contrasted with tautologies, in the other case with values.

Putnam notes that since Quine's (1951) attack on it, 'this overblown form of the analytic–synthetic dichotomy has collapsed. (In effect Quine argued that scientific statements cannot be neatly separated into "conventions" and "facts".)' (Putnam, 2002, p. 8). He will argue later that *both* dichotomies collapsed, in each case because of a kind of *entanglement*: in the one case, because of the entanglement of facts and conventions, in the other case because of the entanglement of facts and values. But we are not ready for this yet. When we are, we shall be in a position to see 'how the very nature of "classical theory" in economics becomes transformed in [Sen's] work, and how that transformation is a direct function of the collapse of the fact–value dichotomy' (Putnam, 2002, p. 9).

A few words on 'distinctions' in ordinary discourse may be helpful here. In the ordinary business of living we are continuously making, using, altering, or abandoning distinctions. Like other important features of a natural language, our distinctions often involve 'defeasible' concepts, so that a claim which involves a distinction may be defeated by some newly discovered fact. Thus, it was once a sufficient answer to the question 'is she dead?' to answer 'yes: her heart has stopped'. If someone says 'his cottage is in the country' the reply may be 'well, the suburbs have pretty well closed it in now'. Our distinctions usually are not based on an abstract metaphysical dichotomy; they are rough and ready, have limited and changing applications, and are fuzzy at the edges. Supporting universal abstract claims is not one of the many work-a-day jobs for which they are intended. The domain of natural language is not a friendly one for the absolutism of the dedicated metaphysical dichotomist, and this will be specially relevant when we come to the fact–value dichotomy. For the moment, consider the logical positivists' famous example 'the cat is on the mat'. Surely one can agree that, on most occasions of use, the purpose of this sentence is to state a fact. But some unkind person who disliked cats, and felt that at least they should be put out at night, might say with an edge (on returning from work after midnight) 'the cat is on the mat!'. Here the factual assertion is clearly dominated by an expression of criticism, comparable to 'George left the washing-up!'.

Now the logical positivists may have been well aware that the capacity for forming distinctions to be found in natural languages was not (by the very nature of such languages) the sort of reinforced concrete foundation which they would need to support their two crucial dichotomies. For the positivists, however, this would not have been seen as a reason for doubting their dichotomies—it would just reinforce their faith in the necessity for the construction of an ideal formal language which would capture these dualisms, fixed like flies in amber. But the project of the 'logical translation' of those things in natural languages which were considered sound enough into an ideal artificial language was simply one of the positivist's hubristic reductionist projects, destined never to be successful. (I have discussed this elsewhere: Walsh, 1996, pp. 17–22, 88–89, 92.)

When the logical positivists first developed their project of a unified science, to be expressed in an ideal formal language, Russellian logic was a new and inspiring edifice. The formalists were in their gilded youth, and the limits and defects of formalism a distant cloud on the horizon.[3] When Putnam was close to some of the greatest figures of logical positivism the cracks were beginning to show in the structure of the system. He became in time a severe critic of the fatal flaws in positivism, and readers of *The Collapse of the Fact/Value Dichotomy* will see him at work demolishing the dichotomies. So it is important to stress two points for non-philosopher readers.

First of all, Putnam does not regard the great founders of logical positivism as having done *nothing* of importance. He deplores the present-day tendency to dismiss them out of hand—often with no real knowledge of their contributions. He himself knows them from inside, not just from reading about their work. His doctoral dissertation at UCLA was supervised by Hans Reichenbach (1949 to 1951), and he has observed that what made philosophy come alive for him, 'made it more exciting and more challenging than I had been able to imagine, was Reichenbach's seminar, and his lecture course, on the philosophy of space and time' (Putnam, 1994, p. 99). Of Rudolph Carnap (whom he also knew) and Reichenbach, he writes that: 'Even if today one cannot accept either Carnap's or Reichenbach's solutions to the problems of philosophy, their attempts represent contributions of enormous value, and there is much to be learned from their study' (Putnam, 1994, p. 101; the reader interested in the legacy of logical positivism should see pp. 85–148).

My second point is that Putnam's rejection of the two dichotomies is by no means confined to the *positivist* version: he rejects earlier versions such as that of Hume as an equally important part of the problem, and also a 'new dichotomy' which has appeared in recent years. The 'new dichotomy' (which we shall have to discuss in due course) is one of a recent crop of philosophical weeds that Putnam shows no desire to allow to grow. As he has remarked of these, 'some of the crude philosophical ideas that are rampant today—claims that neurobiology has solved the problem of intentionality, for example, or that the computer model of the mind has enabled us to answer metaphysical and epistemological questions—are more extreme (and cruder) versions of scientism than logical positivism ever was. Many philosophers think that *because* they have "rejected" a straw man version of logical positivism—refuted a doctrine that never actually existed in the form they describe—they cannot themselves possibly be guilty of the charge of scientism' (Putnam, 1994, p. vii, emphasis in original).

Meanwhile, one of Putnam's greatest influences in philosophy, Willard Van Orman Quine, played a key role in the development of Putnam's views on the analytic–synthetic issue. The positivists, as Putnam notes, with their insistence that all the truths of mathematics were analytic, *and also not ampliative*, had 'stretched the notion of analyticity to the breaking point' (Putnam, 2002, p. 11).[4] Putnam would have us consider that possibly the truths of mathematics 'are *unlike* both paradigm examples of analytic truths (like "all bachelors are unmarried") *and* purely descriptive truths (like "robins have feathers")' (Putnam, 2002, emphasis in original). But, not content with forcing analyticity on mathematics, the logical positivists supposed that the forced question 'analytic or synthetic', 'must make sense as applied to every single statement of theoretical physics' (Putnam, 2002, p. 11). This, of course, Quine attacked in his famous insistence that the lore of our fathers forms a fabric 'black with fact and white with convention' (Quine, 1963, p. 406).

Putnam here argues that 'Quine however, went much too far in his initial attack on the distinction in his famous essay "Two Dogmas of Empiricism" [Quine, (1951), 1953, pp. 20–46], throwing out the baby with the bathwater by, in effect, denying that there is *any* sense to distinguishing a class of analytic truths (for example, "all bachelors are unmarried") from truths that are obviously subject to observational test ("all main sequence stars are red")' (Putnam, 2002, p. 42, emphasis in original).

Putnam launched the argument, which has taken hold (Putnam, [1962], 1975, pp. 33–69), that 'one can accept Quine's insight (that there are large ranges of statements that cannot be simply classified as either analytic truths or statements of observable fact) while retaining the modest idea that there are also cases which fall on either side of the following specifiable distinction: statements of a language that are trivially true in virtue of the meanings of their words and statements that are not; Quine himself later conceded that I was right and attempted to state that difference precisely' (Putnam, 2002, p. 13). He stresses that accepting this does not entail that all the statements regarded as 'other than' trivially true fall into a *single* class. This will be important later, when we see that statements which are 'other than' trivially true may well be *a blend of facts and values*. Meanwhile, he observes that the notion of analytic statements can be 'a modest and occasionally useful notion, but so domesticated that it ceases to be a powerful philosophical weapon, that can perform such marvelous functions as explaining why mathematical truths pose no problem at all for empiricism' (Putnam, 2002, p. 13).

It is important, especially for economists, to see just how deep and unbridgeable a chasm the metaphysical dichotomy was regarded by philosophers as being. *Both* sides of the dichotomy were regarded as *natural kinds*, categories 'whose members possessed an "essential" property in common' (Putnam, 2002, p. 13), So, for example, 'the *non-analytic* statements, were all supposed to have *the* property of being "descriptions of fact", where the original model of a fact is the sort of empirical fact one can *picture*. The possibility that there are many *kinds* of statements that are "not analytic", and the possibility that to identify a statement as not being "analytic" was not (yet) to identify a philosophically interesting *kind* of statement, were missing from the beginning' (Putnam, 2002, p. 13, emphasis in original).

Among these many kinds of statements, which were not analytical, of course, would be statements which, at one and the same time, described *and evaluated* a state of affairs. But here, as we shall see, Quine refused to follow Putnam. In this respect, Quine did not go far enough. As we shall see, the history of the fact/value dichotomy has close family ties to that of the analytic/synthetic.

The history of the fact–value dichotomy

The doctrine that one cannot validly infer an 'ought' from an 'is', although not precisely *stated* by David Hume, is almost universally inferred from the 'observation' which concludes the *Treatise*, Book III, Part 1, Section 1 (Hume, [1738], 1978, pp. 469–470. See further Putnam, 2002, pp. 149–151). Putnam stresses that, while the doctrine attributed to Hume is widely accepted (even called 'Hume's Law'), the specific *reasons* which Hume offered in support of it 'are by no means accepted by those who cite Hume so approvingly' (Putnam, 2002, p. 14).

First it needs to be noticed that Hume is not making a point about the forms of certain statements in English. It is not an answer to him to remark that one can use 'is' to make a moral claim: 'murder *is* wrong', and 'ought' to state a fact: 'given his departure time, he *ought* to have arrived'. Rather, Putnam argues, 'Hume's metaphysics of "matters of fact" constitutes the whole ground of the alleged underivability of "oughts" from "ises"' (Putnam, 2002, p. 15).

The whole argument centers on what Hume meant by a 'matter of fact'. He had a substantial metaphysical position on this, and everything depends on it. Hume believed that *all* the objects of human reason could be divided into two kinds: 'relations of ideas' and 'matters of fact'. The former were what would later be called analytic statements, and Hume chose mathematical examples of these, such as that 15 is half of 30. He pointed out that no investigation of the world was called for to see the truth of these. Not so with 'matters of fact'. Here evidence was needed and, what is more, the evidence was *never undeniable*: matters of fact can be denied without a contradiction. He argued that all reasoning about matters of fact was based on the relation of cause and effect, and that our knowledge of *this* relation arose entirely from experience, and not from a priori reasoning. Thus, all the laws of nature were known to us only by experience, and there could be no demonstrative argument: arguments dependent on past experience could be probable only, depending as they do on the assumption that the future will be like the past.

Putnam examines Hume's particular concept of a 'matter of fact'. In English, the phrase can cover many things, but for Hume it is a precise technical term. Putnam points out that 'Hume's criterion for "matters of fact" presupposes what might be called a "pictorial semantics". [Putnam here cites Elijah Milgram, 1997 and 1995.] Concepts, in Hume's theory of the mind, are a kind of "idea", and "ideas" are themselves pictorial: the only way they can represent any "matter of fact" is by *resembling* it (not necessarily visually, however, ideas can also be tactile, olfactory, and so on)' (Putnam, 2002, p. 15, emphasis in original).

The 'matter of fact' that fire is hot, we sense by coming close to it: we *feel* heat. By what sense, Hume wanted to know, do we sense 'crime', or 'virtue'? As Putnam argues, for Hume, if there *were* matters of fact about *virtue* 'then it would have to be the case (if we assume "pictorial semantics") that the property of virtue would be *picturable* in the way that the property of being an apple is picturable' (Putnam, 2002, p. 15, emphasis in original). Putnam stresses that 'Hume was quite correct, *given his semantical views*, to conclude that there are no such matters of fact' (Putnam, 2002, p. 15). The reader must pursue for herself what is left when Putnam gently removes from Hume 'the discredited seventeenth- and eighteenth-century talk of "ideas"' (Putnam, 2002, p. 15). We may note here that the metaphysical dichotomy, of course, goes, if one wishes 'to *disinflate* the dichotomy implicit in Hume's arguments' (Putnam, 2002, emphasis in original). Suffice it to say for our purposes that, as with the logical positivists, the collapse of the fact–value dichotomy leaves the possibility of a somewhat vague distinction which should not in and of itself even appear 'to solve philosophical problems' (Putnam, 2002, p. 16).

Hume is one of the few philosophers for whom neoclassical economists seem to have had a genuine fondness (and who can blame them!). So it was important for our purposes to draw attention to what claims relevant to our discussion—and derived from Hume—cannot be sustained today. Putnam, those who read him will see, does the minimal necessary surgery on Hume leaving a very small scar. But Hume's crucial metaphysical concept has been removed.

Although Kant certainly played a role in the further development of what was to become the twentieth-century fact–value dichotomy, I have known only a few economists who have seemed eager to climb the rocky heights and take refuge in his high fortress. Those who feel dizzy at such heights may take comfort in Putnam's judgement that, while some distinguished moral philosophers still think Kant's account (especially in a Rawlsian version) 'fundamentally right, most philosophers today find Kant's moral philosophy overly dependent on the rest of Kant's metaphysics, which few if any are able any longer to accept' (Putnam, 2002, p. 17).

Actually, Kant's main influence on the development of the twentieth-century fact–value dichotomy may have been through the *collapse* of a couple of his most famous and influential ideas. When his intoxicating notion of 'synthetic a priori truth' lost its credibility, this 'led the logical positivists to go back to a vastly inflated version of Hume's idea that a judgment is either analytic (deals with "relations of ideas") or synthetic a posteriori (deals with "matters of fact")' (Putnam, 2002, p. 17). And similarly, the collapse 'of Kant's notion of "pure practical reason" (and with it of the Kantian variety of *a priori* ethics founded on that notion) led the logical positivists to go back to a vastly inflated version of Hume's idea that ethical judgments are not statements of fact but either expressions of sentiment or disguised imperatives' (Putnam, 2002, p. 17).

It is important to see that, surprising as this may seem initially, ethics did not fare as badly at Hume's hands as would later be the case with logical positivism. Certainly Hume *was* a non-cognitivist in ethics! But Hume was able to combine this, as Putnam notes, with 'a faith in the existence of such a thing as ethical *wisdom* because he shared the comfortable eighteenth-century assumption that all intelligent and well-informed people . . . would feel the appropriate "sentiments" of approval and disapproval in the same circumstances' (Putnam, 2002, p. 20, emphasis in original). Contrast the logical positivists, by whom all evaluative statements were customarily described as nonsense. It must surely have seemed strange to the logical positivists that Hume should have cared enough about ethics to write a treatise on it! Yet Hume saw it as 'an entire self-standing branch of philosophy—morals—the proper reconstruction of which he took to have broad social and political implications' (Putnam, 2002, p. 22). Not so Carnap, whose purpose was to '*expel* ethics from the domain of knowledge, not to *reconstruct* it' (Putnam, 2002, p. 22, emphasis in original).

This hubristic belief in the possibility of *expelling* ethics was not based on the logical positivists' fact–value dichotomy working alone, however, as is sometimes believed. An important feature of Putnam's analysis is that he shows how the positivists' analytic–synthetic *and* fact–value dichotomies *worked together*, and reinforced each other in their attack on the meaningfulness of moral philosophy. As I put it a number of years ago,

> [m]eaning, or 'cognitive significance' (to use the positivists' barbarous phrase) was supposed to be a characteristic, open to empirical testing, of individual 'propositions'. Consider the 'putative' proposition 'murder is wrong'. What empirical findings, the positivists would ask, tend to confirm or disconfirm this? If saying that murder is wrong is merely a misleading way of reporting what a given society believes, this is a perfectly good sociological fact, and the proposition is a respectable empirical one. But the person making a moral judgment will not accept this analysis. Positivists then wielded their absolute analytic–synthetic distinction: if 'murder is wrong' was not a synthetic (empirically testable) proposition it must be an analytic proposition, like (they believed) those of logic and mathematics—in effect, a tautology. The person who wished to make the moral judgment would not accept this, and was told that the disputed utterance was a 'pseudo-proposition', like those of poets, theologians and metaphysicians.
>
> (Walsh, 1987, p. 862)

But as Putnam tellingly points out, the positivists' confidence that the offending ethical sentences *could not be factual*, 'just like Hume's confidence that "the crime of ingratitude is not any particular fact," derived from their confidence that they knew exactly what a *fact* was' (Putnam, 2002, p. 21, emphasis in original). Putnam now moves to show that in the case of *both* dichotomies, '*it is the conception of the "factual" that does all the philosophical work*' (Putnam, 2002, p. 21, emphasis added). With this much weight pressing on it, their concept of a 'fact' had better be rock solid. Interestingly, Putnam—who knew the original logical positivists well, remember—tells us that their initial notion of a fact 'was somewhat similar to Hume's' (Putnam, 2002, p. 21). Now it needs to be remembered here that the positivists, from Vienna days on, wanted to be *the* philosophers who served the needs of science best, especially the latest physics. So Putnam is right on target in pointing out that the positivists were being forced to abandon their initial *notion of a fact* 'to do justice to the revolutionary science of the first half of the twentieth century' (Putnam, 2002, p. 21).

In treatments of the fact–value dichotomy by economists, attention is usually focused on 'values' and their supposed unreliability. It is assumed that one knows what 'facts' are! Putnam, on the other hand, was seriously involved with the mathematical structure and philosophy of hard science from his early professional years.

Perhaps in Hume's day one could maintain that there were no scientifically *indispensable* predicates that referred to entities not observable by means of the senses. (But see Putnam's qualifications to this in his notes 29 and 30, 2002, p. 152.) Putnam now mounts a detailed argument that follows the positivists in their long retreat, as they were forced to revise their notion of a fact in order to take account of modern science—a process of revision in which, he argues, 'they destroyed the very basis on which they erected the fact–value dichotomy!' (Putnam, 2002, p. 21). This, readers must sample for themselves. Remembering that, as Putnam says '[t]he logical positivists themselves were deeply impressed by the successes of relativity theory, which speaks of "curved spacetime", and quantum mechanics' (Putnam, 2002, p. 22), so that the positivists were being forced into their rearguard action by the victories of the very science they had sought to serve. I do not think even an opponent of logical positivism can fail to feel a certain sadness at Putnam's intimate depiction of brilliant minds forced gradually to relinquish the heart of their life's work.

Preoccupied with challenges to their theory resulting from developments of physical science, it is perhaps no wonder that the positivists should come to see the language of science as language at its truest and best. Ordinary language might be all right in its place they thought, but science called for a 'rational reconstruction' of language. Even after the basis for supporting such a concept had fallen apart, the idea still haunted some philosophers. This led to what Putnam regards as the poverty of the logical positivist conception of a language: 'Carnap thus required that cognitively meaningful language resemble the language of physics' (Putnam, 2002, p. 25).

What is important for economics—indeed for any social science—is to see clearly on what a narrow scientistic picture of 'fact' the logical positivist fact–value dichotomy depended, 'just as the Humean ancestor of that distinction was defended upon the basis of a narrow empiricist psychology of "ideas" and "impressions". The realization that so much of our descriptive language is a living counterexample to *both* (classical empiricist and logical positivist) pictures of the realm of "fact" ought to shake the confidence of anyone who supposes that there is a notion of *fact* that contrasts neatly and absolutely with the notion of "value" supposedly invoked in talk of the nature of all "value judgments"' (Putnam, 2002, p. 26, emphasis in original).

The reader will have noticed already (and will see more of) Putnam's tendency to praise certain properties of natural languages—for example their descriptive richness. So a few words are in order concerning his attitude towards 'ordinary language'. Some aspects of his position are of ancient lineage. The Greek philosophers saw the examination of what was said in ordinary language as a major source of (especially) moral concepts. Aristotelians, in later ages, have tended to pay attention in this way to ordinary speech. In the 1950s, of course, one ran into philosophers who, I fear, made rather a *fad* out of the analysis of ordinary language, talking as if this were the whole *object* of philosophy. A number of years ago I granted that '[t]he various versions of the ordinary language movement ultimately went into mannerist decadence, of course, but not before they had definitively exposed the crude mistakes in the positivist account of "meaning"' (Walsh, 1987, p. 892). Now I know from many conversations with Putnam from the mid-1950s on that he was never affected by this fad. Rather, his growing respect for natural languages over recent years is a result of his intimate knowledge of the formalist movements of the twentieth century, of their hubristic claims, and their unfulfilled reductionist projects. Like Wittgenstein, he *started* by giving formalism a thorough gallop for its wind!

The entanglement of fact, convention, and value

For the re-establishment of an enriched classical economic theory in present day terms, the entanglement which will be essential is of course that of fact and *value* (Walsh, 2000, pp. 6–10). Putnam, however, begins his treatment of entanglements with one which was recognized by philosophy earlier, namely the entanglement of fact and convention. He sets the stage by reminding non-philosopher readers that, by 1950, Quine had 'demolished the (metaphysically inflated) notion of the "analytic" to the satisfaction of most philosophers' (Putnam, 2002, p. 29). Did this mean that every scientific statement should be regarded as a statement of 'fact' (i.e. as synthetic)? No: 'rather, Quine suggested that the whole idea of classifying every statement including the statements of pure mathematics as "factual" or "conventional" (which the logical positivists equated with "analytic") was a hopeless muddle. But if the whole idea that there is a *clear* notion of fact collapsed with the hopelessly restrictive empiricist picture that gave rise to it, *what happens to the fact-value dichotomy?*' (Putnam, 2002, p. 30, emphasis in original).

Putnam now quotes an article of mine, in which I had borrowed Quine's vivid image and suggested that 'if a theory may be black with fact and white with convention, it might well (as far as logical empiricism could tell) be red with values. Since for them confirmation *or* falsification had to be a property of a theory as a *whole*, they had no way of unraveling this whole cloth' (Walsh, 1987, p. 862, emphasis in original).

Putnam comments: 'Thus Walsh (and before him, Quine's friend Morton White [1956]) made the point that after Carnap's abandonment (between 1936 and 1939) of the picture of 'factual' sentences as individually capable of confrontation with sense experience . . . and Quine's critique of the logical positivists' picture of what they called the language of science as neatly divided into a "factual" part and an "analytic" part, *the whole argument for the classical fact-value dichotomy was in ruins*, and that, "as far as logical empiricism could tell" science might presuppose values as well as experiences and conventions' (Putnam, 2002, p. 30, emphasis in original).

It should be noted that, while the phrase 'entanglement of fact and value' is a convenient shorthand, what we are typically dealing with (as Putnam makes clear) is a *triple* entanglement: of fact, convention and value.

Entanglement and classical pragmatism

Despite certain of his views, Quine is known to have been strongly influenced by the classical American pragmatists. As already noted, this has for a number of years been true of Putnam also. He is quick to point out that, for him, 'turning to American pragmatism does not mean turning to a metaphysical theory. Indeed, the pragmatists were probably wrong in thinking that anyone could provide what they called a 'theory of truth', and Peirce was certainly wrong in thinking that truth can be defined as what inquiry would converge to in the long run' (Putnam, 1994, p. 152). What attracts him are certain specific theses, and at least one of these is very relevant right here. Namely, 'the thesis that there is no *fundamental* dichotomy between "facts" and "values"' (Putnam, 1994, p. 152, emphasis in original). According to the classical pragmatists—Peirce, James, Dewey— 'normative discourse—talk of right and wrong, good and bad, better and worse— is indispensable in science and in social and personal life as well' (Putnam, 1994, p. 154). But the classical pragmatists, in claiming that normativity pervades all our experience, so that normative judgements are indispensable even to the practice of science itself, 'did not refer only to the kind of normative judgments that we call "moral" or "ethical": judgments of "coherence", "plausibility", "reasonableness", "simplicity" . . . are all normative judgments in Charles Peirce's sense, judgments of "what ought to be" in the case of reasoning' (Putnam, 2002, p. 31).

Putnam adds that 'Carnap tried to avoid admitting this by seeking to reduce hypothesis-selection to an *algorithm* . . . but without success' (Putnam, 2002, p. 31). He sends the reader to his Chapter 8 for more on this 'and other unsuccessful attempts by various logical positivists (as well as Karl Popper) to avoid conceding that *theory selection always presupposes values*, and . . . that they were, one and all, failures' (Putnam, 2002, p. 31, emphasis in original.). Putnam points out explicitly that his first introduction to philosophy of science was as an undergraduate, studying with C. West Churchman at the University of Pennsylvania: 'Churchman was a pragmatist himself and certainly did not evade the fact that science presupposes value judgments' (Putnam, 2002, p. 136). When he moved from Pennsylvania in 1948, for a year's graduate work at Harvard, he found 'the view that fact and value interpenetrate was defended at Harvard by Morton White, who had also taught me at Pennsylvania' (Putnam, 2002, p. 137). But on transferring to UCLA, he came under the influence of Hans Reichenbach, which took him in a totally opposite direction!

Quine's influence, both when Putnam was at Harvard in 1948–1949 and later, was much more ambivalent—there was, above all, his 'famous doctrine that fact and convention interpenetrate, without there ever being any sentences which are true by virtue of fact alone or true by virtue of convention alone' (Putnam, 2002, p. 138). Why then should fact and *value* not interpenetrate? When I asked this question (Walsh, 1987, 3, p. 862) I did not know that 'Quine's close friend Morton White, tried to convince Quine of this in the 1950s but in vain [White, 1956]' (Putnam, 2002, p. 138).

Different kinds of value judgements

Neoclassical economists typically write as if there were only one sort of value judgement. Of course, if one accepted logical positivism this would make sense, since if *all* value judgements were destitute of 'cognitive significance', why look for differences? Putnam, on the contrary, *stresses* the differences between different sorts of *ethical* value judgements, between these and *epistemic* value judgements, *aesthetic* value judgements, and so on.

Now, of course, during the gilded days of the imperial sway of the canonical neo-Walrasian (or 'Arrow–Debreu') general equilibrium theory, it was the done thing to refer to the famous theorems of the founders of this Augustan age (such as the Arrow negative existence theorem on the possibility of a social ordering) as 'powerful', 'rigorous' and 'elegant' results. These epistemic values, expressed in a language borrowed from the formalist school of mathematics, were the exactly appropriate terms to use (as long as the intellectual empire could be believed to be intact). The classical pragmatists would have understood these uses of evaluative language perfectly, even while rejecting some of the foundations on which the theoretical empire was resting. When disintegration set in it became clear that an increasingly severe critique of the neoclassical axioms of 'rationality' had 'been growing, even from *within* the neoclassical economic and decision theory establishment' (Walsh, 1998a, p. 1. See also Walsh 1996 and the sources cited there).

After the Balkanization of neoclassical theory into a plethora of different (often game-theoretic) models, the value judgements being offered about the erstwhile 'complete' general equilibrium models have noticeably chilled. Christopher Bliss has been one of the most able and imaginative defenders of the canonical complete, neo-Walrasian general equilibrium models of the gilded age (Bliss, 1975 is an elegant example). It is therefore with some sadness that I quote a more recent judgement of epistemic value of his: 'The near-emptiness of general equilibrium theory is a theorem of the theory' (Bliss, 1993, p. 227).

That (despite their belief in 'value-free' science) the models of Arrow, Debreu, and other notable contributors to the formalization of neo-Walrasian general equilibrium theory *did* faithfully adhere to the epistemic values which they endorsed will be seen by anyone (with the taste for this kind of argument) who can read them, and any such reader will do so with pleasure. It should be noted that *aesthetic* claims were often prominent in appraisals of this work: the theorems were judged 'rigorous', but also 'beautiful'. (In an abstract intellectual field one can expect to see epistemic and aesthetic values to be manifested together. I think there is little doubt that the presence of this in their work was felt by the great neo-Walrasians to be evidence of the maturing of their field into a true science).

Putnam turns now to the differences 'between the various ethical values themselves' (Putnam, 2002, p. 31). This can be illustrated by looking at the different roles played by ethical values in classical and neoclassical (neo-Walrasian) theory. In the original classics, and especially in Adam Smith, the whole structure of the theory puts the values involved center stage. The core concepts of the theory are the viability of an economy and (if more than *barely* viable) its ability to generate a surplus. The surplus can then be used for luxurious waste, or for accumulation and human development. Sen's moral argument concerning the development of human capabilities fits perfectly into this kind of model.

In neoclassical theory, the concepts of viability, surplus and economic class are without definition in the model. Production is by means of the services of the 'given' resources, which happen to exist. 'Individuals' have endowments (never mind how they got them). Pedro the night watchman is an individual agent, and so is one of the largest transnational corporations in the world. Each chooses a most highly ranked feasible option. Pedro chooses to do without medical insurance so that his daughter (who is seriously disabled) can have care. The transnational chooses to buy the cooperation of a dictator in obtaining supplies of cheap child labor. If these two choices were the most highly ranked choices available to the two 'agents' they are said to be rational. The model is said to be 'value-free'. However, if any agent in the model (Pedro, for example) cannot be given a little more income without the transnational (whose headquarters he works in) having a little less, then the equilibrium is said to be 'Pareto optimal' (or, more carefully, 'Pareto efficient'). It has been suggested recently that: 'The sections of [*Rationality, Allocation and Reproduction*] devoted to the philosophical roots and significance of Pareto optimality—which characterize Pareto optimality as the product of "a strikingly inconsistent tangle of utilitarianism and logical positivism"—should be read by all economists who continue to use the idea of Pareto optimality as if it were incontestable' (Hamlin, 1997, p. 1593). So I will gratefully not repeat the argument here, merely giving the relevant page numbers (Walsh, 1996, pp. 174–206).

The limitations of the *explicit* value judgements (although their ethical nature is not owned up to) in neo-Walrasian models must not lead the non-economist reader, startled by the moral triviality of these Pareto optimality claims, to miss the fact that there are *other* values lurking out of sight. For the fact is that the axioms of preference, which form a crucial part of the core of these models, involve highly non-trivial ethical assumptions as indeed we shall see when discussing Putnam's Chapter V, below.

Entanglement

That the entanglement of facts, theories, and values can thus be seen at the most abstract levels, where the 'facts' are those of science and the 'values' are the epistemic values Putnam has been discussing, must not lead us to forget that such entanglement persists through the 'facts' of everyday discourse, and the richest, most concrete values—those expressed in what have been called 'thick' ethical concepts. It is now time to consider these. If we do so, 'we will find a much deeper entanglement of fact and value (including ethical and aesthetic and every other sort of value)' (Putnam, 2002, p. 34).

It should be noted that the idea of 'thick' ethical concepts bears a striking resemblance to the idea of 'rich description', which Amartya Sen adopted from Maurice Dobb. As I noted previously,

> [c]ertain descriptions, Dobb had argued, have a vividness that makes it impossible to ignore some vital fact, and this rich and telling description elicits from us a moral judgment, sometimes against our wishes. In a somewhat similar way, Smith saw our recognition of moral obligations as dependent on our ability to enter imaginatively into another's plight or suffering. It is not, I believe, historically improper to use the present day philosophical concept of the 'entanglement' of facts and values for this key property of classical political economy in its philosophically richest manifestation, namely in Adam Smith.
>
> (Walsh, 2000, p. 9)

Putnam has been developing the idea of 'thick' ethical concepts for many years. The beginning of this can be seen as long ago as 1981, when he noted that '[t]he importance of terms like "inconsiderate", "pert", "stubborn", "pesky", etc., has been emphasized by Iris Murdoch in *The Sovereignty of "Good"* [1970]' (Putnam, 1981, p. 139). In 1990, discussing entanglements, he remarked that this was 'a constant theme of John Dewey's writing. But this aspect of pragmatism was neglected in Anglo-American philosophy after Dewey's death, in spite of Morton White's valiant effort to keep it alive [White, 1956], and it was, perhaps, Iris Murdoch who reopened the theme in a very different way.' (Putnam, [1990], 1993, pp. 145–146). Murdoch, he argues, 'was the first to emphasize that languages have two very different sorts of ethical concepts: abstract ethical concepts . . . such as "good", and "right", and more descriptive, less abstract concepts' (Putnam, [1990], 1993, pp. 145–146). Entanglement would clearly be most obviously visible in the case of the thick, richly descriptive, ethical concepts. Murdoch had argued that 'there was no way of saying what the "descriptive component" of the meaning of a word like *cruel* or *inconsiderate* is without using a word of the same kind' (Putnam, [1990], 1993, pp. 145–146, emphasis in original).

In using a word such as 'cruel', one sometimes wishes mainly to *describe* an action or a policy (such as the response to famine), sometimes mainly to convey a moral judgement, sometimes about equally to do both. But, Putnam argues, even the most purely descriptive uses of a thick ethical concept, to be understood, depend on an imaginative grasp of the evaluation involved in the concept's ethical uses. This is seen in the 'all-important distinction that Socrates keeps drawing between mere *rashness* or *foolhardiness* and genuine *bravery*' (Putnam, 2002, pp. 39–40, emphasis in original).

Someone who thought that 'brave' simply meant 'not afraid to risk life and limb' would not understand Socrates, for whom 'bravery' is a virtue. Putnam is arguing that, if one did not at *any* point feel the appeal of the relevant ethical point of view, one wouldn't be able to acquire a thick ethical concept, and that sophisticated use of it requires a continuing ability to identify (at least in imagination) with that point of view.

A telling example of a thick ethical concept, which sounds a theme that keeps recurring throughout Sen's work, is 'exploitation'. In 1978 he cited a passage from Maurice Dobb (1973) where Dobb is clearly replying to Joan Robinson's positivism: 'As such "exploitation" is neither something "metaphysical" nor simply an ethical judgment (still less "just a noise") as has sometimes been depicted: it is a factual description of a socio-economic relationship, as much as is Marc Bloch's apt characterization of Feudalism as a system where feudal Lords "lived on the labour of other men"' (Dobb, 1973, p. 145, cited by Sen, 1978, p. 177). He quotes this passage again in his brief but deeply touching biographical sketch of Dobb for the *New Palgrave* (Sen, 1987b, 1, p. 911). And Dobb's 'descriptively rich' understanding of 'exploitation' is heard again, for example, in Sen (1992, pp. 118–119).

There are, of course, uses of the concept of 'exploitation' in English which are purely descriptive, as when one says 'the site of that house fully exploits the shelter offered by the hills behind it'. It is different when we speak of the 'exploitation' of human beings, and even more especially of children.

> The concept that human labour has been and is exploited is morally signifi-
> cant in a way in which the concept that a machine can be exploited is not. The
> mathematics and analytical economics of reproduction in more than mini-
> mally viable capital reproduction models [i.e. classical models] are highly
> relevant, since they show how *any* input in such models can be said meta-
> phorically to be 'exploited'; that is to say, corn output is more than the corn
> input used in its production. But this is just the beginning of the story. In the
> case of human labour, the use of the word 'exploit' is a different member of
> its family of legitimate uses in English. . . The logical structure of a natural
> language is perfectly able to make distinctions of this sort. The fact that such
> distinctions do not show up in the mathematical language of commodity
> reproduction theory should not be seen as a serious defect of that theory.
>
> (Walsh, 1998b, p. 191)

Considering the necessary inputs into an artistic production, Sen examined the claim that 'Michelangelo made this statue of David' (Sen, 1978, p. 177). It is a remark that must be made thousands of times a year! Yet, as Sen observed, 'the description is remarkably selective on facts: it says nothing about the tools and instruments used in making the statue, it is silent on the ownership of the huge block of marble that Michelangelo used; it eschews the patronage that Michelangelo received. The description is not based on the assumption that Michelangelo would have been able to make the statue even without these other things. In going from all possible factual statements about a phenomenon to a pithy description, there is, in a sense, a loss of information, but there is also, in another sense, a gain of focus' (Sen, 1978, p. 177).

It would, I believe, be hard to overestimate the influence of Dobb's concept of 'rich', or as we would say, 'thick', descriptions in Sen's deep regard for the moral philosophy and political economy of Adam Smith or, indeed, on his work in general.

Is the 'new dichotomy' a 'fact–value' dichotomy?

Having completed his account of entanglement, Putnam now turns to some relatively recent developments in analytic philosophy, and the question of their bearing on Sen's enriched classical economics. He tells us that 'the collapse of the various grounds on which the fact–value dichotomy was originally defended, including the Verifiability Theory of Meaning, has not led to a demise of the dichotomy, even among professional philosophers. What it has led to is a change in the nature of the *arguments* offered for the dichotomy. Today it is defended more and more on metaphysical grounds. At the same time, even the defenders of the dichotomy concede that the old arguments for the dichotomy were bad arguments' (Putnam, 2002, p. 40, emphasis in original).

This passage is virtually the same as a passage from an earlier work (Putnam, [1990], 1993, p. 144), and I find I have the same problem with it that I did on a previous occasion (Walsh, 2000, pp. 7–9). I have no fear that philosophers would misunderstand what Putnam is saying. But I do still believe that economist readers, if they have not been following certain recent debates within philosophy, might do so. They might, in short, get the idea that the dichotomy *in which neoclassical economics has an interest*, namely the fact–value dichotomy, is alive and well, defended by new philosophers for brand new reasons.

So I find I still favor, as I did a couple of years ago, the idea of referring to the dichotomy which is now being defended by philosophers as 'the "new" dichotomy' (Walsh, 2000, p. 7). Perceptive economist readers should have already picked up a whiff of its newness from the statement that 'it is defended more and more on metaphysical grounds' (Putnam, 2002, p. 40). If there is one thing positive neoclassical economists have never wanted to do, it is to depend on a *metaphysical* argument for any of their vital claims. I think economists who investigate the issues will quickly see that the dichotomy that has been developed by philosophers such as Bernard Williams will not do the work for them which the old logical positivist fact-value dichotomy was for so many years believed to do.

Happily, Putnam rapidly assures the reader that

> [w]hat follows from Williams's metaphysical story is, however, not *a fact–value* dichotomy at all, but rather a dichotomy between what is 'absolutely' the case, true independently of the perspective of any observer, and what is only true relative to one or another 'perspective'. Williams, for example, does not deny that ethical sentences can be true or false; what he denies is that they

can be true or false *non-perspectivally* . . . According to Williams, 'Peter is cruel' can be true in the very same sense in which 'Grass is green' is true, while still being an ethical utterance. The point is that for Williams *factual statements* in a natural language like. 'Grass is green' are not treated as possessing the highest kind of truth.

(Putnam, 2002, p. 41, emphasis in original)

'*Absolute* truth', for Williams, is confined to the deliverances to be hoped for from completed physics. So the dichotomy is not between facts (in any sense in which we ever know any) and values, nor is it between *science* and values: the whole of *present-day* science (including physics) is in the same bag with economics, moral philosophy, rich descriptions, and all everyday uses of natural language. Alone in icy majesty on the other side of the dichotomy is the ideal of a perfected physics. Putnam endorses my conclusion of two years ago in this *Review*: 'As Vivian Walsh sums it up (referring both to Williams's views and to my published criticisms of those views):

> So, according to the new dichotomists, we are to wait around for finished science to tell us (presumably in a constructed language which it endorses) what things are absolutely true. Putnam does not mince words: 'This dichotomy between what the world is like independent of any local perspective and what is projected by us seems to me utterly indefensible' . . .
>
> The would be 'positive' economist [and the would be 'positive' lawyer as well, I might add – HP] is unlikely to be cheered up by being offered a dichotomy that rests, not just on a metaphysical argument, but on a demonstrably bad metaphysical argument. But there is a more work-a-day objection that may be even more telling. Economists [and lawyers as well, I add – HP] cannot afford to neglect the failure of an advertising campaign that tried to sell a shade of green which consumers rejected, or the devastating results of a record drought upon grasslands. The things consumers [and clients] want, or buy, or have produced for them, are chosen or rejected in terms of features that arguably would not appear in 'completed science' if it should ever arrive. They live, move, and have their being, just like those who make moral statements, on the 'wrong' side of the dichotomy between 'finished science' and *everything else that anyone ever says.*'

(Walsh, 2000, pp. 8–9, cited (with additions) by Putnam, 2002, p. 42, emphasis in the original)

Any readers desirous of a further critique by Putnam of Williams' concept of the 'absolute conception of the world' will find this in (for example) Putnam (1992, pp. 80–107). I content myself with a short quotation from Putnam's concluding passage:

> Williams wants to acknowledge the entanglement of fact and values and hold on to the 'absolute' character of (ideal) scientific knowledge at the same time.

But there is no way to do this. It cannot be the case that scientific knowledge (future fundamental physics) is absolute and nothing else is; for fundamental physics cannot explain the possibility of *referring to* or *stating* anything, including fundamental physics itself. So, if everything that is *not* physics is 'perspectival', then the notion of the 'absolute' is itself hopelessly perspectival.

(Putnam, 1992, p. 107, emphasis in original)

There is some irony in the fact that 'positive' neoclassical economists, long ago taught by logical positivism to distrust metaphysics, should on *this* occasion be wisely protected against being infected by the metaphysical realism of philosophers such as Williams. The situation also illustrates Putnam's claim that there are scientistic extravagances around in philosophy today which are cruder than the positions taken by the great positivists. It is natural to ask at this point whether economists are safe from philosophy-induced error as long as they reject metaphysical realism? Alas, the answer is that they are *not*. There is another danger.

Disillusioned metaphysical realists and the rush to relativism: another danger

Unfortunately, disillusioned ex-metaphysical realists have often rushed into a position of extreme skepticism that proves (if possible) more damaging to the adoption of a morally responsible position on economics in general, and on human development in particular, than even the position they have given up. Putnam, who has persistently opposed such nihilistic tendencies of thought over a number of years, addresses this issue in Chapter 11.

He chooses the celebrated philosopher Richard Rorty, with whom he has had an ongoing debate on these issues for years, as his representative case of 'a disappointed metaphysical realist' (Putnam, 2002, p. 101). It should be noted at once that it is by no means the case that Putnam and Rorty disagree on *all* major philosophical issues: Putnam remarks of Rorty that 'Dewey is one of his heroes. Rorty hails Dewey's rejection of any supposedly fundamental fact/value dichotomy, either ontological or epistemological [Rorty, 1982, 1991]' (Putnam, 2002, p. 98). But what Rorty disagrees with in Dewey—and in Putnam—is their retention of a firm belief in a world which our thought and languages do not *make*—a world which is out there, whether we choose to attend to it or not: 'Again and again, Rorty argues that the notion of "objective reality" is empty, since we cannot stand outside of our skins and compare our notions with (supposed) objective reality as it is "in itself" [Rorty, 1979, 1991, 1993]' (Putnam, 2002, p. 99).

Of course, being satisfied with nothing as 'real' except reality 'as it is in itself' is the essential mark of the metaphysical realist. As Putnam expresses it, '[i]f the metaphysical sort of realism that posits "things in themselves" with an "intrinsic nature" makes no sense, then, Rorty supposes, neither does the notion of objectivity' (Putnam, 2002, p. 99). The solutions we can find to our problems are then supposed to be 'at best solutions or resolutions by the standards of our culture'

(Putnam, 2002, p. 99). Putnam, on the contrary, happily accepts the demise of metaphysical realism, and is still willing to 'take out life insurance' (Putnam, 2002, p. 100). He does not confuse 'one or another metaphysical interpretation of the notion of objectivity . . . with the ordinary idea that our thoughts and beliefs refer to things in the world' (Putnam, 2002, p. 99).

Some philosophers have seen metaphysical realist ideas as *vital foundations* for our beliefs about the world and its contents. When they become convinced that these 'foundations' have now collapsed, then the place they lived in and all its furniture has (they believe) come tumbling down. 'For Rorty, as for the French thinkers whom he admires . . . [t]he failure of our philosophical "foundations" is a failure of the whole culture. . . By this I mean that, for Rorty or Foucault or Derrida, the failure of foundationalism makes a difference to how we are allowed to talk in ordinary life—a difference as to whether and when we are allowed to use words like "know", "objective", "fact", and "reason". The picture is that philosophy was not a reflection *on* the culture, a reflection some of whose ambitious projects failed, but a *basis*, a sort of pedestal, on which the culture rested, and which has been abruptly yanked out' (Putnam, 1990, p. 20, emphasis in original).

The demise of metaphysical realism is, of course, no loss (quite the reverse!) for Putnam since it leaves the field clear for the 'natural' realism that he supports in the pragmatists, in John Austin, and in Wittgenstein. There was never a great danger, surely, of economists, whether neoclassical *or* classical, flocking to the support of the metaphysical realists. Much more dangerous is relativism. This, again, is not so much a problem for pure theory (neoclassical or classical). But it is a problem for the area in which Sen's capability theory of human development operates, since *policy* can be seriously damaged by relativist attacks.

Putnam notes that 'Richard Rorty has been in recent years one of the most important interpreters of continental philosophy to an American audience. Like the continental philosophers he interprets, Rorty rejects the label "relativist". But almost all of bis readers have classified him as some sort of a relativist' (Putnam, 1992, p. 67). In one work in particular (Rorty, 1979), as Putnam notes, 'he identified truth, at least in what he called "normal" discourse, with the agreement of one's cultural peers' (Putnam, 1992, p. 67).

Putnam remarks that Rorty (1979) 'contains brilliant criticisms of the kinds of metaphysics that Rorty rejects' (Putnam, 1992, p. 68). It would be nice to think that he does later escape from relativism; this, however, is a highly complicated issue which the interested reader must pursue for herself in some of Rorty's works (such as Rorty, 1982, 1989) and Putnam's comments on these (for example, Putnam, 1990, 1994, 1995). But Putnam (1995) has commented on Rorty's 'telling us again and again that . . . all our thought is simply "marks and noises" which we are "caused" to produce by a blind material world to which we cannot so much as *refer*' (Putnam, 1995, p. 75, emphasis in original). Putnam adds in a note on p. 81 that '[t]his is the way Rorty presented his view at a conference on Truth in Paris (May 3, 1990) sponsored by the Collège Internationale de Philosophie' (Putnam, 1995, p. 81). As for relativism as an idea on its own merits, suppose that most American philosophers are *not* relativists. Then 'if, as a matter of empirical fact, the statement "the majority of my cultural peers would not agree that relativism is correct" is true, then, according to the relativist's own criterion of truth, relativism is not true!' (Putnam, 1992, p. 71).

But one must separate the relativism (or apparent relativism!) of certain post-modernist philosophers from their *valid* rejection of metaphysical realism. As Putnam argues, 'Deconstructionists are right in claiming that a certain philosophical tradition is bankrupt; but to identify that metaphysical tradition with our lives and our language is to give metaphysics an altogether exaggerated importance' (Putnam, 1992, p. 124). Metaphysical realism claimed to offer us the world and all its fixtures. But we find that we are left with a promissory note entitling us to some things in themselves—if and when completed physics is ready to deliver them. For *this*, common sense was asked to give up her comfortable tables and chairs and ice cubes! (See Putnam's cautionary tale in 1987, pp. 3–8.)

Putnam notes that some of Derrida's followers interpret him as teaching that logic is itself repressive. He grants that '[i]n certain ways one can understand the reasons for this interpretation. Traditional beliefs include much that is repressive (think of traditional beliefs about various races, about women, about workers, about homosexuals). Our "standards" require not only rational reconstruction but criticism. But criticism requires argument, not the abandonment of argument. The view that all the left has to do is tear down what is, and not discuss what might replace it, is the most dangerous politics of all, and one that could easily be borrowed by the extreme right' (Putnam, 1992, p. 130).

But he hastens to add 'Derrida himself is not guilty of this kind of thinking. He has movingly replied to the charge of nihilism' (Putnam, 1992, p. 130). Putnam does not think Derrida himself an extremist: 'But the philosophical irresponsibility of one decade can become the real-world political tragedy of a few decades later. And deconstruction without reconstruction is irresponsibility' (Putnam, 1992, p. 133).

This issue bears directly on the work of Amartya Sen. Relativism, and moral nihilism, are destructive of everything which it is most important for people to see, and to act on, in the task of human development as Sen and those who work with him regard it. As Martha Nussbaum and Amartya Sen have noted, 'in order to know which changes count as development, that is as beneficial alterations, we need to have not only a description of the practices and the values of a culture but also some sort of evaluation *of* those practices and values' (Nussbaum and Sen, 1989, p. 307, emphasis in original). They are careful to insist that these ideas must not be imposed from *outside*: 'It must be internal, using resources inside the culture itself in order to criticize certain aspects of the culture. Second, it must be immersed rather than detached (i.e. its norm of objectivity should not be one that involves the detachment of the judging subject from the practices, the perceptions, even the emotions, of the culture), stressing, instead, that objective value judgments can be made from the point of view of experienced immersion in the way of life of a culture. And yet, third, it will have to be *genuinely critical*, subjecting traditional beliefs and practices to critical examination. (Nussbaum and Sen, 1989, p. 308, emphasis in original).

They turn (very wisely) to Aristotle for inspiration: 'We do not inquire in a vacuum. Our conditions and ways of life, and the hopes, pleasures, pains, and evaluations that are a part of these cannot be left out of the inquiry without making it pointless and incoherent. We do not stand on this rim of heaven and look "out there" for truth; if we did we would not find the right thing. Ethical truth is in and of human life; it can be seen only from the point of view of immersion' (Nussbaum and Sen, 1989, p. 311, emphasis in original).

Against Plato, (and certain Platonic elements in Rawls today), they refuse to jettison the notion of truth, while holding with Aristotle that *all* of truth is value laden: 'All truth is seen from somewhere; if we try to see from outside of human life, we see nothing at all. Supporting this position, Hilary Putnam has recently argued that once we have the correct understanding of scientific truth, we will see that there is just as much, and the same sort of, truth and objectivity in ethics as in science' (Nussbaum and Sen, 1989, p. 312). They are right to refer to Putnam's many arguments[5] to the effect that matters expressed in natural languages do not constitute a second-class sort of truth, and to his doctrine of natural realism (which they refer to as 'internal realism' using a term which he later gave up, preferring to speak of 'common sense' realism or (after William James) 'natural' realism).

This is consistent with their expressed choice of Aristotle over Plato: Aristotle, and the Aristotelian tradition, has favored common sense realism, as Putnam shows in a section called 'The Return of Aristotle' (in Putnam, 1994, pp. 3–81). This theme of natural realism has been heard before in our discussion in these pages—for example when considering Putnam's interest in the pragmatists. It is now time to attend to it more directly.

The significance of natural realism for Putnam's defense of Sen's enriched classicism

The idea of natural realism is very simple and very old. But it has been defended over the ages by philosophers who believed in it for very different reasons, and with very sophisticated arguments—never more so than in the case of Putnam. Natural realism can appropriately be called 'common-sense' since it is what people normally assume until their heads are turned by speculative metaphysics. It is the comfortable belief that our furniture will be there when we come home—unless stolen, or destroyed by a tornado. It is the belief in a world we do not make, and which will be there after we are gone. (Hence Putnam's taking out life insurance.) This entails beliefs about the ability of the descriptions we give in ordinary language to successfully capture the world around us and what we do in it: to 'hook onto the world' as Putnam likes to say. We can, if common sense is correct, fairly accurately describe important facts—such as that someone we love died because a car ran a red light and rammed our vehicle. Such facts, if true, carry implications of culpability, which a court of law will take seriously. These facts are thoroughly entangled with values. A metaphysical realist defense of the perpetrator would at best be laughed at and at worst lead to a charge of contempt of court.

The claim that famine is imminent in a poor country, unless certain steps are taken at once, depends on facts about entitlement collapse due to a flood, about food supplies destroyed by a natural calamity, about bureaucratic torpidity and irresponsibility—and so on. They are heavily value-laden facts about the world we live in.

Now if these sorts of facts are treated as 'second class' or 'true only from one perspective' then the truth and seriousness of the moral claims involved are demeaned—just as they also are if these moral claims are said to be just the reflection of a particular culture. Whatever might be their 'enlightened' and 'progressive' *intentions*, or postures of concern, the metaphysical realist, the deconstructionist, the cultural relativist, all have in common the fact that the objective consequence of their influence is to undermine the efforts of those, like Sen, who are among the significant and persistent defenders of the poor.

Putnam and Nussbaum find that in Aristotle 'we do not discover something *behind* something else, *a hidden reality* behind the complex unity *that we see* and are. We find what we are in the appearances. And Aristotle tells us that if we attend properly to the appearances the dualists' questions never even get going' (Putnam and Nussbaum, in Putnam, 1994, p. 55, emphasis added). Deeply influenced by Aristotle, Nussbaum is a strong defender of natural realism, and an opponent of skepticism. As she has remarked in a recent work

> [w]hat is deeply pernicious in today's academy, then, is the tendency to dismiss the whole idea of pursuing truth and objectivity as if these aims could no longer guide us. Such attacks on truth are not new, we find them in Thrasymachus and in the ancient Greek skeptics—[Nussbaum, 1994, pp. 714–744; 1990a, pp. 220–229]—But they are forms of sophistry whose influence mars the otherwise promising pursuit of Socratic goals on our campuses. Postmodernists do not justify their more extreme conclusions with compelling arguments. Nor do they even grapple with the technical issues about physics and language that any modern account of these matters needs to confront. For this reason, their influence has been relatively slight in philosophy, where nuanced accounts of these matters abound. Derrida on truth is simply not worth studying for someone who has been studying Quine and Putnam and Davidson. In other parts of the humanities, however, they exercise a large influence (in part because their work is approachable as the technical work of philosophers frequently is not).
>
> (Nussbaum, 1997c, pp. 410–441)

Turning to medieval philosophy, Putnam and Nussbaum seek to show how that great interpreter of Aristotle, 'Saint Thomas Aquinas, was led . . . to adopt [an interpretation] that is very close to ours' (Putnam and Nussbaum, 1994, p. 51).

Among modern philosophers, Putnam has, on a number of occasions, singled out common sense realism as one of the classical American pragmatists' most attractive features (we already know that he credits them with understanding the entanglement of facts and values). Thus, on truth and realism, he notes that

William James, in a letter to a friend towards the end of his life, 'wrote that he never denied that our thoughts have to fit reality to count as true, as he was over and over again accused of doing' (Putnam, 1999, p. 5). On the other hand he does not side completely with James, insisting that 'James's suggestion that the world we know is to an indeterminate extent the product of our own minds is one I deplore' (Putnam, 1999, p. 6). In a note he adds that 'I myself regret having spoken of "mind dependence" in connection with these issues in my *Reason, Truth, and History* (Cambridge: Cambridge University Press, 1981)!' (Putnam, 1999, p. 178). For him, 'the *real* insight in James's pragmatism, [is] the insight that "description" is never a mere copying and that we constantly add to the ways in which language can be responsible to reality. And this is the insight we must not throw away in our haste to recoil from James's unwise talk of our (partly) "making up" the world' (Putnam, 1999, p. 9, emphasis in original).

Increasingly, Putnam has been following 'a lead pioneered by Wittgenstein', but he recognizes that he is 'running against a powerful current of Wittgenstein interpretation' (Putnam, 1999, p. 44). For an analysis of Putnam's interpretation of Wittgenstein, interested readers should see the writings of James Conant, for example his 'Introduction' to Putnam (1994, pp. xi–lxxvi). Conant surveys the reasons why Putnam claims that the 'metaphysical realists' God's eye view of the world has collapsed, and the reasons why nevertheless this collapse does no damage to the furniture of the world as seen by common sense: the tables and chairs and trees and grass. Conant refers continually to the special features of Putnam's interpretation of Wittgenstein, and offers a number of valuable sources.

Putnam recognizes that he is adopting 'a sort of cultivated naiveté' (Putnam, 1994, p. 283) in the position he has taken, and adds 'I mentioned Wittgenstein in connection with it; I could also have mentioned Strawson or Austin or, going back earlier in the century, William James' (Putnam, 1994, p. 283). What he is calling deliberate naiveté was 'what James called "natural realism"' (Putnam, 1994, p. 284). As Conant puts it, '[t]he commonplace which Putnam is most concerned to rescue is the one Wittgenstein expresses as follows: "When we say, and *mean*, that such-and-such is the case, we—and our meaning—do not stop anywhere short of the fact"' (Conant, in Putnam, 1994, pp. xxvi–xxvii, citing Wittgenstein, 1953, Section 95). Putnam wants to rescue our confidence in the ordinary furniture of our world—the real things which surround us—and in our ordinary way of talking about them which, as Conant puts it, 'Putnam sees the metaphysician as having hijacked' (Conant, in Putnam, 1994, p. xxvii). Conant notes Putnam's having quoted Wittgenstein's remark to the effect that 'if the words "language", "experience", "world" have a use, it must be as humble a one as that of the words "talk", "lamp", and "door"' (Wittgenstein, 1953, Section 97, cited by Conant in Putnam, 1994, p. xxvii).

Putnam announced recently that he will from now on use the term 'natural realism' for the common sense view he supports, taking the label 'from William James' expressed desire for a view of perception that does justice to the 'natural realism of the common man' (Putnam, 1999, p. 10). He notes that the opponents of natural realism were 'subjected to a further round of scathing criticism in

Austin's [1962] *Sense and Sensibilia* . . . and, in a much less satisfactory way, in Gilbert Ryle's [1949] *The Concept of Mind*' (Putnam, 1999, p. 11). I remember discussing Ryle's work with Putnam when we first spent time talking together in 1955. Austin's (1962) book, which he so much admires now, would not, of course, be published (posthumously) until some years later. I had been a natural realist in the 1950s, but it was mostly from Ryle's influence and that of people nearer my own age whom he had taught. In those days Putnam and I agreed on many questions of moral philosophy, but not on natural realism! He had a long arduous road to travel, because for him to accept natural realism he had to investigate its consistency with the major twentieth century developments in logic, mathematics, and science. His acquired naiveté is *hard won*—like the anti-war convictions of an old soldier!

Fact and value in the world of Amartya Sen

Putnam heads his third chapter with a telling passage from Sen, which concludes that 'it is precisely the narrowing of the broad Smithian view of human beings, in modern economics, that can be seen as one of the major deficiencies of modern economic theory. This impoverishment is closely related to the distancing of economics from ethics' (Sen, 1987a, p. 28).

Well, Putnam has now handed Sen, through the subtle analysis of the concept of a 'fact' and the philosophical defense of 'entanglement', what is surely the most rigorous and sophisticated philosophical argument for rejecting that 'distancing of economics from ethics' to date. It is not that Sen need now alter his normal *practice*: on the contrary, Sen's works form a massive monument to the successful and sustained entanglement of fact, convention, and value. And of course this is one of the things which make Sen's life's work so appealing to Putnam, and explains Putnam's choice of Sen as a great exemplar of entanglement, even when addressing (as in the Rosenthal Lectures) an audience of lawyers.

What has happened is that Putnam has brought up a powerful force to protect one of Sen's flanks. Readers of Putnam (2002), I think, will be unable to miss seeing how happy he is to come on the field and join Sen's endeavor—which he describes as 'work that has transformed our understanding of what 'classical economic theory' was about in addition to having important implications for questions of global welfare' (Putnam, 2002, p. 49). He begins by referring to my concept of a 'second phase' in the present day revival of classical theory as being 'the right term for the Senian program' (Putnam, III, p. 5). He then surveys the issues that arise in the whole area of what economic rationality requires.

Six concepts of economic rationality

Putnam begins by quoting Sen's remark that '[i]t is fair to say that there are two predominant methods of defining rationality of behavior in mainline [neoclassical] economic theory. One is to see rationality as internal *consistency* of choice and the other is to identify rationality with *maximization of self-interest*' (Sen,

1987a, p. 12, emphasis in original). Predominance, of course, is an empirical question; what is certainly true, however, is that neoclassical economists *use* at least six distinct concepts of rationality—whether they are always aware of this or not. 'Internal' consistency can be disposed of fairly quickly. At the best, it has been shown to apply only to a very restricted class of models (see Sen, 1993b, pp. 495–521, 1994, pp. 385–390). Putnam reasonably doubts 'whether the notion of *purely internal consistency* is itself cogent' (Putnam, 2002, p. 50, emphasis in original). He cites Sen, who had argued *against* its cogency, on the ground that 'what we regard as consistent in a set of observed choices must depend on the *interpretation* of those choices and on some features *external* to choice as such (e.g. the nature of our preferences, aims, values, motivations)' (Sen, 1987a, p. 14, emphasis in original). As Putnam observes 'Once we give up the idea—itself the product of a narrow verificationism which is a hangover of logical positivism—that one's choices must flawlessly "reveal" one's values, it is impossible to avoid the question of the relation of a person's choices to his or her values, as well as the question of the evaluation of those values themselves' (Putnam, 2002, p. 50).

This leads us naturally to the concept of rationality as the maximization of any goal. Robbins, whose concern was the allocation of scarce means among ends which could be ranked in order of importance, was arguing for this concept of rationality, and not for *internal* consistency in the sense discussed above. This concept, which is profoundly reductionist—boiling down 'rationality' to sheer efficient maximization—fits like a glove the mathematics of constrained maximization. For both its formal convenience *and* its emptiness it is beloved of economists. With the goal kept off-stage, this instrumental concept of rationality (as it is sometimes called) is only the *skeleton* of an account of human rational choice. And the impression that it avoids all moral judgments is in fact mistaken, since implicit values will have slipped in through the back door simply as a result of the nature of which matters of choice a given model puts center stage, and what questions it never allows to come up. Thus, Putnam was right to insist that it is impossible to avoid in this way the question of the relation of a person's choices to their values—which, of course give body and content to the formal exercise of maximization subject to constraints, on which the spotlight has been focused.[6]

Many moral theories are (among other things) maximizing theories, and any such theory has some use for the concept of scarcity (or of maximizing subject to constraints). Of course, such theories need to take care that their consequentialism does not ride rough shod over *rights* (see Walsh, 1996). The mathematics of constrained maximization is a widely useful formalism, as already noted, but it is only a skeleton for a concept of rationality.

Putnam considers next the concept of rationality as the pursuit of self-interest. He notes, correctly, that the prestige of this idea owed much to 'a misreading of Smith that Sen has repeatedly and consistently tried to correct' (Putnam, 2002, p. 50). Since I have discussed the role of concepts of self-interest on a number of occasions (Walsh, 1987, 1994, 1996, 1998a, 1998b, 2000) I shall be brief here. One point, I think, is of overwhelming importance. In condemning our rash of transnational exploiters, corporate swindlers, 'imaginative' accountants, inside traders, and assorted barrow boys, it is vital to see that Smith assigned an important and perfectly morally justifiable role to self-interest—*properly defined*. Thus, a sober concern with what will make one's life go best in the long ran, ridden on a tight rein by the humble virtue of prudence, is a necessary and unobjectionable *element* in any human life. An admirable human being will indeed be moved also by higher motives, as Smith insisted, and may even be called upon to sacrifice long-term goals. But, as Aristotle and Smith both saw clearly, attending to one's own long-term interest, *when* no higher obligation demands attention, is in no way morally disgraceful.

It is useful to adopt here a concept originally owing to Henry Sidgwick ([1874], 1907), which has been revived and used with elegance by Derek Parfit (1984): the idea of 'present aims' as distinct from life-long self-interest. The claim that rationality *can* sometimes be a matter of maximizing the attainment of strictly short-term present aims is not invalid. Indeed, in certain situations it is precisely what even pure duty calls for: a fire fighter braving death to enter a burning building, a surgeon about to operate, an air-sea rescue team, are only a few obvious examples of valid present aims. But our society is saturated with the pursuit of strictly selfish, *self-indulgent* present aims. These cause massive social damage, but it should also be observed that they usually do as much, or *more* damage to the persons engaged in their pursuit as they do to others. If there is one thing obviously true of such actions, it is that they are flatly opposed to the Smithian self-interest of those who do them. The annual costs to America (and the rest of the rich countries) of drug, alcohol, and tobacco addiction and of consequent crime and medical expenses, of teen pregnancy or AIDS resulting from *unprotected* sex, of the chemical pollution pumped into our atmosphere by irresponsible corporations, and other clear violations of the true self-interest of those involved, is known to be massive. What nonsense this makes of the 'positive' economist's fond delusion that models that assume their agents to act in accordance with their self-interest will be good predictors! Our 'positive' economists could do much good for society if (abandoning their claim to be 'value-free') they engaged in exhortation of their readers to pursue the hitherto almost unattainable moral heights of Smithian self-interest.

Of course, if one is concerned with Smith as a great *classical* economist, as Sen is, one needs to note specifically that '[Smith's] deepest reason for objecting to luxurious waste came from a moral judgment deriving directly from his classical economic theory which, for the first time, made clear the extraction of surplus throughout industry and the vital importance of the allocation of that surplus to the accumulation of capital . . . Smith saw clearly that the rapid industrialization was imposing terrible moral costs upon the emerging working class. But if the surplus thus obtained were squandered on luxury, those costs would have been borne in vain' (Walsh, 1998b, p. 189).

The responsible use of the net product, or surplus, has been the deepest moral issue for classical political economy from its beginnings, and was of course inherited by Adam Smith, and carried by him out of the early agricultural classicism of the Physiocrats and into the analysis of a multi-sectorial industrial society (cf. Walsh and Gram, 1980). The solution of this problem of the allocation of surplus is more complex today, since it requires the use of models where the most polluting industries are given *negative* growth rates in proportion to the need to eliminate them, while benign industries are developed and given higher positive growth rates in proportion to their helpful potentialities.

Putnam supports Sen's campaign against utilitarianism

Continuing our examination of six concepts of rationality, we now come to the fifth, namely rationality as the maximization of utility. One of Sen's most important contributions to economics and to moral philosophy has been his long sustained campaign to free economic theory from its persistent vestiges of utilitarian philosophy. Sen's whole contribution to the analysis of human well being and development requires the recognition that human flourishing depends on the fulfillment of a *number* of different capabilities which cannot be put in a pot and boiled down into some homogeneous soup, whether of pleasure, utility, or GDP.

The soup of utilitarianism comes in thick and thin versions. The *thick* version, which economics adopted from Jeremy Bentham, *did* offer some human nourishment to the poor, as we shall see. The *thin* version, which is implicit in the structure of neo-Walrasian economic theory, lacks any nutritional value whatever. It is arguable that thin utilitarianism has been nearly as damaging to neoclassical economics as has been its other main philosophical borrowing, logical positivism.

Putnam begins his attack on utilitarianism with Jeremy Bentham, describing him as 'the father of utilitarianism'. Well, Bentham truly *was* the father of utilitarianism in neoclassical economics. Aristotle, of course, had long ago argued in detail against *just* those properties of utilitarian ethics that make it destructive of what today we call capability theory. (This has been analyzed in detail by Nussbaum, especially Nussbaum, 1986 and 1990a.)

As Putnam observes, Benthamite utilitarianism 'held that everyone ultimately "really" desires only a subjective psychological quantity (called "pleasure" by Bentham) and that this "quantity" was a purely *subjective* matter' (Putnam, 2002, p. 51). He notes that '[t]he assumption that people act only on self-interested motives was in former centuries sometimes defended on the basis of the psychology of Jeremy Bentham' (Putnam, 2002, p. 51). This is true: Bentham added psychological hedonism to his ethical hedonism—as it were, for good measure! And this may certainly have influenced some people to adopt the self-interest theory of rationality. But in fairness to the neoclassical economists who were influenced by Bentham it should be remembered that the more brilliant of them—notably Francis Ysidro Edgeworth—were well aware that a utilitarian account could be given of *altruistic* choices with the very mathematical models which they had developed (see Edgeworth, 1881 and my comments in Walsh, 1996, pp. 164–173). By the same token, a coherent statement of the self-interest theory need not involve utilitarianism.

If Bentham's theory is about *pleasure* (we shall see that he was not consistent about this) then he is open to immediate attack. The classical pragmatists once more offer support. Putnam cites Dewey as saying 'of course, pure pleasure is a myth. Any pleasure is qualitatively unique, being precisely the harmony of one set of conditions with its appropriate activity. The pleasure of eating is one thing; the pleasure of hearing music, another; the pleasure of an amiable act, another; the pleasure of drunkenness or of anger is still another . . . Hence the possibility of absolutely different moral values attaching to pleasures, according to the type or aspect of character which they express. But if the good is only a sum of pleasures, any pleasure, so far as it goes, is as good as any other–the pleasure of malignity as good as the pleasure of kindness, simply as pleasure' (Dewey, [1908], 1978, pp. 257–258, cited in Putnam, 2002, p. 51).

The above refutation of hedonism as a moral philosophy has, of course, ancient roots. As Nussbaum has observed of Aristotle, '[a]rguments against pleasure as a single end and standard of choice occupy considerable space in his ethical works' (Nussbaum, 1990a, p. 57). And Aristotle sees that pleasures differ in *kind*, some 'are pleasures only for corrupt people, while some are pleasures for good people' (Nussbaum, 1990a, p. 57).

Lest some hard worked development economist, struggling with the problems of the world's poor, should enquire as to why Putnam (and Nussbaum) take the trouble to demolish crude pleasure/pain theories, let me remark that they appear not to be quite dead issues. T. M. Scanlon, in contributing to a symposium specifically on Amartya Sen's philosophy, begins by stating that 'Sen is much more attracted to consequentialism that I am' (Scanlon, 2001, p. 39). Evidently, other things being equal, this would place Scanlon even further from utilitarianism than that doctrine's celebrated opponent, Sen. Yet Scanlon (accepting Sen's characterization of utilitarianism as the conjunction of consequentialism, welfarism, and sum-ranking) suggests that 'it is welfarism (or historically, hedonism) that provides the support for the other two. Although hedonism does not entail sum-ranking, it is plausible that if pleasure and the absence of pain is the sole ultimate value, then since more of it is better than less, the value of states of affairs should be determined by the amount of happiness they contain' (Scanlon, 2001, p. 40). I am ready to believe that Scanlon's charge does still lie against economists, who have persistently confused the concepts of 'pleasure', 'happiness', 'welfare', 'well-being' and 'benefit' in their work. It would distress me to think that this could be true of philosophers. Even if we suppose, however, that crude hedonism can be dismissed, this does not dispose of *all* the elements in Bentham's utilitarianism. Bentham was not consistent as to what he wanted maximized—and goodness knows he was not the last to suffer from such confusions! He was himself well aware, it should be noted in fairness, that his term 'utility' did violence to distinctions that were recognized, and given importance, in ordinary language.

He wanted 'utility' to stand for 'that property in any object, whereby it tends to produce benefit, advantage, pleasure, good, or happiness (all this in the present case *comes to the same thing*) or (what *comes again to the same thing*) to prevent the happening of mischief, pain, evil, or unhappiness' (Bentham, [1789], 1970, p. 12, emphasis added). But he was riding roughshod over distinctions enshrined in ordinary moral discourse, and his linguistic reductionism was not accepted. The sophisticated utilitarians of later generations typically abandoned 'pleasure', and settled for a word standing for a long-term disposition, such as 'happiness' or chose a concept like 'well-being' or simply 'good'. Bentham's notion of utility with all its warts, however, did play one important role in the evolution of neoclassical economics, and on this something needs to be said. This arises from the fact that the early neoclassicism, from its beginnings in the 1870s up to the early 1930s was fairly strongly influenced by Benthamite utilitarianism. These economists adopted the notion of quantities of utility, and the belief that, as one consumed more of a good, the quantity of utility experienced from each additional unit of the good would diminish.

As Putnam observes 'Arthur Cecil Pigou's enormously influential *The Economics of Welfare*, published in 1920, derived a simple argument for at least some redistribution of wealth from these "neo-classical" premises. If the Law of Diminishing Marginal Utility is right, then the marginal utility of *money* should also diminish.' (Putnam, 2002, p. 53). Pigou had inferred that the redistribution of some income from the very rich to the very poor should increase the total utility of the population as a whole. Unfortunately, as Putnam notes, 'it was during the depths of the Depression that Lionel Robbins, certainly one of the most influential economists in the world, persuaded the entire economics profession that *interpersonal comparisons of utility are "meaningless"* ' (Putnam, 2002, p. 53, emphasis in original).

The seriousness of Putnam's charge is little affected by the fact that there were a *few* neoclassical economists who rejected Robbins' argument—even one or two *at* the LSE—notable instances being Lord Dalton and Sir Alan Peacock. I remember Peacock from my years there, and it is pleasant to be able to cite him. Hugh Dalton, of course, had been among the most famous of Pigou's students and Peacock has described where he stood: 'His main professional interest was in the use of taxation as an instrument for the redistribution of income and wealth, an interest inspired by Pigou's teaching and by his revulsion at the contrast between the sufferings inflicted on younger generations by World War I and the material gains of those who financed or profited from the war itself' (Peacock, 1987, I, p. 747). Peacock adds dryly that Dalton, as Reader in economics at the LSE, was responsible for 'recommending Lionel Robbins to be Professor of Economics, a typical example of his desire not only to "corrupt the young" (as he termed it) but also to promote the interests even of those with whom he disagreed' (Peacock, 1987, I, p. 747). Dalton was Minister of Economic Warfare in Churchill's coalition government during the Second World War, and Chancellor of the Exchequer in the first Labor government afterwards.

Returning to the early 1930s, the long love affair between neoclassical economics and utilitarianism came to a sudden end in the Great Depression. It was now an embarrassment that (to adapt a line of Yeats) the ghost of Jeremy Bentham was beating on the door! The LSE, rallied by Robbins, counterattacked promptly. Two economists, there at the time, produced work which claimed 'to banish what was regarded as the substance of utilitarianism from neo-classical economics'

(Walsh, 1996, p. 35). Sir John Hicks (whom we shall have reason to return to for the major work on capital theory and traverse of his later years), collaborated with Sir Roy Allen in an article that changed the way neoclassical choice theory was presented (Hicks and Allen, 1934).

The object of the exercise is very clear today after the fundamental work of Sen. We know that utilitarianism has several key features, and that one can drop the feature that wholly preoccupied Hicks and Allen and still have what I have called a 'lower octane' utilitarianism left. For Hicks and Allen, the substance of utilitarianism consisted in the claim that one could speak of different *quantities* of utility, and thus argue that giving a sum of money to a rich person would yield a smaller quantity of utility than giving it to a poor person. Classical Benthamite utilitarianism then judged two states of a society according to the *sum* of all the individual utilities. This, of course, was what Sen calls 'sum-ranking' (Sen, 1982, p. 28; 1987a, p. 39; 1992, pp. 13–14). One ranked states of a society by the sum of utilities in each state.

Blithely taking it that all agents in a model possessed complete, perfect information, Hicks and Allen pointed out that rational choice (rationality as the maximization of a goal) only required that an agent make the most *highly ranked* choice that was attainable.[7] What is vital is to see that Hicks and Allen had been wrong on two key issues. First, they had not successfully banished all *'cardinal'* measures (those involving *quantities* of utility), and secondly, utilitarianism can survive where *only rankings* ('ordinal' measures) are allowed.

As for the first, 'cardinality' arguably re-entered the debate once economists confronted choice among risky outcomes.[8] And then Sen pioneered the development of various concepts of 'cardinality' and various different kinds of interpersonal comparability, including partial comparability (Sen, 1982, for example). Many years ago I suggested an ordinary language approach to interpersonal comparability (Walsh, 1964, pp. 149–155), which avoided Benthamite utilitarianism, and was written in the spirit of Ryle and some ideas of Ian Little (Little, [1950], 1957).

Secondly, Hicks and Allen were wrong in their assumption that 'cardinal' utility was a necessary element of utilitarianism. As philosopher readers will be well aware, utilitarianism is still alive and well, but most utilitarian philosophy now is of a strictly 'ordinal' kind, involving only rankings (or orderings) and not *quantities* of utility. Using concepts pioneered by Sen (and others), I have argued that such a strictly ordinal theory 'is nevertheless recognizably utilitarian by virtue of being teleological (or consequentialist) and welfarist, and is thus seen as a version of utilitarianism—albeit a 'thinner' one than the classical—by friend and foe alike. Utilitarianism is a deeper and more complicated doctrine than has sometimes been realized, and a number of its most significant features, as well as its most serious defects, still show up even in its 'thinnest' form (Walsh, 1996, pp. 39–80). An especially revealing feature of present day ordinal utilitarianism (or 'preference utilitarianism', as Putnam calls it) is how happily it takes up residence in the structure provided by the axioms of neo-Walrasian economic theory.

I know of no other philosophical work in which the intimate relationships and affinities between neo-Walrasian economic theory and preference utilitarianism show up in as clear a light as in John Broome (1991). The utilitarianism which Broome probingly discusses is far from crude hedonism. Given that most people would argue that at least *part* of ethics is concerned with good, a teleological ethical theory may then be distinguished (roughly) as one that claims that *all* of moral philosophy is about maximizing good. What is right is then defined in terms of good, as simply what maximizes good. (So rights have lost any independent claim.) There is a *single maximand*—namely what the theory regards as good. (This is the form taken by what Sen called 'welfarism'.) It follows that there is a 'betterness' relation between choices or acts, which has the structure of the 'at least as good as' relation of neo-Walrasian theory. Broome argues that the 'betterness' relation is necessarily an ordering (in particular that it satisfies the standard axioms of completeness and transitivity of canonical Arrow–Debreu theory).

As I noted on an earlier occasion, Broome 'bases his case for the claim that the structure of axiomatic expected utility theory is that required by a utilitarian account of good precisely on the coherence of good. By this he means, roughly, that the betterness relation satisfies the axioms of symmetry, transitivity, completeness and the sure-thing principle. It is significant that he has serious doubts about completeness (Broome, 1991, pp. 7–8, 136–138). He concludes finally that 'one might easily doubt that betterness relations are complete, because there may be incommensurable goods. This is, I think, the most serious gap' (Broome, 1991, pp. 238–239). Yet despite these doubts he clearly believes that the utilitarian conception of good *requires* completeness' (Walsh, 1996, pp. 65–66).

Broome was well aware that just about *all* of the axioms he sees as necessary for utilitarianism had been under attack by mathematical economists and decision theorists since (at least) the 1970s. (See Walsh, 1996, for a discussion and sources.) But he argues tellingly that they are *necessary* for the coherence of utilitarianism. He makes what I believe to be the best case for ordinal utilitarianism, but, aware of its problems, he maintains a certain distance from it.

There is a deep irony about the fate that has befallen ordinal utilitarianism at the hands of neo-Walrasian economics. The support offered by the axioms of canonical Arrow–Debreu theory may once have looked irresistible, but this has proved unreliable. Putnam notes this ironic development in his discussion of the Rationality of Preferences (Putnam, 2002): 'Vivian Walsh points out in *Rationality Allocation and Reproduction* that there can be little doubt that the axioms of completeness and transitivity had gained a great deal of the prestige that they enjoyed outside economic theory from the vital role that they had played *within* economic theory, in the proofs of the canonical existence and optimality theorems of Arrow and Debreu. But by the early 1970s this was no longer true . . . Now the axioms of completeness and transitivity were being dispensed with in the very existence proofs that had once make them famous!' (Putnam, 2002, p. 164, note 3). Meanwhile the decision theorists entered the fray, but with some issues of their own in mind, 'and a debate that is peculiarly their own has raged over the respective merits of weakening the ordering axioms (completeness and transitivity) and keeping another assumption called "independence" versus giving up independence [otherwise knows as the sure thing principle] and retaining orderings' (Putnam, 2002, p. 165, note 3).

Utilitarianism had taken up residence in houses built by neoclassical economists and by decision theorists with axiomatic foundations that once looked rock solid. But the economists and decision theorists have been pulling these down now for years themselves, which has left the utilitarian philosophers who sought shelter in these prestigious, Nobel decorated structures, out in the cold.

Putnam could have chosen any one or more of the axioms involved in this meltdown as the focal point of his critique of preference utilitarianism. In fact he chose the axiom of completeness (or comparability), noting that '[a]s Vivian Walsh and Amartya Sen both pointed out to me, within economic theory, criticism of the axioms of transitivity and completeness have quite a long history' (Putnam, 2002, p. 163, note 3). Indeed this is so, and Putnam supplies the philosopher reader with a number of references to the literature within economic theory and decision theory.

Actually, Putnam and I were involved for a while in discussions on some of these issues soon after we first met since, as I remarked elsewhere, 'Hilary Putnam has recently told me that I was questioning the axiom of completeness by 1958 in some of our long conversations on the relations between philosophy and economics' (Walsh, 1996, p. 9). We began working (around 1960) on a joint paper on this, but alas never finished it. I did publish a paper on choice sets with incompatibilities, with the help of Putnam and Martin Davis, some years later (Walsh, 1967).

Now some younger theorists in both economics and decision theory have rejected the completeness axiom, and worked without it (this is also true of the axiom of transitivity), and there are a *number* of good reasons for doing so. Here I wish to concentrate on just one issue, which I choose because it involves a deep moral question, and is highly relevant to Sen's work on capabilities.

Many of those who have rejected completeness have done so because it demands of the choosing agent a preposterous level of knowledge of *facts*. How can we form a complete ranking of alternatives about many of which we are ignorant? This is true, but here I leave it aside. (It is discussed in Walsh, 1996.) There is another question, less often raised by economists, although it is discussed by philosophers: if, as it must be, our *moral* understanding is sketchy and incomplete, how can we compare every *morally* relevant alternative? The completeness axiom, however, is assuming that there are no moral conflicts we are *unable* to resolve—no tragic choices where, whichever action we choose, we feel a terrible moral loss.

Rationality claims, where these are made subject to the completeness axiom, are made with profound moral issues cut away. A large part of the tacit preference utilitarian morality lurking in neoclassical economics is simply because of this cutting away of all tragic situations, and thus of all 'hard choices', leaving a crude form of ordinal utility based consequentialism as the pervasive moral substructure of neoclassical economics. Philosophers, political scientists, psychologists, and

people concerned with social policy, should be aware that borrowing formalizations of 'rationality' from standard neo-Walrasian economic theory offers them a
stripped down and vulgarized version of the ancient philosophical idea of human
rationality. This is one of the most important messages of the work of Sen over the
last 40 years.

If a formal model of decision *is needed*, then the non-economists will do well
to go to the work of those mathematical economists and decision theorists who
have produced models that characterize rational choice *without* assuming
completeness, and/or without assuming transitivity. Some of these critical writers
are philosophers, but a number (it should be noted) were specialists in the canonical Arrow–Debreu models who sought to bring these models closer to the real
world. It is a rich and fascinating literature. (For a variety of sources, see Putnam,
2002, pp. 163–168; Walsh, 1996, pp. 29–138.)

Putnam's life's work is enough evidence for his respect for mathematics and
symbolic logic. One can give formal proofs their due, however, without making
formalism into a fundamentalist religion. And Maurice Dobb, after all is said and
done, set Sen on a road that honed his formal theory *but* also kept 'descriptive
richness'.

Of the many issues concerning the axioms of completeness and transitivity that
have been discussed in recent literature, Putnam concentrates on the moral issue
of the suppression of tragic conflict. In canonical Arrow–Debreu models and in
standard decision theory, not being able to rank two alternatives was treated as
being 'indifferent' between them. But, as Putnam points out, '[d]enying the very
possibility of a difference between alternatives that the agent regards as perfectly
substitutable and alternatives that the agent regards as presenting her with an existential decision, looks "fishy"' (Putnam, 2002, p. 81).

He makes the highly interesting point that, where an existential choice is at
issue, the agent has the *right* to make it *for herself*, and not to have the matter
'decided for her by the decision theorist (or by a bureaucrat, or a psychologist, or
by a flip of a coin . . .)' (Putnam, 2002, p. 82). If we are truly *indifferent* as to
which of two outcomes we get, then we may be willing to let a random process
decide. But if we are in deep moral conflict between two life goals we may be
desperately searching for a third alternative, or more information, or a change of
heart. In any case we will certainly not accept a choice being made for us by some
busybody.

This is an issue that has been deeply probed by Isaac Levi (1986), who makes
the remarkable claim that, when a person *has* to choose in a situation of unresolved moral conflict, nevertheless criteria for choosing rationally in such situations *can* be developed. Arguing in favor of Levi's position, I noted that Levi
shows how there may be a hierarchy of value structures, so that conflict may be
present at one level yet absent at a higher level: 'It is a salient feature of Levi's
theory, however, that an agent may have to go ahead and make choices with
conflict still unresolved. . . Levi insists that people may have no chance to resolve
the issues—he refuses to construe an action taken when under such pressure as a
commitment to the preferences 'revealed' by the action' (Walsh, 1996, p. 59).

Much of human moral struggle consists in the effort to *do* what is known to be right. But there is a second kind of moral struggle, which is the one that is relevant here. As Putnam observes: 'In this connection, Isaac Levi borrows the concept of a second sense of moral struggle—not to *do* what is right but to *find out* what is right—from Dewey and Tuft's *Ethics* [Volume 5 in *The Middle Works of John Dewey*]' (Putnam, 2002, p. 167, note 25, emphasis in original).

Actually, when Putnam and I first began to have long discussions of philosophy, around 1955, we were concerned specifically with the moral significance of tragic choices, with the question of how to *appraise* the terrible results of tragic loss, deprivations, ill luck, and the scarcity of means, without implying any unjust *blame* of the victims. As Putnam notes, '[t]hat there is a very important class of (ethical) value-judgments that do not praise or blame anyone was one of the central points of Walsh's *Scarcity and Evil*. (Walsh's term for the class was "appraisals".)' (Putnam, 2002, p. 161, note 40). Ethical uses of language intended to convey praise or blame, on the other hand, I referred to as *ascriptions* of responsibility (Walsh, 1954, 1958a, 1958b, 1961).

For Putnam, there are many different significant partitionings of the space of judgments. We can speak of ethical and epistemic values: among ethical values, we can distinguish appraisals from ascriptions, and we can speak of 'thick' and 'thin' ethical values—and so on (see Putnam, 2002, pp. 60–61). Putnam's approach to moral philosophy allows space for the recognition of a structure like Sen's capability theory, in which it is essential that human beings be able to realize a number of *different* capabilities, none of which is dispensable, and with regard to which we may on occasion have to be content with a partial ordering.

Utilitarianism as an ethical theory is clearly at the other extreme: some one objective must be given absolute dominance, and every other goal, every duty, even every human right, must give way before it. A utilitarian must reject the whole idea of value conflict—which is why the Arrow–Debreu axioms of preference suited it so well. Utilitarianism was in the genes of neoclassical theory, and it should be no surprise that the highest realization of that theory seemed to utilitarians to be a natural home.

Rationality in natural language

A carefully distilled concept of rationality freed from all ethical 'impurities', from all human emotions and eccentricities, and presented in the crystal clear formalism of a putatively perfect artificial language, was a natural ideal for those under the spell of logical positivism. For Putnam, on the contrary, turning from formalism like the later Wittgenstein, seeking like Aristotle, not some Platonic form of the good, but (with the classical American pragmatists), rather what is good for human beings leading human lives, another road was clearly indicated. The natural concomitant of his common sense realism and of his insistence on the ubiquitous entanglement of facts and values was an approach to moral philosophy that took seriously the ethical implications of the fabric of natural language. On this view rationality is not what satisfies some axiom set. Claims that someone's actions were or were not rational is, on this view, closer to the claim in a court of law that someone did or did not act as the reasonable person would act. Such claims are often defeasible: the person accused may be able to establish the existence of some state of affairs which defeats the claim of having failed to act reasonably. This is not like the formal proof of a theorem from a finite set of axioms. What defeats a charge of unreasonable action may be something that never arose before. Concepts in natural languages are open textured, they do not have defined limits of use or clear borders in every dimension—as Putnam argued in comparing ordinary language distinctions with metaphysical dichotomies. When I was a child in Ireland 70 years ago, a country doctor would be condemned as unreasonably negligent for failing to go out on a house call on a stormy night—my grandfather would have ridden a hunter when this was the best way to get to a patient. But no one expected him to try and find a new heart for someone who needed one!

Words like 'rational' belong to a closely knit fabric of related words, as is to be expected; as Putnam has remarked 'our values of equality, intellectual freedom, and rationality, are deeply interconnected. But the moral that I would draw from this is more Aristotelian than Kantian; we have a *rich and multi-faceted* idea of the good, and *the parts of this idea are interdependent*' (Putnam, 1987, p. 56, emphasis added). Entanglements of fact, convention and value are clearly at their thickest here. As I noted on an earlier occasion '[w]e would not ordinarily say that a choice or action was rational but unreasonable, nor that it was reasonable but irresponsible, nor that it was responsible but unwise, nor that it was wise but morally indefensible' (Walsh, 1996, p. 1).

It is not a new insight that if you try to drive human nature out the front door, she will promptly climb back in through a rear window. Neoclassical economics, stipulating that an 'agent' was rational if and only if it obeyed the preference axioms of canonical Arrow–Debreu theory, had implicitly identified 'rationality' with acting in a manner consistent with a welfarist consequentialism—in effect, a low-octane utilitarianism. This, as we have seen, is a highly contentious moral position obliterating tragic choices, independent recognition of human rights, etc. Why did anyone ever believe that this was value-free? A number of years ago Sen made an observation to me which may be an important part of the answer. He pointed out that when the canonical Arrow–Debreu work first came out, relatively few economists could follow the mathematics with complete fluency. (This was even truer of other social scientists trying to understand the deep theorems those economists were providing.) Today, he added, every well-trained graduate student in economics could do it.

Well, if a reader has difficulty in just following a language, she may not see some of the implications, which are not exactly advertised or clearly visible on the surface. And readers were not used to seeing moral claims expressed in mathematical formalism. Thus, Arrow's impossibility theory was seen as a formal negative existence theorem that demonstrated the impossibility of valid moral claims about social states, rather than as an essay in mathematical moral philosophy.

What is ironic is that neoclassical economists *themselves* had to appeal to ordinary language appraisals of rationality for their own purposes. Again the practice of the law is a place where this shows up particularly clearly. A corporation, let us suppose, has done something which has caused public outcry and legal remedies are being sought. It might help if the corporation could bring expert witnesses to argue that its actions were reasonable. An economist appearing for the corporation may be able to wave before the jury an elaborate formal model, but what is necessary is to persuade the jury that the corporation's actions satisfy, not the formal model, but what the jury regards as reasonable and responsible behavior in society. So while economists use in their models formal concepts of rationality such as we have been discussing, they have to appeal to the ordinary language understanding of rationality when confronting the public. To borrow a metaphor of Putnam's (which he used of some philosophers, in a different context) economists may find themselves keeping more than one set of books.

Textbooks are a rich source here. Not PhD level texts, which are written for students who have already committed themselves to economics, but undergraduate texts, say in microeconomic theory. All of the concepts of rationality previously discussed are used, often with fast, quiet racing changes from one to another as the terrain suits. But there are also rather frequent appeals to our sixth concept of rationality, namely to what the student will feel is reasonable, and the suggestion that what the student thus supports will be the upshot of rational choice as analyzed by the theory. Need I add that the student is simultaneously assured that the rationality claims being advocated are pure, value-free science?

A good deal of what is treated as self-interested choice in neoclassical theory is in fact *self-goal* choice. Obsession with one goal may well *violate* self-interest, however: one may destroy one's life creating a business empire, for example (see Morton, 1991, p. 166; Walsh, 1996, pp. 121–128, 201). The self-goal obsessed range from saints to terrorists (not forgetting the non-empty intersection of these sets!). As Sen notes: 'Some of the nastiest things in the world happen as a result of "selfless" pursuit of objectives far from one's own well-being, but also from the well-being and freedoms of others' (Sen, 1994, p. 389).

Since such a goal can dominate an agent's *whole life* (and not just a short period), such choice is distinct from the maximization of present aims. Furthermore, since a noble (or base!) self-goal has, as a matter of history, often been *explicitly* announced by an agent as lexically dominating all 'lesser' objectives, it should arguably be included as a concept of rationality. Readers may wish to add this concept to our list, making it number seven, although it has not been as widely debated in the literature.

The capabilities approach as a component of second wave classical theory

'Obviously I do not have the time to explain the capability approach in detail, much less to discuss the rival approaches to questions of poverty, welfare and global justice that Sen considers and rejects' Putnam tells his audience at the third Rosenthal Lecture (Putnam, 2002, p. 57). But that he should offer such an explanation is not necessary, since it has been done by Sen and those who share his views in great detail over a number of years. Putnam's purpose, rather, has been to show 'how welfare economics has found itself forced to recognize that its "classical" concern with economic well being (and its opposite, economic deprivation) is essentially a moral concern and cannot be addressed responsibly as long as we are unwilling to take reasoned moral argument seriously' (Putnam, 2002, p. 57). I shall therefore be concerned here mainly with the two aspects of capability theory that Putnam's argument has singled out as relevant to his discussion, namely its moral implications, and its classical roots.

Economists working on world development have recently been embracing the concept of 'ethical development', which clearly recognizes their involvement with explicit moral judgments. Thus we are told that '"Ethical development" is the project of rethinking and redefining "development", since some development economists have become disenchanted with the view that "economic growth" is the chief objective, and that per capita income is *the* measure of development' (Qizilbash, 1996, p. 1209).

Sen illuminates his capability-based theory by comparing its powers and limitations with those of several rivals, on a number of key issues. I believe that there is no issue where the specific morally relevant differences of capability theory show up more clearly than that of inequality. The capabilities that Sen is concerned with, as Putnam notes, 'are particularly capabilities "to achieve functionings that [a person] has reason to value . . ., and this yields a particular way of viewing the assessment of equality and inequality"' (Putnam, 2002, p. 56, quoting Sen, 1992, pp. 4–5).

It is thus far from accidental that Sen first put his concept of capabilities through its paces in a Tanner Lecture entitled 'Equality of What?' ([1980], pp. 353–369). A few pages suffice him to show how rival approaches neglect deep and potentially tragic inequalities, which the capability approach reveals. Sen has written much on his concepts of functionings and capabilities since that paper, and has modified and added to his statements in response to criticism; nevertheless I think any readers who happen not to be already conversant with the literature on this topic will still gain from going back to Sen's brief and pointed initial statement, and starting there.

As Sen runs through rival concepts of equality, utilitarianism, already deficient in so many ways, does especially badly here; 'Even the minutest gain in total utility *sum* would be taken to outweigh distributional inequalities of the most blatant kind' (Sen, [1980], p. 356). He then introduces an example he had used even earlier, in Sen (1973, pp. 16–20). It is a situation that haunts his writings on inequality, and appears again, for example, in Sen (1992). He compares a healthy vigorous person who is a 'pleasure-wizard' at maximizing utility with someone who is severely disabled (Sen [1980], pp. 357–358). I shall repeat here my presentation of such a situation from an earlier work: 'Consider two young people, both (let us suppose) equally talented and equally eager to realize their potentialities to the fullest possible degree. They could even, for the purposes of the model, be identical twins. There is one serious difference between them: while Augusta is blessed with robust health, Beatrice has suffered an injury which has left her with a severe physical hardship' (Walsh, 1995–1996, p. 557). Beatrice, I assumed, would only be able (as a result of being disabled) to derive *half* as much utility as Augusta from any particular income level. She obviously thus needs to be given *more* income than Augusta, but 'utilitarianism, maximizing the sum-total of utility, would give Augusta a *higher* income than Beatrice, making the latter *even worse off* than she would be on an equal division of income, where her utility level was already stipulated to be only half Augusta's' (Walsh, 1995–1996, pp. 557–558, emphasis in original). As Sen concluded, '[i]t is this narrowness that makes the utilitarian conception of equality such a limited one. Even where utility is accepted as the only basis of moral importance, utilitarianism fails to capture the relevance of overall advantage for the requirements of equality' (Sen, 1982, p. 358).

And, of course, 'utility' in *any* interpretation (even when identified with 'good') *cannot* be accepted as the only basis of moral importance, as Sen has insisted for decades and as we have seen at length. Putnam comments especially on one characteristic argument of Sen's: 'The novel point that Sen makes is that in cases of extreme and long-lasting deprivation, the satisfaction of desires can also be an impoverished information base because a frequent consequence of this sort of deprivation is the reduction in the range of desires owing to the hopelessness of the situation' (Putnam, 2002, p. 58). One might add that grinding poverty will clearly destroy the strength and morale needed to fight for one's rights. As Sen has recently expressed this, '[t]he utility calculus can be deeply unfair to those who are persistently deprived: for example, the usual underdogs in stratified societies, perennially oppressed minorities in intolerant communities, traditionally precarious sharecroppers living in a world of uncertainty, routinely overworked sweat-shop employees in exploitative economic arrangements, hopelessly subdued housewives in severely sexist cultures. The deprived people tend to come to terms with their deprivation' (Sen, 1999, pp. 62–63).

It is completely characteristic of Sen that the test that he has consistently put to concepts of equality (and thus to development theories supposedly offering policy prescriptions leading to greater equality) has always been, from his earliest to his latest work, how these concepts of equality fare when dealing with the most wretched, deprived and exploited of this world.

Utilitarianism falls at this fence, and we have seen at the same time how badly equality of *income* does, since Beatrice even with Augusta's income, may (given her disability) be seriously deprived. Neoclassical growth theory, of course, is still wedded to income per head, which can conveniently conceal the most appalling inequalities *even in* income and wealth, in addition to the inadequacies of the space of incomes as a measure (Sen, 1992, pp. 28–30). There is a case that can be made for *beginning* with income inequality, but '[t]here is, however, an equally good case for not *ending* with income analysis only. John Rawls's classic analysis of "primary goods" provides a broader picture of resources that people need no matter what their respective ends are' (Sen, 1999, p. 72, emphasis in original).

Rawls is one of a number of writers who have approached inequality in terms of a list of primary or basic goods. In the field of development theory, a group of economists, for instance, 'associated with [Paul] Streeten (1981) – argued for giving priority to meeting the basic needs of the most deprived' (Qizilbash, 1996, p. 1209). In the case of Rawls, however, his concept of primary goods comes embedded in a complex political philosophy, leading to a theory of justice. To avoid the complexities of Rawls' theory of justice here, I shall say only a few words about his primary goods before turning to the 'basic needs' school in development economics.

It should be no surprise that Sen would be attracted to theories that single out the different specific needs of the poorest and seek a treatment that would address these. Such analyses clearly deserve to be taken more seriously than the old standbys of utility and incomes. Not only do such theories suggest a renewal of serious moral involvement when compared with the watered down utilitarianism of neoclassical economics, but they also involve (more or less explicitly) a return to some key concepts of classical political economy.

As early as his Tanner Lecture on equality, Sen was turning from 'the obtuseness of welfarism' (Sen, 1982, p. 362) to the fundamentally different rights-based work of Rawls. An analysis of equality in terms of human rights and of a theory of justice, must have seemed ideally suited to blow away the close fog of utilitarianism like a blast of cold New England air from an opened door.

For utilitarianism, the ugly and unhealthy pleasure people take in discriminating against each other must be included in the total of their 'utility', whereas, Rawls argues, '[i]n justice as fairness, on the other hand, persons accept in advance a principle of equal liberty. . . An individual who finds that he enjoys seeing others in positions of lesser liberty understands that he has no claim whatever to this enjoyment. The pleasure he takes in another's deprivation is wrong in itself' (Rawls, 1971, pp. 30–31).

Sen comments that 'It is easily seen that this is an argument not merely against utilitarianism, but against the adequacy of utility information for moral judgments of states of affairs, and is, thus, an attack on welfarism in general.' (Sen, 1982, p. 363). One does not have to accept the whole apparatus of the Rawlsian system in order to defend non-welfarist moral claims in general, or even rights-based claims in particular. But with utilitarian claims being virtually the only ones that were noticed by economic theory and much of social science, Rawls was a powerful wake-up call for neoclassical theory. Sen, on the other hand, could see beyond this: as early as his Tanner Lecture, he points out that 'Herbert Hart has persuasively disputed Rawls's arguments for the priority of liberty [H.L.A. Hart, 1973]' (Sen, 1982).

From the beginning, therefore, Sen's response to Rawls has been qualified: 'If people were basically very similar, then an index of primary goods might be quite a good way of judging advantage. But, in fact, people seem to have very different needs varying with health, longevity, climatic conditions, location, work conditions, temperament, and even body size (affecting food and clothing requirements). So what is involved is not merely ignoring a few hard cases' (Sen, 1982, p. 366). The 'hard cases' are, of course, cases like Beatrice, who would get neither more nor less from Rawls on account of being disabled. But with regard to such hard cases, Sen tells us in a note that 'Rawls is, in fact, just *postponing* the question rather than justifying *ignoring* it' (Sen, 1982, pp. 365–366, note 28, emphasis in original).

In his latter work on inequality, Sen stresses that '[w]hile my own approach is deeply influenced by Rawls's analysis, I argue that the particular informational focus on which Rawls himself concentrates neglects some considerations that can be of great importance to the substantive assessment of equality—and also of efficiency' (Sen, 1992, p. 8). Once again the issue 'turns on the fundamental diversity of human beings. Two persons holding the same bundle of primary goods can have very different freedoms to pursue their respective conceptions of the good (whether or not these conceptions coincide)' (Sen, 1992, p. 8).

This will be his deepest complaint, not just against Rawls, but against *any* theory which judges equality in terms of a list of *goods*. A few years ago we find him, in a work which stresses the crucial role of freedom and rights, nevertheless reminding his readers that the case for a *complete priority* of rights can be disputed: 'Why should the status of intense economic needs, which can be matters of life and death, be lower than that of personal liberties? This issue was forcefully raised in a general form by Herbert Hart a long time ago (in a famous article in 1973)' (Sen, 1999, p. 64). He notes that Rawls has acknowledged the force of Hart's argument in later work (Rawls, 1993, especially Lecture 8).

The basic needs approach has some obvious similarity to one aspect of Rawls' position, namely his concern with primary goods. Aside from this, however, the point of view and purposes of basic needs theory is fundamentally different. It was written in order to advance the project of a morally responsible development analysis and policy. And, in contrast to Rawls, its economic thinking had fairly evident classical roots. For these reasons it will be of more use to us here than Rawls. We need to consider the role of certain necessary, or basic, goods in the original classics and in present day classical theory. This undertaking will enable us to compare the tradition of the classical economists with Sen's capability theory.

Sen, it should be noted, has acknowledged that '[t]he "basic needs" literature and the related studies on the "quality of life" have been enormously helpful in drawing attention to deprivations of essential goods and services and their crucial role in human living' (Sen, 1992, p. 109). He prefers going directly to capabilities, but he makes an important concession to the basic needs approach: 'In so far as the underlying reasoning of the basic-needs approach relates to giving people the *means* of achieving certain basic functionings, the problem of interpersonal variations in "transforming" commodities into functions—discussed earlier—can also be avoided by directly looking at the functioning space rather than at the commodity space' (Sen, 1992, p. 109, emphasis in original).

This feature of the basic needs approach, together with its *disaggregated* nature, enabling a number of different commodities and services to be seen as severally necessary and only together sufficient for a minimally decent human life, render it, I believe, entitled to serious consideration in a way in which I do not think that utility-based or income-based approaches to inequality and development are. I do not advocate the basic needs approach as a *rival* to the capability approach. But I do think that it has a role to play in a discussion of the relationship between Sen's analysis and classical growth theory.

Sen has indeed explicitly noted that the basic needs approach 'has some similarities with the capabilities approach. As Paul Streeten (1981) has pointed out, "the basic needs concept is a reminder that the objective of the development effort is to provide all human beings with the *opportunity* for a full life" (p. 21 [emphasis in original]). It involves the rejection of both utility-based welfare economics and commodity-based growth calculus. These characteristics are shared by the basic needs approach with the capabilities approach, and more specifically the focus on "nutrition, health, shelter, water and sanitation, education, and other essentials" [Ibid.] in the basic needs approach makes it directly concerned with a number of important capabilities' (Sen, 1984, p. 513).

Sen is right to add immediately, however, that there are significant differences between the two approaches to development. Needs are defined in terms of *commodities*—although as Sen notes 'attention is paid to differences in the commodities needed by different persons to satisfy the same human requirements . . . But often commodity requirements may not be at all derivable from a specified set of capabilities, since the relation between commodity bundles and capability bundles may quite plausibly be a *many–one* correspondence, with the same capabilities being achievable by more than one particular bundle of goods and services' (Sen, 1984, pp. 513–514, emphasis in original).

A very important difference, for an economist but also for a philosopher, concerns the *range* of the respective ideas. The analysis in terms of needs *as it arose* in development theory, was concentrated on the truly primary needs of the *desperately* poor. This haunts the treatment, for example, of Streeten *et al.*'s (1981) powerful work. As Sen observes, the implicit preconception of that work is with reaching a *minimal* capability level. Sen's capability theory, on the other hand, 'can be used for judging individual "advantage" at any level. In this sense the basic needs approach involves one particular application of the capabilities framework' (Sen, 1984, p. 514).[9]

A relevant consideration is captured by Sen's claim that '[t]he perspective of fulfilling needs has some obvious advantages in dealing with dependents (e.g. children), but for responsible adults the format of capabilities may be much more suitable in seeing what is involved and in linking it with the issue of freedom' (Sen, 1984, p. 514). Indeed, Sen's concept of capability can probably best be seen in a clear light by investigating its connection with freedom. Phillip Petit has recently done exactly this. He asks us to consider 'a society where an oil-rich potentate decides, perhaps out of idle whim, to use his enormous annual income in order to raise the functioning among the very poor subjects of his regime. Imagine, to make the case vivid, that he does this so successfully that the people flourish' (Petit, 2001, p. 11). What is missing? The potentate might impose his preferences, but Petit takes the case where he does not do so: the potentate is quite happy for people to express their own preferences, using his facilities only as they prefer. Petit grants that the people are much better off than before the potentate's largesse (I might add that they are doing very well as regards basic needs). But it all depends on the potentate's grace and favor. Petit observes that some of Sen's own critics appear to overlook the importance of enjoying favor-independently-decisive preference in matters of functioning. Thus he notes that 'G. A. Cohen supports the idea that what is important is not functioning capability but access to functioning or, as he himself says, to advantage. And he suggests that it does not matter by his lights that this access is dependent on the whim of someone like our potentate.' But Petit (2001, p. 13) rejects this, pointing out that '[f]ew can be prepared to argue that dependence on the grace and favor of a figure like the potentate does not detract seriously from the capability of the benefits he provides to raise the quality of people's lives'

Petit makes it clear that Sen is not demanding that a person who is free be *continually* and *actively* making choices: Sen's conception is one that concerns *preference*, not every occasion of choice. One may depend on the services of others, provided that they are attending to our stated preferences. One cannot, after all, make decisive choices when one is under a general anesthetic, but one can have made known one's decisive preferences, which one's surgeon will carry out (or face a malpractice suit). One *wants* functionings, but not *thrust upon* one. For Sen the *capability* to function *as preferred* is what is most important. Cohen (1993, pp. 24–25) accused Sen of having an 'athletic' image of the person; Petit, however, cogently supports Sen in saying that such athleticism was never intended.

Commenting on Pettit, Sen points out that 'the acceptance of what Pettit suggests would entail a very considerable emendation of the capability perspective' (Sen, 2001, p. 52). Sen is quite explicit that, as he sees it, '[t]he capability approach demands only '*content*-independent effectiveness' and is silent on '*context*-independent effectiveness' (which, Pettit argues, is additionally needed)' (Sen, 2001, p. 52, emphasis in original). In other words, Sen is arguing that if an artist can paint (or sculpt) exactly what he wants, then the fact that he had to kiss the ring of a corrupt old pontiff in order to do this is *insignificant* to the realization of the artist's capabilities. Ordinary language is surely with Sen: we would only say that the full exercise of the artist's capabilities were inhibited if the pope actually *interfered* with the successful execution of the work. Sen, however, does grant that freedom has a *robustness* when it is not dependent on another's will.

Nevertheless, he concludes that the capability approach should not be amended in the way Pettit suggests. This is because the capability approach can surely concentrate on a particular aspect of freedom, even if other aspects have their importance. If Beatrice has a music coach who comes to her own apartment, when he expects non-handicapped students to come to his home, then she may well feel under something of an obligation to him. But arguably her capability to play a Bach partita for solo violin is not impaired by this. That question—is her *progress* impaired—is the one which *specifically concerns* capability theory. If an elderly widow is kept in bearable health only because her doctor (who has known her most of her life) keeps her supplied with 'free samples', what concerns capability theory is that the old woman retains some health. (Some of the medicines really are samples, but not all. But she does not know this, it is one of the things he will never tell her.)

As Sen observes, '[t]he Aristotelian focus on what a person has the capability to do (dependent as it is on the many factors beyond the control of this person) does point to something quite important for public policy (on this see especially Nussbaum, 1988, 1992). We live in a world in which being completely independent of the help and goodwill of others may be particularly difficult to achieve, and sometimes may not even be the most important thing to achieve' (Sen, 2001, p. 56). This brief sketch of Sen's debate with Pettit (the interested reader must go to the original papers for some fascinating details) may perhaps have thrown a rather unfavorable light on the basic needs approach, since the recipients of provision for their basic needs are arguably cast in a rather passive role—that of taking what some bureaucrat decides is good for them. Thus, as long ago as 1981, Streeten was noting that the basic needs approach had 'fallen into disrepute in the North–South dialogue. At international meetings delegates from the developing countries have vehemently rejected the basic needs concept. There has been concern over the potential hypocrisy of such a strategy and suspicion about the intentions of aid-giving governments and international agencies' (Streeten, 1981, p. 168).

If capability theory can defend its flank against invasion from ideas concerning other sorts of freedom, basic needs theory would seem to be much less able to do so. In situations short of destitution, the capability approach surely has more to offer. And this may well explain its having largely displaced the basic needs approach in present day debate.

Sen, however, had defended the approach in terms of basic needs within *some situations*, and rejected its dismissal as being in bad faith: the argument that the concentration on the most elementary needs of the very poor concealed a desire to confine policy against inequality to some small doling out of bare survival to the poorest. He is surely right that if the basic needs approach is seen as just one application of the capabilities approach, it should be clear that other issues related to capabilities (including that of the *equality* of capabilities), is not prejudiced by 'the special concern with basic needs at a certain stage of development' (Sen, 1984, p. 515, emphasis in original).

Necessaries, conveniencies, and classical growth theories

Sen has returned recently to a theme that appears several times in his writings: 'What counts as "necessity" in a society is to be determined, in Smithian analysis, by its need to generate some minimally required freedoms, such as the ability to appear in public without shame, or to take part in the life of the community. Adam Smith put the issue thus: "By necessaries I understand not only the commodities which are indispensable for the support of life, but what ever the customs of the country renders it indecent for creditable people, even the lowest order to be without" ' (Smith, [1776], 1976a, pp. 469–471, cited by Sen, 1999, pp. 73–74).

Sen is right that Smith looks beyond the commodities, such as a linen shirt, to the substantive freedoms—the capabilities—which the shirt conveys to the day laborer who would be ashamed to appear in public without it. It is not so very surprising that Smith should think in this way: as Sen himself notes, the concept of functionings, which reflects the various things a person may value doing or being, 'has distinctly Aristotelian roots' (Sen, 1999, p. 75). And Smith, as Sen has often noted, is part of the tradition which passed these Aristotelian ideas down to us (as was Marx who, when young, read Greek philosophy).

I have no doubt that Smith, Hellenist and moral philosopher, would gladly admit that for many evaluative purposes the appropriate space is that of the substantive freedoms – the fulfilled capabilities which have yielded a valuable life. But Smith, the first mature classic, would also want to look in the other direction, behind the linen shirt to its conditions of reproduction—and especially towards the conditions that governed the reproducibility of such shirts (and other necessaries) on an expanded scale. But to engage in the specifics of these issues in a manner which, while hopefully true to Smith, nevertheless leads into present-day classical theory, we need to introduce some technical concepts.

It will be helpful to begin with a sketch of the simplest present-day classical reproduction structure (asking the indulgence of economist readers, since this is clearly for the benefit of philosophers). I shall be very 'minimalist' about this, since the bare bones are exactly what need to be seen *before* we return to Smithian enrichments. Consider, then, a very simple isolated economy where two commodities, corn and iron, are produced under conditions of constant returns, with no technical choice. A single process is thus available for the production of corn, using corn itself as seed and iron implements for cultivation. Labor is available on the payment of a wage in corn. Likewise, iron agricultural implements are produced using a single process, by means of iron tools and corn (the wage of the iron workers). It should be noted that this is a model of the little economy's *reproduction* structure *only*. So inputs of *given*, non-reproduced resources, such as land, while clearly used, are assumed to be freely available (as indeed land was to homesteaders in the United States during the nineteenth century, and until later in Canada).[10] In a standard notation, one writes Y_c for the total output of corn and Y_i for the total output of iron goods. The per unit input requirements of corn to produce a unit of corn is written a_{cc}, the per unit requirement of corn to produce a unit of iron is a_{ci}, while the input of iron into producing one unit of corn is a_{ic} and the iron input into a unit of iron is a_{ii}.

The first concept of classical theory can now be expressed for our simple model: it has to do with *viability*. For the model economy to be viable, it is necessary that:

> Total corn needed for corn + total corn needed for iron be less than or equal to total corn output, and
> Total iron needed for corn + total iron needed for iron be less than or equal to total iron output.

More formally:

$$a_{cc}Y_c + a_{ci}Y_i \leq Y_c \tag{1}$$

$$a_{ic}Y_c + a_{ii}Y_i \leq Y_i \tag{2}$$

The viability condition expressed rather lengthily by expressions 1 and 2 above can be expressed in a manner that is not *confined* to our simple model, but rather is robust to expansion to any finite numbers of sectors.[11]

Now we need to consider first the case where the viability condition is *barely* satisfied: total outputs remain *just enough* to reproduce the economy on the same scale. Relationships numbers 1 and 2 are satisfied as equations.[12] The seed used in last year's sowing is replaced, worn out tools and implements are replaced, and the corn for subsistence is there.

The commodities that appear in this model are what have come to be called (since Sraffa, 1960) basic commodities. A basic is a commodity that is an input, directly or indirectly, into every other commodity. There are, however, differences. Our iron tools and implements are *Sraffa* (1960) basics, but Smith's 'necessaries' are normal consumption goods, rather than technical means of production. The viability of an economy also depends, however, on its technical basics, so in this respect we should modify Smith.

Questions also arise about the *consumption* basics, which in our baby model are just represented by 'corn'. They need not be so confined, of course—such models, as already noted, can have as many sectors as desired. If we are to be true to the spirit of Smith, and articulate elements of a present day model which can be used to discuss his political economy, we must surely hold onto the consumption basics, and the concept of subsistence which they formalize. The non-economist reader may be surprised to hear that Sraffa (1960) dropped consumption basics. Clearly this would not do for the purposes of a present day discussion of Smith. But to see some of what is at issue we need to develop the little corn and iron model so that a net product, or surplus, arises. This will arise if we make total output *greater than* the total inputs that produce it, so that the economy is more than minimally viable. So now we have *strict* inequalities:

$$a_{cc}Y_c + a_{ci}Y_i < Y_c \tag{3}$$

$$a_{ic}Y_c + a_{ii}Y_i < Y_i \tag{4}$$

We can now introduce a rate of surplus, R, obtaining quantity equations for the two-sector model:

$$(a_{cc}Y_c + a_{ci}Y_i)(1 + R_c) = Y_c \tag{5}$$

$$(a_{ic}Y_c + a_{ii}Y_i)(1 + R_i) = Y_i \tag{6}$$

Here, the surplus is left aggregated; but it could be divided between growth (written g) or luxury consumption (written l with a subscript). If *all* of the surplus is absorbed in luxury, zero growth is possible. Classical theory old and new is quite precise about the fact that all luxury consumption is *at the cost of growth*. Clearly, on the other hand, maximum growth implies zero luxury. More reasonable is a division between the two:

$$(a_{cc}Y_c + a_{ci}Y_i)(1 + g) = (1 - l_c)Y_c$$
$$(a_{ic}Y_c + a_{ii}Y_i)(1 + g) = (1 - l_i)Y_i \qquad (7)$$

Growth in this simple model is assumed to be balanced, something that has to be dropped before a model can come anywhere near capturing Smith's concept of growth (as Walsh and Gram, 1980, p. 274, pointed out). The *l*s are subscripted because luxury consumption does not have to be balanced, even in this simple model.

Now we are ready to explore the implications of whether or not there are consumption basics. Note first that to drop the original classical concept of *subsistence* (an important concept for Adam Smith) is what is implied by the present day classical idea of dropping consumption basics. Gram and I strongly felt in 1980 (and still do today) that a serious difficulty with this move is that, 'if the notion of subsistence is abandoned altogether, it follows by definition that surplus may be positive in a situation in which there is insufficient net output to support even the labor force, much less to allow for growth in the stock of capital . . . Surplus then loses its historical significance since a positive surplus no longer implies the basis for accumulation or for the support of the capitalist class. Of course, the classical economists never fell into this trap since they always treated wages as a necessary input into the process of production' (Walsh and Gram, 1980, p. 318).

I shall argue that an *appropriately* characterized concept of subsistence is *even more vital* today for an *enriched* classical model (inspired by Smith and Sen) than a more Spartan concept of subsistence was for the minimalist classical models of the twentieth century. But a few words are necessary before beginning this, in order to prevent misunderstandings. Not only were the twentieth-century founders of the classical revival minimalist in their concentration on the mathematical formalization of original classicism, they also concentrated on formalizing *particular parts* of the theory. To consider only the two contributors to the Neumann/Sraffa blend, which Gram and I used, Neumann's famous paper (Neumann, [1937], 1945–1946, pp. 1–9) concentrated a bright spotlight on the formal characterization of a model of the reproduction of commodities by means of the same commodities, which is always in maximum balanced growth. Consumption is confined to 'necessities of life' (Neumann, [1937], 1945–1946, p. 2). Neumann assumes that non-produced resources needed in production are available free (as I did in the little corn and iron model sketched above). His model is thus entirely concentrated on the *reproduction* structure, and on *one* situation of this—namely the properties of a model of any finite number of sectors, which is in maximal balanced growth. (For an up-to-date characterization of the Neumann model and its classical properties, see Kurz and Salvadori, 1998b, pp. 25–56, and for comments see Walsh, 2002a, pp. 327–342.)

Piero Sraffa (1960) on the other hand operated within a context that excluded any discussion of growth. But he explored the ultimate significance of the distinction between basic and non-basic commodities, developed the concept of a standard commodity (on which see Kurz and Salvadori, 1998b, pp. 123–147) treated classical models with joint production, and with non-produced resources which are scarce, and much more.

Sraffa indeed begins, in his first chapter, with a model of the production of wheat and iron by means of wheat and iron for subsistence in 'an extremely simple society which produces just enough to maintain itself' (Sraffa, 1960, p. 3). Gram and I were following Sraffa in this (as I was in the sketch of a subsistence model in the present paper). Sraffa extends his subsistence model to cover any number of commodities. Then, in Chapter Two, he treats production with a surplus. He notes that 'now there is room for a new class of "luxury" products which are not used, whether as instruments of production or as articles of subsistence, in the production of others. . . Their role is purely passive' (Sraffa, 1960, p. 7). These, of course, are the non-basics. Only two pages later, he raises the issue of the wage: 'We have up to this point regarded wages as consisting of the necessary subsistence of the workers and thus entering the system on the same footing as the fuel for the engines or the feed for the cattle. We must now take into account the other aspect of wages since, besides the ever-present element of subsistence, they may include a share of the surplus product' (Sraffa, 1960, p. 9).

Sraffa considers the possible option of separating the two components of the wage and regarding 'only the "surplus" part as variable, whereas the goods necessary for the subsistence of the workers would continue to appear, with the fuel, etc., among the means of production' (Sraffa, 1960, pp. 9–10). Seeing the force of this argument, Gram and I followed Sraffa's suggested division of the wage (Walsh and Gram, 1980, pp. 319–343, 380–403). Sraffa, however, preferred to treat the wage as a whole as variable.

However this served his purposes, this would not provide a structure helpful in discussing Smith's enriched classicism. At first glance, indeed, one might suggest that Smith's 'necessaries' can be seen as Sraffa's 'subsistence' component of the wage, and Smith's 'luxuries' as the luxury component in Sraffa. The original classical economists and especially Smith, however, did not mean bare physical survival when they wrote of subsistence: they meant, rather, a customary standard of living. They could—and did—hope that continual prosperity would *raise* the standard (and they knew that hard times could lower it). Indeed, Smith is at pains to detail how an ordinary worker in the Britain of his day enjoyed many comforts not available to an African chieftain. Smith includes things such as a linen shirt and leather shoes in his definition of 'necessaries', explicitly stipulating that this concept covers, not only what commodities are indispensable to support life, but also what 'the customs of the country' (Smith, [1776], 1976a, p. 469) require.

And then there are Smith's 'conveniencies'. Are these the same as his luxuries? Surely not. For one thing, 'necessaries and conveniencies' are linked together. And conveniencies are not condemned, or described as 'gross' or 'unbridled'. Granted, Smith does not *always* condemn luxuries. But on the whole he does. Gram has noted recently that 'Smith's use of "conveniency" goes well beyond the desire to save time and trouble. It refers to "love of system" in the stoical sense, well-captured according to Smith (TMS, VII. Ii. 1. 42), by Seneca in the *Epistles*, where the Latin *convenientia* refers to proper, fit, decent and becoming actions' (Gram, 1998, p. 162).

If we include 'conveniencies' along with 'necessaries' in a present day enrichment of classical theory we can be in the spirit of Smith. As Gram writes 'material necessities which allow for the exercise of prudence provide the basis for an individually defined notion of subsistence; those that allow for the exercise of justice, the basis for a socially defined subsistence. The advance from barbarous to civilized society not only expands the notion of justice to include the protection of rights as well as life and property, but also reduces the need to exercise the respectable virtue of self-denial while making possible the exercise of the amiable virtue of beneficence' (Gram, 1998, p. 164).

My suggestion is that those commodities, which can be seen to be required, not just for physical survival, but for the realization of the vital human capabilities, be given the status of basic commodities. In such modeling, a rate of growth would have moral significance, and the basic/non-basic distinction would mark an important difference between those commodities that could reasonably be regarded as a precondition of human flourishing, and those gross luxuries that serve only for the perverted pursuit of vulgar display and vain distinction.

Remember that no list of basics would give us a nice mapping from any basic or group of basics to the *necessary* flowering of a capability. Any capability, simple *or* sophisticated can be realized by different commodities, as the capability to be nourished is realized by different food stuffs. Again, the *specific* requirements of an individual person cannot be embedded in a model of this kind—all sorts of differences of age, gender, size, health, or handicap can affect these. Yet being handicapped, for example, *does* make the realization of some of our capabilities depend upon certain rather identifiable commodities, such as a wheelchair, and certain facilities such as entry ramps, which could certainly be in our list of basic commodities. 'Growth' in a present-day classical model is the growth of the *specific* components of a list of commodities produced in the different sectors of a basic technology. 'GDP' grows in *neoclassical* theory, if more people become addicted to smoking—and again if the incomes of surgeons go up when they have to operate on the smokers. In a classical model, the non-basics produced appear, as we have seen, as a reduction in the rate of growth from what would otherwise have been possible.

So far, however, we have concentrated on just *two* of the advantages of classical theory for an enriched political economy in the spirit of Sen's interpretation of Smith: first, that growth is always disaggregated, so that one can see exactly *what* is being allowed to grow, and, second that what grows are the *basic* commodities—not gross luxuries, or the great shiny toys desired by militarists. To see that classical models have further advantages, we must go beyond simple models that assume (as Smith could never have done) that growth is balanced.

It might be argued that much of the criticism of balanced growth models stemmed from the fact that neoclassical theory treats all commodities as equivalent in status (something which makes it logically problematic for the theory to cope with a 'war on drugs'). When GDP grows, as even the popular press is aware, many 'bads' grow along with 'goods'. But in a present day classical model what are growing, as we have seen, are all those commodities that are to be found in a non-negative square matrix of basics, and these have a special status. Any classical model, in partitioning the set of commodities into basics and non-basics, is black with fact, white with convention, and red with values. The modern classical models of the last century, for all their formal, minimalist austerity, were a paradigm example of entanglement. The *enrichment* of present day classical theory by Amartya Sen and (as we shall shortly see) by theorists such as Luigi Pasinetti, does not *introduce* entanglement into what was previously a 'value-free' mathematical science. What it does is to bring the moral implications of the theory back to center stage and put a spotlight dead on them, as was done long ago by Adam Smith. Putnam, of course, is well aware of all this, and his argument is designed to show that there is nothing unusual or questionable about the fact that political economy is both a mathematical and a moral science.

Ensuring that the reproduction of our global economy can proceed on an expanding scale without threatening the sustainability of life on our planet, requires that a *classical* model of growth be developed to handle issues beyond steady-state (or balanced) sorts of growth.

The significance of transformational growth for Sen's view of Smith

In Adam Smith, growth is never simply the production of a larger number of each of the existing commodities, by means of existing technologies, year after year. As is well known, he saw growth as bubbling up here and there in the economy, often as some technological innovation, or the greater division of labor, lowered the costs of production. New machinery was being invented; new goods (or goods provided in a new way) were appearing. Since he was not concerned with producing a formal model, Smith described what he saw in the world around him. When the early revivers of classical theory sought to present its core concepts in mathematical models, however, they naturally began with the simplest case, when each of the sectors in a model's basic technology is turning out, say, 5% more output per year. Even John von Neumann, the most sophisticated mathematician ever to have constructed an economic model when he presented his famous paper on an expanding economy (Neumann, [1937], 1945–1946) and one of the twentieth century's great mathematicians on any terms, concentrated on balanced growth.[13] The mathematical convenience of balanced growth, however, could not long compensate for its unreality. Balanced growth from the proportional enlargement of the inputs devoted to reproduction in each sector was *perhaps* possible. But once one wanted to introduce technical progress, that this should take place at exactly the same rate in every sector every year was beyond belief. Clearly twentieth-century classical theory needed to break out of the straitjacket of balanced growth. The escape was not accomplished all at once, and a full treatment would call for distinguishing between several contributing streams of thought. Here it must suffice to glance at two stages.

The first stage in the escape beyond steady-state modeling was confined to depicting a model economy passing from one balanced growth equilibrium to another. One may begin with the work of Adolph Lowe (1955). Ten years later, Sir John Hicks (1965) analyzed the path from one equilibrium state to another and named the process 'traverse'. Lowe's full dress presentation of his ideas then followed (Lowe, 1976). (The interested reader will find this discussed in a number of chapters in Halevi *et al.*, 1992.)

If a model can traverse from a balanced growth path in which one or more industries use a highly pollutant technology to a different technological configuration which is significantly more benign, clearly some progress has been made in the formal depiction of a morally responsible political economy of growth. I suggested some years ago that: 'Most original, perhaps, has been Lowe's treatment of the recycling of production and consumption residuals, thus cutting down the damaging ecological effects of growth, in a specifically classical context, so that these processes of transformation of residuals become another circular flow (Lowe, 1976, pp. 223–231)' (Walsh, 1992, p. 39). It should also be noted that Lowe's approach, unlike that of most theorists of his period, was *explicitly* normative: he proposes the adoption of a prescriptive rather than just a descriptive approach to modeling growth—what he terms '*instrumental analysis*' (Lowe, 1976, p. 12, emphasis in original).

The theory of traverse, however, had its limitations: 'in general it cannot be taken for granted that the sequence, generated by some kind of "disturbance", will eventually lead to a new steady-state equilibrium' (Kurz, 1992, p. 74). What was needed was not just a process whereby a model was shunted from one supposedly steady state to another—as a train is shunted from one main line, over a series of points, to another main line. What was needed, rather, was a modeling of an economy undergoing *continuous* transformational growth. And this had been a preoccupation of Luigi Pasinetti (1965, 1981, 1993) for many years.

Present day classical growth models, from the simplest (like our two sector corn and iron model) to the most sophisticated, have stipulated an input matrix $\mathbf{A}$ of per unit input requirements a_{ij}, for any input i needed to produce a unit of output j. Constant returns to scale processes of production are then assumed to exist for the technology summarized in $\mathbf{A}$. Technical change, if it is introduced, implies a new linear technology, expressed in a new input matrix *with new a_{ij}* for at least *some* processes.[14]

Pasinetti, however, was not content with the sorts of growth that can be analyzed with such models, nor with the element of freedom introduced by the Hicks–Lowe traverse. His much more ambitious goal was to present a dynamic model 'without that fixity of coefficients which had constrained all interindustry analysis into a straightjacket' (Pasinetti, 1981, p. xii). In the sense in which there can be said to be 'equilibrium' in his model, it is a *continually* changing equilibrium. It is not (as in the traverse models) returning to a steady state like the one from which it departed in traversing.

Pasinetti grants that the assumptions of constant returns to scale (standard in balanced growth models) and of zero technical progress are at least *logically* possible. But he insists that the assumption of *balanced* technical progress plus the uniform expansion of demand 'are not only unlikely, they are impossible' (Pasinetti, 1981, p. 66). He assumes the existence of continual technical progress, taking place at *explicitly* different rates in different sectors. This process in turn will result in the appearance of *new* goods, necessarily resulting in shifts of demand, as consumers (satiated with some old goods) transfer their demands to the new goods as these appear.

This stress on major changes in demand might seem at first glance to imply some concession to neoclassical theory, and it is true that Pasinetti regards *classical* theory as having neglected the importance of certain dynamic properties of demand. But he is even more critical of the extensive discussions of demand in neoclassicism: 'The consumers' demand theory that we know today is a highly sophisticated logical framework, built on entirely static premises. It relies on the existence of a perfectly known and consistent set of preferences defined at a given level of per capita income. Such a theory . . . is clearly unable to offer us any guide to the investigation of changes in demand following successive and persistent *increments* to income' (Pasinetti, 1981, p. 69, emphasis in original).[15]

In any case, Pasinetti's models are classical to the bone, as anyone who studies them will see. In particular, he is inspired by Adam Smith—the very subtitle of his earlier book on transformational growth describes the work as '*A Theoretical Essay on the Dynamics of the Wealth of Nations*' (Pasinetti, 1981). Smith, of course, never expected growth to be balanced, and for him technical innovation and growth of demand were interwoven in the fabric of growth depicted in his work. Indeed Pasinetti derives what are arguably the most characteristic concepts of his growth theory explicitly from Smith: the central role of technical innovation occurring unevenly in different sectors, and the method of analysis in terms of vertically integrated sectors, found in an embryonic form in the *Wealth of Nations*. This involves treating the model economy as a set of vertically integrated sectors, in each of which only one final consumption good is produced. No intermediate goods are *explicitly* represented; in the case of each production process, all its inputs are reduced to inputs of labor and of the services of stocks of capital goods. Thus, 'there is a production process behind each final commodity, which goes right back to what have traditionally been called the "factors of production"' (Pasinetti, 1981, p. 30). It is important to stress, as he does, that 'for our purposes, this entails no loss of generality. For, as will be shown in detail later on (Chapter VI), it is always possible, when needed, to re-introduce intermediate commodities by linear algebraic transformations' (Pasinetti, 1981, pp. 29–30. For a brief non-mathematical discussion, the non-economist reader might consult Pasinetti and Scazzieri, 1987, pp. 525–528).

In his more recent book, Pasinetti considers the simplest possible model for his theory, which plays for his (purely classical) theory a somewhat similar role to that played in neoclassical theory by their pure exchange model. This simplest classical model (of structural economic dynamics) is a highly abstract model economy where commodities are produced by pure labor alone.[16] As Pasinetti observes, '[t]he theoretical elements of a pure labour economy can be traced back, in the history of economic thought, to the original insights of Adam Smith' (Pasinetti, 1993, p. 16). Famously, Smith had written of an early and rude state of society; Pasinetti, however, has in mind a sophisticated and developed society which is, however, supposed to have the peculiar characteristic of employing labor *alone*. 'This is—as should be clear—an abstraction' (Pasinetti, 1993, p. 16).

He observes that Smith 'noticed that a process of continual expansion presupposes changes in the structure of employment, notably an increase in the share of 'productive' work (relative to 'unproductive' work)' (Pasinetti, 1993, p. 2). He notes later that: 'After Smith, economists have unfortunately shown less and less interest, with only a few exceptions, in the role played by technical progress' (Pasinetti, 1993, p. 106). Pasinetti's models enrich the production side of present day classical theory by breaking out of the steady state in a manner far beyond traverse, and stimulating the development of a theory of structural economic dynamics. But they also strikingly enrich the demand and consumption side of classicism, and again in a way that revives the richness of Smith and leaves behind the minimalism of Ricardo and of the early classical revival in the twentieth century. These matters call for our attention, since they concern certain links between the work of Pasinetti and that of Sen.

Consumption decisions in a dynamic context: evolving basics and capabilities

Pasinetti stresses 'the great need for a theory of consumers' decisions, both private and public, in a dynamic context' (Pasinetti, 1993, p. 107). We need to begin, however, with a few words on the enduring classical *skeleton* that underlies Pasinetti's continually transforming economy. Despite his going from an analysis in terms of an inter-industry structure to a formalization in terms of vertically integrated sectors, Pasinetti proposes 'that we go on using the analytic tools of inter-industry analysis, *à la* Leontiev (1951)[17] or *à la* Sraffa (1960), as long as we consider the economic system *at a particular moment of time*' (Pasinetti, 1993, p. 13, emphasis added). He argues that we need 'an appropriate set of rules in order to switch from inter-industry analysis, as it has been developed with regard to a given period of time, to vertically integrated analysis, to be used for investigations in time (that is, in a dynamic analysis), with the possibility of returning to inter-industry analysis at any moment when it is necessary or useful. Comparative statics and dynamics would thereby find an appropriate integration, and be used in a complementary manner' (Pasinetti, 1993, p. 13).

Consider, then, a Pasinetti model economy at a given moment of time. We have a familiar present day classical model which will have technical basics determined by the techniques now in use, and in which we can also discover consumption basics—Smith's necessaries and conveniencies. Even in the narrower category of 'necessaries', Smith (it will be recalled) specifically included 'not only the commodities which are indispensable for the support of life, but what ever the customs of the country renders it indecent for creditable people, even the lowest order, to be without' (Smith, [1776], 1976a, pp. 469–471, cited by Sen,

1999, pp. 73–74). Now Smith included a linen shirt (in part of the same passage) among his necessaries, even while admitting that '[a] linen shirt, for example, is, strictly speaking, not a necessary of life' (Smith, [1776], 1976a, pp. 469–471, cited by Sen, 1999, pp. 73–74). What is most interesting is that he recognizes that the list of necessaries *changes* over time: 'The Greeks and Romans lived, I suppose, very comfortably though they had no linen' (Smith, [1776], 1976a, pp. 469–471, cited by Sen, 1999, pp. 73–74). So a linen shirt was not a basic in earlier times. But technology changed, and by Smith's day 'a creditable day-labourer would be ashamed to appear in public without a linen shirt' (Smith, [1776], 1976a, pp. 469–471, cited by Sen, 1999, pp. 73–74). It is the same now, he tells us, with leather shoes. He is describing how the list of consumption basics changes as a result of transformational growth. He is describing a kind of growth where we do not simply have a little more of the *same* things, as time goes on. We have completely *new goods*. Not just goods that were once luxuries, but have now become inexpensive: rather we now have goods that simply *did not exist* before. Structural economic dynamics gives us new goods that do not remain wildly expensive luxuries—they may become new basics. And if they were made by new manufacturing processes, there are of course new *technical* basics, too.

This is the situation at a certain point in time. If we take another cross-section of the model when it has been evolving for a few years, the list of basics (technical and consumption) will have changed in various respects. This is in Smith, but Pasinetti has expanded and enriched its role, and investigated how it can be expressed formally, in a manner consistent with its classical origins. In his models, both technology *and* demand are changing *irreversibly*, and so a new production theory and a new consumption theory are needed. Pasinetti has made remarkable contributions to the handling of production, which has always been where classical theory was strongest. The neoclassics, of course, always regarded rational consumer choice as a specialty of theirs. But they were not concentrating on the question of dynamic choices, which concerns Pasinetti. As he notes, 'a dynamic analysis requires a decisive enrichment' (Pasinetti, 1993, p. 38). Note in passing that this would be an enrichment of a present day *classical*—indeed Smithian—theory, which is just what I mean by 'second phase' or 'enriched' present-day classical economics.

It will, I believe, prove interesting to investigate briefly the character of Sraffa basics (both consumption basics and technical basics) at a few different stages in the evolution of a Pasinetti-type dynamic model. He tells us that 'at low levels of income, the demand for consumption goods is, by necessity, confined to those goods that are essential to survival, such as food, above all' (Pasinetti, 1993, p. 38). Here, a cross-section of the model would show a basic technology of sparsely constructed necessaries and of the commodities needed to reproduce them. On Smith's own account, his linen shirts and leather shoes do not strictly have a place here. Taking a later cross-section, after the model has undergone transformational growth, we might find it had reached the point where Pasinetti writes that 'the primary necessity needs quickly reach saturation and the demand for consumption goods moves towards less necessary goods, while many of the very primary necessity goods (the so-called 'inferior' goods) are replaced by consumption goods of higher quality' (Pasinetti, 1993, p. 38). Here, the basic technology would show an enriched set of technical basics needed to produce them (leather working equipment, etc).

Arguably the 'basic needs'[18] approach would be willing to count the consumption goods in both of these stages in the evolution of a Pasinetti-type model as satisfying their concept of 'basic needs'. Perhaps *not* the consumption goods of later stages, however. As Sen has noted, 'basic needs are "interpreted in terms of *minimum* specified quantities" of particular commodities, and the implicit framework is that of reaching a *minimum* level of capabilities (see Streeten *et al.*, 1981, pp. 25–6)' (Sen, 1984, p. 514, emphasis in original).

Sen's capability approach, on the other hand, is not confined to the treatment of poor countries, or of the poor in rich countries. (As we have seen, some authors have been confused into thinking that this limitation on capability analysis must apply, perhaps because of Sen's lifelong concern with poverty and its analysis (see Sen, 1985a).

Meanwhile as the structural dynamics of a Pasinetti-type model gathered steam, a cross-section might be expected to show saturation having set in with regard to many or most commodities, which would have appeared among any list of 'basic needs'. There would still be Sraffa basics, but to borrow from Smith again, these would be the necessaries and *conveniencies* of a cultivated and enriched life. These conveniencies are not to be confused with the gross luxuries and profusions of the newly moneyed vulgar, for which Smith so often showed his contempt. His conveniencies, rather, are to be construed as the external necessities that Aristotle regarded as needed for the full development of human functioning. Aristotle clearly distinguishes his external necessities for the good human life from vulgar indulgence, as Smith does his conveniencies from vain display and the corruption of a love of beauty.

The capability approach, as Sen has stressed, is not confined as is the 'basic needs' approach, and 'can be used for judging individual "advantage" at any level' (Sen, 1984, p. 514). But this is also true of the progressively enriched set of basic commodities in a model of structural dynamics. Nor is this conceptualization (as Sen has said of 'basic needs') 'a more passive concept than "capability"' (Sen, 1984, p. 514). The capabilities approach indeed asks: what can a person do?—not just what can we *do for* the person. But Pasinetti's transformational growth is all about the transforming effects of human *learning*. This can be a bit athletic on the side of *production*, true. But on the side of changing and evolving consumption, it can be the learning of a fulfillment that brings contentment.

What, then, is the relation between the evolving basics of a structural dynamic model and capabilities? I wish to stress from the beginning that the relationship is *not* a tight mapping (for reasons that are already familiar). But there *is*, I shall argue, a significant relationship nonetheless. To explore it requires making some distinctions.

Sen has always been careful to insist that '[t]here can be substantial debates on the particular functionings that should be included in the list of important achievements and the corresponding capabilities' (Sen, 1999, p. 75, p. 310, note

42). Without prejudice, for the moment, to what exactly should appear on such a list, we need to note that it has been claimed that *any* such list should specify capabilities where attainability is *severally* necessary, and only *together* sufficient for satisfactory human flourishing.

Now, a Pasinetti-type model presents a truly dynamic process in which commodities arguably necessary to the realization of vital capabilities appear sequentially over time. Actually, *two* sequential aspects of Pasinetti's model need to be carefully distinguished, since they arise for different reasons. The first of these is the argument that human needs form a hierarchy, which can (and should) be addressed *sequentially*. Bertram Schefold has argued that '[t]here are certain hierarchies of needs, from basic needs up to higher needs such as the need for self-fulfillment' (Schefold, 1990, p. 187).[19] Schefold argues for the relevance here of lexical orderings (Schefold, 1990, p. 185), and this seems reasonable, especially in the most desperate situation, where the need for water, then food, clearly trump all less immediate needs. Pasinetti expects saturation to overtake the demand for *every* good at some point, a new good replacing the old and enriching the consumer's life. Thus, Pasinetti (1993, p. 38) argues that 'a dynamic analysis requires a decisive enrichment of the reference framework' and he certainly expects various needs to be satisfied in 'a certain hierarchical order' (cf. Walsh, 2000, pp. 16–19). Schefold (and Pasinetti) both assume that human nature reveals the presence of an *extreme* hierarchy of needs, way beyond desperate situations involving the immediate survival needs of famine victims and other life threatening emergencies. Pasinetti models, however, also have a quite different *technically* sequential property: that quite unbalanced growth, stimulated by human learning generates commodities that offer fulfillment, now for one human need and now for another. Sometimes a technical discovery may occur just when the need it can fulfill is becoming dominant, but of course there can be no guarantee in the structure of the model that it will be so.

What Pasinetti's model implies can perhaps be seen most clearly by making an extreme assumption about capabilities of the most non-hierarchical kind. Let us suppose, then, that there is a finite set of crucial human capabilities such that a humanly valuable life required that *all* of these be fulfilled to some level. There is *no* trade off between any of the decisive set of capabilities. Then Pasinetti's structural dynamics lead us to expect that commodities relevant to the higher fulfillment of some of these capabilities will become available over time, but not for all capabilities at once—that would require balanced technical change!

Now suppose the opposite: suppose there is a strict hierarchy of human needs all the way from water and nutrients up to the creative needs of a great artist. Again, there is no reason to suppose that the sequential development of the material basis for needs fulfillment laid out in the path of a Pasinetti model of structural dynamics would map closely onto this structure of needs. Conveniencies that could make life better would indeed be arriving on the scene, and a genuine enrichment of a classical kind taking place, but not necessarily for every important aspect of life at once, nor for one after another in a special order of need.

As to the relations between any particular capability and any commodity or commodities, the Pasinetti dynamic models do not change what Sen has repeatedly said: there is no guarantee that a particular amount of a particular commodity will be necessary (or sufficient) to allow the fulfillment of a particular capability. *Sometimes* it will happen. A particular (generic) drug may be the only cure for a disease, and be needed in a particular dose (irrespective of age, gender, size, or stamina). This drug could have arrived (as a result of recent fruits of scientific learning) as a new component to be found at a particular time slice of a Pasinetti model's set of basic commodities. One could invent a science fiction world in which, for each vital capacity, there was a single basic commodity which, when consumed, gave one all that was needed to fulfill the capability. But it would be science fiction.

What then can transformational growth give us? It can give us something which Adam Smith would understand: an evolving basket of necessaries and conveniencies, continually enriched in one way or another, with pollutant and destructive technologies eliminated one by one, with good things relevant to the flowering of human functionings arriving also one by one. Not a tight mapping to a list of capabilities, but surely a soil and a climate in which capabilities can flourish. There is nothing *minimalist* about Pasinetti's models. They have a definite goal, encapsulated in his concept of the 'natural system', which is an extension to other fundamental economic magnitudes of Smith's concept of 'natural prices'. As Pasinetti puts it, '[t]he natural economic system represents so to speak the fundamental skeleton of the present theoretical construction. It is a set of relations that possess characteristics of analytic relevance and logical consistency, with *strong normative properties*' (Pasinetti, 1993, p. 117, emphasis added). Pasinetti's structural economic dynamics has absorbed the mathematical legacy of the minimalist twentieth-century classical revival, but it has carried this to a newly enriched development which owes more to Smith than to Ricardo, and which exemplifies the entanglement of facts, analysis and values.

Commenting on Sen's work on development, Putnam stresses how 'Sen shows us the need for more sensitive measures of "underdevelopment", poverty, and other forms of economic deprivation' (Putnam, 2002, p. 57). Noting how seriously the 'information base' has been restricted in past work in the field, he draws attention to what one might call the philosophical richness of Sen's concept of capabilities. What this does, as Putnam sees it, 'is invite us to think about what functionings form part of our and other cultures' *notions of a good life*, and to investigate just *how much freedom to achieve* various of those functionings various groups of people in various situations actually have' (Putnam, 2002, p. 60, emphasis added). But for this, as Putnam observes, 'one necessarily becomes involved with questions that have been extensively discussed in the literature of ethics' (Putnam, 2002, p. 63). To these questions we now turn.

Some philosophical origins and implications of capability theory

Philosophical debate concerning concepts that can now be seen to have been concerned with issues related to what we now call capabilities, were typically concerned, not with rudimentary functionings, such as being adequately nourished or having elementary health care, but instead with rather sophisticated flourishings. This raises the issue of the *range* of Sen's concept. Does it, perhaps, have limitations which render it unsuitable for use in philosophical analysis of— for example—Aristotle's moral philosophy?

Putnam pertinently quotes a passage where Sen insists on the range of application of his concept: 'The functionings included can vary from the most elementary ones, such as being well-nourished, avoiding escapable morbidity and immature mortality, etc., to quite complex and sophisticated achievements, such as having self-respect, being able to take part in the life of the community, and so on' (Sen, 1992, p. 5, cited by Putnam, 2002, pp. 56–57).

The reader of Sen will be familiar with the capability of having self-respect, of appearing in public without shame, and being able to take part in the life of the community. These attainments are usually referred to in the context of Smith's day-laborer, who, it will be recalled, needed a linen shirt and leather shoes to pass muster. But even in Smith's day, the attainment of the functionings at issue were available to a day-laborer—they were very elementary ones. They were hardly, these functionings, even in the late eighteenth century 'quite complex and sophisticated achievements' (Sen, 1992, p. 5).

Sen's choice of examples (which were perfectly appropriate in the context of his approval of Smith's ideas on 'necessaries') here, I would argue, sell him short. I would claim that the concepts of capabilities and functionings can be properly used to analyze any human attainments of which humanity is ever capable— Michelangelo carving the statue of David (to use one of Sen's own examples) if you will. By the same token, the language of capability deprivation can encompass any tragic loss that fragile humanity can endure. This, I would suggest, is precisely *why* it has seemed natural to compare capability theory to certain ideas of Aristotle concerning conditions that constrain the attainability of the human good.

Now (although Putnam does not refer to this) there has been some suggestion in the literature on capability theory to the effect that it is really confined to the analysis of poverty. Even in discussing *inequality* it has been suggested, once we are no longer in deep poverty, capabilities are an unreliable guide. Thus, G. A. Cohen, for example, has claimed that 'capability provides a highly suitable measure of the deprivation that poverty imposes, but it is not so evidently serviceable when the object is to identify degrees of inequality as such' (Cohen, 1994, p. 188. Cf. Walsh, 1995–1996, pp. 556–569.) For Cohen, Sen's 'special interest in poverty is shown by [his] choice of capability as the premier space of advantage' (Cohen, 1994, p. 188). But, as has come to be seen, through Nussbaum's work, capability theory is a present day descendent of an ancient philosophical idea, fully and richly explored in ancient Greek philosophy and drama, concerning the perils to which *all* levels of human moral and creative attainment are exposed by the unforeseeable winds of fortune. This is a theme that sounds again in medieval philosophy, in Adam Smith, in some early writings of Karl Marx, and in the middle of the twentieth century.

Sen, however, was not initially influenced by the ancient roots of his concept. As he remarked some years ago, 'at the time of proposing the [capability] approach, I did not manage to seize on its Aristotelian connections' (Sen, 1993a, p. 30, note 2). He adds, however, that 'the most powerful conceptual connections [of the capability approach] would appear to be with the Aristotelian view of the human good' (Sen, 1993a, p. 46). He observes, justly, that '[t]he Aristotelian perspective and its connections with the recent attempts at constructing a capability-focused approach have been illuminatingly discussed by Martha Nussbaum' (Sen, 1993a, p. 46).

Nussbaum's classical scholarship led her straight to the ancient Greek preoccupation with tragic mishaps, and their fatal effects on human moral functionings. This shows throughout her early work, *The Fragility of Goodness* (1986). As she has recently observed: 'My own version of this approach (which began independently of Sen's work through thinking about Aristotle's ideas of human functioning and Marx's use of them) is in several ways different from Sen's, both in its emphasis on the philosophical underpinnings of the approach and in its readiness to take a stand on what the central capabilities are' (Nussbaum, 2000a, p. 70). Indeed this early work (1986) of Nussbaum's had been maturing for many years. Several chapters were clearly published by 1982 (Nussbaum, 1986, pp. xv–xvi) and she tells us that '[t]he entire project began many years ago in my thoughts, but it first took on concrete form . . . in 1972–3' (Nussbaum, 1986, p. xiv).

Putnam correctly notes the fact that (in recent years) 'Martha Nussbaum has also used a 'capabilities' approach to discuss development issues, particularly as they affect women' (Putnam, 2002, p. 57). And in the use she has made of her own work on human development we can indeed see the influence of Sen, and an enrichment of both their ideas. Putnam remarks that '[i]t is appropriate to mention that this notion of "functionings" was anticipated by Walsh in 1961 in *Scarcity and Evil*. Walsh's term was "achievements", and like Sen he connected a very wide notion of achievements or functionings with a concern for the character of a human life as a whole which goes back to Aristotle. The idea of applying this point of view to problems of *development* is, of course, due entirely to Sen' (Putnam, 2002, p. 57, emphasis in original).

Putnam is right that when I first started to work on my version of this approach (which, by the way, was in 1946–1947), I had no thought of applying it to development studies, indeed I never thought of this until I read Sen's work. What I did see was an interface between the concept of scarcity in *economic theory* and questions in moral philosophy concerning responsibility: were we to blame for failures to attain some moral goal when some scarcity, or deprivation had prevented our attainment of the goal? My tutor George Duncan, who had been a Fellow in classics of Trinity College Dublin before he became professor of political economy, led me through the parts of Aristotle which he saw immediately were deeply relevant for my subject, and persuaded me to pursue a doctorate in the (then) bizarre field of the relations between economic theory and moral philosophy! He even secured me a research studentship, to support my work for two years. I did not publish any of these ideas for a number of years, finally doing so in a series of articles (Walsh, 1954, 1958a, 1958b) and then as my first book, *Scarcity and Evil* (Walsh, 1961). From the 1958 articles on, of course, I owed much to Putnam's help and advice.

These days it will be no surprise to readers acquainted with, for example, the work that appears in a journal such as *Economics and Philosophy*, that both of these fields can, on occasion, learn from each other. During the 1950s, however, it was a lonely and little traveled road. Now the philosopher can see, as Putnam does, that Sen's economic theory has illuminated issues in moral philosophy, while the economist can see that Sen's philosophical critique has illuminated issues in economic analysis.

In my early work, I was interested in using economic analysis to explore a particular partitioning of the space of value judgments which had been debated on and off since the ancient Greeks: between events for which we can legitimately be said to deserve praise or blame, and events which some impediment or deprivation prevented us from being able to control. For this I proposed to borrow the concept of scarcity from economics.[20]

Discussing different ways of 'partitioning' the space of value judgments (one is already familiar to us: that between 'thick' and 'thin' ethical concepts), Putnam notes: 'That there is a very important class of (ethical) value-judgments that do not praise or blame anyone was one of the central points of Walsh's *Scarcity and Evil*) . . . . (Walsh's term for the class was "appraisals")' (Putnam, 2002, p. 161, note 40).

When some terrible calamity takes place, our first instinct is to *ascribe* responsibility—to blame. But we may find out that no one involved had available the means to avert the calamity. This does not reduce our *appraisal*, but we have no basis for the distinct kind of ethical judgment involved in ascriptions of responsibility. We abandon the use of words like 'criminal' or 'disgraceful' or 'outrageous' and use only words like 'appalling' or 'tragic'. I argued, however, that while natural language *seeks* to make this distinction justly, it often fails to do so because of incomplete information, or because of the failure to see certain lacks and deprivations, which impeded the agents involved, as relevant in mitigating (or removing) the ascription of blame. It was here that I saw the analytical category of effects of scarcity as helpful. Putative ascriptions were defeasible, on the production of evidence of inability to achieve a morally demanded goal resulting from the scarcity of some necessary means. (A set of feasible attainments can be specified in a Euclidean hyperspace of the relevant number of dimensions, and a moral agent is evidently not to blame for failure to achieve a goal not in her attainable set).

What Sen was later to call 'functionings' I called 'attainments', 'achievements', sometimes 'accomplishments'. Sen wrote of the *capability* to achieve a functioning, I wrote of how scarcities might impede or prevent an attainment. An attainment (or functioning) thus depends on the *absence* of a scarcity (i.e. on an unimpeded capability). The distinction I wanted to make between two sorts of ethical claims can be expressed in Sen's terminology: when something dreadful has occurred, an ascription of blame for this will be withdrawn if it can be shown that the moral agent putatively responsible in fact *lacked* a capability crucial to the required functioning.

Like Nussbaum, I was interested in the moral implications of the tragic nature of life—of human vulnerability. Unlike her, (in her early work) however, I believed that certain economic concepts—the formal structure of maximization subject to constraints, or scarcity—could illuminate strictly philosophical issues. A belief that abstract economic theory could illuminate moral philosophy is of course a life long characteristic of Sen's work, and for me (as for many others) one of its strongest appeals. But Sen, although aware that capability theory had implications for moral philosophy, developed it initially for work in the (morally crucial) economic applied field of human development. That the ideas we share should have such powerful application to a field so vital to human progress is delightful. But I never saw this possibility!

Meanwhile, Putnam was surely right to encourage repeatedly (over the years after 1955) my conviction that the concepts of attainments and their vulnerability to the constraints to which they were subject did have bearing on a significant partition of the set of moral judgments. Later, Putnam would also support and encourage the early philosophical work of Nussbaum, which so brilliantly illuminated the Greek roots of the concepts we are discussing.

Most writers on what we now call 'capability theory' make at least a polite bow towards Aristotle, as a thinker who had some early ideas on the subject. For anyone who wishes to have a grasp of the philosophical issues at stake, however, this is not quite sufficient. What Nussbaum shows (among many things) is that Aristotle's argument concerning 'the ways in which good activity is vulnerable to circumstances' (Nussbaum, 1986, p. 327) is part of his contribution to a great debate which involved a large part of Greek philosophy and tragic drama and led to deep divisions. She notes that Aristotle[21] goes against 'a well-established tradition in moral philosophy, both ancient and modern, according to which moral goodness, that which is an appropriate object of ethical praise and blame, cannot be harmed or affected by external circumstances. For Plato, the good person could not be harmed by the world: his life is no less good and praiseworthy because of adverse circumstances' (Nussbaum, 1986, p. 329).

Fascinatingly (for me) she adds in a note some evidence which I think justifies the claim that Plato maintained his 'invulnerability of goodness' thesis only by turning a blind eye to what would have happened if one more deprivation were added to the plight of this good person. She remarks that Plato (who *did* require at least the capability to engage in contemplative activity for a good life) had insisted 'that contemplative activity is altogether self-sufficient, requiring no special worldly conditions for its attainment beyond life itself' (Nussbaum, 1986, p. 495, note 21).

But even the ability to contemplate is an *attainment* (or functioning) dependent on being able to exercise the relevant capability (free from certain instances of scarcity). If you give someone a philosophical education, they *may* be able to contemplate (or anyway compose philosophical arguments) with shells bursting around them, as Wittgenstein is said to have done. But if they suffer brain damage, this can become impossible. We have become experts at keeping people alive who have lost the capabilities needed for *any* meaningful life, in a way Plato and Aristotle could hardly have foreseen. The good person can be *alive* and *blameless*, but without the capability for *any* attainment. What is invulnerable is only the possibility of the person's blamelessness—this is all Plato's argument validly assures us; over *every possible* attainment, Aristotle's critique holds. And, as I remarked many years ago, 'blamelessness is a bodiless thing for a human being to love' (Walsh, 1961, p. 71).

Greek tragic drama, as Nussbaum shows in tellingly argued detail, often provides searingly vivid depictions of the human state of dependence on capabilities to function which Aristotle deeply understands and Plato seeks to surmount. 'Greek tragedy shows good people being ruined because of things that just happen to them, things that they do not control' (Nussbaum, 1986, p. 25). What is more, tragedy also shows 'something more deeply disturbing; it shows good people doing bad things, things otherwise repugnant to their ethical character and commitments because of circumstances whose origin does not lie with them' (Nussbaum, 1986, p. 25). Notably, Greek tragedy shows, and takes very seriously, situations of 'tragic conflict' in the sense in which we have seen Putnam discuss, and support the reasonableness of, this idea in the work of Isaac Levi (for example). We have seen that those who support the axioms of completeness and transitivity have to try to reject tragic conflict. Nussbaum will in due course show that the attempt to deny the possibility of tragic conflict is very old: in fact, it 'begins with the beginning of moral philosophy' (Nussbaum, 1986, p. 25). Meanwhile Aristotle's own view in such cases, she argues, is this: 'in some such cases we will ascribe blame; in some we will pity, or blame in a reduced way; in still other cases we may even praise the agent' (Nussbaum, 1986, p. 427, note 9). The reader who explores Aristotle with Nussbaum as her guide will be initiated into an understanding of the subtle ways in which human flourishing can be wilted by the deprivations that continually threaten the fulfillment of our capabilities, for which I know of no present-day equal.

The position taken firmly by Aristotle (and approximated, sometimes reluctantly, by ancient Greek philosophy, and by tragic drama *as a whole*) happens, of course, to be *the* philosophical position that would open one's eyes fully to the *immense* importance of those human qualities which are most fragile. Nussbaum avails herself of the 'deeply traditional' (Nussbaum, 1986, p. 422, note 3) imagery of the tender and vulnerable plant, dependent on things beyond its control, at the mercy of fortune or 'luck'.[22] The most striking contrast to this luck-dominated, fragile view of human goodness is of course the position of Kant, as she immediately points out: 'For the Kantian believes that there is one domain of value, the domain of moral value, that is altogether immune to the assaults of luck. No matter what happens in the world, the moral value of the good will remains unaffected. Furthermore, the Kantian believes that there is a sharp distinction to be drawn between this and every other type of value, *and* that moral value is of overwhelmingly greater importance than everything else' (Nussbaum, 1986, p. 4, emphasis in original).

Nussbaum, very sensibly, announces that she will 'try to avoid not only the Kantian moral/non-moral distinction, but all versions of that distinction . . . The Greek texts make no such distinction' (Nussbaum, 1986, p. 5). If she is right, it follows that one may properly look for a sensitively and tellingly argued analysis of the vulnerability of human attainments (functionings) to the cold and ever changing winds of fortune in Greek thought in general and Aristotle in particular, but not for a distinction between moral praise and blame and non-moral appraisals of value.

Indeed, it was because I could find little evidence of the distinction which I was looking for in Aristotle, that I chose to concentrate, in my first philosophical paper on the question, on an examination of Kant's moral philosophy (Walsh, 1954). This does *not* mean, however, that Kant (or other philosophers supporting a moral/non-moral distinction) was taking the position for which I developed (with Putnam's help) my ascriptions/appraisals distinction. In ancient times people used to speak of the 'consolations of philosophy', and this antique view is useful here. The point is that I strongly believed, from the early 1950s on, that philosophers who offered a moral/non-moral distinction were often in the business of offering the world's unfortunates a highly *suspect* 'consolation'. This phony consolation is something the Greeks as a whole *don't* try to sell us. They show us that the depredations of fortune can destroy just about *every* quality that could make a human life worth living—or even *enduring*. They do not just show people of strong character surmounting suitably tolerable doses of adversity, like a good showjumper making a faultless round. They show people being spiritually eviscerated. What is more, they show people facing alternatives where *either* of the only available choices involve doing something *dreadful*. From their own time up to ours, they have been repeatedly misunderstood for this. As Nussbaum points out, these attacks begin with Socrates, who tells Euthyphro that 'stories depicting the collisions of competing claims of right are repugnant to reason, since they assert a contradiction; "By this argument, my dear Euthyphro, the pious and impious would be one and the same (*Euthyphro* 8A)' (Nussbaum, 1986, p. 25). Notice that utilitarianism is not the only moral philosophy that cannot live with partial orderings and incompleteness!

Nussbaum, running up her colors right at the beginning as to her intention to 'avoid' all versions of the moral/non-moral distinction, nevertheless (rightly!) does not feel barred from showing 'the convinced partisan of the [moral/non-moral] distinction that our points about fragility apply even to values that would, on most versions of the distinction, standardly be considered as central moral values' (Nussbaum, 1986, p. 5).[23] This captures exactly why I felt long ago (and still do) that the moral/non-moral distinction *as used* was typically in bad faith—something offered as a (phony) consolation to the unfortunate: don't worry about the wretchedness of your life, and the fact that you have had ground out of you every fine and generous quality you once possessed, and betrayed every love and loyalty you had, if you truly *couldn't help* any of this, then you have lost nothing that matters!

My use of the language of appraising and ascribing, and the concept of scarcity, were intended to *show up* the attempts of moral philosophers to pass off as 'invulnerable' moral qualities in a person, what were in fact *attainments*, as could be shown by making some constraint more severe (reducing some capability to function). Hence my decision to try out this approach on Kant first.

For Kant (as for Plato) the good person could not be harmed by the world. What is morally good in a person is treated by Kant as having to do strictly with the person's *moral will*, and not to do with what the person might or might not be able to attain, given the scarcity of means provided by the parsimony of that step-mother, nature. (In Sen's language, Kant's claim is that the only morally significant human functioning is that of the moral will, and the fact that every other human functioning should lack the capability needed to function effectively has no moral significance.) On the view I held from 1954 in 'The theory of the good will' (Walsh, 1954, pp. 627–637), and equally for the view Sen holds today, Kant's position on goods other than good willing merits rejection.

Plato's view, as to the person's moral invulnerability, as readers of Nussbaum (1986) will see, was not characteristic of Greek thought as a whole, and particularly was in total disagreement with Aristotle (and with Greek tragic drama). It is no wonder that Plato distrusted tragic poetry!

Kant *explicitly* sets up the invulnerability of the moral will as centerpiece of his moral philosophy, surely with the confidence that this would resonate with a pious tradition which (outside the readers of certain enlightenment authors) would indeed retain its hegemony for some time to come in his world. Arguably, Kant's presentation of the moral/non-moral distinction is the classic expression of this idea, and its immense influence on later philosophers shows this. Nussbaum tellingly points out the influence of Kant upon modern commentators on Aristotle, which she says cannot 'be overestimated' (Nussbaum, 1986, p. 329). Thus, for 'Kantian' interpreters, such as Sir David Ross (1910–1952), Aristotle is construed as holding that '*happiness* can be augmented or diminished by fortune; but that which is truly deserving of ethical praise and blame, true moral worth, cannot be' (Nussbaum, 1986, p. 329, emphasis in original). Such interpretations thus soft-pedal Aristotle's insistence on how utterly a human being can be devastated by tragic reversals of fortune, or laid waste by extreme deprivations of all sorts.

Turning to Kant himself, it is perhaps arguable that he goes farther in his evaluation of the moral will than is wise—or *needed*—for his own theory. It seemed to me when I first wrote about these matters that Kant was making (at least) the claim that talk about the moral quality of willing was *category distinct* from talk about the senses in which any flowering of human attainment can be said to be 'good'. To use Putnam's present-day terminology, Kant seemed to be turning the ordinary language distinction between ascriptions and appraisals into a full-blown *metaphysical dichotomy*.

This leads to some very undesirable traits in Kant's writing, which surely are not consistent with his own nobler intellectual characteristics. Here and there, for example, he seems willing to *degrade* all human attainment (functioning), to hint at the suggestion that the human 'tragedy' of its loss *does not really matter*. May we then feel that if children die in misery and starvation, but after all their moral wills were still unsullied and so they died innocent, then all is well? If all they lost was 'happiness', then perhaps a benevolent deity can always give them a good big dollop of this? It is strange that the august splendors of Kant's metaphysic of morals should appear to have implications that would be vulgar even coming from Jeremy Bentham!

The distinction Kant wants to make between moral and non-moral uses of ethical language does not *require* him to degrade the legitimate objects of all the 'non-moral' uses of such language. The sensitivity of Greek philosophy and tragedy to every shade of awfulness in the ravages of ill fortune, as well as to every sublime height of human attainment, make one want to say that Kant has tin ears for all this. The ethical appraisal of terrible loss may be distinct from the ascription of responsibility for that loss, but this need not entail setting up a lexical ordering of importance between the two sorts of ethical claims, and giving ascriptions first place.

Be that as it may, Kant has a more difficult problem. It is vital for his position that the account of the person of moral will should not turn out to be, in fact, an account of someone who has been *allowed* the fulfillment of enough of their capabilities to have a healthy crop of attainments, passing as simply good 'willing'. But Kant's person of good will turns out to have been saved 'from some of the subtlest and therefore the worst instances of scarcity. Kant's analysis of the essential nature of morality is based on the situation of his well-to-do elect' (Walsh, 1961, p. 71). A moral will, for Kant, is said to stand under 'objective laws' (Kant, [1785], 1964, pp. 80–81). What is the force of 'objective' here? What if we sincerely believe an action to be objectively necessary, but in fact are mistaken? Kant, in his treatment of categorical imperatives, often seems to want to say that obeying a categorical imperative entails choosing an action that an adequately informed observer would judge to be objectively necessary. We cannot know what Kant would say if presented with the present-day literature on rational choice. That extensive literature has involved the work, over many years, of economists within the neoclassical tradition, decision theorists, logicians, philosophers and others (Walsh, 1961, pp. 67–73 and Putnam, 2002, pp. 163–165, note 3). Arguably, however, we can say that Kant appears to require that his moral agents be possessed of rankings satisfying the axioms of completeness and full transitivity, otherwise how can he require that they always *know* the objectively necessary choice or action?

Kant's confidence that no tragic damage can be done to good people, even 'by some special disfavour of destiny or by the niggardly endowment of stepmotherly nature' (Kant, [1785], 1964, p. 12) offers 'consolations' which do not speak to the needs of the oppressed and wretched of our world. As Sen has dryly observed in another context, 'the appalling world in which we live does not—at least on the surface—look like one in which an all-powerful benevolence is having its way. It is hard to understand how a compassionate world order can include so many people afflicted by acute misery, persistent hunger and deprived and desperate lives, and why millions of innocent children have to die each year from lack of food or medical attention or social care' (Sen, 1999, p. 282).

Given all this, for any use to be made of the ideas which are *valuable* in Kant's moral philosophy—and there are some—these must be detached from his naiveté about the immense importance and tragic vulnerability of the capabilities upon which our ability to attain more than bare moral good intent all crucially depend. Sen, however, in numerous works, has presented his capability theory in specifically the right ethical tone of voice to highlight the moral importance of the project of human development. Recall one of his most constant objections to utilitarianism: 'The deprived people tend to come to terms with their deprivation because of the sheer necessity of survival, and they may, as a result, lack the courage to demand any radical change, and may even adjust their desires and expectations to what they unambitiously see as feasible. . . These considerations require a broader informational base, focusing particularly on peoples' capability to choose the lives they have reason to value' (Sen, 1999, pp. 62–63, compare Sen, 1992, pp. 54–55).

With this red-blooded view of capabilities and deprivations in view, one may safely take from Kant what he *does* offer of real value to development theory, and this has been clearly put by Nussbaum in a recent work, where she notes that we must consider 'each person as worthy of regard, as an end and not just a means' (Nussbaum, 2000a, p. 32). Writing of those who support the idea of what she calls Aristotelian social democracy (as she does), Nussbaum observes that 'neo-Aristotelians hold the separateness of persons to be a basic fact for normative political thought. Each person should be treated as an end, and none as a mere means to the ends of others. . . Because they thus hold that human dignity is an end in itself and not simply a means to other ends, this neo-Aristotelian tradition draws close to Kant, and I have argued in [*Women and Human Development*] that Marx's reading of Aristotle was in many ways shaped by the Kantian idea of humanity as an end. So it would be no surprise if there were to be a close relationship between such neo-Aristotelianisms and the Kantian thought of John Rawls' (Nussbaum, 2000b, p. 106).

She is right to support, for the enrichment of development theory, Kant's noble idea of humanity as a kingdom of ends (one of his formulations of the categorical imperative, after all, is implicit in this). But she will have no truck with his being used to cause confusion in what Aristotle saw clearly. She shows what is at issue most vividly, perhaps, when she confronts Kant's demand for consistency among the principles of practical reason with Agamemnon's dilemma. There is a deep connection between belief in what we call today the axiom of completeness and the efforts of philosophers such as Kant and Plato to deny the fragility of human attainments. A reading of Aristotle and some Greek tragic drama should persuade anyone who doubts that the flourishing of all our highest functionings depend crucially on the availability of a number of vital capabilities *even if* we happen to have a complete ordering of all our goals. But, if we are *unable* to achieve more than a partial ordering of our most important goals, and especially if we face a choice like Agamemnon's, then the appalling power of events beyond our control to destroy us is revealed in the starkest colors.

In the *Agamemnon* of Aeschylus, as Nussbaum points out, Agamemnon's only choice is between two crimes: 'The sacrifice of Iphigenia is regarded by the Chorus as necessary; but they also blame Agamemnon' (Nussbaum, 1986, p. 33). It is recognized, however, that 'no personal guilt of Agamemnon's own, has led him into this tragic predicament' (Nussbaum, 1986, p. 33). It is accepted by everyone as a given that if he spares his daughter, the fleet of which he is commander will remain becalmed, and everyone, *including* Iphigenia, will die— men have already begun to die of starvation. His clear duty as a commander is to save his fleet. But to do this he must kill his daughter. What the Chorus objects to strenuously is that, once he has accepted the necessity of saving his men, Agamemnon totally accepts what he has to do, and shows no horror at it: he does not *recognize* that he is being forced to a terrible act, but completely embraces it, commanding the attendants 'to lift Iphigenia "like a goat" (232) in the air above the altar' (Nussbaum, 1986, p. 36). The Chorus, Nussbaum observes, contributes 'the only note of compassionate humanity in this terrible scene. Never, in the choral narration or subsequently, do we hear the king utter a word of regret or painful memory' (Nussbaum, 1986, p. 37).

From ancient times to the present day, theorists have sought refuge from recognizing what tragic predicaments can do to the attainments of human character by resorting to earlier versions of what we express today by the claim that rational choice requires an *ordering* (i.e. completeness and full transitivity especially) and that all that can be asked of anyone is that they choose their most highly ranked attainable option—Agamemnon was clearly a past master of 'rationality' thus defined! But as Nussbaum shows, tragedy always was (and still is) an embarrassment to such people (of whom the Kantianizers of Aristotle are examples). She cites a comment on these rationalizers by K. J. Dover: 'They react in this way because the cutting of a girl's throat as if she were a sheep constitutes a pitiable and repulsive event; whether it is necessary or unnecessary, commanded by a god or the product of human malice and perversity' (Dover, 1973, p. 66, cited in Nussbaum, 1986, p. 432).

Those who try to 'solve' a tragic dilemma tend, as Nussbaum observes, simply to 'underdescribe or misdescribe it. . . Aeschylus has indicated to us that the only thing remotely like a solution here is, in fact, to describe and see the conflict clearly and to acknowledge that there is no way out. The best the agent can do is to have his suffering, the natural expressions of his goodness of character, and not to stifle these responses out of misguided optimism. . . If we were such that we could in a crisis dissociate ourselves from one commitment because it clashed with another, we would be less good. Goodness itself, then, insists that there should be no further or moral revisionary solving' (Nussbaum, 1986, pp. 49–50). She cites Rush Rhees, commenting on Wittgenstein's reaction to a dilemma of rather similar structure: 'After describing the tragic choice faced by the agent, in which there is no guilt-free way out and we feel we can only say, "God help him", Wittgenstein surprises Rhees by remarking' "I want to say that this is the solution to an ethical problem." He indicated then, our point: that the perspicuous description of the case, the unswerving recognition of the values it contains and of the way in which, for the agent, there is no way out, is all there is by way of solution here; so-called philosophical solutions only succeed in being misdescriptions of the problem' (Nussbaum, 1986, p. 434, note 65, citing Wittgenstein from Rhees, 1965, pp. 3–26).

Now, as Nussbaum has remarked, 'Aristotle defends the claim of tragedy to tell the truth' (Nussbaum, 1990a, p. 18). This idea of human fragility has never died out. It is massively defended today in quite new intellectual disciplines by Amartya Sen, and by the growing band of those who have joined his project. These people use terms such as 'ethical development' (see Qizilbash, 1996, pp. 1209–1221) and indeed they show no reluctance about doing so, stressing that 'there are good reasons why philosophers must be involved in attempts made by economists to redefine development' (Qizilbash, 1996, p. 1210). We have seen how Hilary Putnam has answered this call, defending Sen's flank with ethics. Indeed, Putnam concluded his Rosenthal lectures by remarking that '[j]ust about every one of the terms that Sen and his colleagues and followers use when they talk about capabilities . . . is an entangled term' (Putnam, 2002, pp. 62–63). And the philosophically rigorous defense of entanglement is exactly what is needed to build a development theory black with the dire facts of the poor world, white with economic analysis, and red with a humane moral appraisal of the fragility of human attainments. For this enterprise Putnam sought 'to provide a philosophy of language that can accommodate and support this second phase [of classical economics]' (Putnam, 2002, p. 64).

Notes

* Steven Pressman's advice played a key role in the writing of this paper, as did the advice and editorial assistance of Lisa Bendall-Walsh; phone conversations with Hilary Putnam, Amartya Sen, Gary Mongiovi, Harvey Gram and Martha Nussbaum helped me to clarify various issues. Kristin Harakal of Trexler Library at Muhlenberg College assisted me in locating needed materials. The usual disclaimers apply.

1 Gary Mongiovi tells me how much Sraffa's unpublished papers (which Heinz Kurz is editing) demonstrate Sraffa's deep interest in the *richer* kind of classical theory. The stark minimalism of Sraffa (1960) can thus give a misleading impression of the range and depth of Sraffa's interests, if taken on its own.

2 Some of the younger economists (and philosophers) who have 'rejected' positivism–or what they believe to be positivism–arguably came by their 'rejection' a little too easily, without ever really knowing the views they were dismissing. See Putnam's comments on this below and the source cited there.

3 For the formalist character of the concepts of rationality in neo-Walrasian economic theory, see Walsh (1996) and for the rising dissatisfaction with formal general equilibrium theory *within* neo-Walrasian economics see also Walsh (1998a) and sources cited there). Putnam has observed that '[m]any years ago, Morton White spoke of a 'revolt against formalism' in connection with pragmatism [White, 1949]. This revolt against formalism is not a denial of the utility of formal models in certain contexts; but it manifests itself in a sustained critique of the idea that formal models, in particular, systems of symbolic logic, rule books of inductive logic, formalizations of scientific theories, etc.—describe a condition to which rational thought either can or should aspire. Wittgenstein, as you all know, began his career on the formalist side and spent the whole latter part of his life as an antiformalist. Indeed, *On Certainty* explicitly uses images of plasticity and fluidity ("In time, the banks and the river may change places")' (Putnam, [1992], 1995, pp. 63–64).

4 For the logical positivists, remember, to say that a statement is analytic *involves* denying that it is ampliative. Contrast Frege, for whom the truths of arithmetic are analytic (can be derived from what he regards as the basic laws of logic), *but* 'nonetheless, they do *extend our knowledge*' (Putnam, 2002, p. 148, note 1, emphasis added).

5 Writing in 1987, they refer to Putnam (1981) and to *The Many Faces of Realism* (the Paul Carus Lectures in 1985, but published in 1987). But as we have seen, there have been many additions to Putnam's arguments since!

6 When I was doing research at Trinity College Dublin in the late 1940s for a PhD on how deprivations, tragic losses, and scarcities could impair moral attainments, I was greatly taken with Robbins' (1932) book: I saw his analysis as a subtler and more flexible conceptual apparatus for identifying those impairments than, for example, Kant's stepmotherly nature. This was a major reason why I accepted with delight Robbins' offer of a junior appointment. I fear that my determined pursuit of the scarcities that destroy moral life was an unexpected and embarrassing application of the scarcity concept for him! However, he always respected my philosophical work, arranged for me to lecture partly in Sir Karl Popper's department (an arrangement I would later negotiate in other universities) and encouraged me to continue publishing in philosophy as well as in economic theory. I also regularly attended Freddy Ayer's seminar at University College during my years at the LSE, and we became friends. But I was never converted to logical positivism, and was much more interested in the work of the young people who visited us from Oxford, so the association of Robbins' ideas with logical positivism never impressed me.

7 It is worth noting that some utilitarian economists of the late nineteenth century possessed, and understood, the formal apparatus for such an analysis of rational choice without involving the use of quantities of utility (Walsh, 1996, p. 36). This possibility was never taken up by the profession as a whole, however, until the embarrassments of the 1930s.

8 Problems arose over the interpretation of choices under risk and the nature of 'expected utility' theory. I have discussed the long struggle between Maurice Allais and the 'American School' elsewhere (Walsh, 1996, pp. 45–67).

9 Some philosophers have suggested that capability analysis works best when dealing with the situation of the very poor: G. A. Cohen, for example, has argued that Sen's 'special interest in poverty is shown by [his] choice of capability as the premier space of advantage' (Cohen, 1994, p. 118). I have discussed this claim elsewhere (Walsh, 1995–1996) and will return to it when considering the specifically philosophical roots, and implications, of the capability concept later in this paper. For the moment the reader might note that the capability which Beatrice's injury put at risk was that of becoming a concert violinist (Walsh, 1995–1996, pp. 557–558, 560–561). Hardly a basic need!

10 Sophisticated present-day classical models, of course, include costly (scarce) *non-reproduced* inputs. Such models also treat questions like joint production—where one produces wool, but gets mutton as well. On all such issues see Kurz and Salvadori (1995).

11 The technique matrix for our simple model may be written as

$$\mathbf{A} = \begin{bmatrix} a_{cc} & a_{ci} \\ a_{ic} & a_{ii} \end{bmatrix}.$$

The column vector of gross outputs for our simple model is

$$\mathbf{Y} = \begin{bmatrix} Y_c \\ Y_i \end{bmatrix}.$$

Where the model contains *any* given finite number of sectors (such as many agricultural products, many manufactures and so on, the technique matrix becomes

$$\mathbf{A} = \begin{bmatrix} a_{11} & a_{12} & \cdots & a_{1n} \\ a_{21} & a_{22} & \cdots & a_{2n} \\ \vdots & \vdots & \vdots & \vdots \\ a_{n1} & a_{n2} & \cdots & a_{nn} \end{bmatrix}. \quad \text{And the vector of gross outputs: } \mathbf{Y} = \begin{bmatrix} Y_1 \\ Y_2 \\ \vdots \\ Y_n \end{bmatrix}.$$

For a model of two or of any number of sectors, one may write the viability condition in condensed notation as $\mathbf{AY} \leq \mathbf{Y}$.

12   Or in condensed notation $\mathbf{AY} = \mathbf{Y}$.

13   Most of those who were involved in the early twentieth-century revival of classical theory explicitly intended to re-establish classical ideas on a more rigorous footing. In the case of Neumann, as Kurz and Salvadori point out, the question whether he was familiar with classical writings is open; 'in all probability he was not and did not care whether his analysis was "classical", "neoclassical" or anything else. What matters is the similarity of the structure of the respective approaches. Interestingly, though, von Neumann may well have come across pieces of economic analysis of classical derivation while he was a *Privatdozent* at the University of Berlin from 1927 to 1929' (Kurz and Salvadori, 1998b, p. 26). Their argument to the effect that the *structure* of Neumann's model is classical should be sampled by the interested reader (see Kurz and Salvadori, 1995, pp. 242–245, 379–426; 1988a, pp. 177–183; 1998b, pp. 25–56). Compare Walsh (2002a, pp. 329–331).

It needs to be remembered that the neo-Walrasian school in America in the 1950s learned a number of vital things about how to use modern mathematics from Neumann (as they also did from the mathematicians who wrote under the name of 'Nicolai Bourbaki'). The use of axiomatic methods, set theory, and so on, was just as possible in neoclassical models as in classical. So Neumann needed to be seen as 'one of the boys' by the neoclassics.

14   Sraffa, it will be recalled, did not treat growth. In fact: 'No changes in output and (at any rate in Parts I and II) no changes in the proportions in which different means of production are used by an industry are considered, so that no question arises as to the variation or constancy of returns' (Sraffa, 1960, p. v).

15   Neoclassics will argue that Pasinetti overstates his case here! (Although he *does* treat Engel curves, and praises some neoclassical work, notably that of Kelvin Lancaster, 1971). But all he needed was the point that neoclassical theory does not put *the dynamic effects of demand* on non-balanced growth *center stage*. Interested non-economist readers might enjoy Joseph Halevi (1996) which makes no explicit use of mathematics (although his argument is sophisticated). Halevi offers some interesting historical background, comparing Pasinetti's work to (for example) the early Dobb—Sen development models; he also appraises the new possibilities arising in development theory from Pasinetti's models. Economist readers may wish to follow the debate into the formalization of Halevi's argument constructed by Araujo and Teixeira (2002). They will find another recent commentary on Pasinetti's work in Hishiyama (1996).

16   Interested non-economist readers might be well advised to look at Pasinetti's simplest model (1993)–for all its abstract qualities–before tackling his models with capital goods (1981).

17   The sketch of the quantity system of a simple present-day classical reproduction structure, which I offered the reader, was described as a Neumann–Sraffa blend. Pasinetti uses a Leontiev–Sraffa blend. The non-economist reader may well be concerned as to how this changes the resulting mixture. The short (somewhat rough and ready) answer is that not much is different! Wassily Leontiev and John von Neumann have similar classical bloodlines. Both writers treat production as a circular flow, as did Sraffa. Leontiev worked on his doctorate at Berlin under the supervision of Ladisilaus von Borkiewicz, a notable early twentieth-century reviver of classicism, and would have been in touch with the early writings on these matters in German (see Kurz and Salvadori, 1995, pp. 390–396). He also spent three years in the late 1920s at the Institute for the World Economy at the University of Kiel, an important center in the early revival of classical theory (Adolph Lowe was also there, for example). Leontiev has remarked of his own work that '[f]rom the outset the development of input-output analysis was marked by a succession of empirical applications' (Leontiev, 1987, 2, p. 862). Moving to Harvard, Leontief's applied input–output models became very famous, and a Nobel Prize

followed in 1973. But '[h]is contribution was always played down from the theoretical point of view; indeed it was normally strictly confined to the field of applied economics' (Gilibert, 1988, pp. 40–41). Giorgio Gilibert suggests that Leontiev was more appreciated by mathematicians (i.e. Gale, 1960) than by neoclassical economists.

18 The non-economist reader needs to be alert to the confusing fact that a *basic* for Sraffa is any *input* which is used directly or indirectly in the production of every commodity— even where, as in Sraffa's later chapters, he is not treating any *consumption* goods as basics, but only oil for machines, machine tools, plows, etc. Whereas a 'basic need' is a *human* need, such as water and food.

19 The reader should note that Schefold's 'need for self-fulfillment' separates him somewhat from the 'basic needs' school of development theory, and places him closer to the psychologists influenced by Abraham Maslow. I find Maslow's work quite fascinating, but of course have no professional opinion on it as a contribution to psychology. The interested reader might consult Abraham Maslow (1970), and economist readers in particular might wish to investigate a book length treatment of Maslow's relevance to economics: Mark A. Lutz and Kenneth Lux (1979). Appropriately, that notably humanist neoclassic, Kenneth Boulding contributed an Introduction, which is critical but favorable. Lutz and Lux start from the position that neoclassical economics has had only one input from psychology: utilitarianism, and argue that it is time it had another, which they argue ought to be the humanistic psychology of Maslow. Alas, humanistic neoclassics are not thick on the ground, while present-day classics are liable to see them as engaged in freshly painting the Titanic. But that work might be embeddable in enriched classical theory.

20 The concept of scarcity has arguably been overused by neoclassical economics and underused by the minimalist phase of the classical revival, so a few words on this may be helpful to the non-economist reader. The story begins with Ricardo. As Pasinetti remarks, Ricardo 'had a clear conviction that, when simplifications are necessary, they ought to be made in the direction of eliminating from the analysis what in practice is least important' (Pasinetti, 1981, p. 6). Ricardo's interest was in all those commodities which can be *reproduced* and which then govern an economy's ability to generate a net product and grow. Natural endowments, which cannot be *produced*, become economically relevant when they are *scarce*. But since they were not part of the reproduction structure, Ricardo simply pushed them off stage: 'he prefers not to consider them at all' (Pasinetti, 1981, p. 7). As Pasinetti observes '[t]his approach presents a difficulty in the treatment of natural resources (in particular of land)' (Pasinetti, 1981, p. 7). Some of those who followed Ricardo in spirit–John von Neumann, for example, simply assumed that any necessary non-reproducible inputs are available free (and for our simple reproduction model we followed him in this). A model does not stop being classical, however, if it has scarce non-produced inputs–it will in fact retain classical features even if it has only *one* reproducible input. Not all classical models of the twentieth century minimalist period chose to eliminate non-reproducible inputs; however, Sraffa (1960) has an important treatment of scarce land. (For an up-to-date account of present-day classical analysis of land as a scarce resource, see Kurz and Salvadori, 1995, pp. 277–320. Compare Pasinetti, 1965, pp. 575–579 and Alberto Quadrio-Curzio, 1980, pp. 218–219.)

Aside from the natural resources that may enter a classical model with the status of being *never* reproducible, even reproducible commodities can be scarce in the *short* period. If the single harvest (in a northern country) is in, then the corn harvested is a *given* resource until the next harvest. Without availability of imports, a bad harvest could then mean serious scarcity before the cycle of reproduction yielded another harvest. Now we are ready to turn to moral philosophy. We may be deprived of some attainment because of a *temporary* scarcity: perhaps we could not feed people in our charge because supplies of food did not come *in time*. Also, however, there are moral 'resources' that we have in limited supply, so that, once depleted, they can never be replenished. We have lost, perhaps, some innocence which can never be replaced (compare Walsh, 1996, pp. 94–101). When I wrote *Scarcity and Evil*, I was a neoclassical economic theorist, but I do not think that any of my uses of the concept of scarcity there (or elsewhere) depended on any interpretation of the concept that is inconsistent with present day classical theory. In the light of increasing concerns about global sustainability, and the depletion of non-renewable resources, scarcity (appropriately analyzed) must inevitably be a topic of increasing interest. Economist readers will find a sophisticated discussion, from a classical perspective, of the role of non-reproducible natural resources in economic growth and development in *Rent, Resources, Technology* (1999) by Alberto Quadrio-Curzio and Fausta Pellizzari, and in Marco Piccioni and Fabio Ravagnani (2002, pp. 1–28).

21 For example in his remarks about Priam in the latter's pitible old age, and in related cases (Nussbaum, 1986, pp. 328–334).

22 She tells us that in speaking of 'luck' she does not 'mean to imply that the events in question are random or uncaused. What happens to a person by luck will be just what does not happen through his or her own agency, what just *happens* to him, as opposed to what he does or makes' (Nussbaum, 1986, p. 3, emphasis in original).

23 Nussbaum is not denying that Greek authors *engage* in praise and blame, simply asserting that they do not (as a whole) have an ethical distinction which leads them to withhold blame wherever they see effects of human vulnerability. The exception, of course, is Plato, who certainly held that moral goodness was something which was not vulnerable to the effects of fortune–although, as we have seen, Plato was taking for granted that misfortune would leave in place at least the capability to contemplate. The interested reader needs to experience directly the depth and subtlety of Nussbaum's argument, of which only a hint can be offered here.

References

Araujo, R. A. and Teixeira, J. R. (2002) Structural change and decisions on investment allocation, *Structural Change and Economic Dynamics*, 13(2), pp. 249–259.

Austin, J. L. (1962) *Sense and Sensibilia* (Oxford, Oxford University Press).

Baigent, N. (1997) Rationality, allocation and reproduction, *European Journal of the History of Economic Thought*, 4(3), pp. 549–551.

Bentham, J. ([1789], 1970) *An Introduction to the Principles of Morals and Legislation*, J. H. Burns and H. L. A. Hart (Eds.) (London, Athlone Press).

Bliss, C. J. (1975) *Capital Theory and The Distribution of Income* (New York, American Elsevier).

Bliss, C. J. (1993) Oil trade and general equilibrium, *Journal of International and Comparative Economics*, 2, pp. 227–242.

Broome, J. (1991) *Weighing Goods: Equality, Uncertainty and Time* (Oxford, Blackwell).

Cohen, G. A. (1993) Equality of what? On Welfare, goods, and capabilities, in: M. C. Nussbaum and A. Sen (Eds.) *The Quality of Life* (Oxford, Clarendon Press), pp. 9–29.

Cohen, G. A. (1994) Amartya Sen's unequal world, *New Left Review*, 203(1) pp. 117–129.

Dewey, J. ([1908], 1978) *The Middle Works of John Dewey*, Vol. 5 (Dewey and James H. Tufts, *Ethics*), J. A. Boydston (Ed.) (Carbondale, IL, University of Southern Illinois Press).

Dobb, M. H. (1973) *Theories of Value and Distribution Since Adam Smith: Ideology and Economic Theory* (Cambridge, Cambridge University Press).

Dover, K. J. (1973) Some neglected aspects of Agamemnon's dilemma, *Journal of Hellenic Studies*, 93, pp. 58–69.

Drèze, J. and Sen, A. K. (1989) *Hunger and Public Action* (Oxford, Clarendon Press).

Edgeworth, F. Y. (1881) *Mathematical Psychics: An Essay on the Application of Mathematics to the Moral Sciences* (London, Kegan Paul).

Gale, D. (1960) *The Theory of Linear Economic Models* (New York, McGraw Hill).

Gilibert, G. (1988) Leontiev Wassily, H. D. Kurtz and N. Salvadon (Eds.) *The Elgar Companion to Classical Economics*, Vol. 2, pp. 40–45 (Cheltenham, Edward Elgar).

Gram, H. N. (1998) Necessaries, conveniencies and luxuries, in: H. D. Kurz and N. Salvadori (Eds.) *The Elgar Companion to Classical Economics*, Vol. 2, pp. 162–166, (Cheltenham, Edward Elgar).

Halevi, J. (1996) The significance of the theory of vertically integrated processes for the problem of economic development, *Structural Dynamics*, 7, pp. 163–171.

Halevi, J., Laibman, D. and Nell, E. J. (Eds) (1992) *Beyond the Steady State: A Revival of Growth Theory* (London, Macmillan).

Hamlin, A. (1997) Rationality, allocation and reproduction, *The Economic Journal*, 107 (444), pp. 1592–1593.

Hart, H. L. A. (1973) Rawls on liberty and its priority, *University of Chicago Law Review*, 40, pp. 534–555.

Hausman, D. M. (1980) On justifying the ways of mammon to man, in: G. R. Feiwel (Ed.) *Joan Robinson and Modern Economic Theory*, pp. 821–832 (London, Macmillan).

Hicks, J. R. (1965) *Capital and Growth* (Oxford, Oxford University Press).

Hicks, J. R. and Allen, R. D. G. (1934) A reconsideration of the theory of value, Parts 1–2, *Economica*, 1, Pt. 1, pp. 52–76, Pt. 2, pp. 196–219.

Hishiyama, I. (1996) Appraising Pasinetti's structural dynamics, *Structural Change and Economic Dynamics*, 7, pp. 127–134.

Hume, D. ([1738], 1978) *A Treatise of Human Nature*, L. A. Selby-Biggs and P. H. Nidditch (Eds) (Oxford, Oxford University Press).

Kant, I. ([1785], 1964) *Groundwork of the Metaphysic of Morals*, (Ed and trans) H. J. Paton (New York, Harper and Row).

Klamer, A. (1980) A conversation with Amartya Sen, *Journal of Economic Perspectives*, 3(1), pp. 135–150.

Kurz, H. D. (1992) Accumulation, effective demand and income distribution, in: J. Halevi, D. Laibman and E. J. Nell (Eds) *Beyond the Steady State: A Revival of Growth Theory*, pp. 73–95 (London, Macmillan).

Kurz, H. D. and Salvadori, N. (1995) *Theory of Production, A Long Period Analysis* (Cambridge, Cambridge University Press).

Kurz, H. D. and Salvadori, N. (Eds) (1998a) *The Elgar Companion to Classical Economics*, 2 vols. (Cheltenham, Edward Elgar).

Kurz, H. D. and Salvadori, N. (Eds) (1998b) *Understanding 'Classical' Economics, Studies in Long-Period Theory* (New York, Routledge).

Lancaster, K. (1971) *Consumer Demand—A New Approach* (New York, Columbia University Press).

Leontiev, W. (1951) *The Structure of American Economy*, 2nd ed. (New York, Oxford University Press).

Leontiev, W. (1987) Input-Output analysis, in: J. Eatwell, M. Milgate and P. Newan (Eds.) *The New Palgrave: A Dictionary of Economics*.

Levi, I. (1986) *Hard Choices* (Cambridge, Cambridge University Press).

Little, I. M. D. ([1950], 1957) *A Critique of Welfare Economics* (Oxford, Clarendon Press).

Lowe, A. (1955) Structural analysis of real capital formation, in: M. Abromavitz (Ed.) *Capital Formation and Economic Growth* (Princeton, Princeton University Press).

Lowe, A. (1976) *The Path of Economic Growth* (Cambridge, Cambridge University Press).

Lutz, M. A. & Lux, K. (1979) *The Challenge of Humanistic Economics* (Menlo Park, California, Benjamin/Cummings).

Maslow, A. H. (1970) *Motivation and Personality* (New York, Harper and Row).

Milgram, E. (1995) Was Hume a Humean? *Hume Studies*, 20 (1), pp. 75–93.

Morton, A. (1991) *Disasters and Dilemmas* (Oxford, Clarendon Press).

Murdoch, I. (1970) *The Sovereignty of 'Good'* (London, Routledge & Kegan Paul).

Neumann, J. von ([1937], 1945–1946) A model of general economic equilibrium, *Review of Economic Studies*, 13, pp. 1–9.

Nussbaum, M. C. (1986) *The Fragility of Goodness: Luck and Ethics in Greek Tragedy and Philosophy* (Cambridge, Cambridge University Press).

Nussbaum, M. C. (1988) Nature, function and capability: Aristotle on political distribution, *Oxford Studies in Ancient Philosophy*, suppl. Vol. 1, pp. 145–184.

Nussbaum, M. C. (1990a) *Love's Knowledge: Essays on Philosophy and Literature* (New York, Oxford University Press).

Nussbaum, M. C. (1990b) Aristotelian social democracy, in: B. Douglas *et al.* (Eds.) *Liberalism and The Good*, pp. 203–252 (London, Routledge).

Nussbaum, M. C. (1992) Human functioning and social justice: in defense of Aristotelian essentialism, *Political Theory*, 20, pp. 202–246.

Nussbaum, M. C. (1993) Non-relative virtues: an Aristotelian approach, in: M. C. Nussbaum and A. K. Sen (Eds.) *The Quality of Life*, pp. 242–269 (Oxford, Clarendon Press).

Nussbaum, M. C. (1994) Skepticism about practical reason in literature and the law, *Harvard Law Review*, 107, pp. 714–744.

Nussbaum, M. C. (1997c) *Cultivating Humanity: A Classical Defense of Reform in Liberal Education* (Cambridge, MA, Harvard University Press).

Nussbaum, M. C. (2000a) *Women and Human Development: The Capabilities Approach* (Cambridge, Cambridge University Press).

Nussbaum, M. C. (2000b) Aristotle, politics, and human capabilities: a response to Anthony, Arneson, Charlesworth, and Mulgan, *Ethics*, 3, pp. 102–140.

Nussbaum, M. C. and Sen, A. K. (1989) Internal criticism and Indian rationalist traditions, in: M. Krauss (Ed.) *Relativism, Interpretation and Confrontation*, pp. 229–325 (Notre Dame, University of Notre Dame Press).

Nussbaum, M. C. and Sen, A. K. (Eds.) (1993) *The Quality of Life* (Oxford, Oxford University Press).

Parfit, D. (1984) *Reason and Persons* (Oxford, Oxford University Press).

Pasinetti, L. L. (1965) A new theoretical approach to the problem of economic growth, *Pontificae Academiae Scientiarum Scripta Varia*, 28, pp. 571–677.

Pasinetti, L. L. (1981) *Structural Change and Economic Growth: A Theoretical Essay on the Dynamics of the Wealth of Nations* (Cambridge, Cambridge University Press).

Pasinetti, L. L. (1993) *Structural Economic Dynamics: A Theory of the Economic Consequences of Human Learning* (Cambridge, Cambridge University Press).

Pasinetti, L. L. and Scazzieri, R. (1987) Structural economic dynamics, in: J. Eatwell, M. Milgate and P. Newman (Eds.) *The New Palgrave: a Dictionary of Economics*, Vol. 4, pp. 525–528 (London, Macmillan).

Peacock, A. (1987) Dalton, Edward Hugh John Neale, in: J. Eatwell, M. Milgate and P. Newman (Eds.) *The New Palgrave: a Dictionary of Economics*, Vol. 1, p. 747 (London, Macmillan).

Pettit, P. (2001) Capability and freedom: a defense of Sen (Symposium on Amartya Sen's Philosophy) *Economics and Philosophy*, 17(1), pp. 1–20.

Piccioni, M. and Ravagnani, F. (2002) Absolute rent and the 'normal price' of exhaustible resources, *Quaderno di Ricerca della Fondazione*, 'Centro di Ricerche e Documentazione "Piero Sraffa"', 2, pp. 1–28.

Pigou, A. C. ([1920], 1952) *The Economics of Welfare* (London, Macmillan).

Pressman, S. and Summerfield, G. (2000) The economic contributions of Amartya Sen, *Review of Political Economy*, 12(1), pp. 89–113.

Pressman, S. and Summerfield, G. (2002) Sen and capabilities, *Review of Political Economy*, 14(4), pp. 429–434.

Putnam, H. ([1962], 1975) The analytic and the synthetic, in: H. Putnam, *Mind, Language and Reality, Philosophical papers*, Vol. 2, pp. 33–69 (Cambridge, Cambridge University Press).

Putnam, H. (1981) *Reason, Truth and History* (Cambridge, Cambridge University Press).

Putnam, H. (1987) *The Many Faces of Realism* (La Salle, IL, Open Court).

Putnam, H. (1990) *Realism With a Human Face*, (Ed.) J. Conant (Cambridge, MA, Harvard University Press).

Putnam, H. (1992) *Renewing Philosophy* (Cambridge, Cambridge University Press).

Putnam, H. ([1990], 1993) Objectivity and the science ethics distinction, in: M. C. Nussbaum and A. K. Sen (Eds.) *The Quality of Life*, pp. 143–157 (Oxford, Clarendon Press).

Putnam, H. (1994) *Words and Life*, (Ed.) J. Conant (Cambridge, Cambridge University Press).

Putnam, H. ([1992], 1995) *Pragmatism: An Open Question* (Oxford, Blackwell)

Putnam, H. (1999) *The Threefold Cord: Mind, Body and World* (New York, Columbia University Press).

Putnam, H. (2000) The Rosenthal Lectures, subsequently published in Putnam 2002.

Putnam, H. (2002) *The Collapse of the Fact/Value Dichotomy, and Other Essays, Including The Rosenthal Lectures* (Cambridge, MA, Harvard University Press).

Putnam, H. and Nussbaum, M. C. (1994) Changing Aristotle's mind, in: H. Putnam, *Words and Life*, pp. 22–61 (Cambridge, Cambridge University Press).

Qizilbash, M. (1996) Ethical development, *World Development*, 24(7), pp. 1209–1221.

Quadrio-Curzio, A. (1980) Rent, income distribution, and orders of efficiency and rentability, in: L. L. Pasinetti (Ed.) *Essays on the Theory of Joint Production*, pp. 218–240 (New York, Columbia University Press).

Quadrio-Curzio, A. and Pellizzari, F. (1999) *Rent, Resources, Technologies* (New York, Springer Verlag).

Quine, W. V. ([1951], 1953) Two dogmas of empiricism, in: W. V. Quine, *From a Logical Point of View*, pp. 20–46 (Cambridge, MA, Harvard University Press).

Quine, W. V. (1963) Carnap and logical truth, in: P. A. Schilp (Ed.) *The Philosophy of Rudolph Carnap*, pp. 385–406 (La Salle, IL, Open Court).

Rawls, J. (1971) *A Theory of Justice* (Cambridge, MA, Harvard University Press).

Rawls, J. (1993) *Political Liberalism* (New York, Columbia University Press).

Rhees, R. (1965) Wittgenstein's lecture on ethics, *Philosophical Review*, 74, pp. 3–26.

Ricardo, D. ([1817], 1951) *On the Principles of Political Economy and Taxation, Works and Correspondence of David Ricardo*, Vol. 1, P. Sraffa and M. H. Dobb (Eds.) (Cambridge, Cambridge University Press).

Robbins, L. R. (1932) *An Essay on the Nature and Significance of Economic Science* (London, Macmillan).

Robinson, J. V. (1980) Introduction, to V. C. Walsh and H. N. Gram, *Classical and Neoclassical Theories of General Equilibrium, Historical Origins and Mathematical Structure*, pp. xi–xvi (New York, Oxford University Press).

Rorty, R. (1979) *Philosophy and the Mirror of Nature* (Princeton, Princeton University Press).

Rorty, R. (1982) *Consequences of Pragmatism* (Minneapolis, University of Minnesota Press).

Rorty, R. (1989) *Contingency, Irony and Solidarity* (Cambridge, Cambridge University Press).

Rorty, R. (1991) *Objectivity, Relativism and Truth*, Philosophical Papers, Vol. 1 (Cambridge, Cambridge University Press).

Rorty, R. (1993) Putnam and the relativist menace, *Journal of Philosophy*, 40 (9), pp. 443–461.

Ross, W. D. (Ed.) (1910–1952) *The Works of Aristotle Translated Into English*, 12 vols (Oxford, Oxford University Press).

Ryle, G. (1949) *The Concept of Mind* (New York, Barnes & Noble).

Scanlon, T. M. (2001) Sen and consequentialism *Economics and Philosophy*, 17, pp. 39–50.

Schefold, B. (1990) On changes in the composition of Output, in: K. Bharadwaj and B. Schefold (Eds.) *Essays on Piero Sraffa: Critical Perspectives on the Revival of Classical Theory* (London, Unwin Hyman).

Sen, A. K. (1960) *Choice of Techniques: An Aspect of the Theory of Planned Economic Development* (Oxford, Blackwell).

Sen, A. K. (1973) *On Economic Inequality* (Oxford, Clarendon Press).

Sen, A. K. (1974) On some debates in capital theory, *Economica*, 41 (163), pp. 328–335.

Sen, A. K. (1975) *Employment, Technology and Development* (Oxford, Clarendon Press).

Sen, A. K. (1978) On the labour theory of value: some methodological issues, *Cambridge Journal of Economics*, 2, pp. 175–190.

Sen, A. K. (1982) *Choice, Welfare and Measurement* (Cambridge, MA, MIT Press).

Sen, A. K. (1984) *Resources, Values and Development* (Oxford, Blackwell).

Sen, A. K. (1985) *Commodities and Capabilities* (Amsterdam, North Holland).

Sen, A. K. (1987a) *On Ethics and Economics* (Oxford, Blackwell).

Sen, A. K. (1987b) Maurice Herbert Dobb, in: J. Eatwell, M. Milgate and P. Newman (Eds.) *The New Palgrave: a Dictionary of Economics* Vol. 1, pp. 910–912 (London, Macmillan).

Sen, A. K. (1989) Economic methodology: heterogeneity and relevance, *Social Research*, 56, pp. 299–329.

Sen, A. K. (1992) *Inequality Reexamined* (Oxford, Clarendon Press).

Sen, A. K. (1993a) Capability and well-being, in: M. Nussbaum and A. K. Sen (Eds.) *The Quality of Life*, pp. 30–53 (Oxford, Clarendon Press).

Sen, A. K. (1993b) Internal consistency of choice, *Econometrica*, 61, 495–521.

Sen, A. K. (1994) The formulation of rational choice, *American Economic Review*, 84(2), pp. 385–390.

Sen, A. K. (1999) *Development as Freedom* (New York, Knopf).

Sen, A. K. (2001) Reply, *Economics and Philosophy*, 17, pp. 51–66.

Sidgwick, H. ([1874], 1907) *The Methods of Ethics* (London, Macmillan).

Smith, A. ([1776], 1976a) *An Inquiry into The Nature and Causes of the Wealth of Nations*, R. H. Campbell, A. S. Skinner and W. B. Todd (Eds.) The Glasgow Edition, Oxford, Clarendon Press).

Smith, A. ([1790], 1976b) *The Theory of Moral Sentiments*, D. D. Raphael and A. L. Macfie (Eds.) The Glasgow Edition, (Oxford Clarendon Press).

Sraffa, P. (1960) *Production of Commodities by Means of Commodities: Prelude to a Critique of Economic Theory* (Cambridge, Cambridge University Press).

Stewart, F. (1958) *Planning to Meet Basic Needs* (London, Macmillan).

Streeten, P., Buski, S. J., Mahbubul Haq, Hicks, N. and Stewart, F. (1981) *First Things First: Meeting Basic Human Needs in Developing Countries* (New York, World Bank and Oxford University Press).

Streeten, P. (1984) Basic needs: some unsettled questions, *World Development*, 12(9), pp. 973–978.

Walsh, V. C. (1954) The theory of the good will, *Cambridge Journal*, 7, pp. 627–637.

Walsh, V. C. (1958a) Scarcity and the concepts of ethics, *Philosophy of Science*, 25(4), pp. 249–257.

Walsh, V. C. (1958b) Ascriptions and appraisals, *Journal of Philosophy*, 55(24), pp. 1062–1072.

Walsh, V. C. (1961) *Scarcity and Evil* (Englewood Cliffs, NJ, Prentice Hall).

Walsh, V. C. (1964) The status of welfare comparisons, *Philosophy of Science*, 31(2), pp. 149–155.

Walsh, V. C. (1967) On the significance of choice sets with incompatibilities, *Philosophy of Science*, 34(3), pp. 243–250.

Walsh, V. C. (1987) Philosophy and economics, J. Eatwell, M. Milgate and P. Newman (Eds.) *The New Palgrave: A Dictionary of Economics*, 3, pp. 861–869 (London, Macmillan).

Walsh, V. C. (1992) The classical dynamics of surplus and accumulation, in: J. Halevi, D. Laibman and E. G. Neil, *Beyond The Steady State, A Revival of Growth Theory*, pp. 11–43 (London, Macmillan).

Walsh, V. C. (1994) Rationality as self-interest versus rationality as present aims, in: *American Economic Review* (AEA Papers and Proceedings) 84, pp. 401–405.

Walsh, V. C. (1995–6) Amartya Sen on inequality, capabilities and needs, *Science and Society*, 59(4), pp. 556–569.

Walsh, V. C. (1996) *Rationality, Allocation and Reproduction* (Oxford, Clarendon Press).

Walsh, V. C. (1998a) Rationality in Reproduction Models, (Conference on Sraffa and Modern Economics, *Centro Studie Documentazione*, 'Piero Sraffa', Rome, Italy).

Walsh, V. C. (1998b) Normative and positive classical economics, in: H. D. Kurz and N. Salvadori (Eds.) *The Elgar Companion to Classical Economics*, Vol. 2, pp. 188–194 (Cheltenham, Edward Elgar).

Walsh, V. C. (1998c) Recent interpretations of Adam Smith, in: H. D. Kurz and N. Salvadori (Eds.) *The Elgar Companion to Classical Economics*, Vol. 2, pp. 270–275 (Cheltenham, Edward Elgar).

Walsh, V. C. (2000) Smith after Sen, *Review of Political Economy*, 12(1), pp. 5–25.

Walsh, V. C. (2002a) Classical long–period theory, in: W. J. Samuels and J. E Biddle (Eds.) *Research in the History of Economic Thought and Methodology, A Research Annual*, 20–A, pp. 327–342 (Oxford, Elsevier Science).

Walsh, V. C. (2002b) Marcuzzo, Pasinetti and Roncaglia's *The Economics of Joan Robinson* and Ciccarelli and Ciccarelli's *Joan Robinson: A Bibliography* in: W. J. Samuels and J. E. Biddle (Eds.) *Research in the History of Economic Thought and Methodology, A Research Annual*, 20–A, pp. 165–193 (Oxford, Elsevier Science).

Walsh, V. C. and Gram, H. N. (1980) *Classical and Neoclassical Theories of General Equilibrium, Historical Origins and Mathematical Structure* (New York, Oxford University Press).

White, M. (1949) *Social Thought in America: The Revolt against Formalism* (New York, Viking Press).

White, M. (1956) *Toward Reunion in Philosophy* (Cambridge, MA, Harvard University Press).

Wittgenstein, L. (1953) *Philosophical Investigations* (Oxford, Blackwell).

Wittgenstein, L. (1969) *On Certainty*, G. E. M. Anscombe and G. H. von Wright (Eds.) (Oxford, Blackwell).

4 For ethics and economics without the dichotomies

Hilary Putnam

Because Vivian Walsh's fine essay reviews such a large part of the philosophy I have done in my life, especially (but by no means exclusively) insofar as that philosophy bears on questions of interest to economists as well as to value theorists generally, it is not feasible to comment on it in detail (and Walsh's fascinating exposition of Pasinetti's work, I am only competent to learn from, and not to comment on). What does seem feasible, and not only feasible but reasonable as well, is for me to review some of the principal topics that I treat in Putnam (2002a) and then to point out connections with some of the other work, for instance, that of Martha Nussbaum, to which he refers.

What I mean by 'the fact/value dichotomy' and what I propose in its place

What the expression 'the fact/value dichotomy' refers to is nothing esoteric or technical. In virtually any discussion of policy or politics one might hear someone challenge a statement, not by saying that the statement in question is false, or the arguments offered in its favor are not good ones, but by asking in a certain tone of voice, 'Is that supposed to be a fact or a value judgment?'—the implication being that if it is a value judgment then it is simply 'subjective', and a further implication being that if it is 'subjective' then 'my value judgments are just as good as yours'—that is, the whole notion of better and worse reasons, not to say correctness and incorrectness, does not apply. The following words by Lionel Robbins (1932, p. 53) (words that were meant to challenge the intellectual legitimacy of claims that redistribution of income would increase welfare—claims that were made at the time by Pigou and others) explicitly endorsed these implications:

> If we disagree about ends it is a case of thy blood or mine—or live and let live according to the importance of the difference, or the relative strength of our opponents. But if we disagree about means, then scientific analysis can often help us resolve our differences. If we disagree about the morality of the taking of interest (and we understand what we are talking about), then there is no room for argument.

It is no accident that Amartya Sen's very first philosophical publication (Sen, 1967, p. 53) disputed this claim of Robbins', and argued that there is indeed room for rational argument about value claims. For the whole enterprise that Walsh and I have called 'second phase classical theory'—economic theory that tries to combine both the best mathematical models of an economy and the best ethical reflection, and, more particularly, the subject of 'welfare economics' in any meaningful sense—*requires* that we be able to make, and meaningfully discuss, precisely claims about 'the morality' of income redistribution, about the 'the morality' of using or not using per capita income as our *sole* measure of welfare, about the priorities that *should* be assigned to education, to reducing levels of disease, to reducing levels of malnutrition, and (as we shall see) a host of other value-laden issues. And this is the enterprise to which Sen has devoted his whole professional life.

I now turn to the question: 'What view do you propose to put in place of the fact/value dichotomy that Robbins endorsed?'

The full answer is, of course, quite long (and Vivian Walsh has done an excellent job of spelling it out), but in a brief statement what I would stress is the idea of *the entanglement of fact and value.* In my book I try to show that value judgment and factual judgment are entangled in many ways, not just one. But one of the most important ways is this: there are facts (using the term as we ordinarily do—not as a term in a metaphysical theory, which, as we shall see, is what the logical positivists did) which only come into view through the lenses of an evaluative outlook. 'Virtue terms', for example—terms such as 'brave', 'wise', 'compassionate,' 'resourceful', and their opposites—have, indeed, figured in philosophical discussion for millennia precisely for this reason. If we define a 'brave' person merely as one who does not feel fear (or does not succumb to fear), then, as Socrates already pointed out, we shall miss the crucial distinction between *bravery* and *foolhardiness*. On the side of the bad rather than the good, if we define a 'cruel' person merely as one who causes unnecessary pain (or causes pain out of malice), and take pain to be merely physical pain, then we shall miss all of the subtler forms of cruelty and all of the subtler motives for, and rationalizations of, cruelty. As Iris Murdoch—a significant moral philosopher as well as a famous novelist—long ago showed us, when it comes to describing the subtle ways in which human beings can excel and fail to excel, the concepts we have to use are 'thick' ones, ones which simultaneously describe and evaluate (Murdoch, 1970). In Putnam (2002a) I try to show (as I did earlier in Putnam, 1981) that the whole idea of dividing up a thick ethical concept, such as cruelty or bravery, into a 'purely descriptive part' (one which can be fully characterized in 'value-free language') and a 'purely evaluative part' is a philosophers' fantasy. The world we inhabit, particularly when we describe human beings for purposes other than the purposes of physics or molecular biology or some other exact science—certainly the world we inhabit when we describe the world for the purposes the economist is interested in—is not describable in 'value-neutral' terms. Not without throwing away the most significant *facts* along with the 'value judgments'.

Towards the end of my Rosenthal Lectures (Putnam, 2002a, pp. 62–63) I connected the idea of 'entangled' terms with the concerns of Amartya Sen (and, as we shall see, Martha Nussbaum) in the following words:

I have shown how the fact–value dichotomy or dualism (in a virulent form, in which ethical questions were considered to be questions of 'thy blood or mine') penetrated neo-classical economics after 1932, and I have shown the resultant impoverishment of welfare economics' ability to *evaluate* what it was supposed to evaluate—*economic wellbeing*. I have discussed Amartya Sen's impressive attempt to enrich the evaluative capacity of welfare and developmental economics by means of the 'capabilities approach'. Let me now make explicit the connection, which I have so far left implicit . . . the capabilities approach requires that we use the vocabulary that one inevitably uses, the vocabulary that one *must* use, to talk of capabilities in the sense of 'capacities for valuable functionings', and that vocabulary consists almost entirely of 'entangled' concepts, concepts that cannot be simply factored into a 'descriptive part' and an 'evaluative part'. Just about every one of the terms that Sen V and his coworkers and followers use when they talk about capabilities—'valuable functioning', 'functioning a person *has reason* to value', 'well nourished', '*premature* mortality', 'self-respect', 'able to take part in the life of the community'—is an entangled term. The standpoint that Sen shows we must take if we are to make responsible evaluations in welfare and developmental economics is not the standpoint which says (as Robbins (1932, p. 134) did) that '. . . it does not seem logically possible to associate the two studies [ethics and economics] in any form but mere juxtaposition. Economics deals with ascertainable facts; ethics with valuation and obligations.' It is a standpoint that says that valuation and the 'ascertaining' of facts are interdependent activities.

The logical positivist notion of a 'fact'

One reason that neoclassical economists (and not just Robbins) were unable to see the incredible diversity of facts, and the complex nature of the various kinds of facts that there are, is that they were under the strong influence of the movement called logical positivism. But one of the many ironies of that influence is that, by the end of the 1930s, although the influence of the positivists' fact/value dichotomy upon economists was, if anything, constantly on the increase, the positivists themselves were desperately worried. *They* knew that their 'criterion of cognitive significance'—the logical positivists' criterion for deciding what was meaningful and what was 'nonsense', on which the their fact/value dichotomy was based—was in deep trouble! As they themselves recognized (Hempel, 1963, pp. 685–710). And the heart of the trouble was that the logical positivist idea of a fact, which, as I show in the first chapter of Putnam (2002a), strongly resembled David Hume's, did not fit even their paradigm science of mathematical physics. (It also did not fit mathematics, nor did it fit philosophical statements of the sort made by the positivists themselves—logical positivists faced the embarrassing problem that if their philosophical views were right, then those views themselves would have to be classified as 'nonsense'!) The death blow was dealt with the publication of 'Two dogmas of empiricism' (Quine, 1953) an essay that demolished a central pillar of the whole logical positivist system, the belief that true scientific statements could be neatly sorted into 'empirical truths' and 'analytic statements', and that mathematical truths were all of the latter sort. Faced by these problems, the positivists replaced their original Verifiability Theory of Meaning, according to which *each individual meaningful statement is required to have its own 'method of verification'* by a holistic criterion: a criterion that says, in effect, that as long as *the 'system' (science as reconstructed in a formalized language) as a whole* enables scientists to predict phenomena more successfully, its predicates are 'cognitively meaningful'. A consequence is that after the positivists' abandonment (between 1936 and 1939) of the picture of 'factual' sentences as capable of confrontation with sense experience one by one (which was just the traditional empiricist picture) and Quine's critique of the logical positivists' picture of what they called 'the language of science' as neatly divided into a 'factual' part and an 'analytic' part, *the whole argument for the classical fact-value dichotomy was in ruins.* For if the system of scientific knowledge depends, as Quine showed, on both the adoption of convention and the formulation of empirical descriptions and hypotheses without there being any single scientific sentence that is true *simply* by convention, independently of contingent experience, or any single scientific sentence that is true simply by virtue of sensory experience, independent of convention—if 'convention' and 'experience' name *factors* which permeate all of science, rather than discrete types of sentences—then the possibility cannot be excluded that *values* are also a factor that permeates science as a whole. As Walsh (1987) put it, 'To borrow and adapt Quine's vivid image, if a theory may be black with fact and white with convention, it might well (as far as logical empiricism could tell) be red with values. Since for them confirmation *or* falsification had to be a property of a theory *as a whole*, they had no way of unraveling this whole cloth.'

To underline the irony in all of this: by the time most neoclassical economists became 'converted' to the logical positivist fact/value dichotomy, sophisticated philosophers—including philosophers who counted themselves as friends of the movement, such as Quine and Hempel—had rejected the basis on which that dichotomy was defended.

What it means to give up the dichotomy

I have discovered that when I say that I 'reject the fact/value dichotomy', I am often misheard as saying 'there is no difference between facts and values'. But that is not what I am saying. And in any case, it would make no sense to say that as long as one has not first criticized the untenable pictures of what a 'fact' is and of what a 'value' is that lie behind the traditional empiricist *cum* positivist version of the dichotomy. For if those pictures were right, it would make absolutely no sense to say that 'there is no difference'. But the pictures are not right.

On the traditional empiricist picture, a fact is something one can *picture.* Fundamentally, facts correspond to sense impressions, simple or complex. But this conception was overthrown more by the progress of science itself than by philosophical argument: as science came to speak of unobservable atoms, and then of 'curved spacetime', 'wave-particle duality', and the like, philosophers of science—and philosophy of science was the favorite subject of the logical positivists—were *forced* to recognize that no simple one-to-one correspondence exists between what a scientific statement asserts about reality and some sensory experiences. The contrary view came from Hume's belief that the only metaphysically 'real' facts *are* facts about experiences; and while the positivists tried to strip this view of its metaphysical flavor by turning into a 'thesis about the logic of science', the attempt was a failure, and, as we just saw, they finally had to give it up. An alternative metaphysical view that one often encounters nowadays, on which the only 'real' facts are the facts of pure physics—of a completely idealized physics, to boot—would be irrelevant to economics even if it were right, for, as Walsh points out in his essay, the things economists talk about are not describable in the language of a completely idealized physics. (The most powerful exponent of this more recent point of view is the British philosopher Bernard Williams. I discuss Williams's views in Chapter 2 of Putnam, 2002a, and in Putnam, 2001.) But the various ideas of a 'value judgment' that one encounters, both among philosophers and among laypersons, are just as untenable as these metaphysical conceptions of 'fact'.

For the positivists, as is well known, value judgments were either expressions of feelings, or commands, or expressions we use to 'commend' one another—anything but genuine *judgments*. But even non-positivists rarely stop to look at the endless many *kinds* of value judgment—even the many kinds of *ethical* judgment—there are. A point I emphasize in my book is that not all value judgments are ethical judgments, or ethical or aesthetic judgments, and some value judgments are even essential to scientific practice itself. On this, see Putnam (2002a, chapter 8).

It is easy to gives examples of the diversity to which I just referred. There are ethical judgments that involve praise or blame and ethical judgments that have nothing to do with praise and blame (a point I first saw in Walsh, 1961). A historically important example of such a judgment is the judgment that the Lisbon earthquake of 1755 was a very bad thing; this judgment is also a counterexample to the idea that all ethical judgments have the function of either 'prescribing' or 'commending' conduct; in addition, there are ethical judgments which imply 'oughts' and ethical judgments which do not imply 'oughts'; and there are a host of ethical judgments which cannot be adequately expressed if we are restricted to the moral philosopher's favorite words *ought, must, mustn't, good, bad, right, wrong, duty*, and *obligation*. The idea that all ethical issues can be expressed in this meager vocabulary is a conspicuous form of philosophical blindness.

Philosophers often contrast ethical statements with *descriptions*. (This is a favorite 'linguistic' version of the old fact/value dichotomy.) But it is wrong to say simply that ethical statements aren't descriptions, because it is a matter of *which* ethical statements one has in mind. The statement that 'The cruelties of the regime provoked a number of rebellions' (a statement one can well imagine encountering in a work of history), is a description, after all; it is a description of the causes of certain historical events. On the other hand, 'Terrorism is criminal' and 'Wife-beating is wrong' *aren't* descriptions; they are universal moral condemnations. (The statement that the rebellions were caused by the cruelty of the regime might also evaluate as well as describe, but I doubt that the *purpose* of historians would normally be to perform the speech-act of 'condemning' long-dead persons; their aim is usually to make the historical events intelligible, and to do this they employ descriptions, which are themselves made available by a moral point of view—this is just the phenomenon of 'entanglement' that I described at the beginning of this essay.) Moreover, as normally used by people who already know the magnitude of the earthquake, 'The Lisbon earthquake was a terrible event' is yet another sort of moral evaluation, one which assesses the moral significance of an event *without* assigning praise or blame. Walsh (1961) calls this sort of evaluation an *appraisal*.

In sum, there are at least *two* problem with the metaphysical dichotomy between facts and values that we encounter in economics (and not only in economics, of course): the first problem is that the metaphysical dichotomy is not a distinction at all but a *thesis*: the thesis that 'no value judgment states a fact', and the second problem is that *in that very thesis* both the notion of a 'fact' and the notion of a 'value judgment' are fatally misconceived. The irony here, of course, is that the Logical Positivists thought they were being *anti-metaphysical* with their fact/value dichotomy and their 'Verifiability Theory of Meaning'. And it is just these metaphysical doctrines of Logical Positivists that influenced neoclassical economists, who likewise wished to be 'anti-metaphysical'!

Amartya Sen and the 'capabilities approach'

The leading idea of 'the capabilities approach,' as readers of this journal will know, is that one cannot adequately judge the success of programs aimed at increasing welfare if one's sole measure of welfare is a monetary one—say, per capita income. One way in which he shows us the need for more sensitive measures of 'underdevelopment', poverty, and other forms of economic deprivation is by observing how feeble a measure of economic wellbeing money and gross economic product are by themselves, and how seriously our 'information base' is restricted when we fail to gather information about what results flow from given levels of income or production under various conditions. (Sen, 2000, Chapter 4). As Sen points out, the ability of a person to translate monetary income into the ability to function in one or another sphere (to exercise one or another 'capability') depends very strongly on such factors as the age of the person (especially if the person is very old or very young), on social role (which may itself depend on gender), and on the specific physical and social conditions in a given country (for example, proneness to flood, drought, disease, etc, and proneness to violence and other forms of insecurity). A striking statistic that he uses to illustrate this point is that men in China and in Kerala—a state in the south of India with very low per capita income—decisively outlive African-American men (and, although less decisively, women) in terms of surviving to older age groups (Sen, 2000, pp. 21–22). He also points out that the high mortality rates among black people in America are not adequately explained by the levels of violence in the inner-city; they also affect older black males and black women who do not experience violence. (He suggests that one would have to examine, among other things, the American health care system to account for these rates.)

'Capabilities', in Sen's sense, are not simply valuable functionings; they are *freedoms* to enjoy valuable functionings, a point that is announced in the title of Sen's most recent book, *Development as Freedom*, and stressed throughout that book. Obviously, there is room for disagreement as to just which functionings are 'valuable' or such that people have 'reason to value them', but this room for disagreement is something that Sen regards as valuable rather than as a disadvantage. Nor does he claim that the capabilities approach includes all the factors one might wish to include in the evaluation of welfare: 'we might, for example, attach importance to rules and procedures and not just to freedoms and outcomes' (Sen, 2000, p.77). And he goes on to ask, 'Is this plurality an embarrassment for advocacy of the capability perspective for evaluative purposes?' to which he responds with a firm negative (Sen, 2000, p. 77):

> Quite the contrary. To insist that there should be only one homogenous magnitude that we value is to reduce drastically the range of our evaluative reasoning. It is not, for example, to the credit of classical utilitarianism that it values only pleasure, without taking any direct interest in freedom, rights, creativity or actual living conditions. To insist on the mechanical comfort of having just one homogenous 'good thing' would be to deny our humanity as reasoning creatures. It is like seeking to make the life of the chef easier by finding something which—and which *alone*—we all like (such as smoked salmon, or perhaps even French fries), or some one quality which we must all try to maximize (such as the saltiness of the food).

Mathematically speaking, what the capabilities approach yields (even when we have agreed on a list of valuable functionings—something which itself, as Sen has told us, requires 'public discussion and a democratic understanding and acceptance') is not a complete ordering of situations with respect to positive welfare, but a partial ordering, and a somewhat fuzzy one at that (Sen, 1992, pp. 46–49). The capabilities approach (sometimes Sen calls it a 'perspective') does not pretend to yield a decision method that could be programmed on a computer. What it does do is invite us to think about what functionings form part of our, and other cultures', notions of a good life, and to investigate just how much freedom to achieve various of those functionings various groups of people in various situations actually have. Such an approach demands that we stop attempting to quarantine ethical reflection from economics in the name of 'science' in the way we have been doing ever since Lionel Robbins triumphed over the Pigovian welfare economists in 1932, and return to the kind of reasoned and humane evaluation of social well-being that Adam Smith saw as an essential part of the task of the economist. My aim, in Putnam (2002a), was to provide both an overview of the reasons that convinced so many economists that their subject *had to* quarantine ethical reflection and, by demolishing those reasons, to provide a philosophy of language that can accommodate and support 'second phase' classical economics in general, and the 'capabilities approach' in particular.

Martha Nussbaum and the capabilities approach

In recent years, Martha Nussbaum, whose valuable contribution to the capabilities approach Walsh refers to in a number of places, has been far more willing than Amartya Sen to 'stick out her neck' and actually propose possible *lists* of what she calls 'The Central Human Capabilities'. The following is one she distributed in connection with her lecture at the University of Chicago Law School, as recently as November 3, 2002:

1   *Life.* (Including freedom from premature mortality.)
2   *Bodily Health.* (Including reproductive health, adequate nourishment and shelter).
3   *Bodily Integrity.* Being able to move freely from place to place: to be secure against voilent assault and domestic violence; having opportunities for sexual satisfaction and for choice in matters of reproduction.
4   *Senses, Imagination and Thought.* (Here Nussbaum included access to adequate education, not limited to scientific and technical education and 'Being able to use one's mind in ways protected by guarantees of freedom of expression with respect to both political and artistic speech, and freedom of religious exercise' and 'Being able to have pleasurable experiences and avoid non-beneficial pain'.)
5   *Emotions.* Not having one's emotional development blighted by fear and anxiety. Nussbaum explained that 'Supporting this capacity means supporting forms of human association that can be shown to be crucial in their development.'
6   *Practical Reason.* Being able to form a conception of the good life and to engage in critical reflection about the planning of one's life. (According to Nussbaum, this entails protection for the liberty of conscience and religious observance.)
7   *Affiliation. A.* (According to Nussbaum, protecting this capacity means protecting institutions that constitute and nourish the ability to 'live with and towards others, to recognize and show concern for other human beings, to engage in various forms of social interaction; to be able to imagine the situation of another.' It also includes protecting the freedom of assembly and political speech.) *B.* 'Having the social bases of self-respect and non-humiliation; being able to be treated as a dignified being whose worth is equal to that of others. This entails provisions of non-discrimination on the basis of race, sex, sexual orientation, ethnicity, caste, religion, national origin.
8   *Other Species.* Being able to live with concern for and in relation to animals, plants, and the world of nature.

9   *Control Over One's Environment. A. Political.* Being able to participate effectively in political choices that govern one's life; having the right of political participation, protections of free speech and association. *B. Material.* Being able to hold property (both land and movable goods), and having property rights on an equal basis with others; having the freedom from unwarranted search and seizure. In work, being able to work as a human being exercising practical reason and entering into meaningful relationships of mutual recognition with other workers.

Here I need to say a word about what Martha Nussbaum intends and what she *does not* intend by this list.

The list is, obviously, a list of capabilities that an individual needs to possess in order to achieve various valuable functionings, ones which are part of human flourishing in Martha Nussbaum's view (which is why Walsh stresses the continuity of Nussbaum's thought with Aristotle's, even though some of these functionings would not be part of *eudaemonia* as Aristotle conceived it in his time). But what is it to say—to say *today*, in a society that values pluralism in a way Aristotle never did—that these functionings are part of human flourishing?

Well, it *isn't* to say that *every* person can possess all of these capabilities, and certainly not to say that every person must be required to strive to possess all of them. Some persons will wish to live lives that they find optimal from within their own conception of the good, which omit or even reject some of them. For some persons sexual activity, or, to take a very different sort of example, political participation, may be no part of what they want for themselves—or even of what they are able to find desirable for others. I have heard Martha Nussbaum explain this point using the Rawlsian notion of a 'political conception', that is, a conception on which the ethical theorist hopes to get an 'overlapping consensus' from holders of very different standpoints—not a consensus on the *value* of all these capabilities, indeed, but a consensus on the desirability of a *democratic society's* providing the means and prerequisites for the exercise of the corresponding functionings to all its members, even though some individuals and some groups of individuals (including some religious groups) will not wish to exercise them themselves and will not even value them in principle.

Because I do not myself share Nussbaum's liking for the notion of a 'political conception', I will argue in terms of a more 'comprehensive moral view' rather than a 'political conception'. (Rawls uses these terms in Rawls, 1993.) The reason I dislike the notion of a 'political conception'—either of justice (Rawls) or of Central Human Capabilities (Nussbaum) is that, in my opinion, it confuses questions of moral principle and questions of political tactics. But this is too large a question to discuss here. For a discussion that touches on it, see Putnam (2000).

What I think needs to be said is that, for the great majority of human beings, being unable to enjoy any of the functionings in Nussbaum's list is a *deprivation*. To be sure, different people have different constitutions, and that is in itself a good thing. But the old idea that (to take one controversial example from the list) 'having opportunities for sexual satisfaction' is at best a necessary concession to our 'fallen' nature and that the ideal, for those who are capable of achieving it, is total abstinence from sexual activity is, I believe, profoundly mistaken, even if it were deeply engrained in the Christian tradition for centuries, and is still subscribed to by some Christians. It is a political fact that must indeed be taken into consideration at the level of democratic *strategy* and *tactics* that some religious groups still believe that there is something 'inherently sinful' about sexual desire as such, but nevertheless such a belief is wrong, and its effects on human lives is frequently terrible. Moreover, even St. Paul recognized—however grudgingly—that for the great majority of mankind sexual activity *is* a necessary part of a satisfactory human life. Similarly, artistic activity (under which term I include enjoyment of the arts, both passive and active), and religious activity, in the widest sense of the term (which, of course, need not involve belief in a transcendent aspect of reality) are valuable functionings and, for vast numbers of people, having no opportunity to engage in them is a deprivation. To say a functioning is important and valuable is not to say it is valuable for *everybody*. On the other hand, the capacity to participate effectively and intelligently in politics is something we would like *everyone* to exercise, because this 'functioning' is not just a part of *individual* flourishing; it is the very lifeblood of democracy.

However, to say that the functionings connected with the capacities on Nussbaum's list are each and every one important and valuable for vast numbers of people is not to deny that each person must have the right to choose which ones to exercise or not to exercise. This too I would defend *not* by arguing that we need a 'political conception' on which we can get an 'overlapping consensus' of the voters, but by saying that, in the democratic conception of human flourishing, autonomy is a central—in many respects, *the* central—value (Putnam, 1989, pp. 46–49). At least from the time of Kant, liberal conceptions— *comprehensive* liberal conceptions—have defended the right of individuals to make choices, including choices that are mistaken from the point of view of those conceptions themselves, not as a grudging concession to political realities, but as something essential to our collective life conceived of as a venture in learning.

Moving now to the use of Nussbaum's list of capabilities in welfare economics and policy making, it is important to realize that the proposal that we support the capacities in some such list represents a set of *directions in which Nussbaum hopes the world will move*, and not an inflexible set of non-negotiable demands. It is consistent with the spirit in which she offers this list (which is, of course, to be modified and added to in the course of discussion) that one strive to attain *minimum* levels of capability provision (and even minimum levels adjusted to political realities in the case of each society, when we come to the context of international development). And, of course, minimum levels that can be *raised*, once the possibility of raising them arrives.

Not surprisingly, a charge I have heard made against this list is that the values it represents are 'parochial' (or 'ethnocentric'). But what I did find surprising is that I have recently heard it from philosophers one would normally expect to be sympathetic to liberal values—but ones, it turned out, in the grip of a metaphysical dichotomy, even if it isn't the positivist's dichotomy between 'facts' and 'values'. The new dichotomy is between so-called 'norms' and so-called 'values', and they take this dichotomy from the writing of Jürgen Habermas. In the course of a major exchange with John Rawls, Habermas wrote:

> Norms inform decisions as to what one ought to do, values inform decisions as to what conduct is desirable . . . norms raise a binary validity claim in virtue of which they are said to be either valid or invalid . . . values, by contrast, fix relations of preference that signify that certain goods are more attractive than others; hence we can assent to evaluative statements to a greater or lesser degree. The obligatory force of norms has the absolute meaning of an unconditional and universal duty . . . the attractiveness of values depends on evaluations and a transitive ordering of goods that has become established in particular cultures or has been adopted by particular groups . . .
>
> (Habermas, 1995)

Like the positivist dichotomy between facts and values, Habermas's dichotomy between norms and values is a metaphysical thesis rather than a logical distinction. I believe that this new dichotomy/thesis is just as untenable as the older one. And just as I found it necessary to show that the positivist's dichotomy is unfounded in order to clear a space for the sort of economics that Amartya Sen proposes, so, I believe, it is necessary to keep this new dichotomy from growing into yet another philosophical bogie—a bogie that may, in the long ran, threaten the capabilities approach just as much as the positivist's fact/value dichotomy did, even if it is proposed by philosophers who think of themselves as strong value objectivists.

A norm/value dichotomy? The danger of creeping Kantianism

By a 'norm', Habermas means a universally valid statement of obligation. Although his treatment of norms is 'Kantian'—in that the binding power of the norms that Habermas has spent his life defending, the norms of 'discourse ethics', is identified with the binding power of rational thought and communication itself—he treats 'values', in contrast, as contingent social products that vary as the different 'life worlds' vary. Where the constraint of morality enters in connection with values is at the 'metalevel'. The Habermasian norm of 'communicative action' requires us to *defend* our values by means of communicative action—sufficiently prolonged discussion among all those affected by the adoption of the values in question. Only values that can survive such a defense are permissible. But among the values that are permissible at all, there cannot be *better* and *worse* in any sense that transcends the 'projects' of a particular group. On Habermas's account, values—as opposed to the universal 'norms' of discourse ethics—are as non-cognitive as they are on the positivist account.

An example may clarify the distinction between values and norms. I myself believe that, other things being equal, a community in which there are a variety of morally permissible conceptions of human flourishing is better than one in which everyone agrees on just one conception. Such *diversity of ideals* is one of my 'values' in Habermas's sense, but not a 'norm', because norms are supposed to tell *individuals* what they *must* do, not *communities* how it would be *good* for them to be. However 'values' do not have to refer to whole communities: the judgement that a *particular* act is kind or cruel, or that a particular person is impertinent or refreshingly spontaneous, or that a child is 'having problems' or 'discovering her identity', are all judgments of *value* in the sense under discussion, and in Putnam (2002a) I maintain that such judgements are, in practice, regarded as true or false, and *should* so be regarded. (Imagine what an impoverished view of human reality would result if we were to dismiss all such judgments to the realm of the 'merely subjective'!)

A similar rejection of 'substantive value realism' appears in the writings of another philosopher I admire, my good friend and Harvard colleague Christine Korsgaard. In fact, the sharpest statements of a reductive naturalism, with respect to what I am calling values, that I know of are found in her chapters in Korsgaard *et al.* (1996) and in her subsequently published replies to various critics, in which she explains and defends those views (Korsgaard, 1998, pp. 49–66). In one of those replies (Korsgaard, 1998, p. 52) she writes:

> . . . as I read him [Kant] he does not accept any sort of substantive value realism. He does not think that the objects of our inclinations are good in themselves. We do not want things because we perceive that they are good: rather our initial attractions to them are natural psychological impulses.

What Korsgaard here calls 'the objects of our inclinations' are not yet 'values' according to her account, nor are these 'initial psychological impulses' yet valuations. We *make* them into values and valuations by adopting a maxim that directs us to value them or not to value them, to act on them or not to act on them. Thus, Korsgaard (1998, p. 57):

> The larger point here is that in Kant's theory *our values* are created from psychological materials, from the natural bases of interest and enjoyment, rather than from nothing. Here as elsewhere in Kant's theory reason works by imposing form on matter that it finds.

But in 'imposing form on matter that it finds', reason is guided by no substantive ends. Thus, Korsgaard writes (Korsgaard, 1998, p. 50): 'There is really only one principle of practical reason—the principle that we should choose our maxims as universal laws.' And making it plain that she is speaking for herself, and not just as a Kant-interpreter, Korsgaard writes, 'I argue for the conclusion that human beings must see ourselves as value-conferring and must therefore value humanity as an end in itself' (Korsgaard, 1998, pp. 60–61).

The problem with the views of both Korsgaard and Habermas is simple to explain: our 'norms', our 'maxims', and the 'laws' that we impose upon ourselves by universalizing our maxims, *contain value terms*; in particular, they contain entangled terms such as 'kind', 'cruel', 'impertinent', 'sensitive', 'insensitive', etc. For instance, it is a 'law' or 'norm' recognized by every Kantian moral philosopher (indeed, by every decent human being) that one should treat those one deals with, and especially those in distress or trouble, with 'kindness', unless there is an overriding moral reason why one should not. Similar rules of conduct direct one to avoid 'cruelty', to avoid 'rudeness', to avoid 'humiliating' others, to be 'sensitive' to the thoughts and feelings of others, etc.

However, disputes often arise as to whether a particular act was, in fact, cruel. And if criteria of cruelty are simply subjective, or at best contingent social products that vary from community to community, rather *than moral beliefs which are subject to rational discussion*, then the maxim 'avoid cruelty' is *empty*. This observation poses the same problem for Korsgaard and for Habermas; but let me apply it to each of them in turn.

The problem, as I would put it to Korsgaard, is that the only sort of moral objectivity she allows is the 'rational' decision to make a 'maxim' that one proposes to oneself into a 'law'. But this simply *presupposes* that the *terms contained in the maxim have objective application conditions*, and, if they are (as they will typically be) entangled terms, terms which evaluate and describe simultaneously, there is nothing in Korsgaard's account to tell us how they *can* have objective application conditions. Like the positivists, she simply has not faced the problem of entangled terms.

The problem as I put in a reply to Habermas, is that it is precisely our thick ethical concepts that give Kantian 'norms' their *content* (Putnam, 2002b, p. 306). The notion of an 'ideal speech situation' is *empty* in the absence of thick ethical concepts. Unless statements containing thick ethical concepts are admitted to be capable of 'validity' *tout court*, of being right, and not merely reasonable *given* the projects, ideals, etc shared by a particular community, then discourse ethics, like Korsgaardian Kantianism, will be an empty formalism.

In a discussion with me that took place just this past November 13 at Northwestern University, Jürgen Habermas appears to have conceded this point. In his remarks—he was kind enough to provide me with a written text—he took the line that certain values—but only *certain* ones—are objective, namely the ones that appear in moral norms. He continued by discussing an example I used in the chapter discussing his norm/value dichotomy, the example of a father who engages in psychological cruelty by teasing his child, while denying that the child's tears, etc, are really 'serious'. 'He has to learn to take it' the father says (Putnam, 2002a, p. 127).

In our discussion, Habermas replied to this example by saying that 'Values that meet the condition of universalizibility become the defining elements of moral norms'. And he continued as follows,

> The same holds for the moral conflict over the behavior of the teasing father, that reflects a somewhat authoritarian socialization pattern. Again, entering moral discourse the father will first reproduce the prevailing virtues of a

community that praises rigor, toughness, etc. ('Ein deutscher Junge weint nicht' ['A German boy doesn't cry']). And the opponents will confront him with what qualifies such a lack of sensitivity [as] 'cruel', with regard to the suffering soul of a vulnerable child. In the case, the matter will be decided as soon as everyone comes to see, as a result of a metalinguistic or hermeneutic discussion, that the term 'cruel' applies to this kind of teasing. That cruelty falls under the moral norm, not to harm anyone, is—as well as this norm itself, I suppose—beyond dispute.

By making this reply, Habermas has admitted my original point, that the objective validity of Kantian 'norms' *presupposes* the objective applicability of the value-terms those very norms contain. But there is still an untenable dichotomy here (one that became quite clear in the discussion that followed his reading the reply from which I just quoted), a dichotomy between *universalizable* values, which he here concedes to be objective, and *non-universalizable* values, which he still regarded as merely subjective—or at best to be judged as instrumental or not-instrumental to the 'projects' of individuals and groups. Those projects themselves, as long as they are not prohibited by a valid 'norm', play in Habermas's thought exactly that role 'preferences' play in neo-classical rational preference theory. And this means that Habermas's concession to my argument still leaves most of the values represented by Martha Nussbaum's list of 'Central Human Capabilities' in the realm of (what is from Habermas's point of view) the culturally relative. If a society wishes to grant its members freedom to make sexual and reproductive choices, or to support the arts, or to allow its members to own personal property, that is, of course permissible; but if it doesn't want to, if the support of these capabilities is contrary to that culture's 'projects', that too is permissible. That explains the fact (that I initially found surprising) that Habermas's followers told me after the discussion that Nussbaum's list is 'ethnocentric'.

The list would indeed be ethnocentric if the judgement that the arts are important or that sexual satisfaction is important or that the ability to own personal property is important were meant as *universalizable* judgments to the effect that every person *ought to* seek sexual satisfaction or seek to cultivate an appreciation of the arts or to seek personal property. But, as I already pointed out, to say that the capabilities in Nussbaum's list (and the corresponding functionings) are part of human flourishing *is not* to say that *everyone* ought to strive to possess all of them. It *is* to say that they are important and valuable for the flourishing of enormously many human lives, and that any society in which some groups lack these capabilities, or possess them to a level that is below any acceptable minimum, is stunting some human lives. Nor can this claim be adequately 'refuted' by saying that 'they' (the members of these groups) 'don't really *want*' these capabilities as long as the persons in those groups have never had the *option* of developing the capabilities in question. As Sen has written,

A thoroughly deprived person, leading a very reduced life, might not appear to be badly off in terms of the mental metric of desire and its fulfillment, if the hardship is accepted with non-grumbling resignation. In situations of long-standing deprivation, the victims do not go on grieving and lamenting all the time, and very often make great efforts to take pleasure in small mercies and to cut down personal desires to modest—'realistic'—proportions. . . . The extent of a person's deprivation may not at all show up in the metric of desire-fulfillment.

(Sen, 1992, p. 55)

What Habermasians (and Kantians generally) can't see

It is not only in the context of economics (and particularly the economics of development) that the norm/values dichotomy needs to be resisted (even in its latest form, as a dichotomy between 'universalizable' and 'non-universalizable' values). For this dichotomy reduces all questions of existential choice to mere subjective preferences. As I pointed out in Putnam (2002, pp. 85–92), if a person asks herself, as it might be, whether she would be living the best life for *her* if she joined *Medecins sans Frontieres*, she is not simply asking whether that would give her more 'pleasure', nor is she simply asking whether it would maximize the achievement of some *already existing* preferences. There may be (indeed, I think there usually is) an objectively right answer to her question; but it would be absurd to suppose that there is a *universalizable* answer to her question. Her problem is not about universal norms at all; and Kantians (and not only Habermas) are unable to see that there are any objective ethical questions that *aren't about* whether one should or shouldn't universalize some proposed norms.

We need, I believe, to recognize the theme of universalizability for what it is, namely *one* among the many interests that ethics subserves, and to see Kant's Categorical Imperative as a useful test but not a sort of sublime foundation for all of ethics. If we do this, then the difficulty in recognizing that an objective value need not be universalizable, disappears. Kantian ethics, as I argued above is empty and formal unless we supply it with content precisely from our other values. Among those other values, one must include concerns with all of Martha Nussbaum's 'Central Human Capabilities'.

Most ethicists, however, down to the present day, still opt for trying to base ethics upon one single concern, whether it be the Kantian concern with universalizable maxims or the Utilitarian concern with maximizing pleasure (the greatest pleasure of the greatest number for the longest period of time, or some successor to that formula) or some other, and either deny the ethical significance of the other concerns or else try reduce them to their favorite concern. It is as if they wanted to see ethics as a noble statue standing at the top of a single pillar.

My image is very different. My image is of a table with many legs. We all know that a table with many legs wobbles when the floor on which it stands is not even, but such a table is very hard to turn over, and that is how I see ethics: as a table with many legs, which wobbles a lot, but is very hard to turn over (Putnam, 2003).

Habermas's epistemological/metaphysical argument

Jürgen Habermas, however, modifies the Kantian idea that to be a valid ethical judgment is precisely to be, or to follow from, a maxim that is binding on all rational beings (more precisely, all beings with a rational and a sensible nature) in two ways. In his view, to be a valid ethical judgment is rather to be, or to follow from, a maxim that would be accepted by all persons affected at the end of a sufficiently prolonged discussion that faithfully observed the norms of the famous 'discourse ethics' associated with his name (see, for example, Habermas, 1990). This inflection of the Kantian view rests on a complex set of metaphysical and epistemological ideas. If we think of the ideas in question as an enormous iceberg, then the tip of the iceberg is visible in the paragraph I quoted earlier, when Habermas writes, concerning the example of the father who doesn't understand that his behavior is cruel, 'the matter will be decided as soon as everyone comes to see, as a result of a metalinguistic or hermeneutic discussion, that the term 'cruel' applies to this kind of teasing.'

The epistemological idea behind this 'the matter will be decided' is that the discourse conducted in accordance with the Habermasian norms of 'communicative action' is a *discovery procedure*. The ethical question (whether the father's behavior is cruel) is portrayed as something that 'will be decided' by following the procedure. The metaphysical idea (which Habermas uses to support the epistemological idea) is that even if (contrary to what Habermas formerly believed) the Peircean definition of truth, as *what would be agreed upon if discussion conducted according to the norms of (ideal) communicative action were sufficiently prolonged*, doesn't work for empirical statements—I argue that it doesn't in chapter 7 of Putnam (2002a)—still, he insists, it does work as a definition of 'validity' for ethical statements (Habermas, 2001). (Strictly speaking, this is the Peircean definition of truth as interpreted by Habermas's old friend Karl-Otto Apel, 1981.)

I believe that a sufficient reason to reject the metaphysical idea, the idea that truth (or 'validity', to use Habermas's language) of ethical statements is 'Peircean' (or Peirce-cum-Apelian) is that it is simply false that the whole community would necessarily come into agreement that the father's teasing constitutes cruelty, even if it does. Why *must* they come into agreement, even if the speech situation is 'ideal'? After all, it might well be that most, or at least a significant minority, of the members of the community share the father's obtuseness. They are not, we may imagine, bad people, in most other respects. They genuinely want to do what is right, and they love rational argument. Indeed, they regard the question as to whether the case is a case of 'cruelty' as a fascinating one, and they discuss it endlessly, No one tries to manipulate anyone else, and everyone listens patiently to everyone else's arguments. But we can perfectly well imagine that the father and others like him never 'get it'. There will never be consensus—although on a straightforward construal of the requirements of an ideal speech situation (speaking honestly, trying one's best to say what is true, trying one's best to say what is justified, trying to win one another over by the force of argument and not by manipulation of any kind, etc) the speech situation may well be 'ideal'. At first blush, this is a straightforward counterexample to a Peircean definition of 'validity' for ethical statements.

In fact, however, there is a fundamental ambiguity in Habermas' position. If one attempts to defend the more ambitious claims that he and Apel have made on behalf of discourse ethics, then either there will be no reason to believe the claims (this will be the case if 'discourse ethics' is restricted to some definite set of norms that are supposed to characterize reason) or the claims will be empty. For if the claim that the correct verdict in an ethical dispute will be arrived at in an ideal speech situations just means that it will be arrived at *if the disputants are ideally morally sensitive, imaginative, impartial, etc*, then the claim is a purely 'grammatical' one; it provides no content to the notion of a 'correct verdict in an ethical dispute' that that notion did not independently possess. Indeed, not only are 'ideally morally sensitive', etc, themselves *ethical* concepts, but giving them content in any actual dispute will require 'thickening' them, replacing them by terms (which are still *value* terms, but) which have more descriptive content.

Unfortunately, Habermas has not yet acknowledged the ambiguity. For what I called Habermas's 'epistemological idea', the idea of communicative action as a *discovery procedure*, presupposes precisely that the norms of communicative action are specifiable *prior* to knowing what the valid ethical judgements are. In short, Habermas's response to my thought experiment of the father who doesn't know that his own behavior is cruel requires precisely the epistemological idea, and the only reason that I can see for Habermas's insistence on the metaphysical idea (that ethical validity is 'Peircean') is that he sees the claim that ethical validity would be discovered if discussion were 'ideal', as something much more substantive than a mere grammatical observation, that he identifies it, in fact, with the untenable epistemological idea.

These remarks do not, of course, bear directly on the work of Christine Korsgaard, for two reasons. First, following Rawls' reading of Kant (in his courses as well as in his beautiful published lectures on moral philosophy), she does not read the Categorical Imperative as any sort of discovery procedure, but rather as a test that maxims we propose to ourselves have to pass. Secondly, she is neither a Peircean nor an Apelian—indeed she does not appeal to theories of truth at all. But this leaves it all the more puzzling why she should regard 'reason' (closely identified with universalizability) as the *sole* objective value.

All of Kant's fundamental psychological distinctions—for example, his sharp separation (at least in the first and second *Critique*) of Reason and Inclination, and his belief that someone guided by Inclination is simply subject to deterministic forces, while someone guided by Reason will *ipso facto* want to live by rules that any 'rational' person could legislate for him or herself are, indeed, deeply metaphysical. It seems to me that Korsgaard is too much influenced, perhaps unintentionally, by this metaphysical psychology. What I would praise is rather the Categorical Imperative, not, indeed, as a practical guide—as a guide it scarcely goes beyond the Golden Rule—but as a powerful statement of the idea that ethics is *universal*, that, insofar as ethics is concerned with the alleviation of suffering, it is concerned with the alleviation of *everyone's* suffering, or if it is concerned with positive well-being, it is concerned with *everybody's* positive well-being. The Capabilities Approach might seem to reject this achievement, in that it is concerned with granting individuals capabilities that not all of them will wish to exercise; but to see this as contrary to universality is a mistake. Kantians have always seen concern with *human rights* as within the scope of universal ethics, although here too the rights in question are rights that not everyone wishes to exercise. Just as in the case of rights, what makes concerns with capabilities universalizable is not that everyone is under an obligation to exercise each of the central capabilities, but that everyone is under an obligation to do what they can to bring about a situation in which everyone enjoys, at least to a reasonable minimum level, the *freedom* to exercise them. Here, as elsewhere, it is a mistake—and another example of the way in which the tendency to dichotomize everywhere distorts our thinking about ethics—to see concern with human flourishing, and concern with norms as irreconcilable concerns, rather than as *interdependent* parts of the large and complex system of concerns that make up a responsive and responsible ethical consciousness.

References

Apel, K. O. (1981) *Charles S. Peirce; from Pragmatism to Pragmaticism* (Amherst, University of Massachusetts Press).

Habermas, J. [German original, 1983] (1990) *Moral Consciousness and Communicative Action*, (Cambridge, MA, MIT Press).

Habermas, J. (1995) Reconciliation through the public use of reason: remarks on John Rawls' Political Liberalism, *The Journal of Philosophy*, 92(3), pp. 114–115.

Habermas, J. (2001) *Kommunikatives Handeln und detranszendentalisierte Vernunft* (Stuttgart, Reclam).

Hempel, C. G. (1963) Implications of Carnap's work for the philosophy of science, in P. A. Schilpp (Ed), *The Philosophy of Rudolf Carnap*, pp. 685–710 (LaSalle, IL, Open Court).

Korsgaard, C. with G. A. Cohen, Raymond Geuss, Thomas Nagel and Bernard Williams (1996) *The Sources of Normativity* (Cambridge, Cambridge University Press).

Korsgaard, C. (1998) Motivation, metaphysics, and the value of the self: a reply to Ginsborg, Guyer, and Schneewind, *Ethics*, 109, pp. 49–66.

Murdoch, I. (1970) *The Sovereignty of Good* (London, Routledge and Kegan Paul).

Putnam, H. (1981) *Reason, Truth and History* (Cambridge, Cambridge University Press).

Putnam, H. (1989) *The Many Faces of Realism* (Peru, IL, Open Court).

Putnam, H. (2001) Reply to Bernard Williams' 'Philosophy as a humanistic discipline,' *Philosophy*, 76, pp. 605–614.

Putnam, H. (2002a) *The Collapse of the Fact/Value Dichotomy* (Cambridge, MA, Harvard University Press).

Putnam, H. (2002b) Antwort auf Jürgen Habermas, in Marie-Louise Raters and Marcus Willaschek (Eds) *Hilary Putnam und die Tradition des Pragmatismus* (Frankfurt a/M, 2002), pp. 306–321.

Putnam, H. (2003) *Ethics without Ontology* (Cambridge, MA, Harvard University Press).

Putnam, R. A. (2000) Neither a beast nor a god, *Social Theory and Practice*, 26(2), pp. 177–200.

Quine, W. V. (1953) Two dogmas of empiricism, in: W. V. Quine, *From a Logical Point of View*, pp. 20–46. (Cambridge, MA, Harvard University Press). [An earlier version appeared in *Philosophical Review*, January 1951.]

Rawls, J. (1993) *Political Liberalism* (New York, Columbia University Press).

Rawls, J. (2000) *Lectures on the History of Moral Philosophy* (Cambridge, MA, Harvard University Press).

Robbins, L. (1932) *On the Nature and Significance of Economic Science* (London, Macmillan).

Sen, A. K. (1967) The nature and classes of prescriptive judgments, *The Philosophical Quarterly*, 17(66), pp. 46–62.

Sen, A. K. (1992) *Inequality Reexamined* (Cambridge, MA, Harvard University Press).

Sen, A. K. (2000) *Development as Freedom* (New York, Anchor Books).

Walsh, V. C. (1961) *Scarcity and Evil* (Englewood Cliffs, NJ, Prentice-Hall).

Walsh, V. C. (1987) Philosophy and economics, in: J. Eatwell, M. Milgate and P. Newman (Eds) *The New Palgrave: A Dictionary of Economics* 3, pp. 861–869 (London, Macmillan).

5 Tragedy and human capabilities

A response to Vivian Walsh

Martha Nussbaum

Vivian Walsh's 'Sen after Putnam' is a tour de force, covering a wide spectrum of issues with both authority and deep moral commitment. Both because I find Walsh's previous work a continual stimulus and a beacon of encouragement in the relatively desolate intellectual landscape of economics, and because the present paper is so impressive, I find it very difficult to know how to reply. This difficulty is compounded by the fact that I am not an economist, and much of the more technical discussion in the paper is beyond my competence. What I think I might do, then, to carry the conversation forward is to comment briefly on four issues touched on in Walsh's paper, concerning which I've been doing some recent thinking and writing: (1) truth and objectivity, (2) tragic conflicts, (3) disability and (4) freedom. On all four of these issues my own present ideas differ to some extent from those of Sen, so it seems important to introduce these differences.

(1) *Truth and Objectivity.* As Walsh correctly states, Sen and I turned to Aristotle for the idea that in both ethics and science we have available a notion of truth and objectivity that is robust, and yet at the same time 'internal', from the perspective of standing human interests and capacities. We were alert to the similarity between our Aristotelian idea and Putnam's ideas, and it was in part for that reason that we were so eager to get Putnam involved in our work at the World Institute for Development Economics Research, where he produced two splendid papers that developed these ideas further with specific application to development economics (Putnam, 1993, 1995).

Meanwhile, however, my own thinking moved on, under the influence of John Rawls's *Political Liberalism* (Rawls, 1996) and the work of my colleague Charles Larmore (1996). I have come to believe that it is very important to distinguish between the ethical sphere and the political sphere. In any modern society, there exists a plurality of competing value conceptions, both religious and secular. Many of these are reasonable, and we cannot expect the disagreements between them to be resolved any time soon. Because these conceptions frequently lie at the heart of people's sense of self and of the meaning of life, respect for persons dictates respect for these comprehensive conceptions of value.

What this means for political life is that, even if we are convinced that we have very good arguments for our own ideas in ethics and religion, we should not build the core political institutions of our nation around them, in a way that disfavors adherents of other religions and conceptions. Instead, we should view the political core of a society as a 'partial moral conception' (to use Rawls's term), which can be attached to many different comprehensive conceptions of value, and concerning which they can ultimately achieve what Rawls calls an 'overlapping consensus'.

But overlapping consensus will be possible only if the political conception is not only partial, concerning itself with some matters (basic justice) and not others (the ultimate destiny of the soul), but also thin, abstaining from using metaphysical conceptions (such as that of the immortal soul) that divide people along lines of their more comprehensive conceptions. In addition, we can achieve consensus only if we are also parsimonious about our epistemological claims. Since each religion and each ethical conception contains an epistemology of value, we must carefully articulate the political conception in terms of a thin epistemology of value that can be shared by people who differ about contentious epistemological matters. Thus, states that declare that their political conception is based on the idea of self-evident truth are showing disrespect for citizens whose religious or ethical idea denies that there are such truths. Rawls spends a good deal of time demonstrating, I think convincingly, that politics may still claim a certain sort of objectivity for its basic principles, but not the same sort that many people would want to claim for their comprehensive ethical or religious doctrines.

In a recent article (Nussbaum, 2001), I have explored and defended the Rawlsian idea of a thin 'political objectivity', describing its implications for my own articulation of the capabilities approach. There are two implications that are significant for Walsh's article. First, although I continue to agree with Putnam about ethical objectivity, I now feel that it is inappropriate to build that conception of ethical objectivity into the foundations of a political conception. Instead, one should seek a thinner 'political objectivity' that can be acceptable to Putnamites, adherents of the idea of self-evident eternal truth, and even, let us hope, people of more relativist inclinations. (In my article I use the example of Stanley Fish.)

The second noteworthy consequence of accepting Rawls's (and Larmore's) idea is that one has strong reason not to base public policy on the idea of freedom of choice as a general all-purpose human good. In another recent article describing my current differences with Sen (Nussbaum, 2003a), I argue that Sen's current tendency to speak of freedom as an all-purpose good seems increasingly to put him in the camp of 'comprehensive liberalism' of the sort espoused by John Stuart Mill and Joseph Raz, rather than in the camp of political liberals such as Rawls, Larmore, and myself. For the political liberal, it is disrespectful to say that freedom is a generally good thing. Adherents of traditional conceptions of value (such as the American Amish) and members of authority-based religion (such as Roman Catholics) cannot accept that proposition. What they can accept, I believe, is the idea that certain freedoms, conceived as capabilities, are and should be basic to a just political order. Both because the list is finite and because it is a list of capabilities, not actual functions, they will feel that the conception is one that respects them. An Amish citizen can support the right to vote for all citizens, even though she thinks it immoral to vote; a Roman Catholic citizen can support the free exercise of religion, even though she thinks that she herself is in no way morally free to choose a different religion. But neither could assent to the proposition that lives based upon freedom or autonomy are better than lives not so based.

(2) *Tragic Conflicts.* What Walsh says about tragic choices is eloquent and deep, and I have no quarrel with it: indeed, I am very grateful for his use of my work in developing his powerful ideas. I think, however, that one can say a little more here about how the idea of tragic choice helps us to criticize some dominant ways of thinking, in public policy as influenced by economics. In a recent volume devoted to critical examination of the idea of cost–benefit analysis (Nussbaum, 2000b), I have argued that what is wrong with common cost–benefit models of public choice is not only (Walsh's point) that they assume the availability of a complete ordering, and thus fail to grapple with the fact of tragic dilemmas, but it is also that they fail to distinguish two quite fundamentally distinct questions, which must be distinguished if we are to make progress on the most tragic choices that people repeatedly face in life.

One question is: what is the best thing I can do now, all things considered? As Walsh says, one can pose this question to oneself even in the most tragic of circumstances, and frequently one can arrive at an answer. For Agamemnon, to slaughter his daughter was probably the best thing available to him, given that the alternative involved the death of his daughter and of all his troops. But now there is a second question on the table: are any of the alternatives available in this situation free from serious ethical wrongdoing? Frequently, even when some answer can be found to the first question (what I call 'the obvious question'), the answer to the second (the 'tragic question') is 'no.'

What do we get out of asking the tragic question? Isn't it just an invitation to moan and groan needlessly? With Walsh, I think not. As he indicates, there is human value in seeing a tragedy for what it is. Seeing that the situation is not free from wrongdoing, whatever one chooses, one reinforces one's determination to avoid such situations in future, and one strengthens dispositions of character that disincline one to such heinous ethical choices. But there is something more, and this is the point that I wish to add to Walsh's account.

As Hegel pointed out, seeing that a choice is tragic also prompts the question, 'Why did people have to face this, and what can institutional and political change do to make sure that they don't face this again?' Sometimes a tragic choice is caused by brute necessity; but more often the causes lie squarely on the human side, where stupidity, obtuseness, and malice are amply to be found. Concerning the *Antigone*, Hegel correctly noted that the tragic conflict between reasons of religion and reasons of state comes about only because religion and the state have been defined in a particular way. But there are other ways, which go a long way toward removing the conflict. If a state understands protection of the free exercise of religion as among its most important *political* principles, then many, at least, of the tragic conflicts in this area will not arise.

I apply this idea to thinking about public planning and the capabilities list. When I speak of my list of the ten central capabilities, economists usually ask me, what are the trade-offs and orderings? What I want to say is, think of these ten as the material for basic constitutional entitlements. This means that *every one of them* is central and non-negotiable up to some suitable threshold level (which, typically, will be specified over time by judicial and legislative action). It is unacceptable for the state to protect one constitutional entitlement by cutting back on another: thus we do not accept major restrictions on the freedom of speech in order to promote other basic capabilities, say, the right to enjoy self-respect. Debates about hate speech will legitimately debate where the threshold of each of these capabilities rightly falls; and this debate ought to take cognizance of the presence of other capabilities that are pertinent. But the aim must be to have a consistent set that can be guaranteed to all citizens over time.

If we see a case that looks really tragic, we must ask, 'What can we do about this? What has made this case so tragic?' Often, the answer is greed and stupidity. The fact that women used to have to choose, tragically, between family and career resulted not from nature but from the absence of male good will and of intelligent planning from both the state and private employers. The fact that many poor parents today must choose, tragically, between starvation for themselves and non-education for their children, reflects the absence of intelligent state planning; since we know that even a very poor state, such as the Indian state of Kerala, can achieve basic literacy for all children without permitting anyone to starve. The fact that this record has not been imitated in other Indian states results from corruption and stupidity.

In short, we should view the presence of tragedy as an invitation to constructive political thinking, with the aim of putting in place (constitutionally) a core group of basic entitlements, and then really securing them to all people.

(3) *Disability*. As Walsh notes, with considerable eloquence, the fair claims of people with disabilities were at the heart of the capabilities approach from the very beginning. Sen's famous example of a person in a wheelchair, introduced by way of criticism of the Rawlsian account of primary goods, shows that understanding primary goods simply as commodities will not give us the intellectual equipment to address some of the most persistent obstacles between people and flourishing lives. The person in a wheelchair needs more resources to be fully mobile than a person whose limbs work well. To that point of Sen's I would add that she needs resources *of a different sort*: special, usually expensive, *social* resources, such as wheelchair ramps, elevators on buses, etc. More money won't do it. If we think of basic entitlements as capabilities, however, we see what is required to treat the two citizens truly equally.

Again, I think that all this is fine so far as it goes. But Sen simply extracted the list of primary goods from Rawls's overall theory, and did not ask about the rest of the structure; he strongly suggests that if we simply replace primary goods with capabilities, all will be well. The primary object of my current work is to show that all is not well: the idea of the social contract itself needs to be called into question. In my Tanner Lectures 2002–2003 (2002 in Canberra Australia, 2003 at Clare Hall, Cambridge), I argue that the idea of the social contract as a bargain for mutual advantage among rough equals must itself be criticized if we are to have an adequate way of including disabled persons adequately in the political conception. (I make a similar argument for the issue of transnational justice between nations who are not rough equals, and for the case of justice between humans and non-human animals.) The argument for this negative conclusion, and in favor of a development of the capabilities approach, is detailed and cannot be summarized here (but see Nussbaum, 2000c, 2003b). I just want to alert readers to this further departure from Sen's thinking about capabilities.

(4) *Freedom*. In his interpretation of Sen, Walsh makes an interesting move: he attributes to Sen a distinction between 'basic commodities' and 'gross luxuries'. And of course at many points throughout his writings Sen does give us a very strong sense of what he does and does not consider basic. But there is a counter-vailing tendency, increasingly in evidence in his recent work: this is, as I have said, to speak of freedom as a general all-purpose human good, and of capabilities as all instances of this general good of freedom.

I argue (Nussbaum, 2003a) that this move is a bad mistake, taking Sen in the direction of 'neoliberal' thinkers and away from his own earlier emphasis on certain 'basic' goods. So I am happy to see Walsh value and highlight what I take to be a central, if under-theorized, feature of the early Sen.

What is at stake here? Quite simply, justice. For if one thinks that the goal of the state should be to promote freedom across the board, no matter which freedoms and no matter for whom, one will likely choose policies that are very different from the ones that Walsh and I would favor. Social justice for the poor requires limiting many freedoms, even many that are traditionally valued: the freedom of big business to make large campaign contributions; the freedom of industry to pollute the environment; the freedom of the rich to keep 'their' wealth, or as much of it as they can get away with. Similarly, social justice for women requires a lot of limitation of traditionally valued male freedoms: the freedom to harass women in the workplace, the freedom to have intercourse with one's wife whether she consents or not, etc.

What I think we should say is, those freedoms are not good. Not only do they not lie at the core of our constitutional conception, they are actually inimical to that conception, and undermine it. (Of other freedoms, for example, the freedom of motorcyclists to drive around without helmets, we might say, these are neither central nor terrible. They do not and should not enjoy constitutional protection, but they don't do a lot of harm either.) But to make this utterly sensible and necessary reply, we need to rank freedoms and pick some as central. We need to be able to say: the freedom of speech is basic, but the freedom to pollute is not basic. In short, we need a list, of the sort I've been working out, and of the sort that a nation could enact as part of its constitutional conception. I believe that Sen's failure to get definite about content is a big mistake. One's view of content may be in error; thus, it is good to be humble about any suggestion one makes. But one must begin somewhere. Only in this way will the idea of capabilities offer good guidance to law and public policy. I believe that Walsh agrees with this proposal, and I welcome his eloquent defense of the idea that some things really are basic for human flourishing, in a way that other things are not.

References

Larmore, C. (1996) *The Morals of Modernity* (New York and Cambridge, Cambridge University Press).

Nussbaum, M. (2000a) *Women and Human Development* (Cambridge, Cambridge University Press).

Nussbaum, M. (2000b) The costs of tragedy: some moral limits of cost-benefit analysis, *Journal of Legal Studies* 29, 1005–1036.Reprinted in M. D. Adler and E. A. Posner (Eds), *Cost-Benefit Analysis: Legal, Economic and Philosophical Perspectives* (Chicago, University of Chicago Press), pp. 169–200.

Nussbaum, M. (2000c) The future of feminist liberalism. A Presidential Address delivered to the Central Division of the American Philosophical Association, April 2000. *Proceedings and Addresses of the American Philosophical Association*, 74, 47–79.

Nussbaum, M. (2001) Political objectivity, *New Literary History*, 32, 883–906.

Nussbaum, M. (2003a) Capabilities as fundamental entitlements: Sen and social justice, *Feminist Economics*, special issue on Sen.

Nussbaum, M. (2003b) Capabilities and disabilities: justice for mentally disabled citizens, *Philosophical Topics*, special issue on *Global Inequalities*, C. Flanders and M. Nussbaum (Eds.).

Putnam, H. (1993) Objectivity and the science–ethics distinction, in: *The Quality of Life*, M. Nussbaum and A. Sen (Eds) (Oxford, Clarendon Press), pp. 143–157.

Putnam, H. (1995) Pragmatism and moral objectivity, in: *Women, Culture and Development*, M. Nussbaum and J. Glover (Eds) (Oxford, Clarendon Press), pp. 199–224.

Rawls, J. (1996) *Political Liberalism*, expanded paperback edition (New York, Columbia University Press [1993]).

6 Openness versus closedness in classical and neoclassical economics

Harvey Gram

Vivian Walsh has drawn a distinction between a completed first phase and a developing second phase in the revival of Classical economic theory. The first phase elaborated upon and led to a fuller understanding of the work of Sraffa (1960),[1] whose avowed purpose was to resurrect the 'standpoint ascribed to the old classical economists [whose work] has been submerged and forgotten since the advent of the "marginal" method' (Sraffa, 1960, p. v).[2] That work established a core set of propositions in the theory of value which left 'open the possibilities of allowing for a number of historical and social influences to enter the analysis' (Bharadwaj, 1990, p. 73). The first phase has set the stage for a second phase in the development of modern Classical theory.

The first phase made clear that the Classical theory of prices *requires* independent determinations of the level of real wages (or the uniform rate of profit under competitive capitalism) *and* the level and composition of output. The claim that it is possible to bring such determinations to the theory of prices, as if from the outside—to claim that the theory of prices has sufficient degrees of freedom to allow for this independence of distribution and output—gains no support from Neoclassical general equilibrium theory whose structure leaves room neither for a Keynesian theory of effective demand, as a determinant of the level of output and degree of utilization of labor and capital, nor for a Sen-inspired theory of capabilities, as a determinant of income distribution and output composition. The first phase in the revival of Classical theory has opened the door to both. Pasinetti (1981) analyzed the Keynesian connection and pointed the way forward in terms of a developing hierarchy of needs and wants. Walsh (2000) has previously argued the case for Sen, building on Smith. He has now added philosophical support from Putnam, recalling earlier contributions of his own. His purpose is to lay the foundation for a richly textured Classical theory of economic development.

In Neoclassical theory, both the distribution of income and the composition of output are endogenously and simultaneously determined by a general equilibrium of supply and demand. The underlying data on the supply side are parametrically given resource inputs and a given technology of production for transforming inputs into outputs; on the demand side, the data are specified in terms of a given distribution of ownership of inputs and a given pattern of preferences for final outputs. Models for the theory would be *over*-determined if either the distribution of income or the composition of output were to be explained in any way *other* than as a balance of the forces of supply and demand. The three questions—What goods are produced? How are they produced? For whom are they produced?—are answered *all at once* in Neoclassical theory. Simultaneity, in this sense, is absent from Classical theory, where these not unrelated questions are treated separately from the theory of value. '[T]he factors determining output levels and composition, the methods of production in use and the pace of accumulation are not entirely subsumed within the domain of price determination. . . . This is not to deny or even undermine the interdependence and interaction between levels of output (and changes therein), distribution and technology, but to recognize that such interrelations are considered diverse and complex enough to require deeper analysis outside the core of the price theory' (Bharadwaj, 1990, p. 56).

This theoretical divide can be traced in large part to a simple distinction. In Neoclassical economics, the obvious fact that resources—the so-called factors of production of land, labor and capital—are to a large extent *produced* inputs as opposed to *endowments* of nature, is immaterial: the fact that commodities are produced by means of commodities simply has no consequences for the structure of the theory. Thus, the standard definition of the economic problem as the allocation of given means among alternative uses (Robbins, 1935) neither insists upon nor does it allow for a formal distinction to be drawn between inputs that are produced and those that are not. Wherever those inputs have come from, the first question to be asked in setting up a Neoclassical model concerns the feasibility of outputs—what restrains or limits production in the immediate present? The familiar production possibilities frontier embodies central organizing concepts: the opportunity cost of one good in terms of another (at points where at least one input is fully utilized[3]) and the implied scarcity of the various given inputs, measured by the value (using opportunity cost ratios) of the extra output that an extra unit of any particular resource would make possible. Inputs can indeed be produced, but it would make no difference if those produced inputs had simply dropped from the sky rather than being the result of past investment decisions.

In Classical economics, the central economic problem is the production, distribution and accumulation of a surplus or net product. This conception immediately raises the dynamic question of viability, as opposed to the static question of feasibility—can the economic system reproduce itself? This is not a question about constraints on output in the immediate present. It is a question about the evolving technology of reproduction in an industrial society. The perspective of the theorist has thus been turned around. What inputs are required to sustain a particular level and composition of output? Are they small enough to allow a surplus to exist? If so, the consequences of allocating this surplus, and the forms of income that correspond to it, come immediately to center stage—questions about income distribution and the problem of economic development cannot be avoided. The *structure* of Classical economics allows separate theories of distribution and output to play a role. Sen's capabilities approach finds a point of entry.

Walsh outlines a two-sector model of surplus and accumulation. That model, in multi-dimensional form, is fully elaborated for the first time in a seminal paper by

John von Neumann (1945 [1937]). It is perhaps the clearest instance of a model so differently interpreted as now to represent a fault line in the debate surrounding the revival of interest in Classical economics. The model shows how a particular composition of output (corresponding to maximum uniform expansion under constant returns to scale) *determines* a corresponding mix of produced inputs. Criticized from the start,[4] this recognition of the circular flow of production of commodities by means of commodities, in place of the Neoclassical one-way flow from initial factors to final outputs, was seen as 'rather poor economics'.[5] Thus, on the occasion of the fiftieth anniversary of its publication, the question was still being asked of von Neumann's model: 'Is [it] to be viewed as a 'culmination' of a long line of models of classical political economy that began with the Physiocratic circular flow, and continued with Ricardo and Marx? Or is it a *special case* of the Arrow–Debreu–McKenzie model of pure exchange, itself a rigorous reformulation of Walras?' (Dore *et al.*, 1987). Neoclassical theorists take the latter view, regarding the Classical interpretation as correct only in the special case of a quasi-stationary state in which the produced inputs happen to be in accordance with what is required for a steady rate of expansion of the economy as a whole. For them, it is essential to ask 'What supplies of produced goods do we begin with as inheritance from the past?' (Samuelson, 1987, p. 102).[6] The modern Classical position is that, because most inputs are produced commodities, that 'inheritance from the past' is neither arbitrary nor should it be seen as any *more* important than a host of other short-run factors, which have only temporary effects on the course of economic development, and for which no general theory can be developed.

The fundamental role of initial factor endowments and the implied criticism of any theory that does *not* give central place to the scarcity of given inputs is part and parcel of Neoclassical economics. What is problematical with this view? One issue appears central. When the dynamic resource allocation problem is treated analytically in the now standard way, as an intertemporal general equilibrium of supply and demand starting from an arbitrary vector of initial endowments given by 'history', the requirements of the theory present its practitioners with an extraordinary difficulty. Solutions to the problem, if interpreted in the manner in which we would wish to interpret them 'as market systems, . . . are dynamically highly unstable—namely saddle-path stable' (Burgstaller, 1994, p. 38). Burgstaller's development of this result, first recognized in the mid-1960s (Hahn, 1966; Samuelson, 1967), provides a Neoclassical perspective on a wide range of models, from pure exchange to pure reproduction. In every case, the same type of instability arises—saddle-path stability.[7] As a result, it is necessary to add 'to the list of "givens" of neoclassical theory an initial price vector for all durables—a vector which must take on that particular value consistent with the future unfolding of a general equilibrium of supply and demand' (Gram, 2001, pp. 159–160). The theory cannot explain what it is intended to explain; namely, prices and rates of change of quantities.

It is important to understand the source of this deep and profound analytical weakness in Neoclassical economic theory for two reasons. First, it has been claimed that dynamic allocation models lend coherence to Classical economics by extending the domain of reproduction models to incorporate the effects of arbitrarily given initial stocks of produced inputs, thereby answering 'the most damning criticism of Neo-Ricardian versions of classical theory inspired by Sraffa' (Burgstaller, 1994, p. 10). This coherence claim has no empirical relevance, in view of the saddle-path nature of the theoretical solution. Secondly, such irrelevance has its root cause in the more basic, underlying claim that what unites Classical and Neoclassical economics is '[f]orward-looking asset arbitrage, . . . a capitalist economy's most fundamental mechanism of decentralized valuation . . .' (Burgstaller, 1994, p. 1). It is this principle, applied universally and without thought as to its relevance in particular contexts, which has made clear the extraordinary entailments of an intertemporal equilibrium of supply and demand in which the role of prices is to reconcile the full employment of an arbitrary historical endowment of resources with a path of accumulation that leads ultimately to a stationary or steady state.[8]

The forward-looking nature of Neoclassical economics was well appreciated by an earlier critic of Classical theory. Bharadwaj (1990, p. 64) quotes the remarkable and, for proponents of intertemporal general equilibrium theory, prescient passage from *The Nature of Capital and Time*, 'When prices find their normal level at which costs plus interest are covered, it is not because the past costs of production have determined prices in advance, but because the sellers have been good speculators as to what prices would be' (Fisher, 1906, p. 188). This role of speculators with correct expectations as to where the economy will end up in the possibly distant future is essential to the coherence of Neoclassical theory. The associated instability of prices (saddle-path stability) is its undoing. Few express discomfort with this result. One such expression was provided by Samuelson in his heuristic discussion of the economic significance of a saddle-path solution. Under the heading, 'Reaiming Behavior of Speculators', he wrote:

> . . . we can imagine ideal futures markets . . . but it takes a strong imagination to indulge in such an unrealistic exercise. Very few activities are able to rely on a viable organized futures market. . . . Heuristically,. . . any path but the convergent one is going to frustrate somebody's expectations and, crudely, is going to lead to bankruptcy for someone and to reaiming for the system. . . . Even if there is something in this heuristic reasoning, one must admit that the system need not—and generally, will not—move from its present position to the golden age in the most efficient way: it will hare after false goals, get detoured, and begin to be corrected only after it has erred. . . . One feels that the real world of tools, plant, and inventory contrasts with the purely financial dream world of indefinite group self-fulfillment.
>
> (Samuelson, 1967, pp. 228– 30)[9]

A telling aspect of various negative assessments of Neoclassical economics by those engaged in refining its structure concerns the role of learning. At one extreme, the theory of rational expectations focuses attention on the way in which producing and consuming agents learn about the underlying structure of dynamic allocation problems whose solutions are saddle-paths. At the frontier of current research, Evans and Guesnerie (2003, p. 43) ask, 'When is it the case that the *saddle-path stable* solution of a dynamical system is a good candidate for expectational coordination . . . ?'. Their answer is that 'the justification of the saddle-path stable solution as the right solution is not necessarily obtained, even with appropriate common knowledge restrictions [sufficient to imply common knowledge of the perfect-foresight path itself] and even when the agents are sufficiently homogenous [in their reactions to expectations]' (Evans and Guesnerie (2003, p. 61). This conception of learning as expectational coordination is a narrow one that appears to be motivated entirely by the need to lend coherence to the notion of an intertemporal equilibrium of supply and demand.

Pasinetti (1981) took a different approach to learning. What is important for economic development is not learning about the equilibrium entailments of a set of constraints imposed by initially given supplies of qualitatively unchanging inputs, but rather the problem of learning about new technologies for producing new goods with new inputs. However, he stopped short of attempting to incorporate a theory of learning about what a society wants to produce. 'Of course, technical progress cannot be taken as automatically leading to *social* progress . . . How to learn systematically in the fields of social progress is perhaps something that has yet to be learnt' (Pasinetti, 1981, p. 22).

Walsh's call for a second phase in the revival of Classical economics is a call for precisely this kind of learning. Others, citing different reasons for abandoning general equilibrium theory, have come to similar conclusions. 'Post-general-equilibrium economics will need a new model of consumer behaviour, new mathematical models of social interaction, and an analysis of the exogenous institutional sources of stability' (Ackerman, 2002, p. 120). What is significant about Walsh's development of a Smith–Sen–Putnam connection is that it places this quest within a specific analytical framework—modern Classical economics—an open theory, which, unlike Neoclassical general equilibrium theory, has sufficient degrees of freedom to allow Sen's capability approach to gain a hearing.

Notes

1 Kurz and Salvadori (1995) have paid special attention to the connection between Sraffa (1960) and von Neumann (1945 [1937]); Pasinetti (1977, 1981) has given greater emphasis to the link with Leontief (1951). Walsh and Gram (1980) contrast Classical and Neoclassical models while paying particular attention to the history of ideas, as do Kurz and Salvadori (1995). Neoclassical reactions to Sraffa's work can be found in Bliss (1975) and Burmeister (1980). The claim of Burgstaller (1994) to have discovered the common structure of Classical and Neoclassical value theory has been the subject of a *Symposium* in *Metroeconomica* where Burgstaller (2001) answers his critics.

2 'Neoclassical' is here used in place of 'marginal'. It should be further understood that 'Neoclassical' refers to the theory that descends from Walras at the hands of Kenneth Arrow, Gerard Debreu and Lionel McKenzie. It is certainly granted that an earlier neoclassical tradition, associated with Alfred Marshall and many others, shared with Classical theory what has been called the long-period method (Petri, 2001; Garegnani, 1976). In modern texts—especially undergraduate texts–there remain many vestiges of that earlier tradition.

3 The conception of choice of technique as a substitution of one input in place of another implies (under commonly made assumptions concerning the unlimited opportunities for such substitution) *full employment* of all inputs at limit points of the feasible set.

4 In his initial assessment, Champernowne (1945, p. 18) asked, 'How can a country acquire the equipment needed to achieve the best system of production?'

5 In defending this assessment, Koopmans (1964, pp. 356–357) remarked: '. . . it seems quixotic to ignore completely the historically given capital stock available at the beginning of the time period under consideration, and to assume instead that out of some fourth dimension one can . . . pull forth a capital stock of precisely that composition that enables proportional growth to take place at a maximal rate. . . .'.

6 Another theorist finds the same weakness in Sraffa (1960): '. . . I have treated endowments as unknown. This is required for the Sraffa price equations to make sense in a world where inputs precede output. But neoclassical economics can study the economy for an arbitrary history; Sraffa cannot' (Hahn, 1982, p. 368).

7 To understand why a *stable* saddle-path is a source of *instability*, consider aiming a marble from a point on a saddle, chosen so carefully as to ensure that the marble rolls along the surface of the saddle to settle at its 'center'. This is the stable saddle-path, as opposed to the unstable saddle-path, which the marble would then follow if it were slightly disturbed from its position of rest. The stable saddle-path is a source of instability for the same reason that it is very hard to stand an egg on its head—it is very hard to place the marble at a point from which it will roll down to the 'center' of the saddle and not slip off before reaching its precarious point of rest.

8 The theoretical significance of saddle-path instability is of particular relevance in the context of capital theory and in many recent macroeconomic models where one finds saddle-paths at every turn. However, lack of uniqueness and instability, even within the more limited framework of pure exchange, is now recognized as a general and robust result (Ackerman, 2002).

9 Samuelson's concern with the difference between a 'financial dream world' and a full employment equilibrium of the real economy in which all stocks of goods are willingly held is central to the critical comments of Foley (2001) and Petri (2001).

References

Ackerman, F. (2002) Still dead after all these years: interpreting the failure of general equilibrium theory, *Journal of Economic Methodology*, 9, pp. 119–139.

Bharadwaj, K. (1990) Sraffa's return to classical theory, in: K. Bharadwaj and B. Schefold (Eds), *Essays on Piero Sraffa: critical perspectives on the revival of Classical Theory* (London, Unwin Hyman).

Bliss, C. J. (1975) *Capital Theory and the Distribution of Income* (Amsterdam: North-Holland).

Burgstaller, A. (1994) *Property and Prices, Toward a Unified Theory of Value* (Cambridge, Cambridge University Press).

Burgstaller, A. (2001) Some metatheoretical reflections and a reply to critics, *Metroeconomica*, 52, pp. 197–216.

Burmeister, E. (1980) *Capital Theory and Dynamics* (Cambridge, Cambridge University Press).

Champernowne, D. G. (1945) A note on J. v. Neumann's article on 'A model of economic equilibrium', *Review of Economic Studies*, 13, pp. 10–18.

Dore, M., Chakravarty, S. and Goodwin, R. (Eds) (1987) *John von Neumann and Modern Economics* (Oxford, Clarendon Press).

Evans, G. W. and Guesnerie, R. (2003) Coordination on saddle-path solutions: the educative viewpoint—linear univariate models, *Macroeconomic Dynamics*, 7, pp. 42–62.

Fisher, I. (1906) *The Nature of Capital and Income* (New York, Kelley).

Foley, D. K. (2001) Notes on Burgstaller's *Property and Prices, Metroeconomica*, 52, pp. 137–148.

Garegnani, P. (1976) On a change in the notion of equilibrium in recent work on value and distribution, in: M. Brown, K. Sato and P. Zarembka (Eds), *Essays in Modern Capital Theory* (Amsterdam, North-Holland).

Gram, H. N. (2001) Critical comments on André Burgstaller's *Property and Prices, Toward a Unified Theory of Value, Metroeconomica*, 52, pp. 149–61

Hahn, F. H. (1966) Equilibrium dynamics with heterogeneous capital goods, *Quarterly Journal of Economics*, 80, pp. 633–645.

Hahn, F. H. (1982) The neo-Ricardians, *Cambridge Journal of Economics*, 6, 353–374.

Koopmans, T. C. (1964) Economic growth at a maximal rate, *Quarterly Journal of Economics*, 78, pp. 355–94.

Kurz, H. and Salvadori, N. (1995) *Theory of Production, A long-period analysis* (Cambridge, Cambridge University Press).

Leontief, W. W. (1951) *The Structure of the American Economy 1991–1939*, 2nd edn (New York, Oxford University Press).

Neumann, J. von (1945 [1937]) A model of general economic equilibrium, *Review of Economic Studies*, 13, pp. 1–9; Uber ein okonomisches Gleichungssystem und eine Verallgemeinerung des Brouwerschen Fixpunktsatzes, *Ergebnisse eines mathematischen Kolloquiums*, 8, pp. 73–83.

Pasinetti, L. (1977) *Lectures on the Theory of Production* (New York, Columbia University Press).

Pasinetti, L. (1981) *Structural Change and Economic Growth: a theoretical essay on the dynamics of the wealth of nations* (Cambridge, Cambridge University Press).

Petri, F. (2001) Burgstaller on the common core of classical and Walrasian economics, *Metroeco-nomica*, 52, pp. 162–180.

Robbins, L. (1935) *An Essay on the Nature and Significance of Economic Science* (London, Macmillan).

Samuelson, P. A. (1967) Indeterminacy of development in a heterogeneous-capital model with constant saving propensity, in K. Shell (Ed) *Essays on the Theory of Optimal Economic Growth* (Cambridge, MA: MIT Press).

Samuelson, P. A. (1987) A revisionist view of von Neumann's growth model, in M. Dore, S. Chakravarty and R. Goodwin (Eds) *John von Neumann and Modern Economics* (Oxford, Clarendon Press).

Sraffa, P. (1960) *The Production of Commodities by Means of Commodities: prelude to a critique of economic theory* (Cambridge, Cambridge University Press).

Walsh, V. (2000) Smith after Sen, *Review of Political Economy*, 12, pp. 5–25.

Walsh, V. and Gram, H. (1980) *Classical and Neoclassical Theories of General Equilibrium* (New York, Oxford University Press).

7 Walsh on Sen after Putnam

Amartya Sen

Introduction

There may well have been some writing of Vivian Walsh I have read without learning something important. But I cannot readily think of one. The reach and discernment of Walsh's critical analyses, in plentiful evidence in Walsh (1954, 1987, 1994, 1996) and Walsh and Gram (1980), have been a major source of understanding and stimulation for many of us, particularly in comprehending the demands of rational evaluation with an adequate involvement in psychology, ethics, economic allocation, social relations and political responsibility.

I regard myself as particularly fortunate that Vivian Walsh has given such careful and penetrating attention to my work in his new paper, 'Sen after Putnam' (Walsh, 2003), adding greatly to my personal debt to him, which is already large, because of his earlier critiques (Walsh, 1995–1996, 2000), which had made me rethink and reassess my views. As I expected when I received Walsh's new paper, I have benefited greatly, once again, from the insights that Walsh has offered on both the motivation and the content of what I have tried to do, allowing me to see my own limited attempts in a much broader context.

At a personal level too, it is difficult for me to give adequate expression to my appreciation of Vivian Walsh's willingness to take such a deep and involved interest in my work. A great many years ago, I remember an occasion when some of us – all quite young and with much time to fritter away – were trying to persuade a friend, George Akerlof, to come with us to see a light movie (I think it was Danny Kaye's 'Knock on Wood'). Among George's arguments for his refusal to join us in seeing this film was a remarkable reason: 'You see, Amartya, I am not really that interested in other people's personal lives.' While I had to postpone my hope of taking George Akerlof to a movie until a film was made on his *own* personal life (hopefully, not too far off now), I am utterly delighted that Vivian Walsh has been willing to examine my personal intellectual life with such care and attention. I should also take this opportunity to record my enormous debt to Hilary Putnam (2002), not only for the far-reaching understanding that he has provided on the intellectual impediments to achieving the apparently simple goal of a fact-value dichotomy, but also for the light he has thrown on my own work, particularly on *Development as Freedom* (Sen, 1999). Since I had, in that book, silently ignored the exacting demands that allegedly follow directly from the unrestrained power of the fact–value dichotomy, it is also very agreeable – as well as exculpating – for me to see the force of Putnam's reasoning against that dichotomy.

Of the various things I have learned from Walsh's contextual re-examination, I will comment here on only a couple. They may not be the most important of the points to emerge from Walsh's analysis (there are so many departures in his analysis that it would be hard to construct a linear order of their respective significance), but the particular points to be taken up here certainly have had an immediate impact on my ability to think clearly about the appropriate framework for assessing some of my efforts in the areas with which Walsh has been particularly concerned. In contrast, Walsh's investigation of the general bearing and continuing relevance of classical economics, which influences his characterization and assessment of the two phases of its revival in contemporary economics, while potentially perhaps the weightiest of Walsh's conclusions, will call for a much more extensive examination than can be presented here. For one thing, I shall have to think more on those historical and interpretational issues, helped by Walsh's guided tour.

Entanglement and rich description

The first point I want to comment on is Vivian Walsh's discussion of my attempt to argue for the value of 'rich description'. Walsh (2004) rightly notes that I was led in that particular direction by my teacher Maurice Dobb, through both our conversations and his work (see Dobb, 1937, 1955). Dobb had seen the significance of the labour theory of value, as developed by Smith, Ricardo and Marx, not mainly in terms of prediction, nor primarily in terms of its direct ethical implications, but in the richness of the description of the world of work, production and exchange that it provides. I found that argument persuasive, and also argued that the need for richer description is quite pervasive in the subject of economics, despite the minimalist inclinations of contemporary economics. Indeed, 'rich description' is a general directional priority that, I argue, is both important and badly neglected in contemporary economics.

Vivian Walsh is entirely supportive of the thesis of priority, but there is an interesting issue as to what kind of an object a 'rich description' really is. In Walsh (2002), he had already argued that 'it is not, I believe, historically improper to use the present-day philosophical concept of the 'entanglement' of facts and values for this key property of classical political economy in its philosophically richest manifestation, namely in Adam Smith' (Walsh, 2002, p. 9). In his more recent essay, Walsh (2004) provides a much more extensive defence of this claim; that is, to see a rich description as a manifestation of a description that does not shun entanglement of facts and values. In the process, Walsh also links this issue with the philosophical writings not only – and most importantly – of Hilary Putnam (2002), but also of Iris Murdoch, Morton White and, of course, John Dewey. This is certainly an extremely illuminating way of seeing the demands of enriching descriptive exercises by not avoiding value entanglement and paying specific attention to the fact that the interest in many descriptions lies precisely in the intimate connections with valuational issues.

All this is entirely persuasive to me. I am, however, left with the question as to whether Maurice Dobb was mistaken in seeing the labour theory of value and related descriptions as being not specifically ethical (in addition to not being primarily predictive). I think the important point to note here is that ethical values are not the only kind of values, and the significance that we may be inclined to attach to who is labouring away in producing goods is not just ethical (even though they do have ethical bearing as well). We can have many different reasons for seeking particular knowledge, and while ethical concerns often are among these reasons, there can be other types of reasons as well.

I may perhaps be allowed to take the liberty of using an illustration I had employed in Sen (1982, p. 441):

> Consider the statement 'Michelangelo produced the statue of David.' There is an obvious sense in which this would be accepted as a realistic description, despite its being informationally selective and the selection process not being primarily motivated by prediction or prescription. The production process in making the statue actually involved not merely Michelangelo, but his helpers, a huge block of stone, chisels, scaffoldings, etc., but the description quoted focuses on Michelangelo only as the most relevant bit of information. Note that the discrimination cannot be based on any marginal productivity consideration in the usual neoclassical sense. Without Michelangelo no statue, but without stone, no statue either! . . . The selection process involves other motivations, in particular, that of capturing the source of the imagination displayed in the statue. The labour theory of value, in its descriptive interpretation, shows a similar – but not the same – type of discrimination, focusing – in this case – on the human effort directly and indirectly involved in the process of production and exchange of commodities.

It is, of course, a kind of valuation to be interested in human imagination or human effort over other features that could have figured in the description, but it would be a mistake to reduce the reach of that valuation to mainly ethical or prescriptive interest. What Walsh's – and obviously Putnam's – analyses, in my interpretation, demand is the need to distinguish (but not, I hasten to add, dichotomize) different types of values that may be 'entangled' in the selection process involved in relevant and rich description. There is no real conflict between Dobb's claims and Walsh's, but there is a need for some elaboration here, particularly since many economists are evidently tempted to see values mainly in ethical terms. The interest in knowing who made the statue of David may not be geared only towards arriving at a recommendation about who should be paid for it, and may not even be entirely captured by the ethics of who should receive credit for the work. Those ethical concerns may fit well into the epistemology of entangled description, but there can be other interests underlying our inquisitiveness – and in the values involved in it – than just our implicit ethical interest.

Convention and entanglement

In another important passage, Vivian Walsh observes: 'As for common sense, the economist who hankers after some of this after recent invasions of the field by exotic philosophical imports will find that in fact Putnam is a true friend of common sense.' Elsewhere Walsh argues that 'while the phrase "entanglement of fact and value" is a convenient shorthand, what we are typically dealing with (as Putnam makes clear) is a *triple* entanglement: of fact, convention and value.' The role that an understanding of conventions plays in making sense of economic inquiries is particularly worth emphasizing. The understanding that Michelangelo 'made' the statue of David may reflect our values about what we have reason to want to know, but it is the common understanding of such reasons that make our communication on such subjects (not just on sculpture, but also on real income, poverty, inequality, in addition to theories of value) possible and productive.

In a recent essay, called 'Elements of a Theory of Human Rights' (Sen, 2004), I have tried to discuss what is involved in the assertion and use of human rights and the role of public discussion and mutual understanding that makes sense of the very concept of human rights, which is of course a heavily 'entangled' notion. One of my main points there is the possibility that this reasoning can extend beyond the borders of a country and can, therefore, take a less parochial form than is sometimes assumed, to some extent even by as great a thinker as John Rawls, particularly in his *The Law of Peoples* (Rawls, 1999). Without going into that particular issue here, which has relevance for the universalist versus relativist understanding of human rights, I would like to take this occasion to emphasize how extensive a role reasoned convention plays in our communications on subjects of this kind.

Consider the demand that justice should not only be done, but must also be 'seen to be done' – an admonition that has received ringing endorsement and approving reiteration right from the time it was first uttered by Lord Hewart, in 1923 (in 'Rex v. Sussex Justices'), articulating an insistence that justice 'should manifestly and undoubtedly be seen to be done.' It is not, in fact, hard to guess some of the reasons for attaching importance to the need for a decision to be *seen* to be just. For one thing, the administration of justice can, in general, be more effective if judges are seen to be doing a good job, rather than botching things up. Indeed, disbelief in the justice and sagacity of judgments made by the legal establishment can be generally destabilizing for the polity.

These are important enough grounds for going towards Hewart's principle. And yet it is hard to dismiss the suspicion that something more than instrumental importance of the visibility of justice is involved in Lord Hewart's maxim. If others – not charged with dispensing justice – cannot see that a judgment is, in fact, just, then not only its implementability and instrumental use, but even its *correctness*, would seem to be called into question. There has to be a deeper connection between veracity and visibility in matters of justice.

It would, of course, be odd to claim that some judgment is just, precisely 'because' – exactly 'for the reason' that – most people think it to be just. Justice cannot, without some kind of a categorical metamorphosis, be foundationally only a matter of approval by others. It is plausible to think that the connections relate, in one way or another, to some understanding of the objectivity of justice, and to the importance of others being able to see actual justice in a putative claim to justice. This need not require that everyone must share exactly the same sense of justice, or that all must endorse precisely the same principles of justice. But there has to be some shared comprehension of the sense in which justice is being pursued and an understanding that this sense is not altogether implausible (this does not foreclose the possibility that someone who shares that understanding, including an agreement on the minimal plausibility of the principles involved, can still think that the sense of justice that is being invoked can possibly be bettered). The entangled discernment of justice can both invoke established convention and valuational plausibility.[1]

Vivian Walsh and Hilary Putnam have presented persuasive arguments in favour of the '*triple* entanglement: of fact, convention and value.' I will not try to supplement those general arguments, but will confine myself here to telling a story – a made-up story – which has a bearing on the triple entanglement.

Brenda was walking along the Embankment, quietly enjoying the smooth flowing Thames, thinking about what she had just learned in her class on 'the methodology of social science', in particular why value judgements are both altogether distinct from facts and could not possibly be derived from facts. Her train of engaging thought was pleasantly interrupted when Brenda ran into her old friend Ed who is a meteorologist at the Met Office. 'What a nice day, Ed,' said Brenda, 'but tell me also what kind of a day are you predicting for tomorrow?' 'Much better than today,' Ed answered, looking at the half-cloudy sky. 'In fact,' Ed added, 'marvellously good.' Brenda went home happy. But next morning when she saw through her window a very dark day, with massive rain, messy sleet, and blinding fog, Brenda called up Ed: 'Why did you mislead me? Or did you just get the forecast wrong? Why did you say last evening that the weather today would be good – marvellously good – much better than yesterday?'

'But it *is*, I think, a marvellously good day,' said Ed. 'What better can you ask for than the lovely fog, the elegant darkness, the bracing cold rain, and the challenging slippery sleet? I did not get my forecast wrong – only your value judgements are quite different from mine.' 'But Ed,' Brenda protested, 'just look outside – you can *see* it is simply a nasty day. Ask anyone!' 'How can looking help, since it is a valuational issue, not resolvable by factual observation?' replied Ed. 'Also, how can talking with other people possibly help to resolve our differences? You must understand that "nasty", "good", "better" are normative terms – not matters of fact, nor matters of observation. Dear, dear, Brenda, you really must learn some philosophy, a great subject – very popular at the Met Office.'

Brenda pondered on the fact that even though 'good', 'nasty' and 'better' are evaluative terms, it is not hard to understand why they are so firmly linked to things one can see. It is not only that people by and large agree on these uses, but also understand well enough why agreements emerge so easily on such subjects – what reasons make us take certain weather conditions to be better than others.

The rules connect with our experiences and priorities, and they are reasonably obvious rules to appreciate given the kind of creatures we human beings are (for example, how adversely affected – physically and mentally – we typically are by slipperiness, messiness, darkness, or extremes of temperatures). Brenda wanted to tell all this to Ed, but he had hung up.

As it happens, Brenda is forced again to get into ethics and justice the next day. When she calls Tom – another friend of hers – she tells him about her experience with Ed. At this, Tom fumes and says, 'Ed has behaved very badly, Brenda. How irresponsible of him! Justice requires that Ed should be killed without further ado.' 'You are joking, of course,' says Brenda. 'No, no,' replies Tom, 'people like Ed make me very angry. I think it is because the society is so tolerant of bad behaviour that homeland security has become so difficult to manage. I know, of course, that we cannot in fact kill Ed, given the way the laws stand. But I must insist that given his behaviour Ed deserves to be killed forthwith and people should jubilate if he were to be actually executed.' Brenda has now a different problem to deal with, and says, 'But Tom, we don't kill people forthwith – at least not on this side of the Atlantic – nor jubilate at execution. But really, Ed's was a very minor fault, if fault indeed it was. Surely Tom, you too, like others, should be able to see that justice cannot possibly demand that Ed be killed on this trivial ground!'

It is now Tom's turn, the well-trained economist that he is, to lecture Brenda that they are dealing with an evaluative problem; there is no question of objectivity here; and his own views are 'just as good' as Brenda's. Since Tom is very fond of Brenda, he does not want to go on quarrelling with her, and only notes that on this evaluative question (to wit, who should be executed and for what reason), he and Brenda simply must differ. 'Brenda, my silly love!' Tom says with his usual gallantry. 'On this valuational matter, let us agree to disagree. There is no point in considering how it appears to others. You are entitled to your opinion, I am entitled to mine – and all others are entitled to theirs.' Brenda wants to respond very loudly to Tom's lofty imposition of trace, but meanwhile Tom has hung up.

Clearly, the most immediate conclusion to emerge from this story is that Brenda needs some new friends. But perhaps there is also a less immediate issue here about the need to take note of 'triple entanglements', which throws some light on Brenda's problems with her philosopher friend at the Met Office and her economist friend, freely distributing values as well as punishments. All this will come as no surprise at all to readers of Putnam and Walsh, but it is important to see that the reach of their contentions goes well beyond academic studies. Entanglement is a general issue in social living, not just a special concern in economics and philosophy. We are dealing here with some of the most sweeping connections that influence our thoughts, understanding and communication.

I end by expressing again my happiness and appreciation that Hilary Putnam and Vivian Walsh have taken such a powerfully illuminating interest in my work and speculations. I conclude on that note of entangled indebtedness.

Note

1 It is, thus, possible to distinguish between two distinct lines of disputation that justice is being done:
  (1) the observable (or 'seeable') demands of the established rules of justice are not fulfilled, and
  (2) the established rules of justice are not at all plausible.

References

Dobb, M. H. (1937) *Political Economy and Capitalism* (London: Routledge).

Dobb, M. H. (1955) *On Economic Theory and Socialism* (London: Routledge).

Putnam, H. (2002) *The Collapse of the Fact/Value Dichotomy and Other Essays* (Cambridge, MA: Harvard University Press).

Rawls, J. (1999) *The Law of Peoples* (Cambridge, MA: Harvard University Press). Sen, A. K. (1982) *Choice, Welfare and Measurement* (Oxford: Blackwell [reprinted Cambridge, MA: Harvard University Press, 1997]).

Sen, A. K. (2004) Elements of a theory of human rights, *Philosophy and Public Affairs*, 32 (4), pp. 315–356.

Walsh, V. C. (1954) The theory of the good will, *Cambridge Journal, 1*, pp. 627–637.

Walsh, V. C. (1987) Philosophy and economics, in. J. Eatwell, M. Milgate & P. Newman (Eds) *The New Palgrave: A Dictionary of Economics*, Vol. 3, pp. 861–869 (London: Macmillan).

Walsh, V. C. (1994) Rationality as Self-interest versus Rationality as Present Aims, *American Economic Review*, 84, pp. 401–405.

Walsh, V. C. (1995–1996) Amartya Sen on inequality, capabilities and needs, *Science and Society*, 59, pp. 556–569.

Walsh, V. C. (1996) *Rationality, Allocation and Reproduction* (Oxford: Clarendon Press).

Walsh, V. C. (2000) Smith after Sen, *Review of Political Economy*, 12, pp. 5–25.

Walsh, V. C. (2003) Sen after Putnam, *Review of Political Economy*, 15, pp. 315–394.

Walsh, V. C. and Gram, H. (1980) *Classical and Neoclassical Theories of General Equilibrium* (New York: Oxford University Press).

8 Facts, theories, values and destitution in the works of Sir Partha Dasgupta

Hilary Putnam and Vivian Walsh

But the lack of concern about the poor was not just a matter of views of markets and government, views that said that markets would take care of everything and government would only make matters worse; *it was also a matter of values*.

(Joseph Stiglitz, 2003, pp. 85–86; emphasis added)

Even if prices were to be got right in a poor economy, the market mechanism, unless acting upon a reasonable distribution of productive assets, can be relied upon to be *an unmitigated disaster*.

(Partha Dasgupta, 1993, p. 498; emphasis added)

The passages quoted above rest upon facts about the poor, theoretical advances in economics, and humane values. They exemplify what we call a *triple entanglement* of facts, theory, and values.[1] It is to the credit of the economics profession that it contains people who write as Stiglitz and Dasgupta do. They are by no means a tiny minority. But it would be unwise to claim that they are a majority.

We have argued for many years now that all economics (and indeed all science) *is* a triple entanglement. But it is far from being the case that all economics *clearly displays* this, and some economics allegedly devoted to the world's poor may be sailing under false colors. Thus, we are warned by Jagdish Bhagwati (2004, p. 163) 'even altruistic institutions will occasionally be run by men whose private ambitions, rather than social good, are the primary determinants of their policies.' Indeed, one can easily see why some economists, whose services are paid for by corporate or government interests (or by the substantial intersection of these sets) might wish to revive the old logical positivist claim that values can be excluded from all scientific work.

However, Dasgupta has long been well aware that entanglement was unavoidable. He cites Putnam (1981, 1989), and tells us that entanglement 'will influence the way I will throughout argue in this book' (Dasgupta, 1993, p. 6). And he offers as an example what is perhaps the *leitmotiv* of his whole book: the concept of *destitution*: 'The 'descriptive' and 'evaluative' components of concepts like destitution cannot be separated. They are entangled' (Dasgupta, 1993, p. 7). The reader may imagine our surprise on reading his recent article (Dasgupta, 2005, pp. 221–278).[2] Now he claims that 'in professional debates on social policy, economists speak or write as though they agree on values but differ on their reading of facts' (Dasgupta, 2005, p. 221). Clearly we must begin by trying to clarify where we, and Dasgupta, respectively stand on the relations of facts and values.

Dasgupta's views on facts, theories, and values; and Putnam's

On the second page of his recent paper, Dasgupta (2005, p. 222) quotes Putnam's (1993, p. 146) rhetorical question, 'When and where did a Nazi and an anti-Nazi, a communist and a social democrat, a fundamentalist and a liberal . . . agree on the facts?' He continues: 'The point Putnam was making was that facts can be as subject to dispute as are values, in part because facts and values are often entangled. In this paper I make a different but stronger claim: *in professional debates on social policy, economists speak or write as though they agree on values but differ on their reading of facts.*'

This first remark of Dasgupta's is difficult to interpret, for several reasons.

In logic, if A is a 'stronger claim' than B, then A implies B. Thus, by referring to his claim as 'stronger' than Putnam's, Dasgupta seems to say that he *endorses* the claim that 'facts and values are often entangled' (and hence, as explained in Putnam, 2002, the idea of a 'fact/value dichotomy' is deeply confused). But (1) Dasgupta's claim has no such logical relation to Putnam's. Dasgupta's is an empirical claim about how economists 'speak or write' and Putnam's is a logical claim about the unclarity and confusion in both the supposed 'fact/value dichotomy' and the arguments for it, and neither claim either implies or is implied by the other; (2) if we suppose, as much of his paper suggests we should, that his real claim is not that economists 'speak or write' *as if* this were so, but that they do in fact agree on values but differ on their reading of facts, *that* claim is not 'stronger' than Putnam's, but inconsistent with the latter. For to say that economists agree on values but differ on their reading of facts is to *assume* a clear distinction between values and 'readings of facts', and Putnam's claim was that the distinction is unclear. Perhaps this was just careless on Dasgupta's part. In any case, it is clear from Dasgupta's paper as a whole that he does not understand the issue of entanglement of fact and value, and so we must begin by explaining it.

The entanglement of fact, theory and value

Dasgupta lists three publications by Putnam (1990, 2002, 2003) that describe two major ways in which 'facts' and 'values' become entangled.

First, even in the so-called hard sciences, methodological disputes frequently involve what Putnam called 'epistemic values'—coherence, simplicity, the 'beauty' of a theory (Dirac's term) or its 'inner perfection' (Einstein's term), as well as the familiar values of successful prediction. As Putnam (2002, p. 142) pointed out:

An example in this connection is the following: both Einstein's theory of gravitation and Alfred North Whitehead's 1922 theory (of which very few people have ever heard) agreed with Special Relativity, and both predicted the familiar phenomena of the deflection of light by gravitation, the non-Newtonian character of the orbit of Mercury, the exact orbit of the Moon, etc. Yet Einstein's theory was accepted and Whitehead's theory was rejected fifty years before anyone thought of an observation that would decide between the two.[3] A great number of theories must be rejected on non-observational grounds, for the rule 'Test every theory that occurs to anyone' is impossible to follow.

In short, judgments of coherence, simplicity, etc, are presupposed by physical science. Yet coherence and simplicity and the like are *values*. Indeed, each and every one of the familiar arguments for relativism (or radical contextualism) in ethics could be repeated without the slightest alteration in connection with these epistemic values; the argument that ethical values are metaphysically 'queer' (because, *inter alia*, we do not have a sense organ for detecting 'goodness') could be modified to read 'epistemic values are ontologically queer (because we do not have a sense organ for detecting simplicity and coherence)'; the familiar arguments for relativism or non-cognitivism from the disagreements between cultures concerning values (arguments which are often driven by the fashionable, but we believe wholly untenable, pictures of different cultures as 'incommensurable') could be modified to read that there are disagreements between cultures concerning what beliefs are more 'coherent', 'plausible', 'simpler as accounts of the facts', etc; and in both the case of ethics and the case of science there are those who would say that when cultures disagree, saying that one side is objectively right is mere rhetoric. Thus, even when the first-order judgments in dispute are the paradigmatic cases of the 'factual' in our time—the judgments of theoretical physics—the decision as to their warranted assertability involves value choices. Such choices are not necessarily *ethical* value choices, of course; but disagreements about these epistemic values in politics are intricately connected to disagreements in ethical values, as Putnam's example of 'a Nazi and an anti-Nazi, a communist and a social democrat, a fundamentalist and a liberal' was meant to illustrate. And we do not suppose that Dasgupta would want to deny that economists' views are entangled with their politics—or would he? It is because he quoted this passage with apparent approval that we are led to conclude that he missed the point—and with it, the whole issue of entanglement became invisible to him.

A second type of entanglement arises from the fact that the fact/value dichotomy was originally the legacy of David Hume, as Putnam (2002, pp. 7–27) explains, but neither Hume nor his logical positivist successors in the twentieth century were able to provide a tenable account of what a 'fact' was, or of what sorts of statements failed to describe 'facts' and why they so failed. (Not only ethical statements, but also statements of mathematics, statements of metaphysics, and even—in one publication of Carnap (1934)—statements of epistemology, were denied the status of 'fact', although mathematical statements, unlike the others, were held to be 'analytic', that is true by virtue of linguistic conventions, and therefore legitimate parts of the language of science.)

The logical positivists followed Hume quite closely. For Hume, a fact had to be something one could have a sense impression of. For the positivists, in the Vienna circle period, 'facts' had to be directly observable—they had to be either about 'sense data' or else about 'observable things' and 'observable properties' of those observable things. But this notion of 'fact' left such terms as 'bacteria', 'electric current', 'proton', or 'gene' without factual content!—something the positivists themselves came to find intolerable. At first, they tried to find some way to 'reduce' these 'theoretical terms', as they called them, to other terms referring to observable properties ('observation terms'), but by 1939 Carnap himself had given up on this project.[4]

Even then the positivists continued to hold that the 'empirical content' of any meaningful factual statement could be given by a set of statements about observables. In effect, a dichotomy between facts and theories (with theories failing the positivist test of 'empirical significance' unless and until they could be 'reduced' to claims about observable facts) was replaced by a dichotomy between the surface semantics of scientific theories, according to which, for example, 'Electrons are negatively charged' is a statement about unobservable particles, and the properly analyzed 'empirical content' of those theories, according to which 'Electrons are negatively charged' is really a statement about 'observable things'. This new dichotomy presupposed, however, that the 'empirical content' of scientific theories could be parceled out among the individual sentences of those theories one by one: otherwise talk of *the* empirical significance of any given *sentence* in the language of science could make no sense. In his celebrated paper 'Two dogmas of empiricism,' Quine (1950) decisively exploded this new dichotomy (which he characterized as 'reductionism' and as the 'second dogma' of empiricism—the 'first dogma' being the belief in an analytic/synthetic or empirical fact/convention distinction, with mathematics on the 'analytic' or 'conventional' side). In sum, Quine showed that theories and observable facts are entangled (just as Putnam argued, values and facts are entangled).

The logical empiricists' constant modifications of their 'criterion of empirical significance' (revisions forced as one inadequacy after another became apparent), combined with Quine's destruction of their notion of the 'empirical content' of individual theoretical statements, left them with only a holistic notion of empirical significance—a notion that was not applicable to individual sentences, but only to the system of scientific assertions as a whole. Quine (1963, p. 406) summarized this holistic conception in the concluding paragraph of another famous paper, when he wrote: 'The lore of our fathers is a fabric of sentences . . . it is a pale grey lore, black with fact and white with convention. But I have found no substantial reason for concluding that there are any quite black threads in it, or any white ones.' As Walsh (1987, p. 862) put it: 'To borrow and adapt Quine's vivid image, if a theory may be black with fact and white with convention, it might well (as far as logical empiricism could tell) be red with values. Since for them confirmation or falsification had to be a property of a theory *as a whole*, they had no way of unraveling this whole cloth.' In time, it turned out that the positivists had no tenable way of demarcating either the analytic from the synthetic or the factual from the evaluative![5]

Moreover, as Putnam (2002, pp. 28–45) explains, once we begin to examine the notion of a 'fact' without the logical positivist blinders just described, we see that the very vocabulary in which we describe human facts, either in the social sciences or in literature or in daily speech, frequently fails to be factorable into separate and distinct 'factual' and 'evaluative' components. The term 'well-being' is a case in point.

Perhaps Dasgupta does not deny any of this. Perhaps his reply to us is that all this does not matter, because economists all have good values. None of them, for example, would say that someone who is starving enjoys 'well-being'. That is true enough. But is that enough to constitute 'agreement on values'? No one would call a quaking coward 'courageous', either, but as Plato taught us, there is more to the notion of courage than not being overcome by fear; and similarly there is much more to well-being than not starving. But it is time to look at a dispute that Dasgupta himself offers as a clear case of economists disagreeing about facts and not about values. He writes:

> In their influential World Bank monograph on the incidence of undernourishment in poor countries, Reutlinger and Pellekaan wrote, 'long run economic growth is often slowed by widespread chronic food insecurity. People who lack energy are ill-equipped to take advantage of opportunities for increasing their productivity and output. That is why policymakers in some countries may want to consider interventions that speed up food security for the groups worst affected without waiting for the general effect of long-run growth.'
>
> Then there are economists who advocate policies based upon an opposite causal mechanism, such as the one in World Bank (1986: 7): 'The best policies for alleviating malnutrition and poverty are those which increase growth and the competitiveness of the economy, for a growing and competitive economy facilitates a more even distribution of human capital and ensures higher incomes for the poor. Progress in the battle against malnutrition and poverty can be sustained if, and only if, there is satisfactory economic growth.'
>
> There doesn't appear to me to be a conflict of values here. Rather, it reads as though there is a disagreement over the most effective means for eliminating destitution.
>
> (2005, p. 272)

Dasgupta closes by saying 'That the publications are from the same institution and the same year should not cause surprise: we are all still woefully ignorant of the ways in which human societies and Nature respond to policies' (2005, p. 272).

Well, there is 'ignorance' and there is what Michelle Moody-Adams (using a phrase of Aquinas's) calls 'affected ignorance'.[6] The World Bank (1986) Report affects not to know that not every economy can be transformed into a 'growing and competitive one' in the near (or even the foreseeable) future; another thing they affect not to know is that prosperity does not always 'trickle down' in the form of 'higher incomes for the poor'; and a third thing they affect not to know is that there is no obvious and universal incompatibility between aiming at 'satisfactory economic growth' in the long term and taking immediate steps to alleviate the 'widespread chronic food insecurity.' Indeed, this last point (that there is no logical incompatibility here) is something Dasgupta himself overlooks. Nevertheless, he is right to cite this as a 'disagreement'—for, even if the *words* of World Bank (1986) are not *logically* incompatible with the *words* of Reutlinger and Pellekaan (1986), it is clear to any intelligent reader that the *values* of World Bank (1986) are profoundly different from the values of Reutlinger and Pellekaan (1986), and for that matter, the values of Dasgupta (1993).

Why do we say this? Because simply assuming that the sort of measures Reutlinger and Pellekaan urge upon us are *incompatible* with 'increasing growth and competitiveness of the economy'[7] is no argument at all—rather it is a sound-bite. And when world-class economists resort to sound-bites, one can be sure that deeply held values are involved.

Recall, once again, that early in his essay Dasgupta wrote 'The point Putnam was making was that facts can be as subject to dispute as are values, in part because facts and values are often entangled.' Here the reader seems to be meant to gather that Dasgupta *agrees* with the thrust of Putnam's rhetorical question that he quoted, namely, 'When and where did a Nazi and an anti-Nazi, a communist and a social democrat, a fundamentalist and a liberal . . . agree on the facts?' And he understood—or seemed to understand—on the second page of his essay that the social democrats' and the fundamentalists' 'facts' and their 'values' are deeply entangled. But on the last page of the same essay he is blind to the way in which the 'disagreement' between his two quotations is exactly of the same entangled character—indeed, he explicitly *denies* that this is a case of entanglement!

A different issue

When Dasgupta reports another view of Putnam's he seriously distorts it. This happens because he wants to defend the view that 'social well-being is a scalar' (p. 237). Amartya Sen and Putnam (p. 247) are listed as claiming that 'to imagine that choices are made on the basis of an underlying ordering is to misconceive personhood.' Already, in this sweeping summary of our views, the fact that we insist that *partial orderings* are both possible and valuable is simply not mentioned. One would hardly guess that it is only the idea that all choices are based on a pre-given complete ordering that we regard as 'misconceiving personhood'. And then he goes on to give 'tragic choices' as our concern, and to say that 'we are not offered reasons why one cannot rank tragic choices'. But tragic choices are not by any means the only reason Sen thinks we must be content with partial orderings, and they were not even *mentioned* in Putnam's chapter on partial orderings. (Putnam used an *existential* choice—between a hedonistic life and a life of public service—as his example, and we would hardly describe this choice as 'tragic').

More important, it is just false that 'we are not offered reasons' in that chapter. The whole chapter is devoted to explaining why, if the choices are, for example, 'a hedonistic life freely chosen by Jane' and 'a life of public service—e.g., in *Doctors Without Borders*—freely chosen by Jane', no rank ordering is possible prior to the choice itself. Dasgupta may not agree with Putnam's reasons, but to say Putnam didn't offer any is a strange mistake.

Values expressed in formal languages

The fact that economics is a mathematical science may be responsible for some of the misunderstandings Dasgupta feels he has suffered. Ethicists and public intellectuals must recognize the fact that important parts of economics have *required* the use of a formal mathematical language. And economists in return must strive to find the most minimally formal guise to present their results when addressing a non-specialist audience. In his recent books, Dasgupta (1993, 2001) presents his arguments concerning the deeply serious issues of poverty and destitution with the minimum formalism; and *his* mathematical equipment is chosen for honest work, not for fashion and display, as has been the case with some.

Stiglitz, who wanted to reach a mass audience, referred in only a *single note* (Stiglitz, 2003, p. 261) to the formal results that underlay his attack on the market fundamentalism of Washington-consensus economists.[8] Once he presented the real-world implications of this research in a natural language, vividly illustrated by examples of the disastrous results of market fundamentalism for poor countries, the values involved were visible for all to see.

Part of the problem may be that, in present-day society, people still retain a view of science that makes sense only when supported by the arguments of logical positivism: we still *expect* scientific statements to be value free. People are not used to being offered pieces of mathematical moral philosophy.

Dasgupta (2005, p. 221) tells us that a number of ethicists have concluded 'that modern economics must be an ethical desert.' Well, it could be that they are assuming (mistakenly) that pages of mathematics surely cannot be making value claims. But when economists are developing a new theory they are entitled to use their formal language and not pause to offer natural language translations until they are sure what results they can really claim to be sound. So in this phase of their work there may be no evidence of values that would be *visible* to anyone not *at home* in the mathematical language involved. In an unfamiliar mathematical language, like an unfamiliar foreign language, subtle inflections are lost.

We are not arguing for an *unlimited* license for economists to hunt *any* mathematical fox totally without regard for where it takes them—high theory does have its costs! Paul Samuelson (1983, p. xix), no foe of mathematical economics, wisely observed that: 'more can be less. Much of mathematical economics in the 1950s gained in elegance over poor old Pareto and Edward Chamberlin. But the fine garments sometimes achieved fit only by chopping off some real arms and legs. The theory of cones, polyhedra, and convex sets made possible "elementary" theorems and lemmas. But they seduced economists away from the phenomena of increasing returns to scale and nonconvex technology that lie at the heart of oligopoly problems and many real-world maximizing assignments. Easy victories over a science's wrong opponents are hollow victories—at least almost always.'

The reader of Dasgupta's books will see that the sort of mathematical hubris which Samuelson is laughing at is *not* a characteristic of the work of Dasgupta—it was, however, a characteristic of some work done in the 1950s and later (to which Samuelson is referring), and which underlies the market fundamentalist orthodoxy of the Washington-consensus economists. We suggest that possibly Dasgupta might do well to disassociate his position a little more obviously from this tradition, as, after all, Stiglitz has done. Meanwhile, we wish it to be clear that we do not see Dasgupta as a *natural* opponent. In a world (and a country) whose economists are better known for their labors to make the new rich richer than for any preoccupation with the poor and destitute, we see Dasgupta as someone we would always expect to find with those who (like Sen) have consistently supported the claims of the poor.

Nor are we any happier with some of Dasgupta's critics! Had they read his recent article (2005), and nothing else of his work, we might understand them somewhat. But if they read him at all they were reading earlier work which we believe to be admirable. Fortunately, part of the problem can, we believe, be attributed to misunderstanding. Until the issues over globalization drove major economists like Stiglitz to write deliberately for a wide audience, the economists who were *most visible* to ethicists and public intellectuals *supported* the Washington consensus. And we doubt if any criticism of these economists by ethicists or public intellectuals can compete with the severity of the comments that have now been made by leading *economists* on just those champions of the Washington consensus.

Dasgupta on Bergson–Samuelson welfare theory

To clear the ground of certain confusions concerning economic welfare theory and values, we need to clarify certain matters which arise from Dasgupta's appeal to the Bergson–Samuelson analysis of welfare economics. He tells us right at the beginning that 'Ethics has taken a back seat in modern economics not because contemporary economists are wedded to a 'value-free' enterprise, but because the ethical foundations of the subject were constructed over five decades ago and are now regarded to be a settled matter' (2005, pp. 221f.). He makes it perfectly clear what these 'ethical foundations' are in his eyes: he is referring to the fact that 'over a half century ago (Bergson) Burk (1938) and Samuelson (1947) established the foundation of policy evaluation on a broad, ethical structure' (2005, p. 226).

Now in choosing to stress that the position upon which he depends truly begins as early as 1938, with Bergson's youthful paper, Dasgupta is following the view taken by Samuelson (who did most to develop and establish the Bergson argument in later years). As Samuelson observes, in the first edition of his *Foundations of Economic Analysis* ([1947], 1983, p. ix) '[t]he reader will note my dependence upon the sterling contribution to Welfare Economics of Professor Abram Bergson.'

He adds that Bergson 'is the first who understands the contributions of all previous contributors, and who is able to form a synthesis of them. In addition, he is the first to develop explicitly the notion of an ordinal social welfare function in terms of which all the various schools of thought can be interpreted, and in terms of which they for the first time assume significance . . . The analysis that follows is simply an enlargement and development of his important work' (Samuelson, [1947], 1983, p. 219).

Given then, that the Bergson–Samuelson analysis existed in its essentials since 1938, and that the arguments of Lord Robbins (1935, 1938) concerning economics and values were published at roughly the same time, we are somewhat puzzled by Dasgupta's dismissal of these works by Robbins simply on the grounds that 'Robbins wrote over 70 years ago, and the discipline I know to be economics has moved on since then' (2005, p. 225).

Our puzzlement is increased by the fact that the work of Bergson and Samuelson was undertaken in order to *meet* and *avoid violating* precisely Robbins's critique of the older welfare economics. Robbins and Bergson–Samuelson go together like a horse and carriage. Both Bergson (1938) and Samuelson [1947] make this clear. Bergson (1938, p. 323), for example, tells us that:

> In general, any set of value propositions which is sufficient for the evaluation of all alternatives may be introduced, and for each of these sets of propositions there corresponds a maximum position. The number of sets is infinite, and in any particular case the selection of one of them must be determined by its compatibility with the values prevailing in the community the welfare of which is being studied. For only if the welfare principles are based upon prevailing values, can they be relevant to the activity of the community in question.

He adds in a note: 'This conception of the basis for the welfare principles should meet Professor Robbins's requirement that the economist take the values of the community as data' (Bergson, 1938, p. 323, note 2).

Samuelson, once again, strongly endorses this interpretation by Bergson of what this welfare theory essays and of what it *avoids*: 'It is fashionable for the modern economist to insist that ethical value judgments have no place in scientific analysis. Professor Robbins in particular has insisted upon this point, and today it is customary to make a distinction between the pure analysis of Robbins *qua* economist and his propaganda, condemnations, and policy recommendations *qua* citizen. In practice, if pushed to extremes, this somewhat schizophrenic rule becomes difficult to adhere to, and it leads to rather tedious circumlocutions. *But in essence Robbins is undoubtedly correct*' (Samuelson, [1947], 1983, pp. 219–220; emphasis added).

He adds that 'it is not valid to conclude from this that there is no room in economics for what goes under the name of 'welfare economics'. It is a legitimate exercise of economic analysis to examine the consequences of various value judgments, whether or not they are shared by the theorist, just as the study of comparative ethics is itself a science like any other branch of anthropology . . . It is only fair to point out, however, *that the theorems enunciated under the heading of welfare economics are not meaningful propositions or hypotheses in the technical sense. For they represent the deductive implications of assumptions which are not themselves meaningful refutable hypotheses about reality*' (Samuelson, [1947], 1983, pp. 220–221; emphasis added).

It will be clear to readers that Samuelson was adopting the logical positivist position on facts and values, and that this position arguably lies behind part of his keen interest in Bergson's contribution. Bergson, after all, had demonstrated that there was a way to *sail around* the obstacle which Robbins' position represented. Thus, Bergson's welfare theory elegantly defined the limits of what an economist could do *without* violating the logical positivist constraints imposed by Robbins. As long as neoclassical economics did not explicitly reject logical positivism, this was clearly the policy to adopt for any neoclassical economist of humane sentiments—which Samuelson, notably, always was. But logical positivism, as a philosophy of mathematics or of science, fell largely as a result of the work of Quine; and the work of Putnam has shown that the fact/value dichotomy cannot survive the fall of the fact/theory dichotomy. When entanglement is an essential trait of the hard sciences, why should a social science like economics expect to stand aloof from it? Why should it even *want* to try?

When one reads the work of economists who cling to the Robbinsian position, relying on the Bergson–Samuelson tradition to support their limited use of values, their major motive becomes clear. It seems that they are largely driven by a fear of relativism. That they can discover real hard facts which are the case, and prove rigorous theorems, are (as is right and proper) precious to them. They fear that if values invade the very core of their subject, its scientific status is fatally compromised. But what they have to accept is *fallibilism*. not relativism, and they surely cannot expect to be more immune to entanglement than physics or mathematics!

This glance at the Bergson–Samuelson tradition, however, raises some puzzling questions about parts of Dasgupta's article. First, the position adopted by Bergson and Samuelson was their response to the logical positivist claim that, as Samuelson ([1947], 1983, p. 219) himself noted: 'ethical value judgments have no place in scientific analysis.' Dasgupta, on the contrary, has assured us that it is *not* the case that present-day economists, like him, 'are wedded to a "value-free" enterprise' (2005, p. 221). But this involves an explicit abandonment of the position that, for Samuelson, turned Bergson's youthful paper from simply the clear presentation of a mathematically convenient welfare function to the presentation of a major strategy which allowed economists to *do* welfare economics *without being convicted of violating scientific procedure*. As if this were not enough, Dasgupta proceeds to add insult to injury by interpreting Bergson and Samuelson as having taken an *explicitly ethical* position: 'the *ethical foundations* of the subject were constructed over five decades ago' (2005, p. 221f.; emphasis added), and again later: '(Bergson) Burk (1938) and Samuelson (1947) established the foundations of policy evaluation on a broad *ethical* structure' (2005, p. 226; emphasis added). Finally, the picture Dagupta presents, of Bergson–Samuelson welfare theory as a *solid structure* built in 1938 and still essentially unchallenged today, is at best a sweeping simplification of the complicated history of what used to be called the 'new welfare economics.'

What is important here is to see that Dasgupta's major works contain a treatment of values that is enriched by a serious study of *recent* work by moral philosophers and political scientists, including (for example) a well-informed discussion of the role of rights of various kinds, as well as a broad concept of well-being. It is *anything but* a rehash of the tired old 'new' welfare economics—something that is about as new today as the 'new look'! (see Dasgupta, 1993, pp. 3–72; 2001, pp. 1–40).

One simple example must suffice here. He is criticizing the customary approach to interpersonal comparisons. Dasgupta (1993, p. 5, note 4; emphasis added) tells us that:

> the ingredients which result in various experiental states are [treated as] a mere surrogate for what we are ultimately after, namely, the interpersonal comparison of *experiental states*. This is a wrong way of stating the matter. D. Davidson (1986) has made the powerful claim that it isn't a mere surrogate; he has argued that the meaning we attach to the idea of such comparisons involves our own judgments on the value *of such ingredients* . . . See also Scanlon (1992).

He does not use the word 'capabilities' in the passage which follows, but the 'ingredients' he lists are things that would *sustain* vital capabilities. He points out that such things as appear as 'ingredients' include a person's freedom 'to form associations and friendships, to speak her mind, to do what she rationally desires to do . . . in fact, precisely those items that loom prominently in right-based ethical theories. There is then the agreeable fact that these determinants of a person's good *are* measurable and comparable, and that this is so irrespective of what a person's conception of her good happens to be. This itself is symptomatic of the objectivity of ethical truth, and it provides a reason why the shop-worn distinction between facts and values is far less sharp than it has typically been taken to be' (Dasgupta, 1993, p. 6).

It should be noted that, while Dasgupta (1993, p. 4f.) *defends* what he sees as valid insights of utilitarianism in this discussion, he is quick to add that '[t]he notion of rights is central to the present study' (Dasgupta, 1993, p. 7). The reader of Dasgupta (1993, 2001) will quickly see that these are not works in which ethics 'has taken a back seat' (2005, p. 221).

Dasgupta contrasts the enrichment which economics has derived from some special sciences with what he sees as the lack of such help from ethics. But here again he is ignoring the fact/theory/value entanglement. The special sciences which Dasgupta has found helpful—like all sciences—*are* an entanglement: so *values* are an element in what economics has taken over from these branches of knowledge, and thus benefited from. The special sciences had values in their luggage!

Nussbaum's vital capabilities, and John Rawls

Dasgupta takes Martha Nussbaum to task for her list of non-negotiable capabilities (2005, p. 234f.). But Nussbaum, like Rawls, is not writing of a society with a significant fraction of its population in a state of destitution. Dasgupta, however, himself remarks that Rawls 'notably restricted applications of his theory of justice to countries that are not overly poor' (2005, p. 234, note 15). So it is not clear why Dasgupta failed to see the obvious fact that Nussbaum (who announced the influence of Rawls on her recent work), was simply *following Rawls* on this issue: on the very first page of her paper Nussbaum (2003, p. 413) observes that 'my own thinking moved on, under the influence of John Rawls's *Political Liberalism*' (Rawls, 1993).

It is not always remarked that Rawls *himself* was moving towards capability theory in his latest work. He writes that 'it should be stressed that the account of primary goods does take into account, and does not abstract from, basic capabilities' (Rawls, 2001, p. 69). It should also be noted that Rawls's choice of societies without widespread deep poverty (let alone destitution) as models for his theory was brought up years ago by his critics from the left. Sen wrote about issues related to this (much as he always admired Rawls's work), in particular he wrote about the strains which a Rawlsian society would undergo if confronted with bitter class conflict (Sen, 1992, pp. 76–79). But Rawls's work throughout his life shows that he was well aware of how terrible many real societies are; and he reminds his readers that, after all, he had been concerned with studying what properties we should seek to attain in an *ideal* society. He was primarily concerned 'with ideal theory' (Rawls, 1999, p. 555).

So her deep interest in Rawls arguably may have moved Nussbaum somewhat in the direction of ideal theory, and thus of *ideal lists of capabilities*. The plight of the actually starving surely calls for action best modeled in terms of lexical orderings: they need water immediately, then food, then emergency health care. But consider the case of the seriously poor, but not destitute. Dasgupta (1993, p. 401) rightly observes that '[n]utrients to an extent display complementarities among themselves . . . in that a person can't make up for deficiencies in one by consuming a lot of another.' Here, it would seem, a situation where *balanced* intake is a serious policy aim would appear to emerge at a much humbler level than that which Nussbaum was considering. Alas, the fact that balanced growth of needed goods can be *desirable* has no tendency to show that it will be technically *attainable*—as Adam Smith was well aware, and as are those who have been concerned to express his insights in formal models today (see Walsh, 2003, pp. 363–377 for a brief sketch of the issues).

The disenfranchised and destitute

Dasgupta (1993, p. 476) remarks that '[i]t is often said that even when a person owns no physical assets she owns one asset that is inalienable, namely *labour power*. The last two chapters here revealed the important truth that this is false.

What an assetless person owns is *potential* labour power, nothing more.' The economically disenfranchised are those too weak to work: they are thus excluded from the labor market. If many are assetless, 'markets on their own would be incapable of enabling all to obtain an adequate diet' (Dasgupta, 1993, p. 476). The involuntary unemployment resulting is *not* due to demand deficiency, and it will inexorably take place even when 'were the distribution of assets sufficiently equal, the labor market would be capable of absorbing all, and no one would suffer from malnutrition' (Dasgupta, 1993, p. 476). However widespread the destitution, all equilibria are Pareto-efficient!

Dasgupta (1993, p. 476, emphasis added) points out that 'there are no policies open to the government for alleviating the extent of undernourishment other than those that amount to *consumption or asset transfers*. A common wisdom is that such policies impede the growth of an economy's productive capacity because of their detrimental effect on saving and investment, incentives, and so forth.'

Let us point out that what Dasgupta calls politely 'a common wisdom' was *a leading dogma* of the market fundamentalist economists associated with the Washington consensus. Dasgupta, however, will have none of the 'common wisdom'. He insists that 'this is only one side of the picture. Our model will stress the other side, which is that a transfer from the well-off to the undernourished can enhance output via the increased productivity of the impoverished . . . We don't know in advance which is the greater effect, but to ignore the latter yields biased estimates of the effects of redistribution policies' (Dasgupta, 1993, p. 476). He tells us that '[b]y developing the economics of malnutrition, I will offer a final justification for the thesis that *it is the singular responsibility of the state to be an active participant in the allocation mechanism guiding the production and distribution of positive and negative freedoms*. This justification is built on the idea that *in a poor economy markets on their own are incapable of empowering all people with the opportunity to convert their potential labor power into actual labor power*. As a resource allocation mechanism, *markets on their own simply aren't effective*' (Dasgupta, 1993, p. 477; emphasis added). He adds that the theory he will develop 'also shows how a group of similar people can become fragmented over time *into distinct classes*. facing widely different opportunities. Risk and uncertainty will play no role in this. *It is a pristine theory of class formation*' (Dasgupta, 1993, p. 477; emphasis added).

The ethicists and public intellectuals, like the late Sir Bernard Williams and Nussbaum, whose comments on the state of neoclassical economics clearly offended Dasgupta, were *not* wholly wrong: the market fundamentalists (now forever associated with the Washington consensus) *have* been justly accused of propagating a discredited theology, *long before* the recent critics wrote. For example, Peter Hammond (1989, pp. 186–257) totally outdid present critics (from a distinguished position *within* the economics profession) in his detailed critique of 'Some assumptions of contemporary neoclassical economic theology.' Hammond (1989, p. 248) sums up in a phrase which comes amazingly close to Nussbaum: 'The serious student is often attracted to economics by humanitarian feelings . . . orthodox teaching deflects these feelings into the dreary desert of so-called Welfare Economics.'

But Hammond would *never* have confused the work of brilliant critics of the 'theology' like Stiglitz or Dasgupta with the denizens of the 'dreary desert'! He argues powerfully for the existence of 'a residual neoclassical theory, purged of theology' (Hammond, 1989, p. 248), and hopefully *any* intellectual who reads the passages which we have just quoted from Dasgupta's work will see unmistakable signs that *he belongs* with Hammond's band of reformers. A few simple instances will illustrate this.

Dasgupta (1993, p. 168) notes that the canonical theory of a competitive market is still what is known as the '*Arrow–Debreu equilibrium,* in honor of the two economists who presented the definitive modern version of it' (Arrow and Debreu, 1954; Debreu, 1959; Arrow, 1964). In models for this theory 'where labor skills are the only endowments of many agents . . . trade is necessary for survival' (Dasgupta, 1993, p. 170). He adds that he will study circumstances where 'many are driven to destitution' (Dasgupta, 1993, p. 170). He is referring to the models later in Dasgupta (1993) which we have already discussed above. We can now see that they have roots in a major criticism of Arrow–Debreu theory concerning the survival of destitute agents (he cites work of his own, and that of Hammond, 1991). The debate on survival has been an important critical literature concerning Arrow Debreu theory, but it is by no means the only one: we have noted Stiglitz's work on incomplete and asymmetric information (which is a distinct issue); and there are other critical issues which cannot be developed here.

One other matter deserves a few words here. We have seen how Dasgupta (1993, p. 477) has claimed that his model of destitution 'also shows how a group of similar people can become fragmented over time into distinct classes, facing widely different opportunities.' And this is *not* a case of the effects of asymmetric information, since we are told that risk and uncertainty play no role. The emergence of a theory of class formation in a model where all actors are individuals, making rational decisions, has been developed by a well-known neoclassical economist, John Roemer. He starts from an Arrow–Debreu model of competitive equilibrium, and uses game theoretic methods. Coalitions emerge, and he is able to specify '*the* canonically exploited class in the economy' (Roemer, 1982, p. 244).[9] Dasgupta's derivation of conflicting classes from a model in the Arrow–Debreu tradition is thus not unique. But it is certainly *not* a characteristic of market fundamentalist interpreters of the Arrow–Debreu tradition, and it again puts him squarely in the company of authors like Stiglitz, Hammond, Roemer, and other reformers. It is an honorable group to belong to, and one which (we believe) deserves the esteem and the support of all who care about political economy.

Models of the reproduction and allocation of surplus

The models of Dasgupta referred to above (like those of Roemer) bring the concept of opposed classes center stage. Dasgupta's destitute, as we have seen, lack even labor power to offer in exchange for food. The more fortunate of the landless offer their labor power in exchange for minimum subsistence; illness, age or other emergencies will cause some of them to drop down among the destitute.

There is a class of landowners, who receive rental income and can choose not to work—this is especially true of the richer landlords, whom Dasgupta (1993, p. 492) calls 'pure *rentiers* (or the *gentry*).' His models put a spotlight on the existence of a surplus in the hands of the better-off, and on his conclusion that 'a transfer from the well-off to the undernourished *can enhance output* via the increased productivity of the impoverished' (Dasgupta, 1993, p. 476; emphasis added).

Neo-Walrasian models were formulated in such a way as to keep such issues as the ability to survive without trade and the destitution of the unemployed off-stage.[10] In explicitly modeling what may happen to those who cannot sell, or even offer to sell their own labor, Dasgupta is distancing himself from mainstream neo-Walrasian theory, but he is in line with Adam Smith ([1776], 1976, p. 84), who noted that '[m] any workmen could not subsist a week, few could subsist a month, and scarce any a year without employment.' Even in some of his earliest work (the 'Early Draft' of the *Wealth of Nations*. not published until last century), Smith (1978, p. 563) shows his acute awareness of how much of the surplus is extracted and devoted to luxurious waste: '[i]n a civilized society the poor provide both for themselves and for the enormous luxury of their superiors.' The moral judgment, which is the *leimotiv* of all of Smith's economic writings, is the vital responsibility for the productive use of the surplus—not squandering it on 'the slothful and oppressive profusion of the great' (Smith, 1978, p. 566) but rather 'in setting to work industrious people' (Smith, [1776], 1976, p. 65). Dasgupta's use of the concepts of class, and of needs and subsistence—and of the surplus in the hands of the richer landlords, a transfer of some of which could save the poorest from destitution and *increase* output— these are legitimately descended from Adam Smith, and in that sense their use is truly classical. This shows especially in the way he draws attention to how *starkly* he is interpreting the concept of *needs*: he is by no means thinking of what might be seen as needs by those who live in a developed country, and have in mind a decent standard of living: 'The sense in which I am thinking of the notion here is starker. In classical political economy, this sense found an illustration in Marx's account of the transformation of food and fuel into labour power' (Dasgupta, 1993, p. 37). He argues that '[o]ne advantage of appealing to the concept of needs is that we are able to see commodity consumption as an input, political and civil liberties as the background environment, and welfare and individual functionings as an output vector, of what is in effect a complex "production process"' (Dasgupta, 1993, p. 37). He cites, among others, Sen's (1982, 1985) '. . . focus on human functionings'. He adds in a note: 'In pure production models in economics a commodity is called "basic" if it is a necessary input for the production of pretty much anything else. See Sraffa (1960)' (Dasgupta, 1993, p. 38, note 29).

Sraffa's work has been a vital component in the development of present day classical theory. But Sraffa *alone* will not do for Dasgupta, since Sraffa chose to abandon the idea of *consumption* basics: 'The drawback of this course is that it involves relegating the necessaries of consumption to the limbo of non-basic products' (Sraffa, 1960, p. 10). A discussion of these problems appears in Walsh and Gram (1980, pp. 317–319, 337–340).

Sraffa's reason for dropping consumption basics was that 'besides the ever-present element of subsistence [wages] may include a share of the surplus product' (Sraffa, 1960, p. 9). And this is clearly not an issue in a very poor economy such as is depicted in the models of Dasgupta with which we have been concerned. There are, however, other reasons why present-day classical theorists have found that Sraffa needed to be supplemented—notably the fact that he does not set up his models in a way that facilitates treating growth. For this reason Walsh and Gram (1980) used a Sraffa–Neumann blend, as do Kurz and Salvadori (1995) and many others. A sketch of these matters appears in Walsh (2003, pp. 363–369).

It is a telling feature of 'the appalling world in which we live' (Sen, 1999, p. 282) that Dasgupta's laborers in a poor country today can only be assumed to have the means of bare physical survival, while Smith, writing in the eighteenth century, early in the industrial revolution, included little comforts like a linen shirt and leather shoes among the 'necessaries' required for even a day laborer in Britain to be said to have subsistence. Smith might well have expected conditions in the poor world to have advanced, by the end of the twentieth century, to equal or surpass the conditions of labor in eighteenth-century Scotland! We are mindful here of Sen's use of his concept of 'rich description' adopted from his mentor Maurice Dobb when up at Cambridge, and never forgotten (see Sen, 2005).

Like other people at Cambridge in Sen's student days, Dobb tended to favor Ricardo as the original classic of choice. But he was aware of Smith's understanding of surplus (see Dobb, 1973, pp. 45f.). And, whereas the other Sraffians and Joan Robinson adopted the logical positivist rejection of values,[11] Dobb (1973, pp. 11–12, 15) was skeptical of the fact/value dichotomy *specifically* as applied to mathematical modeling in economics. Be that as it may, Sen left Cambridge with a rejection of the fact/value dichotomy, and when he began to develop the classical interests which are increasingly evident in his work today, these interests were centered on Adam Smith—and especially on the ethical implications of Smith's classical theory. Sen and Dasgupta thus share the property that their emerging classical tendencies are unmistakably those of what we have been referring to in recent work as the second phase in the present-day classical revival (Walsh, 2000, 2003; Putnam, 2002, 2003).

It is notable how *early* modern classical work began to appear which was explicitly an entanglement of facts, theories and values. Luigi Pasinetti's (1965) paper is a striking example. Another is Adolph Lowe (1976), who, like Pasinetti, presents specific models which are self-consciously classical and have overt ethical implications. By the early 1980s we have Roemer's (1982) models of the emergence of a most exploited class.

A theme that can be heard in much of this work is that morally responsible growth must pay attention to the most urgent human needs and the development of the most vital human capabilities. Bertram Schefold (1990, p. 187), for example, has observed that '[t]here are certain hierarchies of needs, from basic needs up to higher needs such as the need for self-fulfillment.' For Schefold, this implies the importance of modeling, which uses lexical orderings. This fits Sen's capability theory of development and Pasinetti's theory of transformational growth.

Schefold (1990, p. 180) expects 'shifts in the composition of output determined by Engel elasticities,' which reflects what Pasinetti anticipated to be an important feature of his non-balanced growth. This would also be a feature of the changing needs of the previously destitute in Dasgupta's models, if redistributive policies lifted them from semi-starvation to the recovery of their labor power. As Dasgupta (1993, p. 39f.) writes:

> The claims of needs suggest a sense of urgency. They hint, but only hint, at a preemptory argument. Basic needs display these features in a sharp form. We can postpone listening to a piece of music or going to a party, but we can't postpone the consumption of water when thirsty, or food when hungry, or medical attention when ill. Such needs have lexicographic priority over other needs.

In a Pasinetti model, as it evolves, the needs or functionings which are physically (and morally) most pressing are treated in just this manner, and get the highest growth rates. So Dasgupta's destitute would come first, restoring their power to labor, and so to contribute to the growing output of basic commodities.

Viability and sustainability

At first glance, the classical concept of viability and the current concept of sustainability might appear to have much in common. They both address the question of whether or not an economy can continue reproducing itself and whether it can do so on an expanded scale. Yet on investigation one finds that the original classics characteristically tended to limit quite severely what they regarded as the relevant requirement of viability. Perhaps the most extreme case was Ricardo, who notoriously assumed that the original powers of the soil were indestructible.

Among the founders of *neoclassical* economics, William Stanley Jevons stands out as a pioneer of the recognition of the exhaustibility of resources for his first book, *The Coal Question: An Inquiry Concerning the Progress of the Nation and the Probable Exhaustion of our Coal Mines* (Jevons, 1865). He was also actually aware of scientific issues concerning the rigorous development of economic theory, which might interfere with the ability of the science to tackle straight away some of the deepest questions of economic life: economics must be formalized, but this need for mathematics would be at the cost of making it initially a very contracted science (see Walsh and Gram, 1980, pp. 124–131).

As neoclassical theory developed in the twentieth century, and became more appropriately called neo-Walrasian, its formal structure tended to lead to the natural environment being regarded as *given* by the model builder. Jevons, perhaps, would not have been surprised by this. The present authors agree with Dasgupta's (2005, p. 260f.) appraisal of what happened:

> Twentieth century economics . . . has in large measure been detached from the environmental sciences. Judging by the profession's writings, we

economists see Nature at best as a backdrop from which resources can be considered in isolation and we regard the processes that characterize the Earth System to be linear. Moreover, macroeconomic forecasts routinely exclude environmental resources. Accounting for Nature, if it comes into the calculus at all, is an afterthought to the real business of 'doing economics.'

One might hope that development economics would have done better, since it has been supposedly concerned with poor people who have less protection from the wrath of nature. But Dasgupta (2005, p. 261) dashes such hope: 'In ignoring the role of natural capital in economic activities, development economists have merely followed their professional colleagues.' He notes the bitter irony of this neglect by economists studying 'the lives of the rural poor.' It should be noted that Dasgupta has published extensively on these issues, and nature has never been marginalized in his work (see the references in his 2005 paper).

Can one claim that twentieth-century classical theory paid any more attention to the environment? In the case of the minimalist first wave of the classical revival we do not think so. Without wishing to claim that the second phase has yet come near to meeting Dasgupta's standards, we believe that it has shown significant improvements. Indeed, we would suggest that this change is a noticeable feature of the second phase of the classical revival. Those modern classics who take overtly ethical positions *also* tent to take explicit environmental positions, and their treatment of viability includes features that are familiar from the literature on sustainability. Thus, Lowe (1976, pp. 223–231, 290–325), whose modeling had an explicitly normative dimension, included a treatment of the recycling of production and consumption residuals. (For a discussion of the approaches to non-balanced growth in the *traverse* models of Lowe (1976) and Hicks (1965) versus the *transformational* growth models of Pasinetti, see Hagemann (1992, pp. 235–263) and Walsh (1992, pp. 30–39).)

Wassily Leontief, like Lowe, absorbed at first hand the early (German language) beginnings of the twentieth century revival of classical theory. His doctoral research at the University of Berlin was supervised by Ladislaus von Bortkiewicz and, like Lowe, he also spent a few years at the Institute for the World Economy at Kiel, which is noted for its work on the revival of classicism (see Kurz and Salvadori, 1995, pp. 390–396; Dorfman, 1987, pp. 164–166). Also like Lowe, Leontief (1986) paid serious attention to environmental damage, and pioneered its empirical investigation.

The German language revival of the classical tradition had established itself in American with the arrival of Lowe, Leontief and especially John von Neumann. In America, Neumann's work had been developed by his collaboration with Oskar Morgenstern and by Kemeny, Morgenstern and Thompson (1956), and later by Morgenstern and Thompson (1967, 1976).[12] Among many other developments, as Morgenstern and Thompson (1976, p. 8) noted, '*maximum expansion* can be placed under constraints such as "no pollution," "no poison production," "protection of the environment," etc. While this is hardly surprising, the point is that previous models could not include them. Rigorous existence theorems for such models are only established in this work on the firm basis of the open model.' They introduce the existence of luxuries, which Neumann had not treated in his famous model, and then 'pollution disposal industries' (Morgenstern and Thompson, 1976, pp. 141, 145).

Kurz and Salvadori (1995) discuss environmental issues, as does Bertram Schefold (1997, pp. 525–549; 1989), who has written extensively on many aspects of present day classical theory, and has considered Leontief's treatment of environmental questions when comparing classical and neoclassical approaches to this issue.

The present-day classical theorist who has made the gradual elimination of destructive industries, and the selective growth of the most benign production, a core feature of his models of growth and human development, however, remains in our view Pasinetti. Having said this, we wish to add that, for us, one of the most appealing features of Dasgupta's models of class conflict, subsistence, surplus and destitution, is their unmistakably deep engagement with both the moral implications of these matters and the interface between these core issues of classical theory and the most pressing facts of nature.

Acknowledgments

We wish to thank Harvey Gram, Steve Pressman, Lisa Bendall-Walsh and Kristin Brodt for their help. The usual disclaimers apply.

Notes

1 See Putnam (1981, pp. 127–149; 1990, pp. 135–178; 2002; 2003; Walsh (1987, pp. 861–869; 1998, pp.188–194; 2003, pp. 321–338; 2008, pp. 192–232).
2 Subsequent references to this article will be indicated by the date and page numbers only.
3 The refutation of Whitehead's theory was the work of C.M. Will (1971, pp. 409–412).
4 See Putnam (2002, pp. 19–24) for an account of the changes in the positivists' criterion.
5 So what *there is* for values to be entangled with is a pale gray lore, an entanglement of *fact and theory*. So '*both* dichotomies collapsed, in each case because of a kind of *entanglement*: in the one case, because of the entanglement of facts and conventions, in the other because of the entanglement of facts and values' (Walsh, 2003, p. 323). So strictly speaking '[i]t should be noted that, while the phrase "entanglement of fact and value" is a convenient shorthand, what we are typically dealing with (as Putnam makes clear) is a *triple* entanglement: of fact, convention and value' (Walsh, 2003, p. 331).
6 Moody-Adams (1997, pp. 101ff.) defines it as 'choosing not to know what one can and should know.'
7 We do not charge the World Bank (1986) with simply assuming this; whether they do or not, Dasgupta assumes it by giving these two quotations as an example of a straightforward disagreement about 'effective means' to a shared end.
8 Greenwald and Stiglitz (1986) showed 'that when information is imperfect or markets are incomplete, competitive equilibrium is not (constrained Pareto) efficient' (Stiglitz, 2003, p. 261, n1).
9 On Roemer's work see Walsh (1996, pp. 262–270).
10 See the comments of Koopmans (1957, p. 59), Arrow and Hahn (1971, pp. 116–122), Sen (1981, pp. 172–173), and Coles and Hammond (1995).

11 Readers interested in new evidence concerning the implicit logical positivism underlying the work of Sraffa, will find much of interest in the articles in the *Review of Political Economy* (17(3), 2005). See also Walsh (2003, pp. 321–338; 2008, pp. 192–232).

12 During his last years, Oskar Morgenstern read, and commented in detail on, an early draft of Walsh and Gram (1980). The help he provided with the classical theory was invaluable, and his unfailing kindness, will never be forgotten by those authors.

References

Arrow, K. (1964) The role of securities in the optimal allocation of risk bearing, *Review of Economic Studies*, 31, pp. 91–96.

Arrow, K. and Debreu, G. (1954) Existence of equilibrium for a competitive economy, *Econometrica*, 22, pp. 522–590.

Arrow, K. and Hahn, F. (1971) *General Competitive Analysis* (San Francisco: Holden Day).

(Bergson, A.) Burk, A. (1938) A reformulation of certain aspects of welfare economics, *Quarterly Journal of Economics*, 52, pp. 310–334.

Bhagwati, J. (2004) *In Defense of Globalization* (New York: Oxford University Press).

Carnap, R. (1934) *The Unity of Science* (London: Routledge & Kegan Paul).

Coles, J. and Hammond, P. (1995) Walrasian equilibrium without survival: existence, efficiency and remedial policy, in: K. Basu, P. Pattanaik and K. Suzumura (Eds) *Choice, Welfare and Development: A Festschrift in Honour of Amartya Sen* (Oxford: Clarendon Press).

Dasgupta, P. (1993) *An Inquiry Into Well-being and Destitution* (New York: Oxford University Press).

Dasgupta, P. (2001) *Human Well-Being and the Natural Environment* (New York: Oxford University Press).

Dasgupta, P. (2005) What do economists analyze and why: values or facts?, *Economics and Philosophy*, 21, pp. 221–278.

Davidson, D. (1986) Judging interpersonal interests, in: J. Elster and A. Highland (Eds) *Foundations of Social Choice Theory* (Cambridge: Cambridge University Press).

Debreu, G. (1959) *Theory of Value* (New York: Wiley).

Dobb, M. (1973) *Theories of Value and Distribution since Adam Smith* (Cambridge: Cambridge University Press).

Dorfman, R. (1987) Leontief, Wassily, in: J. Eatwell, M. Milgate and P. Newman (Eds) *The New Palgrave: A Dictionary of Economics*, Vol. 3, pp. 164–166 (London: Macmillan).

Greenwald, B. and Stiglitz, J. (1986) Externalities in economies with imperfect information and incomplete markets, *Quarterly Journal of Economics*, 101, pp. 229–264.

Hagemann, H. (1992) Traverse analysis in a post-classical model, in: J. Halevi, D. Laibman and E. Nell (Eds) *Beyond the Steady State: A Revival of Growth Theory* (London: Macmillan).

Hammond, P. (1989) Some assumptions of contemporary neoclassical economic theology, in: G.R. Feiwel (Ed.) *Joan Robinson and Modern Economics* (London: Macmillan).

Hammond, P. (1991) Irreducibility, resource relatedness and survival in equilibrium with individual non-convexities, in: R. Becker *et al.* (Eds) *General Equilibrium and Growth: The Legacy of Lionel McKenzie* (New York: Academic Press).

Hicks, J.R. (1965) *Capital and Growth* (Oxford: Clarendon Press).

Jevons, W.S. (1865) *The Coal Question: An Inquiry Concerning the Progress of the Nation and the Probable Exhaustion of Our Coal Mines* (London: Macmillan).

Kemeny, J., Morgenstern, O. and Thompson, G. (1956) A generalization of the von Neumann model of an expanding economy, *Econometrica*, 24, pp. 115–135.

Koopmans, T. (1957) *Three Essays on the State of Economic Science* (New York: McGraw-Hill).

Kurz, H. and Salvadori, N. (1995) *Theory of Production, A Long Period Analysis* (Cambridge, Cambridge University Press).

Leontief, W. (1986) *Input-Output Economics.* 2nd edn (New York: Oxford University Press).

Lowe, A. (1976) *The Path of Economic Growth* (Cambridge: Cambridge University Press).

Moody-Adams, M. (1997) *Fieldworks in Familiar Places; Morality, Culture and Philosophy* (Cambridge, MA: Harvard University Press).

Morgenstern, O. and Thompson, G. (1967) Private and public consumption and savings in the von Neumann model of an expanding economy, *Kyklos*, 20, pp. 387–409.

Morgenstern, O. and Thompson, G. (1976) *Mathematical Theory of Expanding and Contracting Economies* (Lexington, MA: Lexington Books).

Nussbaum, M. (2003) Tragedy and human capabilities: a response to Vivian Walsh, *Review of Political Economy*, 15, pp. 413–418.

Pasinetti, L. (1965) A new theoretical approach to the problem of economic growth, *Pontifiae Academiae Scientiarum Scripta Varia*, 28, pp. 571–677.

Putnam, H. (1981) *Reason Truth and History* (New York: Cambridge University Press).

Putnam, H. (1989) Objectivity and the science/ethics distinction, WIDER Working Paper 70. Republished in Putnam, 1990, pp. 163–78.

Putnam, H. (1990) *Realism with a Human Face* (Cambridge, MA: Harvard University Press).

Putnam, H. (1993) Objectivity and the science–ethics distinction, in: M.C. Nussbaum and A. Sen (Eds) *The Quality of Life* (Oxford: Clarendon Press).

Putnam, H. (2002) *The Collapse of the Fact/Value Dichotomy, and Other Essays, Including the Rosenthal Lectures* (Cambridge, MA, Harvard University Press).

Putnam, H. (2003) For ethics and economics without the dichotomies, *Review of Political Economy*, 15, pp. 395–412.

Quine, W.V.O. [1950] (1953) Two dogmas of empiricism, in: *From a Logical Point of View* (Cambridge, MA: Harvard University Press).

Quine, W.V.O. (1963) Carnap and logical truth, in: P. Schlipp (Ed) *The Philosophy of Rudolph Carnap* (Open Court).

Rawls, J. (1993) *Political Liberalism* (New York: Columbia University Press).

Rawls, J. (1999) *Collected Papers* (Cambridge: MA, Harvard University Press).

Rawls, J. (2001) *Justice as Fairness: a Restatement* (Cambridge, MA: Harvard University Press).

Reutlinger, S. and Pellekaan, H. (1986) *Poverty and Hunger: Issues and Options for Food Security in Developing Countries* (Washington, DC: World Bank).

Robbins, L. [1932] (1935) *An Essay on the Nature and Significance of Economic Science* (London: Macmillan).

Robbins, L. (1938) Interpersonal comparisons of utility: a comment, *Economic Journal*, 48, pp. 635–641.

Roemer, J. (1982) *A General Theory of Exploitation and Class* (Cambridge, MA: Harvard University Press).

Samuelson, P. [1947] (1983) *Foundations of Economic Analysis* (Cambridge, MA: Harvard University Press).

Scanlon, T. (1992) The moral basis of interpersonal comparisons, in: J. Elster and J. Roemer (Eds) *Interpersonal Comparisons of Well-being* (Cambridge: Cambridge University Press).

Schefold, B. (1989) *Mr. Sraffa on Joint Production and Other Essays* (London: Unwin Hyman).

Schefold, B. (1990) On changes in the composition of output, in: K. Bharadwaj and B. Schefold (Eds) *Essays on Piero Sraffa: Critical Perspective on the Revival of Classical Theory* (London: Unwin Hyman).

Schefold, B. (1997) Ecological problems as a challenge to classical and Keynesian economics, in: *Normal Prices, Technical Change and Accumulation* (London: Macmillan).

Sen, A.K. (1981) *Poverty and Famines: An Essay on Entitlement and Deprivation* (Oxford: Clarendon Press).

Sen, A.K. (1982) Rights and agency, *Philosophy and Public Affairs*, 11, pp. 113–132.

Sen, A.K. (1985) *Commodities and Capabilities* (Amsterdam: North Holland).

Sen, A.K. (1992) *Inequality Reexamined* (Oxford: Clarendon Press).

Sen, A.K. (1999) *Development as Freedom* (New York: Knopf).

Sen, A.K. (2005) Walsh on Sen After Putnam, *Review of Political Economy*, 17, pp. 107–113.

Smith, A. [1776] (1976) *An Inquiry Into The Nature and Causes of the Wealth of Nations* (Oxford: Clarendon Press).

Smith, A. (1978) *Lectures on Jurisprudence: Early Draft of Part of The Wealth of Nations.* in: R.L. Meek, D.D. Raphael and P.G. Stein (Eds) (Oxford. Clarendon Press).

Sraffa, P. (1960) *The Production of Commodities by Means of Commodities: Prelude to a Critique of Economic Theory* (Cambridge: Cambridge University Press).

Stiglitz, J. (2003) *Globalization and its Discontents* (New York: W. W. Norton).

Walsh, V. (1987) Philosophy and economics, in: J. Eatwell, M. Milgate and P. Newman (Eds) *The New Palgrave: a Dictionary of Economics*, Vol. 3, pp. 861–869 (London: Macmillan).

Walsh, V. (1992) The classical dynamics of surplus and accumulation, in: J. Halevi, D. Laibman and E.J. Nell (Eds) *Beyond the Steady State: A Revival of Growth Theory*, pp. 11–43 (London: Macmillan).

Walsh, V. (1996) *Rationality, Allocation and Reproduction* (Oxford: Clarendon Press).

Walsh, V. (1998) Normative and positive classical economics, in: H. Kurz and N. Salvadori (Eds) *The Elgar Companion to Classical Economics* (Cheltenham: Edward Elgar).

Walsh, V. (2000) Smith after Sen, *Review of Political Economy*, 12, pp. 5–25.

Walsh, V. (2003) Sen after Putnam, *Review of Political Economy*, 15, pp. 315–394.

Walsh, V. (2008) Freedom, values and Sen: towards a morally enriched classical economic theory, *Review of Political Economy*, 20, pp. 192–232.

Walsh, V. and Gram, H. (1980) *Classical and Neoclassical Theories of General Equilibrium, Historical Origins and Mathematical Structure* (New York: Oxford University Press).

Will, C.M. (1971) Relativistic gravity in the solar system, II: Anisotrophy in the Newtonian gravitational constant, *Astrophysics Journal*, 169, pp. 409–412.

World Bank (1986) *World Development Report* (New York: Oxford University Press).

9 Freedom, values and Sen

Towards a morally enriched classical economic theory

Vivian Walsh

Rationality is interpreted here, broadly, as the discipline of subjecting one's choices—of actions as well as of objectives, values and priorities—to reasoned scrutiny. Rather than defining rationality in terms of some formulaic conditions that have been proposed in the literature . . . rationality is seen here in much more general terms as the need to subject one's choices to the demands of reason.

(Amartya Sen, 2002, p. 4)

Rationality: entanglement of fact, theory and value

I read with great joy Amartya Sen's (2005, pp. 109–110) declaration of his 'enormous debt to Hilary Putnam'. Putnam and Sen deeply influenced the position about rationality that I adopted in several recent works (Walsh, 1996, 2003). I had written that:

> Our ordinary concept of rationality is embedded in a delicate fabric of inter-connected ideas which can be understood only in the context of the family of uses of words and expressions which are employed in making, explaining, and defending rationality claims. The concept of rationality in formal, axiomatized economic theory is not like this; it can be given a formal defini-tion. A 'rational agent' in such a model is simply one who obeys certain axioms, and that is the end of it. When we ordinarily claim of someone that they acted rationally, on the other hand, we are not claiming that they satisfied a certain finite set of necessary and sufficient conditions. Our claim is a defea-sible one—very crudely, it may be defeated by the production of various different sorts of evidence, some of which we may never have anticipated.
>
> (Walsh, 1996, p. 1)

For me that passage has a long history. While lecturing on both economics and philosophy at the London School of Economics in the early 1950s, I regularly attended Sir Alfred Ayer's seminar at University College; Freddy Ayer and I became friends. I was never converted to logical positivism, but by then he had mellowed and invited the Oxford 'ordinary language' people to visit and give papers. In this way I got to know them. I heard Gilbert Ryle in Oxford, and one or two of the younger people stayed in my flat in Knightsbridge when in town. This influence can be seen in some of my earliest papers. When I met Hilary Putnam and we became friends, in the fall of 1955, I often talked to him of these matters. From then on, he read and commented on everything I wrote in philosophy and I never recall his seeking to lead me away from paying serious attention to natural languages, especially in *moral* philosophy, which was my main concern. Neither of us accepted the faddish idea that the sole object of philosophy was minute analysis of ordinary usage. Of course, since Putnam's early work was largely in the fields of mathematical logic and the philosophy of science, he was naturally concerned with constructed languages. But his early work took issues concerning natural languages seriously (Putnam, [1962], 1975, pp. 62–69).

Putnam recently reminded me that the first draft of this paper was actually written by 1957. There is also a piece (in Putnam, 1975) entitled 'Review of *The Concept of a Person*', which was written in the 1960s, but not previously published. Here Putnam ([1962], 1975, p. 135) remarks that 'Wittgenstein and Austin, in fact, were two highly original and highly independent philosophers, each of whom contributed radical new ideas to philosophy'. And as those who know his more recent work will be aware, Putnam's regard for Austin and Wittgenstein has increased over the years.

Putnam, like Wittgenstein, felt the power of formalism when young. But, also like Wittgenstein, he came to a deep understanding of the hubristic nature of some claims that had been made for the power and range of constructed languages.[1] This results in a just balance between natural and constructed languages and their several strengths and weaknesses. This gives his work a recognizably different sound, as he moves with ease among languages of different sorts, including the sound he and I heard from the Oxford people in the days when we were young.

The introduction to Sen's (2002) book contains a tone that resembles Putnam's. Sen has known (and brilliantly participated in) some of the high points in the application of axiomatic mathematics to questions of economic theory. But like Putnam, he has seen the withering of unsubstantiated claims – and often been the agent of such claims' exposure and rejection.

The view of rationality that Putnam and I share with Sen implies that the treatment of rational choice in neoclassical economics is in need of serious revision. Sen has shown this to be true of individual choice, but also of social choice. This underlies Sen's (2002, p. 4) continuing argument that the famous proofs of the 'impossibility' of rational social choice were proofs only of the lesser claim that social choices satisfying 'some formulaic conditions' were demonstrably impossible. Social choices satisfying a different and deeper concept of rationality were thus unaffected, and it could be shown that they might well be possible. Sen shows this by examining the indefeasible narrowness of the neoclassical concept of rational choice and, more generally, the impoverishment of the informational base which neoclassical theory presupposes.

Having said this, it must immediately be added that Kenneth Arrow, in the early 1950s, chose an axiom set that reflected the informal assumptions of the neoclassical economic theory of his period. The 'preference utilitarianism' (to use

Putnam's term) put in place in the early 1930s by Sir John Hicks and Sir Roy Allen (see Walsh, 1996, pp. 34–45) is reflected in Arrow's axiom set. Arrow proved what followed from the assumptions adopted, and his proof is a magnificent comment on those assumptions. But the 1950s were tense and difficult times for an intellectual, and we (who also live in difficult times) should not be without understanding.

In Sen's severe critique of neoclassical rational choice theory, it would be a grave mistake to see any rejection of the use of formal mathematical modeling – when conducted with a clear understanding of its power and limits. On the contrary, beginning with individual choice, he carefully shows that an axiomatization rejecting the use of certain unnecessarily restrictive assumptions (normally used in neoclassical formal theory) can be constructed to allow the embedding, in models of rational choice, of some deeply important values. Such enrichments of the properties of individual rational choices are not irrelevant for the proper development of social choice theory.

Sen (202, p. 27) describes the term 'rational choice theory' as 'a naming that bestows on a specialized school of thought the entire mandate of rationality of choice, *tout court*, by the hidden force of a definition . . . To avoid ambiguities, and to acknowledge the big fact that rationality of choice can also be seen differently, I shall refer to the so-called "rational choice theory" as RCT'. His point of contention is that 'insofar as moral or socially principled behavior is accommodated within RCT, this is done through the device of complex instrumental arguments that are combined with ultimately self-interested behavior' (Sen, 2002, p. 28). This 'has led to a remarkably large literature on skillfully "elongating" the self-interest model to deal with these challenges' (Sen, 2002, p. 24). But insisting 'that the high-minded oversimplification of intensely ethical behavior (favored by some moral romantics) be comprehensively replaced by the low-minded oversimplification of ubiquitous selfishness is as much an *a priori* prejudice as the alternative it tries to supplant' (Sen, 2002, p. 26).

As I remarked on a previous occasion, '[b]y 1987, Sen's critique of traditional views of the role of self-interest in Smith was in full flower' (Walsh, 2000, p. 12). And as Putnam (2002, pp. 48–49) comments 'if we are to understand Sen's place in history, the reintroduction of ethical concerns and concepts into economic discourse must not be thought of as an *abandonment* of "classical economics"; rather it is a *reintroduction* of something that was everywhere present in the writings of Adam Smith and that went hand-in-hand with Smith's technical analysis . . . Walsh's term "second phase classical theory" is thus the right term for the Senian program'. Thus, it is natural that, in his critique of those neoclassical economists who try to stuff more and more inappropriate choices into their one-size-fits-all stocking of self-interest, Sen (2002, p. 22) again contrasts Smith with his vulgarizers, who see Smith as claiming that each human being is 'tirelessly promoting his own particular interest (and nothing else)'.

One question Sen does not address is why neoclassical economists engage in this time-consuming and somewhat Jesuitical activity of economic and ethical casuisistry? It surely cannot be to please their political or corporate clients. One possible explanation is that economists 'have to appeal to the ordinary language understanding of rationality when confronting the public'. And in the important work of writing undergraduate texts, they must appeal 'to what the student will feel is reasonable' (Walsh, 2003, p. 356). It should also be noted that the declining influence of neoclassicism's last great unifying system, the canonical Arrow–Debreu models, has reduced the pressure on younger neoclassicists to conform to the axiom set of a ruling orthodoxy, and has led to a Balkanization of the literature (Walsh, 2003, pp. 351–353).

Sen's axiomatic changes to capture rational choices not included in RCT

To understand the changes that Sen proposes in the axiomatizations of rational choice, one must bear in mind his argument that the forms assumed by RCT have been influenced by efforts to avoid acknowledging the inevitable entanglement that is a feature of all theory. As Sen (2002, pp. 28–9) puts it: 'This has given the explanatory role of RCT an almost forensic quality, focusing on the detection of hidden instrumentality rather than any acknowledgement of direct ethics Things, it is darkly hinted, are not what they seem (or at least seemed to simple-minded observers like Smith or Kant)'. Thus, what would be obvious moral choices to Smith or Kant must be smuggled in under self-interest.

Sen (2002, p. 33) prepares the ground by distinguishing 'three different ways in which the self may be central to one's self-interested preferences and choices: (1) "self-centered welfare", (2) "self-welfare goal", and (3) "self-goal choice"'. He notes that these 'requirements are independent of each other, and can be used—or not used—in any combination' (Sen, 2002, p. 34). His taxonomy progressively broadens the concept of self-interest. In self-centered welfare, a person maximizes her own well-being, which is assumed to be completely uninfluenced by what happens to others. In the self-welfare goal, while a person's goal is to maximize her own well-being, this may depend on her sympathy (or antipathy) for others. Finally, in the self-goal choice, a person's goals may include objectives other than the maximization of her own well-being, but her choices will still be based solely on maximizing her own goals. She may be motivated only by duty (and not at all by feelings of sympathy), but she chooses which causes to support. Beyond these three different ways in which the self may be central to one's choices, Sen places choices that reject the exclusive dominance of one's self goals. This, he notes 'reflects a type of commitment that is not able to be captured by the broadening of the goals to be pursued' (Sen, 2002, p. 219).

Sen then develops an account of rational individual choice that goes beyond self-goal choice – noting dryly that 'it is fair to say that of the three elements in the privateness of behavior, namely self-centered welfare, self-welfare goals, and self-goal choice, the denial of the first two does not meet with the kind of resistance that disputing the third does' (Sen, 2002, p. 216).

To do this, he needs, first of all, to reject the requirement of optimization and replace it with the weaker requirement of maximization. 'There is far less difficulty in accommodating the general maximization approach within the characterization of rationality used here (demanding systematic reasoning and scrutinized choice) . . . The maximization approach is quite permissive, and does not rule out sensible possibilities (such as an altruistic or socially committed maximization) and at the same time, its demands are not vacuous' (Sen, 2002, p. 37). Maximization, however, is often defined too narrowly in neoclassical writings on rational choice. For Sen, maximization does not require completeness: 'The basic contrast between maximization and optimization arises from the possibility that the preference ranking R may be incomplete' (Sen, 2002, p. 182). His theorem 5.1 'tells us that while a best alternative must also be maximal, a maximal alternative need not be best' (Sen, 2002, p. 183). Nor does he 'presume that any incompleteness must necessarily be tentative' (Sen, 2002, p. 183), noting '[t]he need to accommodate incompleteness in preference theory has been illuminatingly discussed by Putnam' (1996).[2] His Theorem 5.2 then 'shows the reach of maximization—in particular that it works whenever there is the weak property of acyclicity (neither completeness nor transitivity is needed)' (Sen, 2002, p. 184). He adds in a note that acyclicity 'is the absence of any strict preference cycle of finite length' (Sen, 2002, p. 184, n42).

From the point of view of the present work, it is worth noting that Sen (2002, p. 160, n3) explicitly recognizes that, while incompleteness can arise simply from limited information, it can also arise 'from "unresolved" value conflicts'. His references include works[3] that treat what philosophers have called 'tragic choices'. But then he is designing his formalization of rational choice theory to allow room for ethically serious aspects of choice to show up on the radar screen, so this should cause no surprise.

While the move to maximization is important for Sen, and gives him the broad framework he needs, it is not enough. We must also require, he tells us, 'that maximizing behavior is at most a necessary condition for rationality, and can hardly also be sufficient for it' (Sen, 2002, p. 39). We may be engaged in maximizing stupid goals, and so we need to scrutinize our goals. 'This is the view of rationality that corresponds closely to the approach pursued here (and in Chapters 3–76). It is partly captured by the discipline of maximization, but cannot, in this broader view, be reduced just to maximizing behavior' (Sen, 2002, p. 40). So Sen prepares to go beyond self-goal choice: 'For example, a person may have reason not to pursue her own goals relentlessly when this makes it very hard for others to pursue their goals. This type of reasoning (related to going beyond the limits of "self-goal choice") has a "social" basis which both Immanuel Kant (1788) and Adam Smith (1790) have extensively discussed' (Sen, 2002, p. 40) He naturally wants our maximization to be open to such possibilities. But for this he now needs to drop from his theory two axioms adopted as standard (explicitly or implicitly) by RCT. These are concerned with what is often referred to as 'internal consistency of choice'.

Sen (2002, pp. 121–122) points out that 'there is no way of determining whether a choice function is consistent or not *without* referring to objectives, values, or norms'. The argument he presents illustrates Putnam's concept of the triple entanglement of theory, fact and value. Sen begins by stressing that he is not arguing against consistency itself, but only against the neoclassical claim that we can determine the consistency or inconsistency of choices simply by examining the choices themselves. The standard attempt to establish this internal consistency – using only properties of the choices involved – has habitually been advanced through the adoption (explicitly or implicitly) of two axioms, involving the concepts of 'contraction consistency' and 'expansion consistency' respectively. These internal consistency assumptions have played a significant role in the effort by the original developers of RCT to establish the existence of purely formal rationality properties, supposedly free from any entanglement with values. Sen's critique of these internal consistency axioms appears in the context of his defense of the rationality of menu-dependent choice. He shows that menu-dependent choices can be perfectly rational, but that they are ruled out by the axioms at issue.

Consider contraction consistency first. This requires that an alternative x_1, which is chosen from a set S, and belongs to a subset T of S, must be chosen from T as well. So if the set S contains $\{x_1, x_2, x_3,\}$ and x_2 is chosen, then if T contains $\{x_1, x_2\}$, x_2 must still be chosen (Sen, 2002, p. 128). Expansion consistency, on the other hand, requires that if an alternative x_1 is chosen from every set in a particular class, then it must be chosen from their union. Consider the sets $\{x_1, x_2\}$ and $\{x_1, x_3,\}$ and suppose that x_1 is chosen from each set; expansion consistency requires that x_1 must also be chosen from the union of these sets $\{x_1, x_2, x_3,\}$.

Now consider a simple menu-dependent choice. Sen takes the case where an agent chooses x from the attainable set (or menu) containing x and y, but chooses y when z is added to the menu. He notes the apparent problem arises from 'the fact that x is chosen and y *rejected* in one case, and y is chosen and x rejected in the other' (Sen, 2002, p. 129, n14). The appearance of inconsistency can be removed if we suppose the agent prefers y to x and z to y, but has a reason always to choose the second best attainable option.

It is important to note that the model set for such choice is vast, ranging from the sublime to the ridiculous. Consider the case of Kate in the following situation described by Sen. She 'faces a choice at a dinner table between having the last remaining apple in the fruit basket (y) and having nothing instead (x), forgoing the nice looking apple. She decides to behave decently and picks nothing (x), rather than the apple (y). If, instead, the basket had contained two apples, and she had encountered the choice between having nothing (x), having one nice apple (y) and having another nice one (z), she could reasonably enough choose one (y), without violating any rule of good behavior' (Sen, 2002, p. 129).

Sen's agent may have acted from the humble virtue of good manners. But suppose Kate is solely concerned with maximizing her self-centered welfare. She behaves 'decently' only because she is an avid social climber and wants to pass muster at dinner parties! Her pattern of choices is still a valid model for the theory of menu-dependent choice. This should cause no surprise: the space Sen opens for deeply moral choices also lets in trivial (or evil!) choices that involve violating the contraction and expansion consistency axioms. Having discussed menu-dependent choices where the agent is simply maximizing the protection of their social reputation, like Kate, Sen investigates the use of menu-dependent maximization in discovering and understanding moral choices. An agent's choices can exhibit menu dependence because of her commitment to moral imperatives.

Leaving aside pure reputation effects on an agent, the process of choice may 'occur in various mixed forms' (Sen, 2002, p. 162). Those where reputation remains part of the mixture are, arguably, 'most in harmony with the established conventions of standard neoclassical economies' (Sen, 2002, p. 162). Consciously reflective use of ethical rules (he instances Kant) clearly lie at the opposite end of the spectrum of models for menu-dependent choice. Sen (2002, p. 163) notes that a Kantian approach 'has been pursued in different forms in modern ethical writings'. A notable instance is, of course, John Rawls. 'Right', a fundamental concept of Rawlsian analysis, enters Sen's spectrum of models for menu-dependent choice when he depicts an agent who rejects an act that would increase her personal comfort on the ground that she 'may not think it morally right' (Sen, 2002, p. 162).

As Sen (2002, pp. 177–178, n32) observes, 'altruism through sympathy is ultimately self-interested benevolence, whereas doing things for others through commitment may require one to "sacrifice some great and important interest of our own" as Adam Smith put it'. Sen (2002, p. 162, n5) earlier noted the similarity of Smith and Kant on this issue. He remarks that 'Adam Smith also discussed how various moral values . . . can alter our choice behavior'. We are here beyond self-goal choice, and have arrived where models of menu dependence can embody deep moral issues. For Kant, of course, a perfectly moral being (were such to exist) would have *self*-goals, mapped one-to-one to what was morally right. But for humans, as Kant famously insisted, morality appears as a categorical imperative, subjecting our goals to its law. In effect, Kant was claiming that imperfect humans are typically moral only if their choices go beyond their self-goals.

Smith is remarkably close to Kant when he recognizes that we may have to sacrifice some great and important interest of our own in order to do what is right for others, and Sen, in developing a theory of rational choice that can embed this, exemplifies what makes him a pioneer of the enriched, second phase, revival of classical economic theory.

Sen, however, is aware that freeing rational choice theory from concentrating on self-interested choices is not all that must be done. He remarked in an earlier work, '[s]ome of the nastiest things in the world happen as a result of "selfless" pursuit of objectives far removed from one's own well-being but also from the well-being and freedoms of others' (Sen, 1994, p. 389). Unfortunately, Kant's categorical imperative has failings. Consider two dedicated scientists, Tom and Mary, who are both willing to sacrifice their health and even their lives to find a cure for a deadly disease. They can each sincerely hope that such dedication will be adopted universally by anyone in their position. And they both treat humanity as an end – indeed one worth dying for! – and never simply as a means. So they can sail past Kant untouched.

Unfortunately, they are at opposite poles in their approach to the specific research problem they face. After collaborating for several years, they reach a point where they see success as requiring moving in opposite directions. Not only do they see no possibility of cooperating – each sees the other as merely wasting resources and does everything in their power to turn the scientific community and public and private funding away from the other. Suppose that, had they stayed together, their joint talents would have yielded a third and superior path, which they really needed to take. They were willing to sacrifice everything but concentration on their dogged self-goal choices. The contrast between 'self interest' and 'altruism' (as these words are ordinarily used) fails to capture their disastrous mistake.

As Sen (2002, p. 219) notes in his recent book, where he returns to these issues in a game-theoretic context, 'while self-centered welfare and self-welfare goal have both been quite extensively scrutinized in the literature, self-goal choice has received less attention. However, it turns out that in an understanding of cooperation and success in certain game situations, the denial of self-goal choice (and of goal priority) has a role that cannot be taken over by the denial of the other two components of private behavior'. Leaving aside the well-known problems posed by self-interest, Sen (2002, p. 211) asks the reader to suppose 'that both players are completely non-selfish but have different *moral* views about what will be good for the world, and act entirely in pursuit of moral goodness, as they respectively see it'. Using the standard assumptions of Prisoner's Dilemma games (except that self-goal choice is substituted for the usual self-interest assumption), 'each person would end up in a state that he or she regards as morally inferior compared to a state that is feasible'.

Sen (2002, p. 212) points out that

> in terms of the standard format of game theory—not to mention the more limited structure of traditional economic theory—anything short of unwavering pursuit of one's own goals is seen as simply 'irrational' . . . However, this response only reveals *a limitation of the language of game theory in particular and that of the theory of rational behavior in general.* If the recognition that we can all better pursue our respective goals by jointly departing from goal priority makes us do exactly that, why should that departure change the nature of the goals that we are trying to pursue? (emphasis added)

Sen offers an interesting example of the powers and limitations of constructed versus natural languages. In a natural language it is perfectly correct to describe the adjustment by each of the parties of some of their goals, in order to achieve cooperation, as 'rational'. As he remarks, the 'nature of our language often underlines the forces of our wider identity. "We" demand things; "our" actions reflect "our" concerns; "we" protest at injustice done to "us". This is, of course, the language of social intercourse and of politics, but it is difficult to believe that it represents nothing other than a verbal form, and in particular no sense of identity' (Sen, 2002, p. 215).

Sen (2002, p. 217) notes that

> acceptance of rules of conduct towards others with whom one has some sense of identity is part of a more general behavioral phenomenon of acting

according to fixed rules, without following the dictates of goal-maximization. Adam Smith had emphasized the importance of such 'rules of conduct' in social achievement: 'These general rules of conduct, when they have been fixed in our mind by habitual reflection, are of great use in correcting misrepresentations of self-love concerning what is fit and proper in our particular situation'.

He also notes the evolutionary advantage of 'behavior modes that favor group success, and these can be very different indeed from individual profit maximization (or goal maximization in general) in the presence of interdependencies of certain kinds' (Sen, 2002, p. 217). These advantages of social rules of conduct, well understood by Adam Smith, play a role 'that cannot be captured in the standard characterization of rationality' (Sen, 2002, p. 220).

Rationality and freedom

As we have seen, at its core, Sen's approach to rationality explicitly embraces entanglement. This is also true of his treatment of the other major topics that he will discuss, notably his analysis of freedom and social choice. Indeed, he runs up his colors on this at the beginning of his recent book:

> There is a reciprocal relationship between rationality and freedom . . . Even though the idea of freedom is sometimes formulated independently of values, preferences and reasons, freedom cannot be fully appraised without some idea of what a person prefers and has reason to prefer. Thus, there is a basic use of rational assessment in appraising freedom, and in this sense, freedom must depend on reasoned assessment of having different options . . . [T]he converse also holds: rationality, in its turn, depends on freedom. This is not merely because without some freedom of choice, the idea of rational choice would be quite vacuous, but also because the concept of rationality must accommodate the diversity of reasons that may sensibly motivate choice. To deny that accommodation in favor of conformity with some preselected neoclassical axioms . . . would involve, in effect, a basic denial of '*freedom of thought*'.
>
> (Sen, 2002, p. 5)

An enriched understanding of rationality, one that restores its moral implications, thus demands an enriched understanding of freedom. Neoclassical economics, by avoiding overt discussion of the moral implications of its arguments, impoverishes its understanding of freedom. Ironically, the moral theory that covertly persists in neoclassicism reinforces this impoverishment.

Since the 1870s, one moral philosophy has been deeply embedded in neoclassical economics – utilitarianism. Until the 1930s, neoclassical economists acknowledged this, and some (A.C. Pigou, Lord Dalton and Sir Alan Peacock) even used it to support humane policies (Walsh, 2003, pp. 349–350). It was then mistakenly thought that abandoning cardinality during the 1930s removed all vestiges of utilitarianism (Walsh, 1996, pp. 37–40; 2003, pp. 350–352). But, a low-octane utilitarianism has led a second life in the formal structure of neoclassical theory. Modern philosophers interested in formalizing utilitarianism, such as John Broome (1991), recognized preference utilitarianism as providing a structure in which they could set up housekeeping. (Unfortunately, unknown to such philosophers, the economists had moved out and abandoned the mansions of canonical Arrow–Debreu theory.) But as Sen knew for many years, and even demonstrated, any utilitarianism fails by riding roughshod over rights and therefore over freedoms. Insofar as neoclassicism still has a covert moral philosophy, this moral position disempowers it from doing justice to rights and freedoms.

Sen's acute awareness of the moral significance of human rights is an important part of what leads him to argue 'that we must distinguish between two different and irreducibly diverse aspects of freedom, namely "the opportunity aspect" and "the process aspect"'(Sen, 2002, p. 10). As he notes later,

> [f]reedom is valuable for at least two distinct reasons. First, more freedom gives us more *opportunity* to achieve those things that we value, and have reason to value. This aspect of freedom is concerned primarily with our *ability to achieve*, rather than with the process through which that achievement comes about. Second, the *process* through which things happen may also be of importance in assessing freedom. For example, it may be thought, reasonably enough, that the procedure of free decision by the person himself (no matter how successful the person is in getting what he would like to achieve) is an important requirement of freedom.
>
> (Sen, 2002, p. 585)[4]

Sen (2002, pp. 585–586) adds that recognizing 'this distinction does not . . . rule out the existence of overlaps between the two aspects. For example, if a person values achieving something through free choice (and not through the end-product being delivered to him by someone else), . . . then the process aspect of freedom will have a direct bearing on the opportunity aspect as well'.

Given that Sen has deliberately developed a theory of rational choice with a structure designed to include moral choices, an important part of the content of freedom must be the freedom to implement such choices. It is thus no accident that Kant is repeatedly cited in Sen (2002): this aspect of Sen's position has deep Kantian roots.

Sen (2002, p. 11) observes that in 'the political, social and philosophical literature on freedom, we can detect the diverse inclination of different authors to go in one direction or another . . . [T]he concentration of Robert Nozick (1973, 1974) is on the *rightness* of libertarian *procedures* that may be involved. Economists have tended, on the whole, to concentrate—when they take any note of freedom at all—on the *opportunities* offered by freedom' (emphasis added). This is, of course, what one would expect: Nozick was a 'rights' philosopher, while the low-octane utilitarianism at the heart of neoclassical economics is a consequentialist welfarism that dictates concentrating on a narrow class of (utility-based) opportunities. To consider the value of processes would force the neoclassic to confront the independent value of rights, thus violating their (tacit) ethical position and, more importantly, making that position visible. The narrowness of RCT would be in plain view.

It would be a mistake, however, to think that the neoclassic only has problems with *process* freedom. Sen's axiomatizations of rational choice specifically recognized that an agent may be rational in rejecting her best available option (best in terms of her own criteria), to leave it for someone she loves. This is one of many situations where a person may rationally resist being given the 'best' opportunity. As Sen (2002, p. 16) asks '*Is the best option an adequate measure of a person's opportunity?*'. He adds that 'a person may resist being given the "best" option, *as if nothing else mattered*' (Sen, 2002, p. 18, emphasis added). The 'best' option may be important to us, precisely because we want to be able to reject it. For Mahatma Gandhi: 'fasting is possible not just through starving, but through starving *out of choice*' (Sen, 2002, p. 18). Formalizations of rational choice theory blind to such issues offer a deficient account of opportunity freedom. If Gandhi had been involuntarily starving anyway, his famous attack on the violations of rights embodied in the British Raj would have been impossible.

It is time to consider the bearing of starvation (on a massive scale) on libertarian rights. Sen (2002, p. 638) has pointed out that 'famines can take place in an economy that fulfills all the libertarian rights specified in Nozick's system'.

At the heart of neoclassical theory is the concept of free exchange. If an exchange is offered by one party and accepted by another, and there has been no coercion, this exchange is said to be free. For Sen, on the contrary, an exchange is free only if (in addition to the absence of coercion) both parties were able to reject the exchange if they chose. If one of the parties 'accepts' the exchange simply because she will starve if she does not, Sen refuses to call the situation a free exchange. To use a term Sen (1981, pp. 154–184) employs extensively, a person can be said to make a free exchange, only if she has trade-independent security – i.e. can survive without entering in the proposed trade. Massive numbers of people in the poor world, if offered a trade which gives them conditions of semi-starvation, are in no position to refuse it. The notion of 'free' trade as being possible between the poor and rich worlds is simply absurd. Even Nozick saw the necessity of modifying his system of consequence-independent libertarian rights because it would lead to catastrophic moral horrors.

Neoclassical rational choice theory, on which Arrow (1950, 1951, 1963) based his negative existence theorem, assumed that every agent had a minimal endowment sufficient to guarantee the opportunity to choose – what Sen has characterized as possessing trade-independent security. Arrow also took for granted that the laws of society would guarantee every agent the procedural freedoms necessary to support free choice. Later, Rawls would explore the depth and complexity of these matters. Sen (2002) is at pains to illuminate the intricate complexity of the relationship between these freedoms, and their entanglement with questions of fact, theory, and value. What is required is the free development of all the vital human capabilities of individuals, through processes under their own control.

Sen's enrichment of the impoverished information basis of social choice theory

For years, Sen has been steadily and consistently working to increase the amounts and kinds of opportunities that social choice theorists must include in their models, and the nature and extent of the information about such opportunities that the models must recognize as relevant. The results of this lengthy campaign can be seen in Sen (2002); we saw some of this when looking at the ethical enrichment of the concept of rational choice.

Turning to the informational base of Arrow's social choice theory, it is necessary in fairness to recall that the economics of the time offered Arrow only the thin gruel of a preference utilitarianism, which provided no basis for interpersonal comparisons of utility. He was likewise denied all value judgments by the absolute dominance of the logical positivist fact/value dichotomy.

But Arrow had one advantage over most of his peers, which guaranteed his immediate celebrity (although it did not enable him to enrich his informational basis for appraising social states). This advantage came from using methods of proof which, at the time, were still new to most economists. Arrow was not the first economist to use the axiomatic methods of formalist mathematics. But he showed the power of these methods, by confronting a question of great social concern, and proving a negative existence theorem on the possibility of rational social choice or policy. This appeared to free economists from having to commit themselves on deeply controversial social issues.

Early in his book, Sen (2002, p. 70) noted that social 'choice difficulties apply to welfare economics with a vengeance. By the middle 1960s, William Baumol (1965) judiciously remarked that "statements about the significance of welfare economics" had started having "an ill-concealed resemblance to obituary notices". . . . This was certainly the right reading of the prevailing views'. Arrow's theorem naturally led to instant celebrity, but for the wrong reasons. 'It also led to the diagnosis of a deep vulnerability in the subject that overshadowed Arrow's immensely important constructive program of developing a systematic social choice theory that could actually work' (Sen, 2002, pp. 69–70). The chilling effects of the popular (purely negative) interpretation of Arrow's result spread rapidly from economics into political science and philosophy: 'Two centuries after the flowering of the ambitions of social rationality, in Enlightenment thinking and in the writings of the theorists of the French Revolution, the subject seemed to be inescapably doomed. Social appraisals, welfare economic calculations, and evaluative statistics would have to be, it seemed, inevitably arbitrary or unremediably despotic' (Sen, 2002, p. 69). Sen (1999, pp. 250–251) thus had to demonstrate that the 'Arrow theorem does not in fact show what the popular interpretation frequently takes it to show. It establishes, in effect, not the impossibility of rational social choices, but the impossibility that arises when we try to base social choice on a limited class of information'.

Arrow offered several different versions of his theorem. Considering the version in Arrow (1963), Sen (2002, p. 266) shows 'that it is impossible to have a social welfare function with universal domain, satisfying independence, the Pareto principle, and nondictatorship'. Given that there are at least three distinct social states to be considered, and some finite number of individuals, Arrow wanted his social welfare function 'to yield a social ordering for every possible combination of individual preferences; that is, it must have a *universal domain*' (Sen, 2002, p. 266). Arrow's condition specifying the independence of irrelevant alternatives has been defined in several ways; Sen chooses a simple form: 'The way a society ranks a pair of alternative social states x and y should depend on the individual preferences only over *that pair*' (Sen, 2002, p. 266). A group of people will be said to be 'decisive' in ranking x over y if they can get x ranked over y in the social ordering despite what the preferences of the rest of society may be. Arrow then required that no individual can be decisive (his assumption of nondictatorship) and also that all the individuals in the society taken as a group shall be decisive. This latter is his 'weak' version of Pareto optimality: if x is preferred to y by all the individuals in the society, then x is socially preferred to y.

Sen (2002, p. 271) asks how we might avoid the impossibility. He reminds the reader that Arrow's theorem came at a time when utilitarian interpersonal comparisons had been dropped, while non-utility information was still excluded: 'This barren informational landscape makes it hard to arrive at systematic judgments of social welfare. Arrow's theorem can be interpreted, in this context, as a demonstration that even some very weak conditions relating individual preferences to social welfare judgments cannot be simultaneously satisfied given this informational privation'.

'We do care about the size and distribution of the overall achievements; we have reasons to want to reduce deprivation, poverty, and inequality; and all of these call for interpersonal comparisons – either of utilities or of other indicators of individual advantages, such as real incomes, opportunities, primary goods, or capabilities. Once interpersonal comparisons are introduced, the impossibility problem, in the appropriately redefined framework, vanishes' (Sen, 2002, p. 273). Applications to policy questions are cited in extensive footnotes (Sen, 2002, p. 274, n25, n26) and Sen (2002, p. 274) concludes by noting that Arrow's impossibility theorem has led to 'many constructive developments'.

We may begin with a general point about the habit of regarding Arrow's theorem as a generalization of the famous voting paradox, discovered in the 18th century by the Marquis de Condorcet and Jean-Charles de Borda. Sen (2002, p. 330) points out that Arrow

> encourages this view, and motivates the presentation of his impossibility result by referring to the voting paradox (Chapter 1, p. 5; Chapter 3, p. 53; Chapter 4, p. 72). Person 1 prefers x to y and y to z; Person 2 prefers y to z and z to x; Person 3 prefers z to x, and x to y. The result is that in majority voting, x defeats y, y defeats z and z defeats x. This is certainly a convincing enough demonstration that majority voting may not yield a consistent ordering, and also that there may be no majority winner at all. There is no doubt also that this voting paradox played a part in making Arrow think along the lines that he did.

Approaching rational social choice through voting paradoxes has two fatal flaws. The first arises from the unsuitability of this form of modeling for treating issues concerning the distribution of well being. The second flaw can be seen from the fact that Arrow's result can also arise in models where voting paradoxes cannot occur. Voting paradoxes apply only to a subset of the model set for the Arrow theorem.

Sen takes first the issue of unsuitability. Granting that voting paradoxes are important 'in settling political differences', he asks: 'can it be argued *in general*, that the majority method is really "a plausible way of aggregating preferences"? Arrow seems to assert this belief strongly' (Sen, 2002, p. 330). Can we count on a majority decision being egalitarian, for example? Sen (2002, pp. 331–332, n12) notes that

> in most societies the poor are very much more numerous than the rich, and improving the lot of the poor at the cost of the rich would typically be favored by a majority, if the majority votes according to personal gains. But even in such a society, it might be possible to pick the poorest person, and pass on a part of whatever he owns to the others, and to secure a majority for this inequality – increasing change.

In fact, Sen did not need to pick a single poor individual. The history of the Indian sub-continent yields the vivid example of a poor and downtrodden caste, oppressed by the majority of the population. Likewise, rich countries are developing an underclass, comprising a minority of the population. Sen rightly concludes that

> [t]he majority method does have a good deal of plausibility for some types of problems, but an exercise in income distribution is not one of them. Arrow has suggested that 'perhaps the deepest motivation for study of the theory of social choice, at least for the economist, is the hope of saying something useful about the evaluation of income distributions' (Chapter 6, p. 87). If this is indeed so, then the promise of the majority rule as a social choice procedure is clearly very limited, even if problems of intransitivity were never to arise.
>
> (Sen, 2002, pp. 331–332)[5]

Turning to the second problem with using voting procedures in social choice theory (Arrow's result does not depend on voting paradoxes), we must confront the issue of intransitivity. In standard axiomatic choice theory, a preference ranking is said to be transitive if and only if, when an agent prefers x to y and y to z, then she prefers x to z. Now the paradox of voting may be expressed as the inability, given three person's transitive individual rankings, to derive a unique majority ranking which is also transitive. However, as Sen points out, Arrow suggests an illustration of a social choice problem in a situation where no intransitivity arises. This is in the well-known cake dividing problem, where 'a number of individuals with completely egoistical preferences use the method of majority decision to divide up a fixed total of a single commodity' (Arrow, 1951, p. 87) Arrow notes that: 'For any allocation which gives some individual, say 1, a positive amount, there is another, which given 1 nothing and divides up his share in the first allocation among all the others; the second is preferred to the first by all but one individual' (Arrow, 1951, p. 87).

Sen (2002, p. 331) argues:

> let the feasible set of options consist exactly of the two alternatives referred to in the quoted sentence of Arrow, more completely specified thus: x when the cake is equally shared by persons 1, 2, and 3, and y when 1 gets nothing and the whole cake is divided up between 2 and 3. There is no problem of intransitivity here (because there are only two distinct states), and no absence of a majority winner (y wins over x by two-to-one majority). But in what sense is y a 'satisfactory' welfare-economic outcome in this choice problem? Person 1 has been driven completely to the wall and 2 and 3 have been fattened some more. It is hard to maintain that the majority rule is 'a plausible way of aggregating preferences' for these welfare-economic judgments.

If 'the hope of saying something useful about the evaluation of income distributions' (Arrow, 1951, p. 87) is our deepest motivation for studying social choice theory, Sen (2002, p. 332) is surely right that 'the promise of the majority rule as a social choice procedure is clearly very limited, even if problems of intransitivity were never to arise'. Of course, one cannot say something useful about the evaluation of income distribution without making interpersonal comparisons. But Arrow ruled out these comparisons. Given his acceptance of this drastic assumption, as Sen dryly observes, 'Arrow may have been overgenerous in his belief that addressing problems of income distribution can be an effective motivation for choice theory (not to mention its "deepest motivation")' (Sen, 2002, p. 332). Yet amazingly, as Sen shows, there was an escape route that Arrow could have taken.

Interpersonal comparisons entered neoclassical economics in the nineteenth century from utilitarian philosophy. In the early 1930s, when economists found the utilitarian discussions of inequality an embarrassment, they tried, unsuccessfully, to free themselves from these issues by eliminating utilitarian elements from economics. So it was natural for Arrow to assume in 1951 that an interpersonal comparison would be a comparison of different person's utility. However, in a natural language, one continually makes all sorts of comparisons of various properties of persons, some obviously true, some possible to check, some false, and some malicious! Logical positivism, on which the neoclassics had (unwisely) relied to defend them from comparisons of utility, offered them no defense against a statement like 'Tom is much richer than Dick' or 'Mary has had a far better education than Jane.' As Sen rightly points out, in assessing inequality, there are simpler approaches than through utility, 'for example, comparing incomes or wealth. The inequality between the rich and the poor is not primarily a matter of utility, or who *feels* what, but one of who *owns* what. There is no obvious reason why abstaining from interpersonal comparisons of utility must have the effect of making it impossible to consider economic inequality in social welfare judgments' (Sen, 2002, p. 332).

Unfortunately, Arrow was prevented from 'dealing plausibly with judgments concerning income distribution' by a neutrality result 'that Arrow obtains on the way to establishing his impossibility theorem' (Sen, 2002, p. 333). This neutrality is not a property Arrow assumes, but a form of neutrality is nevertheless derivable from the conjunction of the axioms' (Sen, 2002, p. 334). As Sen (2002, p. 334, n16) points out, the

> term *neutrality* makes the property sound a lot more attractive than it is. Arrow's [1963, p. 167] interpretation of the term as meaning that 'the social choice procedure should not have a built-in bias toward one alternative or another' is also too kind. Neutrality rules out any direct use of the non-utility information regarding states of affairs, and that is a big loss in many problems, one of which is judgment about distribution of income.

Summing up the matter: 'From the perspective of welfare economics, once the neutrality result is established in Arrow's framework (in addition to the eschewal of interpersonal comparisons of utility), there are really no interesting social choice procedures left' (Sen, 2002, p. 334).

The neutrality property stipulates that social choices must not depend on the characteristics of the states of society (i.e. who is rich and who is poor, who has rights, whose capabilities are being allowed to wither unrealized), but only on the preferences of individuals concerning each of the states of society. Sen understood the damaging force of the neutrality property early in his investigation of social choice theory and developed a formal analysis of this (Sen, 1970). He has explained its relationship to the axiomatic structure of Arrow's work and to the work of numerous commentators on Arrow (in Sen, 1982). So his treatment of this question in recent work can be said to rest on a lifetime of investigation.

A simple illustration (adapted from Sen, 1982) will make vivid what is at issue. Consider a cake-dividing problem, and two different cases (Figure 9.1) In the first case, Tom is very rich while Dick and Harry are poor. In the second case, Tom is poor while Dick and Harry are very rich. We now investigate the result of cutting a bit from Tom's slice of cake and dividing it between Dick and Harry. We follow Arrow's assumption that each person has purely egoistic preferences, and prefers more cake for himself. In both cases a majority (Dick and Harry) prefers the social state after the redistribution. In Arrow's social choice model 'the two cases are *informationally identical*, and exactly the same judgment must be made about the change in both the cases, since the individual preference orderings are identical in the two cases' (Sen, 1982, p. 20). But in the case where Tom was rich, the redistribution reduced inequality. When Tom is the poor one, the redistribution increases inequality. If we try to say that Tom now has less utility, this is ruled out by Arrow's assumption that one cannot make interpersonal comparisons of utility, while if one wants to say that Tom is now poorer (in terms of quantity of a good,

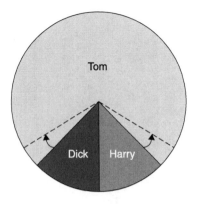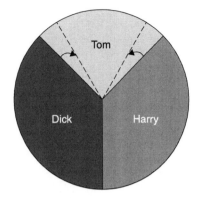

Figure 9.1 The cake dividing problem.

or of income, or of capabilities), this is ruled out by Arrow's ban on non-utility information.

Among the most important kinds of relevant non-utility information, which Sen has consistently insisted it is fatal to leave out of social choice and policy arguments, is information about rights and freedom. As he has noted, the

> conception of rights can, of course, extend beyond the sphere of personal liberty. Nozick (1974) has recently proposed an 'entitlement system' with a very wide scope, incorporating a variety of rights, including those relating to private property. While Marx's . . . conception of 'exploitation' belongs to the other end of the political spectrum, both systems share a rejection of welfarism, and relate social evaluation to historical information (e.g., dated labour in the case of Marx, and past savings and inheritance in the case of Nozick).
>
> (Sen, 1982, p. 249)

This would require extending the meaning of 'social state', to incorporate such information about the past. It could only be done 'by eschewing neutrality and anonymity' (Sen, 1982, p. 250). Thus, he concludes that to 'accommodate values such as liberty, it is necessary to reject the informational constraints of neutrality and anonymity. The same applies to systems of entitlements and rights envisaged in "historical" theories as different as those of Marx and Nozick' (Sen, 1982, p. 258).

I have offered only a sketch of the role played by one or two of Arrow's concepts. It must be remembered that all Arrow's players are in play at once, and his conclusion draws on the implications of their joint action. Sen's recent work, in turn, draws together all the special contributions that he (and numerous others) have made to the analysis and appraisal of each component of Arrow's argument and analysis of their joint effect on the result and its limitations.

Sen and the enrichment of social choice theory

Sen never fails to stress that Arrow was searching for ways to escape from the negative results of his analysis. The axioms that proved lethal to any possibility of rational and morally significant social choice were not Arrow's invention: they simply formalized standard assumptions from neoclassical economics of the period. And almost as early as Arrow's struggle to break free of the bonds in which he found himself enmeshed, was Maurice Dobb's determined encouragement – dissenting from his close Cambridge friends – of Sen's project.

The escape route Arrow (1951) initially concentrated on involved restricting the domain of the individual preferences to a set that would satisfy certain requirements, resulting in the availability, for example, of majority voting. Sen (2002, p. 337) argues that 'this line of escape is really not very interesting for welfare economics, whatever its importance might be for political theory. If the analysis presented earlier is correct, then intransitivity is *not* the main problem in using the majority method (and other voting procedures) in making judgments or decisions about welfare economics'. Sen notes that even in his original presentation Arrow was aware of the crucial role of ruling out interpersonal comparisons of utility. 'He was, however, too convinced then of "the difficulties of interpersonal comparison" to see much hope in remedying the impossibility result through that means' (Sen, 2002, p. 338). Despite this, the 'escape route that receives the largest share of Arrow's attention in the later essays is the possible use of interpersonal comparisons of utility. This extension is of obvious relevance not only in avoiding the impossibility result itself, but also in bringing welfare economic analysis in line with moral philosophy, e.g., using the utilitarian approach, for which Arrow clearly does have considerable sympathy'. Introducing interpersonal comparisons, Sen observes, would also be a way of 'linking up normative social choice theory to ethical traditions that go back a long way and that have received a good deal of critical attention in recent philosophical discussions' (Sen, 2002, p. 338). Sen (2002, p. 339) adds that by the 1970s there had been a great revival 'in making and using interpersonal comparisons, and for this purpose Arrow's original social choice format has been appropriately adapted. Arrow himself contributed to this revival through some remarks in the second edition of his book'. He reasonably concludes that the escape route from impossibility 'that receives the largest share of Arrow's attention in the later essays is the possible use of interpersonal comparisons of utility' (Sen, 2002, p. 338). This would have been understandable at the time, since the interpersonal comparisons at issue among economists in the 1970s, were comparisons of utility.

Today, I think it is more interesting to draw attention to the fact that Arrow had been considering an idea that is close to Sen's concept of capabilities (see Arrow, 1967, 1977). He argues for extended sympathy by pointing out that we 'seem prepared to make comparisons of the form: Action A is better (or worse) for me than Action B is for you. This is probably in fact the standard way in which people make judgments about appropriate income distributions; if I am richer than you, I may find it easy to make the judgment that it is better for you to have the marginal dollar than for me' (Arrow, 1967, p. 19). Arrow begins with income comparisons, but then proceeds, not to utility, but to the specification of increasingly subtle human characteristics, which can nevertheless be compared:

> In this form, the characteristics that define an individual are included in the comparison. In effect, these characteristics are put on a par with the items usually regarded as constituting an individual's wealth. The possession of tools is ordinarily regarded as part of the social state that is being evaluated; why not the possession of the skills to use those tools, and the intelligence that lies behind those skills? Individuals, in appraising each other's states of well-being, consider not only material possessions but also find themselves 'desiring this man's scope and that man's art'. The principle of extended sympathy as a basis for interpersonal comparisons seems basic to many of the welfare judgments made in ordinary practice. It remains to be seen whether an adequate theory of social choice can be derived from this and other acceptable principles.
>
> (Arrow, 1967, p. 20)

He adds in a note: 'The moral implications of the position that many attributes of the individual are similar in nature to external possessions have been discussed by V. C. Walsh, *Scarcity and Evil*' (Arrow 1967, p. 21, n10). Did Arrow have the idea of interpersonal comparisons of what we now call capabilities and functionings in 1967? The argument Arrow uses was derived from *Scarcity and Evil*. So it makes sense to ask how close this argument was to Sen's argument in terms of functionings and capabilities. On this I bow to Putnam (2002, p. 57), who notes that 'this notion of "functionings" was anticipated by Walsh in 1961 in *Scarcity and Evil*. Walsh's term was "achievements", and like Sen he connected a very wide notion of achievements or functionings with a concern for the character of a human life as a whole, which goes back to Aristotle. The idea of applying this point of view to development is, of course, due entirely to Sen'. The time was not yet ripe, however, for a full scale application of a theory of capabilities and functionings in either development theory or social choice theory.

I have sometimes been asked the following. Granted that Arrow recognized the argument of *Scarcity and Evil* had moral implications for social choice. Then why did he not investigate the possibility of dropping utility and making interpersonal comparisons based on how people's attainments were affected by instances of scarcity? One might say, for example, that Beatrice may not get a first at Oxford because her handicap deprives her of mobility and the strength which healthy students possess. (As Sen would later put it, her disability deprives her of the capabilities necessary to function at a first rate level.)

The short answer is that to ask why an epoch-making work (like *Social Choice and Individual Values*) did not also include a treatment of something more is usually silly. In this case there are longer answers that may be worth pursuing. One might begin with the fact that the neoclassical theory of the period was still drenched in the preference utilitarianism that survived the Hicks–Arrow revolution, saved the profession from cardinal utility, and was deeply entrenched as an article of faith. Interpersonal comparisons were still seen as an issue concerning utility.

There is also, I believe, an explanation of why economists did not see *Scarcity and Evil* contributing anything further to economics, as distinct from moral philosophy. It was not that the terminology I used was unfamiliar to economists. The concept of scarcity has deep roots in Austrian economic theory, and was explored by Robbins by 1932. By 1960, it had passed into the first chapters of elementary textbooks of microeconomics, and was regarded as a core concept of neoclassical theory. The formal models of advanced theory put it in their core; as Hicks (1967, p. 111) remarked 'If we take the famous definition, given so many years ago by Lord Robbins—"The relationship between ends and scarce means that have alternative uses"—economics . . . is very well covered by linear theory'.

Scarcity impeded or wholly prevented the attainment of human goals. Scarcity of clean water could kill a child, and scarcity of expert instruction could impede the attainment of a career as a concert violinist. This language of scarcity and attainments translates easily into Sen's language of capability deprivation and functionings (Walsh, 2003, pp. 381–382.) But I do not think that a neoclassical economist in the 1960s, looking for interpersonal comparisons that could be made, would have found this easier to see in terms of capabilities and functionings than in terms of the role of scarcity in impeding attainments – if anything, the scarcity language would have been more familiar. So it surely couldn't have been a matter of language. But, as Putnam (2002, p. 57) noted, when I borrowed the concept of scarcity from neoclassical economics I promptly took it off into moral philosophy, making no effort to use it in economic theory. I never thought of using this idea, as Sen was later to use capability theory – to propose a non-utilitarian way of making interpersonal comparison. I left this vital link in the chain missing.

Minimal liberty and social choice

In utilitarian moral systems, as we know, rights (including rights to enjoy various freedoms) take a back seat; they are defended only if they increase utility. So it should occasion no surprise that the neoclassical economics from which Arrow drew his axioms had little to say about rights. It defended the right to free exchange, but only because this arguably maximized the utility of both trading parties. Perhaps it should not have caused shock when, early in his career, Sen (1970) proved a theorem showing that the tiniest bit of freedom violated a key assumption of Arrowian social choice theory.

Sen did not ask whether a reasonable amount of freedom could be guaranteed; rather, he offered the minimum freedom a society could have and showed that even this violated Arrow's axiom of Pareto optimality. We need here only a weak form of the concept, which Sen (2002, p. 384) specifies as follows: 'if every individual prefers a social state x to a social state y, then x must be socially preferred to y'. What is the minimum liberty which violates this? Suppose persons 1 and 2 both prefer a full time job (1) to a half-time job ($\frac{1}{2}$) and the latter to unemployment

(0). 'But, spoiled as they are by the competitive society in which they live, each prefers that the other be jobless (that is, 0 to $\frac{1}{2}$ to 1, for the other). Indeed, each is green-eyed enough to get more fulfillment out of the joblessness of the other than from his own job' (Sen, 2002, p. 387). Suppose there are four alternative states for each person, letting the first number in each of the four pairs of numbers represent person 1's situation and the second number person 2's situation. Here are their preferences, in descending order:

Person 1	Person 2
$\frac{1}{2}$, 0	0, $\frac{1}{2}$
1, $\frac{1}{2}$	$\frac{1}{2}$, 1
0, $\frac{1}{2}$	$\frac{1}{2}$, 0
$\frac{1}{2}$, 1	1, $\frac{1}{2}$

Minimum Liberty (ML) consists of giving each person a personal sphere over which he has control. Thus, Person 1 is free to work or not as he prefers, and so has choice over the pair $(1, \frac{1}{2})$ and $(0, \frac{1}{2})$. Likewise, Person 2 is free to work or not, and can therefore choose $(\frac{1}{2}, 1)$ or $(\frac{1}{2}, 0)$ How should one interpret social preference? A judge will undertake this, bearing in mind both minimal liberty and the Pareto principle. Sen (2002, p. 388) tells us that:

> On grounds of minimal liberty, the judge puts $(1, \frac{1}{2})$ over $(0, \frac{1}{2})$, since Person 1 actually prefers $(1, \frac{1}{2})$, Person 2 isn't directly involved in this decision about 1's job, and in fact the pair is in 1's personal sphere. On similar grounds, $(\frac{1}{2}, 1)$ is put above $(\frac{1}{2}, 0)$, in line with 2's preference, noting that 1 is not directly involved in this particular choice and that in fact the pair is in 2's personal sphere. But if the judge also adheres to the Pareto principle, then he must put $(\frac{1}{2}, 0)$ over $(1, \frac{1}{2})$, since both prefer the former, and on exactly similar grounds place $(0, \frac{1}{2})$ over $(\frac{1}{2}, 1)$. And this combination involves a cycle of social preference: $(1, \frac{1}{2})$ is better than $(0, \frac{1}{2})$, which is better than $(\frac{1}{2}, 1)$ which is better than $(\frac{1}{2}, 0)$ which is better than $(1, \frac{1}{2})$. Every state is worse than some other state.
>
> The impossibility of the Paretian liberal is based on the inconsistency of three conditions, viz. unrestricted domain, the weak Pareto principle, and the condition of minimal liberty. To avoid the inconsistency, at least one of the conditions has to be dropped or weakened in some substantial way. In the literature on the subject, each of these three avenues has been extensively explored.
>
> (Sen, 2002, p. 389)

Sen goes through an immense range of different contexts and interpretations of social choice, showing that the Paretian liberty impossibility 'holds under each of the interpretations, but has correspondingly different – though related – contents'

(Sen, 2002, p. 406). Applying game-theoretic methods, while interesting in its own right, does not solve the problem. Considering the possibility of the agents engaging in contracts, Sen notes that 'the possibility of Pareto-improving contracts does not – contrary to some claims – eliminate (or "resolve") the impossibility problem under any of the alternative interpretations' (Sen, 2002, p. 406, also see pp. 408–460).

It must not be thought that this argument is all about technicalities. Technical distinctions do abound, but they correspond to humanly acute issues. Consider what Sen (2002, p. 446) calls 'choice inhibition': 'The courage to do something that is frowned upon by powerful people may not be easy to muster even when the game form gives the person the right to do just that'. He instances the case of a woman summoning 'the courage to appear in public with an uncovered head (in a tradition-bound society where such behavior is unconventional), even when the right to this action is actually given to a woman by the accepted game form. In an illuminating clarification, the 'realization of rights' as well as the 'conferment of rights' takes us beyond the 'formal structure' of game forms' (Sen, 2002, p. 446).

Here he discusses authors who mounted a frontal attack on the whole moral mind-set that induced neoclassical economists in the 1950s to treat the Pareto criterion as a sacred cow[6] and led Arrow to adopt it as an axiom. He begins with a passage from Nozick (1974, pp. 165–166) stating the main issue:

> each person may exercise his rights as he chooses. The exercise of these rights fixes some features of the world. Within the constraints of these fixed features, a choice can be made by a social choice mechanism based upon a social ordering, if there are any choices left to be made! Rights do not determine social ordering but instead set the constraints within which a social choice is to be made, by excluding certain alternatives, fixing others, and so on.

Nozick here has cleared a huge space for rights and not just allowed the minimal rights of Sen's Paretian liberty proof.[7] Arrowian social choices can only be made by free agents. Now apply Sen's concept of the requirements for an agent to make free choices: trade-independent security. Social choices are only possible for agents whose vital human capabilities are fulfilled to some satisfactory minimal subsistence level. Nozick is the true enemy of the Pareto principle, which was the last home of the low-octane preference utilitarianism lurking for so many years in axiomatic neoclassical economics. As Sen (2002, pp. 442–443) rightly stresses, Nozick's proposed solution of the Paretian liberty paradox 'was not seen by him as a vindication of the compatibility of individual rights and the Pareto principle . . . In the Nozickian framework, the Pareto principle does not have any priority over the rights (as it does in "welfarist" frameworks, including Paretian welfare economics) and the removal of the "impasse" need not lead to the fulfillment of the Pareto principle'.

The rights Nozick made room for were his libertarian rights. As Sen stresses, these rights can be in place in a country where millions die of famine. Sen's point comes into action here: procedural liberty is a fundamental right, even for libertarians, and procedural liberty can be violated for the wretched of the earth because of their utter lack of trade independent security.

It is time to return to the distinction between the procedural aspect of freedom and the opportunity aspect. Sen (2002, p. 443) notes that the 'social choice formulation of rights, including that presented in Sen (1970), is much concerned with outcomes. This feature was seen as a "mistake" in the criticism that motivated Nozick's departure and the literature that followed that lead'. Nozick's criticism was legitimate; but once the role of procedural freedom is secured by rejecting the dominance of the Paretian requirement, procedural rights can move center stage and trade-independent security can be made a procedural prerequisite before any social choices can take place. This accomplished, the opportunity aspect of freedom comes into its own, and social choices, now made by procedurally free agents, can focus again on outcomes. This is certainly a vindication of the social choice approach to rights. So we 'need to supplement the formalities of the game-form formulation of rights by more substantive concerns. This applies particularly . . . to those rights for which "the outcomes are the primary focus"' (Sen, 2002, pp. 443–444). But he does agree that '(1) there are types of rights in which the exercising of freedom of action is the central issue, and the game-form formulations are quite adequate in fully characterizing such rights, and (2) for those rights for which outcomes are important, the game-form formulations need substantive supplementation' (Sen, 2002, pp. 443–444).

If the utilitarian-based requirements of the weak Pareto principle are to be abandoned, something must be put in its place. Sen (2002, p. 518) offers 'Weak efficiency of opportunity–freedom. A state of affairs is weakly efficient in terms of opportunity–freedom if there is no alternative feasible state in which everyone's opportunity–freedom is surely expanded'. He turns immediately to the question of the space in which these achievements are to be judged. 'The freedom in question must include the freedom to live the way one would like, rather than judging freedom simply by commodity holdings' (Sen, 2002, p. 519). Nor can the interpersonal comparisons be defined simply in commodity or income terms:

> two persons with identical commodity holdings [or identical incomes] may have very unequal freedoms to lead the lives they value, because one person may be disabled . . . A disabled person with the same commodity bundle may be just as rich as another, but still lack the capability to move about freely and to achieve other functionings . . . Even such elementary freedoms as the capability to be well nourished may vary greatly . . . depending on the person's metabolic rate, body size, climatic conditions, parasitic disease, age, gender, special needs (such as those of pregnancy), and so on.
>
> (Sen, 2002, p. 519)

So the space in which opportunity freedoms are considered must be the space of the relevant functionings and capabilities.

Sen (2002, p. 527) notes that this freedom-based analysis 'makes it redundant to assume that the individual preferences and choices must be taken to be aimed exclusively at one's own welfare – the pursuit of the respective self-interest. That staple assumption in welfarist assessment turns out to be essentially irrelevant not only to the process aspect of freedom, but also for efficiency results in terms of opportunity freedoms'.

Doing justice to the importance of opportunity freedom brings Sen to what one cannot accept from Nozick. Sen (2002, p. 635) notes that '[i]n the *independent approach* to rights, the relevance of rights as unrelaxable requirements takes precedence over their "goodness" and significance for valuation, and the force of these rights, in this view, is essentially independent of their consequences. In the preeminent formulation of this approach (Nozick's [1974] "entitlement theory"), all such rights take the form of "side constraints" that simply must not be violated'. But, as we have already noted, 'it is not hard to show that even gigantic famines can take place in an economy that fulfills all the libertarian rights specified in Nozick's system' (Sen, 2002, p. 638). Sen (2002, pp. 638–639) recognizes that 'Nozick (1974) does make exceptions to consequence-independence in cases where the exercise of rights would lead to "catastrophic moral horrors"'. In this concession, Nozick recognizes the importance of consequences – i.e. of opportunity freedom. For Nozick, in the end freedom proved to be a pluralist notion.

For Sen, opportunity freedom requires the freedom for all agents to realize some minimal level of vital human capabilities. But this attainment of functionings must be based on a special kind of growth and development. Until this is achieved, the world's wretched 'accept' the exchanges offered to them only in the sense in which the old slaves 'accepted' their slavery – they simply have no viable alternative.

The legacy of John Rawls

In rejecting utilitarianism, putting rights center stage, and developing a new informational base for social choice theory, Sen has consistently drawn attention to what he owes to Rawls. He is not uncritical: he never accepts Rawls's primary goods, for example. But his esteem for Rawls equals his regard for Arrow. His first book on social choice theory (Sen 1970) contains an extensive discussion of Rawls, and he thanks 'Kenneth Arrow, Maurice Dobb, and John Rawls, for stimulating discussions over a great many years' (Sen, 1982, p. 327). Sen (1992, p. xi) tells us (in discussing equality and freedom) that 'my greatest intellectual debt is undoubtedly to John Rawls'; adding that 'even when I go in a different direction ... that decision is, to a considerable extent, based on an explicit critique of Rawls's theory'. And Sen (2002, p. 307) notes that the 'theory of justice that has had the greatest impact on social choice theory is undoubtedly that of John Rawls'.

Rawls offers three important ideas to Sen's project. First, he offers a model of rational social arrangements with no dependence on utilitarianism – indeed, he rejected it outright. Second, Rawls's analysis is explicitly based on values. Sen did not learn about the importance of values from Rawls – he had had it from his student days, and was encouraged in this by Dobb. But Rawls's value-entangled treatment of society can hardly have failed to be strongly supportive. Third, Rawls gave priority to rights over any concept of the good (not just utilitarianism). So while individual preferences (no matter how morally outrageous, irresponsible or trivial) were a sacred cow for Arrow, Rawls showed how preferences incompatible with justice as fairness were stripped of their special status.

Neoclassical economists also felt the power of Rawls's work. How wedded they were to a low-octane utilitarianism can be seen from the fact that Rawls did not persuade them to forsake this – rather, they set about trying to utilitarianize Rawls. Indeed, a bastard Rawlsianism emerged, and has survived into fairly recent times. There have been one or two distinguished rejections of this tendency by neoclassical economists (see Roemer, 1987; Tungodden, 2003).

If Rawls offered Sen an escape from the restraints of powerful neoclassical positions, there were also aspects of Rawls from which it was necessary for Sen to dissent. The most obvious is the Rawlsian dependence on primary goods. Over the years Rawls (2001, p. 168) made concessions to Sen, finally stressing his wish to 'clarify the idea of primary goods by noting their connection with Sen's important idea that interpersonal comparisons must be based, in part at least, on a measure of what he calls a person's "basic capabilities"'.

Making use of his conception of the two moral powers, which he assumes persons possess (namely the capacity for a sense of justice and the capacity for a conception of the good), Rawls (2001, pp. 18–19) argues that

> it should be stressed that the account of primary goods does take into account, and does not abstract from, basic capabilities: namely, the capabilities of citizens as free and equal partners in virtue of their two moral powers. It is these powers that enable them to be normal and fully cooperating members of society over a complete life and to maintain their status as free and equal citizens. We rely on a conception of citizen's capabilities and basic needs, and the equal rights and liberties are specified with these moral powers in mind.

Describing the framework of his theory of justice as fairness as a whole, he claims that

> we see that it does recognize the fundamental relation between primary goods and persons' basic capabilities. In fact, the index of those goods is drawn up by asking what things, given the basic capabilities included in the (normative) conception of citizens as free and equal, are required by citizens to maintain their status as free and equal and to be normal, fully cooperating members of society. Since the parties know that an index of primary goods is part of the principles of justice, . . . they will not accept these principles unless that index secures what they think is required to protect the essential interests of the persons they represent.

(Rawls, 2001, pp. 169–170)

Rawls's tragic death cut off the possibility of a complete consensus being found. But it is not unreasonable to hypothesize that, had he lived, Rawls might well have embraced capability theory.

The 'political conception' of justice

In his later work, Rawls stressed a 'political conception' of justice. If this implied that Rawls was backing away from the ethical commitments of his original theory, it might have serious implications for Sen's appraisal of the relationship between Sen's position and that of Rawls's. However, an exploration of Rawls's last major work shows that any notion of his flirting with a 'value-free' political theory would be completely mistaken.

Rawls (2001, p. 9) concedes that 'given the fact of reasonable pluralism, a well-ordered society in which all its members accept the same comprehensive doctrine is impossible. But democratic citizens holding different comprehensive doctrines may agree on political conceptions of justice. Political liberalism holds that this provides a sufficient as well as the most reasonable basis of social unity available to us as citizens of a democratic society'. But he stresses the two moral powers vital for his citizens to possess and declares that 'the conception of the person as free and equal is a normative conception: it is given by our moral and political thought and practice' (Rawls, 2001, p. 24). The concepts of justice and fairness, the bedrock of his theory, are always presented throughout his work, from the earliest to the latest, as explicitly moral concepts. This is never truer than in his last book, especially when he is setting out what he sees as the features which a conception of justice should have: '(a) While it is, of course, a moral conception, it is worked out for a specific subject, namely, the basic structure of a democratic society . . . [and] (b) Accepting this conception does not presuppose accepting any particular comprehensive doctrine' (Rawls, 2001, p. 26).

Philosophers who support the work of Sen and Rawls can hold different opinions on the concept of a 'political conception' as proposed by Rawls (see Nussbaum, 2003, pp. 413, 417; Putnam, 2003, pp. 403–404). But Rawls's final work does not support the old value-free position on social theory, which Sen has always opposed. To the end, Rawls offers work which is an explicit blend of theory, fact, and value.

Sen, and criticism of Rawls's contractarianism

Rawls always had critics on the left, from whom it is possible to pick up the idea that his contractarian social model might constrain Sen's ability to do justice to the most destitute and excluded of this world. Could there be a loss (as well as notable gains) from Sen's attraction to Rawls?

The first thing to observe is that Sen himself has in fact been one of the critics of Rawlsian contractarian theory from the left. And he has noted Rawls's efforts to meet his critics. Sen (2002, p. 637) notes that Rawls seems willing to make some room for a sensible compromise in dealing with the claims of pressing material needs. This problem was raised in a general form by Herbert Hart, when he disputed the presumption that in the Rawlsian 'original position' there must be 'a preference for liberty over other goods which every self-interested person who is rational would have' (Hart, 1973, p. 555). In his later writings, John Rawls has acknowledged the relevance of this argument, and suggested ways of accommodating it within his system.

Again, in discussing Rawls's characterization of his conception of justice, Sen (1992, p. 76) notes that 'the crucial "political" feature is the "toleration" of possibly divergent comprehensive doctrines'. The problem was the extent to which Rawls was assuming the acceptance of debate characteristic of an established democracy. But, as Sen (1992, pp. 76–77) pointed out, there may well be 'important issues of justice and injustice in the choice of "political, social, and economic institutions" *even when* pluralist tolerance of the kind outlined by Rawls does not obtain.'

When the civility necessary for civil society disintegrates into a brush fire of bitterness, there may well be no tolerant side, 'and yet there may be very perspicuous problems of inequality, deprivation and injustice in the dispute between the different sides' (Sen, 1992, p. 77). As I have remarked, 'Sen concludes that to be offered a theory that can deal with these great issues *only* when the different sides are tolerant, and thus to see such disputes where neither side is tolerant as lying *outside* the purview of the so-called political conception of justice, would appear to be oddly limiting for the domain of a political conception of justice' (Walsh, 1995–1996, p. 551). I felt at the time that a theory, which could cope only with an idealized Denmark or Sweden, might have little to offer to those who have always been Sen's first preoccupation, namely the most destitute of the world. But these doubts never made me worry about Sen's interest in Rawls, since it was obvious that Sen was aware of the issues involved!

I now think that I was somewhat unfair to Rawls. He is, after all, seeking to characterize a *just* society. Rawls (1971, p. 8) acknowledges that just people, in an unjust regime, may be forced to resort to civil disobedience, militant resistance, revolution and rebellion. In his last years, he reminds us that he has been concerned 'with ideal theory', but notes the importance of 'questions arising from the highly nonideal conditions of our world with its great injustices and widespread social evils' (Rawls, 1999, p. 555). He adds that while 'I think the difference principle is reasonable for domestic justice in a democratic society, it is not feasible as a way to deal with the general problem of unfavorable conditions among societies' (Rawls, 1999, p. 558).

As for the economic arrangements needed for a society to approach his idea of justice, Rawls consistently rejected all authoritarian governments. With this proviso, 'the choice between a private property economy and socialism is left open; from the standpoint of the theory of justice alone, various basic structures would appear to satisfy its principles' (Rawls, 1971, p. 258). He adds that, in a society where 'distributional shares satisfy the principles of justice, many socialist criticisms of the market economy are met. But it is clear that, in theory anyway, a liberal socialist regime can also answer to the two principles of justice' (Rawls, 1971, p. 280).

It may be replied that, in 1971, many people were saying similar things. But in his last work Rawls rejects laissez-faire capitalism (and even welfare-state capitalism) since, among other things, they 'permit very large inequalities in the ownership of real property (productive assets and natural resources) so that the control of the economy and much of political life rests in few hands' (Rawls, 2001, p. 138). He approves property-owning democracy and liberal socialism that 'include arrangements designed to satisfy the two principles of justice' (Ibid). Rawls (2001, p. 178) stresses that we must be careful 'not to compare the ideal of one conception with the actuality of the other'. He warns us that 'political philosophy is always in danger of being used corruptly as a defense of an unjust and unworthy status quo, and thus of being ideological in Marx's sense. From time to time we must ask whether justice as fairness, or any other view, is ideological in this way: and if not, why not?' (Rawls, 2001, p. 4).[8]

In his last works, Rawls was disturbed by the extent to which the control by a few of vast economic resources was being used to bend out of shape the political decisions of democratic governments. But I know of no references to the bearing on this of the revival of classical theory in his work. The economics he learned appear to be all neo-Walrasian – as was only to be expected, given which of the two Cambridges he made his home. So one can only speculate how he would have responded to the analysis of the central role of the extraction and control of a growing surplus which constitutes the core of even the most minimalist forms of revived classical theory that was to be found in the debates at the other Cambridge. The contrast between the intellectual backgrounds of Rawls and Sen is striking. And there are new developments concerning the revival of classical theory, and Sen's relationship to it. But as we turn to these we leave Rawls behind.

Sraffa, Wittgenstein and Dobb: recent comments by Sen and others

We begin with Sen (2003), a short version of the paper he gave at a conference in Rome for the twentieth anniversary of the death of Piero Sraffa. Here he stresses the entanglement of Sraffa's economics and philosophy. Specifically, he describes the role Sraffa played in persuading Wittgenstein to turn away from his early formalism and toward a respect for natural languages, and the possibility that Sraffa was influenced in this matter by his friend Antonio Gramsci. As Sen (2003, pp. 1242–1243) observes 'it is useful to see how Gramsci's notes relate to the subject matter of Sraffa's conversations with Wittgenstein, including the part played by rules and conventions and the reach of what became known as "ordinary language philosophy"'. Here, Sen is making explicit an attitude towards the later Wittgenstein that he has developed over the years, and which can be seen when he wrote some years ago that '[a]s Wittgenstein has taught us, we communicate with each other and understand what others are saying by following certain rules. The rules of communication about welfare are governed by mutually recognized standards, which, for example, permit us to say that a starving wretch is worse off than a healthy, wealthy and happy person' (Sen, 1996, pp. 59–60).

There is a certain irony in Sraffa's influencing Wittgenstein in this direction. As we know now, it would provide an important element in the philosophical defense of an enriched present-day classical economics. But it is becoming apparent from the first fruits of the scholarly examination of Sraffa's unpublished papers that Sraffa displays here the same minimalism with respect to economic theory as characterizes his published work.

Sen, of course, was protected from the minimalist stance of people like Joan Robinson. He was encouraged by Dobb and the concept of rich description. Here there is another irony: recent scholarship highlights all the ways in which Dobb and Sraffa were close (if not always in agreement!). For whatever reason, Dobb never caught the logical positivist infection. The concept of descriptive richness is not one that could be embraced with enthusiasm by a thinker who was concerned to keep values out of political economy. This is true even if the values at issue happen not to be what are normally regarded as 'ethical' values – descriptive richness can take the form of many different kinds of values.

In a recent paper, Sen (2005, pp. 110–11) commented that

> there is an interesting issue as to what kind of an object a 'rich description' really is. In Walsh (2000), he had already argued that 'it is not, I believe, historically improper to use the present-day philosophical concept of the "entanglement" of facts and values for this key property of classical political economy in its philosophically richest manifestation, namely in Adam Smith' (Walsh, 2000, p. 9). In his more recent essay, Walsh (2003) provides a much more extensive defense of this claim: that is, to see a rich description as a manifestation of a description that does not shun entanglement of facts and values. In the process, Walsh also links this issue with the philosophical writings not only – and most importantly – of Hilary Putnam (2002), but also of Ms Murdoch, Morton White and of course, John Dewey. This is certainly an extremely illuminating way of seeing the demands of enriching descriptive exercises by not avoiding value entanglement and paying specific attention to the fact that the interest in many descriptions lies precisely in the intimate connections with valuational issues.

Sen is, of course, right to stress that the values involved need not be ethical – to use his own example, when we say 'Michelangelo produced the statue of David' we concentrate on the aesthetic values created by Michelangelo, leaving all the other necessary inputs in the shadows.

Thus, Sen got from Dobb what he could not get from Sraffa's published work – and, it would appear, could not have got from Sraffa's unpublished writings, as far as they have been reported on.

Signorino (2005) offers a valuable account of Sraffa's 'Lectures on the Advanced Theory of Value', 1928–1931, where Sraffa first presented his interpretation of classical economics, including the role of surplus. Signorino (2005, p. 370) provides strong textural evidence that the 'history of economics as reconstructed by Sraffa is a history of how the various economic theories have been forged within debates concerning questions of economic policy, and of how they have been employed to support the economic interests of one class against another. The discovery of truly and permanent scientific results appears to Sraffa to be a sort of (often unintentional) joint-product emerging from economists' research activity'. To support this claim, Signorino (2005, p. 370) cites Sraffa on Adam Smith: 'That the necessities of his polemics against mercantilism led him to the formulation of general laws, and that this result has a permanent scientific value, may be regarded almost as a by-product of the way in which he advocated a practical policy'.

We eagerly await publication of Sraffa's lectures in complete form. Meanwhile, the above quotation does show that Signorino's interpretation of Sraffa's position warrants serious consideration.

Note that Sraffa contrasts Smith's 'polemic against mercantilism' with a result having 'permanent scientific value', implying that, for these to be found together can only be in an accidental manner – with one being a 'by product' of the other – a by-product, it should be noted, of the work of a propagandist supporting his class interest.

Here I think it will be helpful to recall a few historical facts about Smith, and the rapidly changing character of the British economy in which he lived. Descended on both sides of his family from Scottish lairds, and on his mother's side from that old scoundrel, Sir William Douglas of Lockleven, later Earl of Morton, Smith may have owed some of his advancement to his descent from the aristocracy and landed gentry of Scotland. Be that as it may, what is only too evident is that his pen was *not* at the service of their interest! Already, in the 'Early Draft of Part of the *Wealth of Nations*' he is describing 'the slothful and oppressive profusion of the great' (Smith, 1978, p. 566).

If there *is a* class which he supports, it is the struggling class of emerging little capitalists, who were – whatever their ruthlessness – devoting virtually all the surplus they extracted to growth and not to luxury consumption. As I remark in an earlier work, Smith's: 'deepest reason for objecting to luxurious waste came from a moral judgment deriving directly from his classical economic theory which, for the first time, made clear the extraction of surplus throughout industry and the vital importance of the allocation of that surplus to the accumulation of capital . . . Smith saw clearly that the rapid industrialization was imposing terrible moral costs upon the emerging working class. But if the surplus thus obtained were squandered in luxury, those costs would have been born in vain, and the one hope of an ultimately brighter future for the British working class would have been destroyed' (Walsh, 1998, p. 189).

I find no reason to alter the view that what Smith wrote about was a legitimate triple entanglement (to use Putnam's term) of a mature moral philosophy with a deep understanding of the facts of the economic world of his day, and interpreted correctly in terms of the first mature classical theory. I continue to regard what

Smith presented as important scientific results. As for Smith's 'polemic' against mercantilism, this was of course legitimate, since the mercantilist confusions and archaic restrictions were interfering with the industrial revolution, upon which the fate of the overwhelming majority of Britain's poor ultimately depended.

We are all in Signorino's debt for presenting somewhat dark facts about the motivation for Sraffa's well-known minimalism. Harvey Gram and I knew from many years of personal experience that Joan Robinson's work suffered from an unthought-out logical positivist element (Walsh, 1996, pp. 258–262). With regard to Sraffa, however, I have left this question open in the past, lacking definitive information (Walsh 1996, pp. 256–258). But whatever logical positivist elements may be found in Sraffa's papers, they are outweighed by the gains of his influence on Wittgenstein.

It is certainly becoming clear that, as Mathieu Marion (2005, p. 388) points out, Sraffa 'profoundly disliked the "subjective, moral point of view"'. Marion shows in detail how this is reflected in the minimalism of Sraffa's mathematics, as distinct from just his theoretical approach in general. On several questions concerning Sraffa's use of mathematics (including his avoidance of matrix algebra) Marion is a valuable source, and on some deep questions as to the relationship between Sraffa's view of mathematics and that of Wittgenstein, the interested reader should consult his paper.

Sraffa's dislike for the subjective is further explored by Kurz and Salvadori (2005, p. 438), who offer a fascinating account of the long road traveled by Sraffa in his effort to present 'a representation of the production and circulation of commodities in strictly material terms'. They inform us that, in the 1920s, Sraffa was reading about the new science and its philosophy, including the unity of science project. This project was, of course, one of the great hubristic reductionist proposals of the early twentieth century and intimately related to logical positivism. The scope of 'cognitively meaningful' discourse was to be reduced to empirical propositions and tautologies, mathematics was to be reduced to Russellian symbolic logic, sciences were to be reduced to physics, and 'rationally reconstructed' science was to be expressed in an ideal constructed language. Material object language was to be reduced to sense datum language, and natural languages, which were incurably permeated with (for example) material object talk and 'moral' pseudo-propositions were to be regarded as second rate and useful only for buying groceries (see Walsh 1996, pp. 20–21, 92; Putnam, 2002, pp. 22–30).

Kurz and Salvadori do not discuss Sraffa's ideas in relation to the great logical positivist philosophers, but provide interesting information about the development of Sraffa's views, which is pertinent to such questions. For example, they note that 'Sraffa's concept of objectivism changed over time'. But even in his final position, when Sraffa discusses 'the use of two methods of production employed side by side on land of a given quality,' what was significant for Sraffa about this situation, was that '[t]hese two methods *were observable and thus an objective fact*' (Kurz and Salvadori, 2005, p. 440, emphasis added).

The fascinating issue of the *Review of Political Economy*, together with the recent conference on Sraffa, which included Sen's contribution, show an evolving interest in the revival of classical theory in general and of Sraffa in particular. Sraffa's work will always rank as one of the most vital contributions to the formal core of revived classical theory. Within that context, however, matters that Sraffa chose not to treat need to be added.

The severe limitations of balanced growth theory have been realized for many years, and justify the efforts to escape from this straitjacket by Adolph Lowe (1955, 1976) and Sir John Hicks (1965). The limitations of the escape from steady state growth theory offered by the concept of traverse are also well known. I have suggested that a promising line to pursue might be found in Pasinetti.

> Pasinetti's models [of growth] are classical to the bone, as anyone who studies them will see. In particular, he is inspired by Adam Smith—the very subtitle of his earlier book on transformational growth describes the work as "A Theoretical Essay on the Dynamics of the Wealth of Nations" (Pasinetti, 1981) . . . Indeed Pasinetti derives what are arguably the most characteristic concepts of his growth theory explicitly from Smith: the central role of technical innovation occurring unevenly in different sectors, and the method of analysis in terms of vertically integrated sectors, found in an embryonic form in the *Wealth of Nations*. This involves treating the model economy as a set of vertically integrated sectors, in each of which only one final consumption good is produced.
>
> (Walsh, 2003, p. 372)

I added that 'Pasinetti's models enrich the production side of present-day classical theory by breaking out of the steady state in a manner far beyond traverse, and stimulating the development of a theory of structural economic dynamics. But they also strikingly enrich the demand and consumption side of classicism, and again in a way that revives the richness of Smith' (Walsh, 2003, p. 373).

So we are back with descriptive richness: Pasinetti's study of the growing production, by means of vertically integrated sectors, of a changing and growing array of improved necessaries and conveniences, is treated by him as consciously designed to fulfill ethical goals concerning the developing enrichment of human life. Thus he stressed 'the great need for a theory of consumer's decisions, both private and public, in a dynamic context' (Pasinetti, 1993, p. 107). I think that Pasinetti needs Sen's capability theory. But I also think that Sen needs Pasinetti's approach to growth theory. What can *transformational* growth offer Sen? It can offer something that, arguably, Adam Smith would understand and approve of 'an evolving basket of necessaries and conveniences, continually enriched in one way or another, with pollutant and destructive technologies eliminated one by one, with good things relevant to the flowering of human functionings arriving also one by one. Not a tight mapping to a list of capabilities, but surely a soil and a climate in which capabilities can flourish' (Walsh, 2003, p. 377).

In a recent paper, Sen (2005, p. 110) identifies an aspect of classical theory he has not yet fully explored: 'Walsh's investigation of the general bearing and continuing relevance of classical economics, while potentially perhaps the weightiest of Walsh's conclusions, will call for a much more extensive examination than can be pursued here'.

I recently discussed what Sen's capability theory needs from the classics with Hilary Putnam (November 13, 2005, phone conversation), and he put the point at issue very succinctly: 'capability theory needs to be cashed out by supplementing it with the kind of socially responsible growth theory provided by Pasinetti'.

This is why we (Putnam and Walsh, 2007) were so impressed by Dasgupta's models of class conflict, surplus, subsistence, and destitution. Dasgupta was in effect supplying what we saw as the greatest need of second phase classical theory – going past *informal* talk about capabilities and exploring possible *formal models* of classical reproduction structures with *explicit* moral implications.

Acknowledgments

Parts of this work were originally published in *Science and Society*. I am grateful to the editors for permission to republish this material here. I am indebted for helpful advice to David Laibman, Steven Pressman, and Hilary Putnam, and to Lisa Bendall-Walsh for advice and editorial assistance. Kristin Brodt of Trexler Library at Muhlenberg assisted me in obtaining needed materials. The usual disclaimers apply.

Notes

1 This is not intended to imply that Putnam accepted all of Wittgenstein's views on the philosophy of mathematics. Nevertheless, Putnam (1994, pp. 245–263) was deeply influenced by Wittgenstein's views on this topic.
2 Putnam's (1996) paper 'Über die Rationalitet von Präferenzen' is reprinted in Putnam (2002, Chapter 5).
3 Such as Levi (1986), Putnam (1996), Walsh (1996).
4 Cf. Putnam (2002, pp. 83–86) on the importance of free decision by the person concerned. Sen cited the earlier German version of this passage.
5 The reader should note Arrow's obvious longing for a positive result in social choice theory in the passage cited by Sen above. On the issue of lack of majority concern for the plight of a poor minority one should recall an important exception revealed by Sen's studies of famine. Discussing this, he remarks on 'the phenomenon that no major famine has ever taken place in any country with a multiparty democracy with regular elections and with a reasonably free press' (Sen, 2002, p. 287). Noting that typically 5% or less of a population are struck by a famine, 'how does it become such a potent force in elections and in public criticism? This is in some tension with the assumption of universal self-centeredness' (Sen, 2002, p. 288).
6 See Walsh (1996, especially pp. 174–206) for background on this.
7 Recall that Sen chose minimal rights to prove that even those violated the Pareto Principle.
8 For an interesting argument, which suggests that there is a way in which the left can learn more from Nozick than from Rawls, see Varoufakis (2002–2003).

References

Arrow, K. (1950) A difficulty in the concept of social welfare, *Journal of Political Economy*, 58(4), pp. 328–346.

Arrow, K. (1951) *Social Choice and Individual Values* (New York: Wiley).

Arrow, K. (1963) *Social Choice and Individual Values* (New York: Wiley).

Arrow, K. (1967) Public and private values, in: S. Hook (Ed.) *Human Values and Economic Policy: A Symposium* (New York: New York University Press).

Arrow, K. (1977) Extended sympathy and the possibility of social choice, *American Economic Review*, 67(1), pp. 219–225.

Baumol, W. (1965) *Welfare Economics and the Theory of the State*, 2nd edn (Cambridge, MA: Harvard University Press).

Broome, J. (1991) *Weighing Goods: Equality, Uncertainty and Time* (Oxford: Blackwell).

Hart, H. L. A. (1973) Rawls on liberty and its priority, *University of Chicago Law Review*. Reprinted N. Daniels (Ed.) (1975) *Reading Rawls* (Oxford: Blackwell).

Hicks, J. R. (1965) *Capital and Growth* (Oxford: Clarendon Press).

Hicks, J. R. (1967) Linear theory, in *Surveys of Economic Theory*, Vol. III, *Resource Allocation* (New York: St. Martin's Press).

Kant, I. [1788] (1956) *Critique of Practical Reason*, trans. L. W. Beck (New York: Bobbs–Merril).

Kurz, H. and Salvadori, N. (2005) Representing the production and circulation of commodities in material terms: on Sraffa's objectivism, *Review of Political Economy*, 17 (3), pp. 412–441.

Levi, I. (1986) *Hard Choices: Decision Taking under Unresolved Conflict* (Cambridge: Cambridge University Press).

Lowe, A. (1955) Structural analysis of real capital formation, in: M. Abramovitz (Ed.) *Capital Formation and Economic Growth* (Princeton: Princeton University Press).

Lowe, A. (1976) *The Path of Economic Growth* (Cambridge: Cambridge University Press).

Marion, M. (2005) Sraffa and Wittgenstein: physicism and constructivism, *Review of Political Economy*, 17(3), pp. 381–406.

Nozick, R. (1973) Distributive justice, *Philosophy and Public Affairs*, 3, pp. 45–126.

Nozick, R. (1974) *Anarchy, State and Utopia* (New York, Basic Books).

Nussbaum, M. (2003) Tragedy and human capabilities: a response to Vivian Walsh, *Review of Political Economy*, 15(3), pp. 413–418.

Pasinetti, L. (1981) *Structural Change and Economic Growth: A Theoretical Essay on the Dynamics of the Wealth of Nations* (Cambridge: Cambridge University Press).

Pasinetti, L. (1993) *Structural Economic Dynamics: A Theory of the Economic Consequences of Human Learning* (Cambridge: Cambridge University Press).

Putnam, H. [1962] (1975) The analytic and the synthetic, in: *Mind, Language and Reality, Philosophical Papers, Vol. 2*, pp. 62–69 (Cambridge: Cambridge University Press).

Putnam, H. (1994) Rethinking mathematical necessity, in J. Conant (Ed.) *Words and Life*, pp. 245–263 (Cambridge, MA: Harvard University Press).

Putnam, H. [1996] (2002) On the rationality of preferences, in *The Collapse of the Fact/Value Dichotomy and Other Essays* (Cambridge, MA: Harvard University Press).

Putnam, H. (2002) *The Collapse of the Fact/Value Dichotomy and Other Essays* (Cambridge, MA: Harvard University Press).

Putnam, H. (2003) For ethics and economics without the dichotomies, *Review of Political Economy*, 15 (3), pp. 395–412.

Putnam, H. and Walsh, V. (2007) Facts, theories, values and destitution in the works of Sir Partha Dasgupta, *Review of Political Economy*, 19 (2), pp. 181–202.

Rawls, J. (1971) *A Theory of Justice* (Cambridge, MA: Harvard University Press).

Rawls, J. (1999) *Collected Papers* (Cambridge, MA: Harvard University Press).

Rawls, J. (2001) *Justice as Fairness: A Restatement* (Cambridge, MA: Harvard University Press).

Roemer, J. E. (1987) Egalitarianism, responsibility, and information, *Economics and Philosophy*, 3 (2), pp. 215–244.

Sen, A. K. (1970) *Collective Choice and Social Welfare* (San Francisco: Holden–Day).

Sen, A. K. (1977) On weights and measures: informational constraints in social welfare analysis, *Econometrica*, 45 (7), pp. 1539–1572.

Sen, A. K. (1981) *Poverty and Famines: An Essay on Entitlement and Deprivation* (Oxford: Clarendon Press).

Sen, A. K. (1982) *Choice, Welfare and Measurement* (Cambridge, MA: MIT Press).

Sen, A. K. (1992) *Inequality Reexamined* (Cambridge, MA: Harvard University Press).

Sen, A. K. (1994) The formulation of rational choice, *American Economic Review*, 84, pp. 385–390.

Sen, A. K. (1996) On the foundations of welfare economics: utility, capability and practical reason, in: F. Farina, F. Hahn and S. Vannucci (Eds) *Ethics, Rationality and Economic Behaviour* (Oxford: Clarendon Press).

Sen, A. K. (1999) *Development as Freedom* (New York: Alfred Knopf).

Sen, A. K. (2002) *Rationality and Freedom* (Cambridge, MA: Harvard University Press).

Sen, A. K. (2003) Sraffa, Wittgenstein and Gramsci, *Journal of Economic Literature*, 41, pp. 1240–1255.

Sen, A. K. (2005) Walsh on Sen after Putnam, *Review of Political Economy*, 17(1), pp. 1–7.

Signorino, R. (2005) Piero Sraffa's lectures on the advanced theory of value 1928–31 and the rediscovery of the classical approach, *Review of Political Economy*, 17(3), pp. 359–380.

Smith, A. [1790] (1976) *The Theory of Moral Sentiments*, D. D. Raphael and A. L. Macfie (eds) (Oxford: Clarendon Press).

Smith, A. (1978) Early Draft of Part of the *Wealth of Nations*, *Lectures on Jurisprudence*, R.L. Meek and D.D. Raphael (eds) (Oxford: Clarendon Press), pp. 562–581.

Tungodden, B. (2003) The value of equality, *Economics and Philosophy*, 19 (1), pp. 1–44.

Varoufakis, Y. (2002–2003) Against equality, *Science and Society*, 66 (4), pp. 448–472.

Walsh, V. (1961) *Scarcity and Evil* (Englewood Cliffs, NJ: Prentice Hall).

Walsh, V. (1995–1996) Amartya Sen on inequality, capabilities and needs, *Science and Society*, 59(4), pp. 556–569.

Walsh, V. (1996) *Rationality, Allocation and Reproduction* (Oxford: Clarendon Press).

Walsh, V. (1998) Normative and positive classical economics, in: H. Kurz and N. Salvadori (Eds.) *The Elgar Companion to Classical Economics*, Vol. 2, pp. 188–194 (Cheltenham: Edward Elgar).

Walsh, V. (2000) Smith after Sen, *Review of Political Economy*, 12(1), pp. 5–25.

Walsh, V. (2003) Sen after Putnam, *Review of Political Economy*, 15 (3), pp. 315–394.

Walsh, V. and Gram, H. (1980) *Classical and Neoclassical Theories of General Equilibrium: Historical Origins and Mathematical Structure* (New York, Oxford University Press).

10 Entanglement through economic science

The end of a separate welfare economics

Hilary Putnam and Vivian Walsh

Welfare economics versus scientific (predictive) economics

Neoclassical economists have for many years been using arguments, borrowed from a long discredited philosophy of science, to the effect that, while welfare economics carries an ineradicable taint of values, 'predictive' or 'analytical' economic theory does not. The great battles that were won in the establishment of entanglement, however, took place on the terrain of the established mathematical and physical sciences, and in trying to be more scientifically pure than these, the vigorous but fledgling science of economics has been trying to be more catholic than the pope.

As long as logical positivism was taken seriously by philosophers – especially philosophers of science – economists and other social scientists were arguably entitled to take from the positivists a claim that values had no place in science. Thus, Paul Samuelson, writing when logical positivism was still accepted by philosophers of the established sciences, could legitimately adopt a view which at that time had recently filtered down into economics: 'It is fashionable for the modern economist to insist that ethical judgments have no place in scientific analysis' (Samuelson, [1947], 1983, p. 219). He had some reservations, finding this rule 'difficult to adhere to' (Samuelson, [1947], 1983, p. 220). However, he allowed scientific propriety to trump his sensible instincts, and added: 'But in essence Robbins is undoubtedly correct . . . and ethical conclusions cannot be derived in the same way that scientific hypotheses are inferred or verified' (Samuelson, [1947], 1983, p. 220).

Samuelson did everything he could, in his warm support of Bergson (see Putnam and Walsh, 2007a, pp. 9–11; 2007b, pp. 360–361) to shield enthusiasts of the new welfare economics from the more dangerous fires of values. As George Feiwel (1984, p. 17) observed, for Samuelson 'the McCarthy years had a lasting negative imprint.' Samuelson did not promise, however, that the approach to welfare theory which he proposed would offer a *complete* protection from values: 'I pass over as being obvious from our discussion . . . that it is not literally true that the new welfare economics is devoid of *any* ethical assumptions. Admittedly, however, its assumptions are more general and less controversial [than those of the old welfare theory]' (Samuelson, [1947], 1983, p. 249). However, the new welfare theory would remain incomplete in an important sense, since its 'full significance emerges only after one has made interpersonal comparisons' (Samuelson, [1947], 1983, p. 249). And this, of course, was the dangerous step.

Here is an example of how he regarded the filleted new welfare economics with interpersonal comparisons cut out: 'A limited significance remains for the new welfare economics if we hold that a welfare function is definable but undefined, and if we look for conditions which hold true uniformly for all possible definitions. It cannot tell us which of *any* two situations is better, but it can occasionally rule out one given situation as being worse than another in the sense that everyone is worse off' (Samuelson, [1947], 1983, p. 250).

What the new welfare economics got from logical positivism was a justification for avoiding any and all value judgments. What became habitual, however, was to avoid only interpersonal comparisons. They appealed to the philosophy of science to excuse their avoiding these politically dangerous value judgments! One can easily see why brilliant young theorists, even if they sometimes wrote on welfare economics, would not consider this sort of work, with its shady choice of assumptions, to approach the scientific standing of their work in 'predictive' economics. In time, as the political climate changed, economics began to go back to using interpersonal comparisons, thus giving up what to us had been the really unscientific property of the new welfare theory, a property that had rendered it trivial – as Samuelson had seen years before.

Sen and the re-enrichment of welfare economics

The old welfare economics of Arthur Cecil Pigou and of LSE economists (such as Lord Dalton and Sir Alan Peacock) was never afraid to make interpersonal comparisons, but it was confined by the narrow and unsatisfactory moral theory of utilitarianism. The roots of Amartya Sen's attack on what he called 'the impoverishment of welfare economics' (Sen, 1987, p. 51) of course go back to the influence of Maurice Dobb when Sen was at Cambridge (see Walsh, 2000, pp. 6–10, 17–22; 2003, pp. 319–320; Sen, 2005, pp. 110–111). In mounting his attack, Sen made extensive use of the reasonableness of many kinds of interpersonal comparisons, which are prominent features of any natural language. Rejecting all this would require a revisionist argument of heroic proportions concerning natural languages, which neoclassical economists were in no position to provide. (For a recent example, which shows Sen balancing the respective claims of constructed, axiomatic formalizations and natural language insights, see Sen 2002, especially pp. 3–220; Walsh, 2008).

Rationality and Freedom (Sen, 2002) is a massive source of references to thinkers who have aided and extended this work (Sen has always been notable for the generosity of his acknowledgements). One of the book's many theoretical results is our main concern here: the establishment of a philosophically enlightened and morally rich array of interpersonal comparisons (encompassing any vital human need, capability, or right) in a position of safety from serious and informed challenge.

Some of this work, of course, was in place by the 1980s, and as Dasgupta has recently pointed out '[i]t was not vacuous of Sen (1985) to dub an ethics based directly on the Bergson-Samuelson social welfare function "welfarism". But welfare economics had moved beyond Samuelson's version of welfarism a lot earlier' (Dasgupta, 2007, p. 368). Dasgupta himself is a fine example of the ethical re-enrichment of welfare economics. He endorses the inclusion of ethically valuable characteristics of social states such as 'democracy and civil liberties' (Dasgupta, 2007, p. 368). And he was already writing in 1993 that 'a person's prospects for flourishing are dependent upon the nature and extent of the freedom she enjoys. So we need a measure of her freedom' (Dasgupta, 1993, p. 68). Such matters affect the construction of his 'social evaluation function' – for instance, he tells us that '[t]he idea of *equality* is embedded in the social evaluation function' (Dasgupta, 1993, p. 73).

Despite this massive development, there is surely no reason why Bergson and Samuelson cannot be regarded as distant ancestors of this concept. What does concern us is Dasgupta's evident desire to continue framing this sort of work as 'welfare theory'. We have come to believe that, however enriched this work may become, as long as it gets put into a box labeled 'welfare economics' its influence will be seriously impaired. Consider a point made by Sen (1987, p. 29):

> The position of welfare economics in modern economic theory has been a rather precarious one. In classical political economy there were no sharp boundaries drawn between welfare economic analysis and other types of economic investigation. But as the suspicion of the use of ethics in economics has grown, welfare economics has appeared to be arbitrarily dubious. It has been put into an increasingly narrow box, separated from the rest of economics. Contact with the outside world has been mainly in the form of a one-way relationship by which findings of predictive economics are allowed to influence welfare economic analysis, but welfare economic ideas are not allowed to influence predictive economics, since actual human action is taken to be based on self-interest only, without any impact of ethical considerations or of welfare-economic judgments . . . Welfare economics has been something like an economic equivalent of the 'black hole'—things can get into it, but nothing can escape from it.

Sen offers an interesting reason for wanting to take down the walls that have boxed in welfare economics. He writes: 'The impoverishment of economics related to its distancing from ethics affects both *welfare economics* (narrowing its reach and relevance) and *predictive economics* (weakening its behavioral foundation)' (Sen, 1987, p. 57 (emphasis in original)). This weakening of the behavioral foundations of 'predictive' economics is explored in great detail in the early chapters of *Rationality and Freedom* (Sen, 2002). The point at issue here, however, never explicitly surfaces. It goes way beyond certain particular elements of welfare theory impinging on 'predictive' economics – however true the claim that this can and does happen. Our point is that entanglement is known to be a characteristic of a science *as a whole* (see, Putnam 2002, Ch. 8). Although the entanglement Putnam describes involves epistemic values as 'coherence', 'plausibility', and what Dirac[1] called the beauty of a theory, in the case of a science (like economics), one of whose principal theoretical concepts is 'rationality', it is impossible to separate judgments of those epistemic virtues from judgments as to better and worse ways of taking that ethically loaded term.

The idea that part of a science can be logically walled in and kept separate, so that entanglement can grow only inside the walls, is an incoherent residue of logical positivism, which no longer has legs to stand on. There is no pure, 'predictive' economic science, and no special kind of economics that can be put in a box marked 'welfare' and isolated. Economists who assert the existence of a dichotomy between 'welfare economics' and 'predictive economics' are assuming the truth of a separation theorem that they have never attempted to prove. They are presenting economic theory as decomposable into a scientifically respectable part, which fully satisfies the epistemic values of being 'predictive' and purely 'analytic', and off in another part of town a welfare economics as a sort of *demi monde* to which economists can supposedly go when they want to do things which they would not do in the respectable areas of economics!

When the whole treatment of neoclassical economics' core concept of rationality (for example) is shown to be loaded with both epistemic *and ethical* values, the impossibility of such a separation should be unmistakably clear (see Sen, 2002; Putnam, 2002; Walsh, 1996, 2003, 2008; Putnam and Walsh, 2007a).

A farewell to arms

We believe that we have no quarrel on matters of substance with Dasgupta. As we pointed out in a previous paper in *Review of Political Economy*, 'for us, one of the most appealing features of Dasgupta's models of class conflict, subsistence, surplus and destitution, is their unmistakably deep engagement with both the moral implications of these matters and the interface between these core issues of classical theory and the most pressing facts of nature' (Putnam & Walsh, 2007a, p. 19).

Imagine our surprise when Dasgupta writes that 'If I had been trying to establish that the literature on the economics of development is "value-free", I would understand the relevance of PW's [Putnam and Walsh's] exposition here of the "entanglement". As I wasn't trying to do that, I don't understand the point of their discussion of this' (Dasgupta, 2007, p. 370). This passage convinced us that Dasgupta had not seen Putnam & Walsh (2007a) when he wrote it. Any reader of the latter work will see that from page 13, beginning with a section called '*The Disenfranchised and Destitute*', we present Dasgupta as the very model of an economist whose analytic work contains explicit, fully acknowledged and deeply humane values. It is precisely because of our appreciation for this that we wish to persuade him to haul down the tattered and inappropriate flag of welfare economics. It should be noted that it is possible to accept the validity of entanglement (as Dasgupta was explicitly doing by 1993, pp. 6–7), and still see this as consistent with the belief that what it licensed was simply the unashamed ethical enrichment of welfare economics, rather than the simple destruction of the predictive/welfare economics dichotomy. In his recent book, Putnam (2002) still argued that 'if there is to be such a subject as welfare economics at all, . . . then welfare economics cannot avoid substantial ethical questions' (Putnam, 2002, p. 56). And he adds that his purpose 'is to see how welfare economics has found itself forced to recognize that its "classical" concern with economic well-being (and its opposite, economic deprivation) is essentially a moral concern and cannot be addressed responsibly as long as we are unwilling to take reasoned moral argument seriously' (Putnam, 2002, p. 57). This is essentially the position taken by Sen (1987), which Putnam has been quoting. It is the position we have described in this paper as the moral re-enrichment of welfare economics, and which is characterized by the adoption of ethically enriched interpersonal comparisons of capabilities, freedoms and rights. It is the position that underlies the argument in Sen (1999), and Sen (2005) implies that he had not yet thought through the full implications of entanglement when he wrote that paper. It is a very understandable first reaction to confronting entanglement, but we would now argue that it is not what the recognition of entanglement logically entails.

The deep significance of shared unspoken values

A *leitmotiv* throughout Dasgupta's work, appearing as early as the book we have just been discussing (Dasgupta, 1993) is the idea that 'economists speak or write as though they agree on values but differ on their reading of facts' (Dasgupta, 2005, p. 221). We believe that there is an important truth here, but it needs careful statement. He tells us that 'development economists . . . share the same moral concerns Nussbaum, Putnam, and Sen want us to display' (Dasgupta, 2007, p. 336). This is probably true: the development economists he would want to talk to would be concerned with making the poor less desperate, not with making the multinationals richer. The moral implications of their thick ethical concepts would always be there, implied in their discourse. Since these concepts were left implicit, an innocent public intellectual who overheard their discussion might well think it was all about boring soulless technicalities. Our recent paper in the *Review of Political Economy* (Putnam and Walsh, 2007a, pp. 194–195) drew attention to the existence of a morally serious critical minority within the neoclassical economics profession, people such as Hammond, Stiglitz, and Dasgupta being noted examples.

Post mortem?

A few words are called for about the 'death' of welfare economics. An old friend of both of the present authors announced this death a long time ago: 'By the middle 1960's, William Baumol (1965) judiciously remarked that "statements about the significance of welfare economics" had started having "an ill-concealed resemblance to obituary notices" (p. 2). This was certainly the right reading of the prevailing views. But, as Baumol himself noted, we have to assess how sound these views were' (Sen, 2002, p. 70).

Baumol was right to suspect that the reports of the death of welfare economics had been exaggerated. Largely due to the successful justification of much broader and more philosophically secure interpersonal comparisons by Sen, and the rich development of this by a number of theorists influenced by his work, welfare economics revived and flowered, as we have seen. What then has died when the implications of entanglement are pursued to their logical conclusions? Simply the segregation of discussions of well being, and the development of human capabilities and rights, into a closed off area of economics – the imposition of a sort of conceptual apartheid. Theories of human flourishing and deprivation have broken out of this assigned area and demanded the recognition of their right to be admitted as necessary constituent elements in all areas of economic science.

This is something that has to be thought through by economists – with perhaps some support from philosophers of science used to the mathematical languages of established sciences. The last people to understand it will be public intellectuals who appear to see only a desert waste land when confronted with even the morally impassioned models of a theorist like Dasgupta. Dasgupta himself, on the other hand, has a tendency (when understandably hurt by the sillier criticism he has received) to write as if the whole neoclassical profession were made up of people like the development theorists whom he rightly admires. But Peter Hammond's critique of the elements of interested dishonesty deeply embedded in neoclassical theory (Hammond, 1989, pp. 186–257) has only been confirmed by the growth of market idolatry in the years since it was written. We went on record recently with the claim that Hammond had been right to insist on 'the existence of "a residual neoclassical theory, purged of theology" (Hammond, 1989, p. 248)' (Putnam & Walsh, 2007a, p. 14). This was very much an approval of a minority, however, not an endorsement of the whole neoclassical profession.

Acknowledgments

The authors wish to thank Steven Pressman, Jane Hudak and Kristen Buodt, and Lisa Bendall-Walsh for her editorial advice and assistance. The usual disclaimers apply.

Note

1 Dirac's statements about beauty are reported in many places. They are not in his published papers, which are purely technical. See Kragh (1990, pp. 275–292).

References

Baumol, W.J. (1965) *Welfare Economics and the Theory of the State* (Cambridge, MA: Harvard University Press).

Dasgupta, P. (1993) *An Inquiry Into Well-being and Destitution* (New York: Oxford University Press).

Dasgupta, P. (2005) What do economists analyze and why: values or facts? *Economics and Philosophy*, 21, pp. 221–278.

Dasgupta, P. (2007) Reply to Putnam and Walsh, *Economics and Philosophy*, 23, pp. 365–372.

Feiwel, G. (Ed.) (1984) *Samuelson and Neoclassical Economics* (Boston: Kluwer–Nijhoff).

Hammond, P.J. (1989) Some assumptions of contemporary neoclassical economic theology, in: G.R. Feiwel (Ed.) *Joan Robinson and Modern Economics*, pp. 186–257 (London: Macmillan).

Kragh, H. (1990) *Dirac: A Scientific Biography* (New York: Cambridge University Press).

Putnam, H. (2002) *The Collapse of the Fact/Value Dichotomy, and Other Essays, Including the Rosenthal Lectures* (Cambridge, MA: Harvard University Press).

Putnam, H. and Walsh, V. (2007a) Facts, theories, values and destitution in the works of Sir Partha Dasgupta, *Review of Political Economy*, 19, pp. 1–22.

Putnam, H. and Walsh, V. (2007b) A response to Dasgupta, *Economics and Philosophy*, 23, pp. 359–364.

Samuelson, P.A. ([1947], 1983) *Foundations of Economic Analysis* (Cambridge, MA: Harvard University Press).

Sen, A.K. (1985) *Commodities and Capabilities* (Amsterdam: North Holland).

Sen, A.K. (1987) *On Ethics and Economics* (Oxford and New York: Basil Blackwell).

Sen, A.K. (1999) *Development as Freedom* (New York: Alfred Knopf).

Sen, A.K. (2002) *Rationality and Freedom* (Cambridge, MA: Harvard University Press).

Sen, A.K. (2005) Walsh on Sen after Putnam, *Review of Political Economy*, 17, pp. 107–113.

Walsh, V. (1996) *Rationality, Allocation and Reproduction* (Oxford: Clarendon Press).

Walsh, V. (2000) Smith after Sen, *Review of Political Economy*, 12, pp. 5–25.

Walsh, V. (2003) Sen after Putnam, *Review of Political Economy*, 15, pp. 315–394.

Walsh, V. (2008) Freedom, values and Sen: towards a morally enriched classical economic theory, *Review of Political Economy*, 20, pp. 199–232.

11 The fall of two dichotomies, and the need for a macro-theory of capabilities

Hilary Putnam and Vivian Walsh

A tale of two dichotomies

Gasper (2008: 248) notes that we often face a choice between weaker and stronger versions of a position, and he correctly argues that in such cases we should 'attend to the stronger not the weaker!' When dealing with a science, even a young science like economics, where there has been serious and extensive development of theory, the stronger approach necessarily requires attention to the interconnected fall of *both* dichotomies. What is involved can be seen most clearly by looking at the great battles that were fought in the philosophy of modern physics. This was, after all, the very model of a science for the logical positivists, and the original positivists naturally regarded it as the test case for whether or not their analysis, and the dichotomies central to it, really worked. It is in the nature of modern physics, however, that in showing why fact and convention are necessarily entangled, one is *also* showing why it cannot avoid epistemic values. Facts, epistemic values and convention prove to be *all* entangled.

To see this we must leave the cosy and familiar world of ordinary language, John Austin's endearing 'moderate sized specimens of dry goods' (Austin, 1962: 8), and enter instead the humanly alien world of 'the most fundamental physical theory we have (quantum physics)' (Putnam, 1990: x). We must continually be aware that 'while there is an aspect of conventionality and an aspect of fact in everything we say that is true, we fall into hopeless philosophical error if we commit a "fallacy of division" and conclude that there must be a part of the truth that is the "conventional part" and a part that is the "factual part" ' (ibid.).

The credit for launching the attack on the fact/convention dichotomy has been given mostly to Willard Van Orman Quine, for his paper of January 1951 (reprinted with minor revisions in Quine, 1953). But Quine himself sends the reader to Morton White (1950: 316–330) '[f]or an effective expression of further misgivings over this distinction' (Quine, 1953: 46, n. 22). The fact of the matter is that these close friends were vigorously debating these issues at Harvard, and so which of them appeared in print first was largely a matter of chance – as it happened, Quine followed on White's heels. It should also be noted that, while Quine and White brought this issue centre stage and under a spotlight *just when* logical positivism was beginning to falter under the problems caused by the peculiar 'facts' being delivered by the new physics, the fact/convention dichotomy, *has* a pre-history. It was challenged much earlier by scholars some of whom are referred to by Quine – for example, Pierre Duhem (1954 [1906]) and Armand Lowinger (1941). Also, it goes without saying that rejecting such dichotomies was a strongly characteristic feature, virtually a *leitmotif*, of classical American Pragmatism.

Quine's response to these issues suffered from a mild excess and a serious defect. The mild excess is all over his early paper. He did not in the least need to deny that there were *any* analytic statements: admitting the evidently analytic character of assertions such as 'all bachelors are unmarried' would have entailed no loss of philosophical ground – as Putman showed (see Putnam, 1975 [1962], 2002: 12–13). Indeed, Quine later seems to concede this to Putnam (Quine, 1960: 54–57). The most Quine *needed* was expressed in his early paper when he wrote that 'our statements about the external world face the tribunal of sense experience not individually but only as a corporate body' (Quine, 1953 [1951]: 41).[1] This led, in a later work, to his famous metaphor of our science as a 'pale grey lore' (Quine, 1963: 406). This tightly-woven fabric could not be ripped apart or, more formally, a scientific theory was not decomposable into individual propositions, each testable on its own (if factual) or true by convention on its own.

White clearly saw what this implies – the other dichotomy (of fact and value) can no longer survive on its own. Quine's dogged refusal to see this was the serious defect to which we referred above. On this issue Quine would never give in. By the mid-1950s, White had an elegant argument against the fact/value dichotomy in the context of natural languages, tailored to fit the requirements of the ordinary language philosophy then dominant at Oxford (White, 1956). But he was well aware that this would not sit well with Quine, and his later work concentrated on Quine. The question for White was: what kind of argument would force Quine to see that he could not now retain the fact/value dichotomy? White saw his way into the breach blown open by Quine's assault on the analytic/synthetic dichotomy as lying in the direction of Quine's *holism*. Arguably, this holism was Quine's one consistently pragmatist property.

White then goes back to Duhem who, he tells us, has argued 'that scientific explanation and prediction puts to the test a whole body of beliefs, rather than the one which is ostensibly under test alone' (ibid.: 255). But this 'may be generalized so that it becomes evident that not only other scientific principles, but also the logic and mathematics we use in our explanatory and predictive reasoning, are implicated (ibid.). Noting that this view has been 'most recently advocated by Quine', he now argues for its expansion; just as this position has destroyed the analytic/synthetic dichotomy, 'so the view we have advocated will break down the remaining dualism between logic-cum-empirical science and ethics' (ibid.: 256).

To make a way in for values, he examines how logical positivism went about constructing its artificial language. How did they arrange their artificial language so that no embarrassing terms appear? 'What must be emphasized is the fact that they do no more than *resolve* to apply the word "meaningless" to certain terms' (ibid.: 108). He then asks: 'How different is this from saying, as the moral philosopher does, that certain things ought not to be done? Not altogether different' (ibid.: 109). He turns the tables on positivism:

> Incidentally, it would seem that stealing is a fairly clear notion by comparison to being an observable predicate, so far from sniffing at the obscurity of ethical rules, positivistic theorists of meaning should recognize the respects in which ethical rules might even be clearer than their own
>
> (ibid.)

In effect, the positivists were compelled to seek shelter behind the structure they had built onto an artificial language, so that their ability to *exclude* value claims was in fact the result simply of which predicates they had *stipulated* as being excluded while constructing their artificial language, not the result of a proof legitimately devised from the properties of logic, the structures of mathematics, or the laws of science.

White seeks (as neither Duhem nor Quine sought) to bring values into smaller and smaller corporate bodies. Thus, he argues that values 'may sometimes be components of limited, heterogeneous bodies of belief that are tested in a corporate manner' (White, 1981: 29). It should be noted that in his later work his 'wholes' are much smaller than Quine's. This tendency reaches its peak in White (1986), and he catches Quine insisting on the force of an epistemic value in science:

> Quine himself expresses a normative epistemological principle when he writes as follows of an 'ultimate duty': '. . . the purpose of concepts and of language is efficacy in communication and in prediction. Such is the ultimate duty of language, science, and philosophy, and it is in relation to that duty that a conceptual scheme has finally to be appraised'.
>
> (Quine, 1953 [1951]: 79, cited by White 1986: 652)

There is actually *more*! Quine went on to discuss the epistemic value of 'elegance':

> Elegance, conceptual economy, also enters as an objective. But this virtue, engaging though it is, is secondary – sometimes in one way and sometimes in another. Elegance can make the difference between a psychologically manageable conceptual scheme and one that is too unwieldy for our poor minds to cope with effectively . . . but elegance also enters as an end in itself – and quite properly so as long as it remains secondary in another respect; namely, as long as it is appealed to only in choices where the pragmatic standard prescribes no contrary decision'
>
> (Quine, 1953 [1951]: 79 Quine sends the reader to Duhem (1954 [1906]: 34, 280, 347) or Lowinger (1941: 41, 121, 145).[2]

This is the closest Quine ever came to recognizing that the collapse of the analytic/synthetic dichotomy entailed that physics was also entangled with epistemic values. Quine's talk of making 'the laws of experience, simpler and more manageable' (1953 [1951]: 44) would seem to be in accord with taking such a direction. However, in a 'Reply to Morton White', Quine (1998: 663–665) writes explicitly about what he believes to be the status, for him, of epistemic values:

> naturalization of epistemology does not jettison the normative and settle for the indiscriminate description of ongoing procedures. For me normative epistemology is a branch of engineering. It is the technology of truth-seeking, or in a more cautiously epistemological term, prediction . . . There is no question here of ultimate value, as in morals; it is a matter of efficacy for an ulterior end, truth or prediction. The normative here, as elsewhere in engineering, becomes descriptive when the terminal parameter is expressed. We could say the same of morality if we could view it as aimed at reward in heaven.

Moral values do occasionally intertwine with epistemological norms, but not inextricably. Falsification of an experiment is immoral, and also it is epistemologically inefficacious, however rewarding in respect of fame and fortune. When, in a passage quoted by White, I referred to 'the ultimate duty of language, science and philosophy' I was using the word somewhat as when we speak of a heavy-duty cable or tractor. It was what language, science and philosophy are for, as eyes are for seeing (Quine, 1998: 664–665).

One thing at least is clear from this brief reply: 'Quine is determined to make no concessions to White's normative holism. Somewhat surprisingly, Quine chooses to confront White on the ground of moderate-sized dry goods: heavy-duty cables and tractors (Quine, 1998: 665). White, long before then, had become a fair match for Austin or Strawson on *that* turf' (see White, 1956, 1981, 1986).

As for specifically *epistemic* values, White was not Quine's only critic. Arguably, the best criticism is by Roderick Firth (1998 [1981]) who argued that epistemic instrumentalism collapses into epistemic vacuity on *any* theory of rational acceptability *or* truth. For, he pointed out, whatever we take the correct epistemology or the correct theory of truth to be, we have no way of *identifying* truths except to posit that the statements that are currently rationally acceptable (according to our epistemic norms) are probably true. Thus the claim that rationally acceptable statements tend to be true (and not just justified according to our epistemic norms) has no empirical content whatsoever.

Nor does it help if we take the purpose of our epistemic values to be prediction rather than truth, as Quine seems to suggest. For, as Quine recognizes, scientific predictions are *universal* statements, statements of the form (oversimplifying somewhat), 'Whenever observable property P, obtains at a space-time region X, then P_2 also obtains at X' (Quine calls these 'observation conditionals'); and no observer can be in very many different space–time regions in her working life-time. Universal statements, as we used to say, require 'induction' to 'confirm': that is to say, predictions are not simple reports of what Quine calls 'stimulation of nerve endings', but require the application of epistemic norms to singular observations and to background knowledge. Indeed, even our judgments as to which of our *memories* of past observations we should trust require estimations of *coherence*. So Firth's argument applies here too: the claim that our norms are the ones that best lead to correct prediction, like the claim that they lead to truth, has no empirical content.

That doesn't mean that our norms are non-revisable (as, we regret to say, Firth himself believed). They can be revised holistically, as Quine saw, by applying judgments of simplicity and elegance and the like to the whole combination of factual beliefs and epistemic norms that we inherit. But there is no 'instrumental purpose' that all this serves which can be identified from outside the whole combination.

In a previous work, Putnam wrote:

> . . . it is not, for us, any longer just a sociological-descriptive fact that choosing theories for their power and simplicity, and fostering democratic cooperation and openness to criticism in the generation and evaluation of theories, are part of the nature of scientific inquiry; these norms describe the way we ought to function when the aim is knowledge. Saying this is not the same as saying that inquiry which follows these norms produces knowledge in the way fire produces warmth; we are not dealing with mere empirical correlation here. Nor is it 'analytic' that inquiry which does not meet these standards does not produce justification and knowledge . . . Concepts of knowledge are essentially contested concepts; they are always open to reform. What we can say is that the applicability of our present conception to practice is constantly being tested (it is not a priori that, for example, the concept of 'probability' can be successfully used in practice) *and* that that conception itself is partly constituted by norms which represent values which are now terminal but not immune to revision. And this 'messy' state of affairs is one that, I would say, Dewey wanted us to see as typical.
>
> (Putnam, 1994: 173–174)

As we have seen, however, Quine's reaction to White was simply an unqualified rejection.

Entanglement in physics

Quine wrote a good deal about questions such as whether scientific theories are 'underdetermined' by the totality of observable facts and whether there is any objective 'fact of the matter' as to what the ontology of a scientific theory really is (see the papers in Quine, 1981). But with respect to the question as to how we are to *select* among theories, Quine had no recommendations to make whatsoever. He simply ignored the question of whether theory selection presupposes values.

Of course, Quine had a comeback to this sort of criticism. His answer to those wanting an epistemology that concerns how scientists select theories was the famous injunction to 'settle for psychology' (Quine, 1969: 69–90); *how* psychology is supposed to help a *physicist* decide between theories is something Quine didn't say – beyond telling us that the problem is to make successful predictions.

The two most famous logical empiricist philosophers, Rudolf Carnap and Hans Reichenbach, also tried to evade the issue of entanglement. They attempted to produce algorithms that would describe how scientists should select hypotheses. Reichenbach's (1938: 340) principle of induction is inconsistent (Putnam, 1994: 131–150), while the only algorithms Carnap was able to devise were limited to very simple sampling problems (such as estimating the relative frequency of red balls in an urn given a sample of balls selected from the urn).[3] Today no one holds out any hope for Carnap's project.[4]

Karl Popper (1959) rejected the ideal of inductive logic (in fact, he thought empirical science needs only deductive logic and observation), but he too hoped to reduce the scientific method to a simple rule: test all strongly falsifiable theories, and retain the ones that survive. But that doesn't work either: for when a theory conflicts with what has previously been supposed to be fact, we sometimes give up the theory and we sometimes give up the supposed fact, and as Quine famously put it the decision is a matter of trade-offs that are 'where rational, pragmatic' (Quine, 1953 [1951]: 46) – and that means (although Quine doesn't say so) a matter of informal judgments of coherence, plausibility, simplicity, and the like. Nor is it the case that when two theories conflict, scientists wait until the observational data decide between them, as Popperian philosophy of science demands they should. And last but not least, the idea that scientists test all strongly falsifiable theories that anyone thinks of is not only false as a matter of historical fact; scientists *couldn't* test all the strongly falsifiable theories that we can think of. For example, consider an arbitrary series of 18 or more digits, say, 525537834119638227, and consider the hypothesis that if I wait ten minutes in silence, and then recite that series of digits with due solemnity, and then wait another ten minutes, a pile of gold will appear on the table. This is a strongly falsifiable theory, but we cannot test all such theories because the number of sequences of 18 digits (and hence the number of such 'theories') is larger than the number of seconds the universe has existed!

In sum, judgments of coherence, simplicity, and other epistemic values are *presupposed* by physical science. An example that Putnam has used in this connection is the following: both Einstein's theory of gravitation and Alfred North Whitehead's (1922) theory (of which very few people have ever heard) agree with Special Relativity, and both predicted the familiar phenomena of the deflection of light by gravitation, the non-Newtonian character of the orbit of Mercury, the exact orbit of the Moon, etc. Yet Einstein's theory was accepted and Whitehead's theory was rejected 50 years before anyone thought of an observation that would decide between the two (see Will, 1971: 409–412).

But epistemic values are not only essential to the decision that one theory is worth testing and another too *ad hoc* to warrant the expenditure of effort, time, and material resources required for a test. They are also essential for the decision that a theory (such as Einstein's General Relativity) is confirmed enough to be accepted as the best currently available account and another (such as White-head's) not to be taken seriously, even though it is not actually experimentally refuted. Epistemic values also guide the process of *discovering* theories at every stage. Carnap and Reichenbach probably wouldn't have denied this. According to them, the 'context of discovery' is a matter for psychology to study; 'logic of science' can study only the 'context of justification' (by producing the algorithms for confirming theories that they sought). But there is no evidence that such algorithms, if they exist, are simpler to describe than the psychology of an ideal scientist. Indeed the dichotomy between a 'context of discovery' (which is supposedly outside the sphere of rationality) and a 'context of justification' (which precisely describes what rationality *is*) is just another variant on the fact/value dichotomy.

One example of the way in which an epistemic value may guide discovery is the use of elegant mathematical analogies. Here it may be useful to give an example of the way in which new theories are generated by looking for elegant mathematical analogies. Mark Steiner (1998: 85–89) has referred to this as 'Pythagorean' reasoning.

A 'Pythagorean' discovery

An electron has a magnitude analogous to angular momentum called 'spin'. However, 'spin' has only two values, called 'up' and 'down', unlike classical angular momentum, which has non-denumerably many possible values. A second difference from classical angular momentum is that in classical mechanics if a ball is rotated by 360°, it returns to the state it started out in; whereas if an electron is rotated by 360°, its Ψ function (the complex-valued function that represents the 'state' of the electron) is multiplied by -1 – a change that does not affect the predicted results of measurements when there is only one electron, but does show up as a physical change when the electron is allowed to interact with a second, un-rotated, electron. In short, a 360° rotation *does* make a difference to the state. Mathematically, the possible spin-states are represented by the group SU(2), the group of all 2×2 unitary matrices with determinant $+1$. The -1 that the electron wave function receives upon a 360° rotation while an amazing fact, is less amazing[5] than it seems with the recognition of two facts: (a) The SU(2) group is a 'double cover' of SO(3) the group of ordinary rotations in 3D Euclidean space,[6] and (b) SO(3) is topologically *not* a 'simply connected space'. So once one grants the possibility of angular momentum with a half-integral Lz component (and *that* is amazing since this is completely impossible for regular orbital angular momentum), the fact that spin 1/2 is represented by SU(2) is (almost) a tautology, and the -1 factor is inevitable. Heisenberg (1932) conjectured that the proton and the neutron are two states of the same particle, 'spinning' in opposite directions in an *abstract* three-dimensional space. According to this theory, now a fundamental part of nuclear physics, the nucleus of the atom has a property (now called 'isospin') which is mathematically represented by SU(2), just as spin is. Heisenberg postulated that the neutron is obtained from a proton by a continuous 'rotation' of 180° in this abstract space ('isospin space'), and that to return a proton or a neutron to its original isospin space one must 'rotate' the particle by 720°. However, matrices of any dimension can 'represent' SU(2). The power of purely 'Pythagorean' reasoning was exemplified when Nicholas Kemmer (1938) took the physical meaning of this mathematical fact to be that there can be particles capable of being in 3 or more isospin states), predicted the properties of an entirely different class of particles, *pions*, years before those properties were experimentally verified. As Steiner (1998: 88) writes: 'Kemmer's analogy was simply an extension of Heisenberg's and equally Pythagorean.'

Since Pythagorean reasoning argues from the epistemic *merits* of purely mathematical analysis to what may be the case, it is using an entanglement of epistemic values and mathematical theory to probe towards possible facts. It thus amounts to a counter argument to the validity of *both* dichotomies.

The need for a macro-theory of capabilities

Both of the two topics with which we deal in this paper concern issues where the *weaker* version of a position has been being adopted, although a stronger, more effective presentation of the position was available. In the first topic, the fact/ value dichotomy has been being treated *on its own*, while the *other* dichotomy, of fact and convention, has been doing the heavy lifting, and is more vital to attack. Our second topic concerns the tendency of writers on development, such as Amartya Sen, to concentrate on how poverty deprives individual poor people of the ability to fulfil vital capabilities – which might be called the *micro*-theory of capabilities – rather than to attend to why whole *classes* are currently poor, or destitute (see Gasper, 2008: 248–250). Accepting Gasper on this, we would go somewhat further, noting a tendency to focus on the *consumption* side of poor countries, rather than on the macroeconomic conditions of *reproduction*, and the control of the distribution of the net product, which *underlies* such poverty or destitution.

As it happens, we have been arguing for what amounts to a macro-theory of the reproduction conditions which determine the class distribution of capability fulfilment for some years now, although expressed in a different terminology from Gasper's. (We used the language of the second phase of the classical revival.)

Gasper does note an awareness that '[o]ccupational groups are frequently in competitive class relationships with each other, with some dominating and exploiting others. Critics . . . argue that the micro-focus has led attention away from essential issues'. He refers to important criticisms of Sen's work, which focus on its tendency not to address relations of power and class dominance (see Gasper, 2008: 248 and the references cited therein).

To be fair to Sen, however, we must note that his famous entitlement collapse theory of famines *turns* on an analysis of the situation of a most exploited class (or classes), defined by their not having trade-independent security (see Sen, 1981: 167–173, for a formal treatment). Thus, his models do have a *class structure*: 'The exchange entitlements faced by a person depend, naturally, on his position in the economic class structure as well as the modes of production in the economy' (ibid.: 4). He adds that 'even with the same ownership position, the exchange entitlements will be different depending on what economic prospects are open to him, and that will depend on the modes of production and his position in terms of production relations' (ibid.: 4–5). Lest the reader mistake what Sen means by 'modes of production', he refers readers to Marx (1938 [1867], 1973 [1857–8]) and for the classic treatment of modes of production to Sen (1981: 5, n. 5). He offers a study of the class basis of destitution, and the economic background of the destitute, issues of which he would write in rich detail and with telling force in later writings. This work of Sen's is as 'macroeconomic' as it needs to be, encompassing studies of large populations in the grip of famine. It brings centre stage Smithian concepts of 'necessaries' and 'conveniencies', adapted to present-day situations.

What we *do* find missing is an explicit analysis of the structures of production and *reproduction* that goes with the class-based deprivations and exploitations described. Where is the *surplus* that results from the deprivations? How much of it is devoted to luxurious waste – which Smith deplored – and how much to setting to work industrious people so as to produce more of the necessaries and conveniencies needed by the poor and deprived?

Sen tells us that:

> An adequate conception of development must go much beyond the accumulation of wealth and the growth of gross national product and other income-related variables. Without ignoring the importance of economic growth, *we must look well beyond it.*
>
> (Sen, 1999: 14 [emphasis added])

And again: 'economic growth cannot sensibly be treated as an end in itself' (ibid.). Well, if your only concept of growth is that insisted on for poor countries by the Washington Consensus, this would be true!

But, an elegantly formalized theory of growth, where *only the increased fulfilment of vital human capabilities counts as growth*, has been in existence since Pasinetti (1965) and elaborated in Pasinetti (1981, 1993). Pasinetti's growth theory is totally different from GDP growth theory; where every vulgar extravagance of our ignorant new rich, every imperialist military spending, and every earth destroying addition to our atmosphere, counts as growth! Of course, no one need be surprised that a totally different approach to growth should have existed for so many years; studied in some international journals, but ignored by the American mainstream economics profession – anyone can see that Pasinetti would be anathema to neo-liberals!

Now, however, neoliberalism is admitted to be in ruins even by the filleted American mainstream media! So, now perhaps at least America's daring progressives will take courage and read Pasinetti on *transformational* growth. After all, the first sketch of his growth theory (Pasinetti, 1965) was presented as one of the *Pontificae Academiae Scientiarum Scripta Varia* (28: 571–677) of the Vatican City. This should be a source unfrightening even to the most timorous (cf. Walsh, 2008: 229–230, 371–378).

Pasinetti has richly developed his early sketch (in works published in 1981 and 1993). There is a certain irony in the fact that the classic most cited and admired by Sen, namely Adam Smith, is also the original classic whose treatment of growth Pasinetti seeks to generalize in formal modelling, even describing his first book on the subject (Pasinetti, 1981) in his subtitle as 'A Theoretical Essay on the Dynamics of the Wealth of Nations'. And Smith, it will be noted, is as safe and acceptable as the Vatican and should cause no heart flutters. Pasinetti's formal modelling may be a little daunting for non-mathematical social scientists, but such readers will find a simple informal sketch of Pasinetti's essential message, set in the context of the present day revival of classical theory in a previous work by Walsh (2003: 363–378).

A word or two may be necessary to avoid misunderstanding. The word 'growth' has (with justification) come to be regarded as a dirty word by most well-informed and enlightened people. Pasinetti's concept of 'transformational growth', however, is something *quite* different. Industries which serve only what Smith called 'the oppressive profusion of the great' are given *negative* growth rates, as are the most environmentally destructive, and those producing big expensive toys for our imperialist cowboys. *Positive* growth rates are given to the production of necessaries and conveniencies for the fulfilment of vital capabilities. In fact the concept of sustainability finds its natural formal realization in the mathematical structure of a Pasinetti model.

Acknowledgements

We wish to thank Steven Pressman, Lisa Bendall-Walsh, Ariel Sternberg, Jane Hudak and Kristin Brodt. The usual disclaimers apply.

Notes

1 Quine could actually have done with even less. To controvert Dogma 2, 'We need only argue that *many* scientific sentences inseparably share empirical content ... it would suffice to argue that *many* sentences that are synthetic by popular philosophical acclaim can be held true come what may, and *many* that are analytic by acclaim can be declared false when a theory is being adjusted to recalcitrant evidence' (Quine, 1998: 619).
2 'Duhem's holism just applies to theoretical physics, as distinct from pure mathematics on the one hand and natural history on the other. Mine does not respect these boundaries ... It may seem from these comparisons that my holism is more radical than Duhem's. In other and vaguer ways, mine is more moderate, however' (Quine, 1998: 619).
3 Carnap (1950).
4 In fact, Carnap (1963) backs away significantly from the hopes for an algorithm that would enable us to reproduce the judgments of an ideal inductive judge that he expressed in Carnap (1950).
5 The authors thank Amiel Sternberg for pointing this out to us.
6 For a visualization of this fact see the Wikipedia article on 'Feynman's plate trick': http://en.wikipedia.org/wiki/Plate_trick

References

Austin, J. L. (1962) *Sense and Sensibilia* (Oxford: Clarendon Press).

Carnap, R. (1950) *Logical Foundations of Probability* (Chicago. IL: University of Chicago Press).

Carnap, R. (1963) 'Hilary Putnam on degree confirmation and inductive logic', in P. A. Schilpp (ed.), *The Philosophy of Rudolph Carnap* (LaSalle, IL: Open Court), pp. 761–784.

Carnap, R. (1967) *The Logical Structure of the World* (London: Kegan Paul).

Duhem, M. (1954 [1906]) *The Aim and Structure of Physical Theory*, trans. P. P. Wiener (Princeton, NJ: Princeton University Press).

Firth, R. (1998 [1981]) 'Epistemic merit, intrinsic and instrumental', in J. Troyer (ed.), *In Defense of Radical Empiricism* (Lanham, MD: Rowan and Littlefield), pp. 259–271.

Gasper, D. (2008) 'From "Hume's Law" to problem-and-policy-analysis for human development: Sen after Dewey, Myrdal, Streeton, Stretton and Haq', *Review of Political Economy*, 20(2): 233–256.

Heisenberg, W. (1932) 'Über den Bau der Atomkerne', *Zeitschrift für Physik*, 77: 1–11.

Kemmer, N. (1938) 'The charge-dependence of nuclear forces', *Proceedings of the Cambridge Philosophical Society*, 34: 354–364.

Lowinger, A. (1941) *The Methodology of Pierre Duhem* (New York: Columbia University Press).

Marx, K. (1938 [1867]) *Capital, Vol. 1* (London: Allen & Unwin).

Marx, K. (1973 [1857–8]) *Grundrisse: Foundations of the critique of political economy* (Harmondsworth: UK: Penguin).

Pasinetti, L. L. (1965) 'A new theoretical approach to the problem of economic growth', *Pontificae Academiae Scientiarum Scripta Varia*, 28: 571–677.

Pasinetti, L. L. (1981) *Structural Change and Economic Growth: A theoretical essay on the dynamics of the wealth of nations* (Cambridge: Cambridge University Press).

Pasinetti, L. L. (1993) *Structural Economic Dynamics: A theory of the economic consequences of human learning* (Cambridge: Cambridge University Press).

Popper, K. R. (1959) *The Logic of Scientific Discovery* (London: Hutchinson).

Putnam, H. (1975 [1962]) 'It ain't necessarily so', in *Philosophical Papers, Vol. 1* (Cambridge: Cambridge University Press), pp. 237–249.

Putnam, H. (1963) ' "Degree of confirmation" and inductive logic', in P. A. Schilpp (ed.), *The Philosophy of Rudolph Carnap* (La Salle, IL: Open Court), pp. 761–784.

Putnam, H. (1990) *Realism with a Human Face* (Cambridge, MA: Harvard University Press).

Putnam, H. (1994) *Words and Life* (Cambridge, MA: Harvard University Press).

Putnam, H. (2002) *The Collapse of the Fact/Value Dichotomy and Other Essays* (Cambridge, MA: Harvard University Press).

Quine, W. V. O. (1953 [1951]) 'Two dogmas of empiricism', in *From a Logical Point of View* (Cambridge, MA: Harvard University Press), pp. 20–46.

Quine, W. V. O. (1960) *Word and Object* (Cambridge, MA: MIT Press).

Quine, W. V. O. (1963) 'Carnap on logical truth', in P. A. Schilpp (ed.) *The Philosophy of Rudolph Carnap* (La Salle, IL: Open Court), pp. 761–784.

Quine, W. V. O. (1969) 'Epistemology naturalized', in *Ontological Reality and Other Essays* (New York: Columbia University Press), pp 69–90.

Quine, W. V. O. (1981) *Theories and Things* (Cambridge, MA: Harvard University Press).

Quine, W. V. O. (1998) 'A reply to Morton White', in L. E. Hahn and P. A. Schilpp (eds) *The Philosophy of W. V. Quine* (Chicago and La Salle, IL: Open Court), pp. 663–665.

Reichenbach, H. (1938) *Experience and Prediction* (Chicago, IL: University of Chicago Press).

Sen, A. K. (1981) *Poverty and Famines, an Essay on Entitlement and Deprivation* (Oxford: Clarendon Press).

Sen, A. K. (1999) *Development as Freedom* (New York: Knopf).

Steiner, M. (1998) *The Applicability of Physics as a Philosophical Problem* (Cambridge, MA: Harvard University Press).

Walsh, V. C. (2003) 'Sen after Putnam', *Review of Political Economy*, 15(3): 315–394.

Walsh, V. C. (2008) 'Freedom, values, and Sen: Towards a morally enriched classical economic theory', *Review of Political Economy*, 20(2): 199–232.

White, M. G. (1950) 'The analytic and the synthetic: An untenable dualism', in S. Hook (ed.) *John Dewey: Philosopher of science and freedom* (New York: Dial Press), pp. 316–330.

White, M. G. (1956) *Toward Reunion in Philosophy* (Cambridge, MA: Harvard University Press).

White, M. G. (1981) *What Is and What Ought to be Done: An essay on ethics and epistemology* (New York: Oxford University Press).

White, M. G. (1986) 'Normative ethics, normative epistemology, and Quine's holism,' in L. E. Hahn, and P. A. Schilpp (eds), *The Philosophy of W. V. Quine* (Chicago and La Salle, IL: Open Court), pp. 663–665.

Whitehead, A. N. (1922) *The Principle of Relativity with Applications to Physical Science* (Cambridge: Cambridge University Press).

Will, C. M. (1971) 'Relativistic gravity in the solar system, II: Anisotropy in the Newtonian gravitational constant', *Astrophysics Journal*, 169: 409–412.

Index

Bold indicates figure